STUDIES IN BAPTIST HISTORY AND THOUGHT
VOLUME 35

A Catholic Reformed Theologian
Federalism and Baptism in the Thought of
Benjamin Keach, 1640-1704

STUDIES IN BAPTIST HISTORY AND THOUGHT
VOLUME 35

STUDIES IN BAPTIST HISTORY AND THOUGHT
VOLUME 35

A Catholic Reformed Theologian
Federalism and Baptism in the Thought of Benjamin Keach, 1640-1704

D. B. Riker

Foreword by Timothy George

WIPF & STOCK · Eugene, Oregon

Wipf and Stock Publishers
199 W 8th Ave, Suite 3
Eugene, OR 97401

A Catholic Reformed Theologian
Federalism and Baptism in the Thought of Benjamin Keach, 1640 - 1704
By Riker, D. B.
Copyright©2009 Paternoster
ISBN 13: 978-1-60899-451-9
Publication date 2/19/2010
Previously published by Paternoster, 2009

This Edition published by Wipf and Stock Publishers
by arrangement with Paternoster

Series Preface

Baptists form one of the largest Christian communities in the world, and while they hold the historic faith in common with other mainstream Christian traditions, they nevertheless have important insights which they can offer to the worldwide church. Studies in Baptist History and Thought will be one means towards this end. It is an international series of academic studies which includes original monographs, revised dissertations, collections of essays and conference papers, and aims to cover any aspect of Baptist history and thought. While not all the authors are themselves Baptists, they nevertheless share an interest in relating Baptist history and thought to the other branches of the Christian church and to the wider life of the world.

The series includes studies in various aspects of Baptist history from the seventeenth century down to the present day, including biographical works, and Baptist thought is understood as covering the subject-matter of theology (including interdisciplinary studies embracing biblical studies, philosophy, sociology, practical theology, liturgy and women's studies). The diverse streams of Baptist life throughout the world are all within the scope of these volumes.

The series editors and consultants believe that the academic disciplines of history and theology are of vital importance to the spiritual vitality of the churches of the Baptist faith and order. The series sets out to discuss, examine and explore the many dimensions of their tradition and so to contribute to their on-going intellectual vigour.

A brief word of explanation is due for the series identifier on the front cover. The fountains, taken from heraldry, represent the Baptist distinctive of believer's baptism and, at the same time, the source of the water of life. There are three of them because they symbolize the Trinitarian basis of Baptist life and faith. Those who are redeemed by the Lamb, the book of Revelation reminds us, will be led to 'fountains of living waters' (Rev. 7.17).

Series Editors

Anthony R. Cross, Fellow of the Centre for Baptist History and Heritage, Regent's Park College, Oxford, UK

Curtis W. Freeman, Research Professor of Theology and Director of the Baptist House of Studies, Duke University, North Carolina, USA

Stephen R. Holmes, Lecturer in Theology, University of St Andrews, Scotland, UK

Elizabeth Newman, Professor of Theology and Ethics, Baptist Theological Seminary at Richmond, Virginia, USA

Philip E. Thompson, Assistant Professor of Systematic Theology and Christian Heritage, North American Baptist Seminary, Sioux Falls, South Dakota, USA

Series Consultant Editors

David Bebbington, Professor of History, University of Stirling, Scotland, UK

Paul S. Fiddes, Professor of Systematic Theology, University of Oxford, and Principal of Regent's Park College, Oxford, UK

Ken R. Manley, Distinguished Professor of Church History, Whitley College, The University of Melbourne, Australia

Stanley E. Porter, President and Professor of New Testament, McMaster Divinity College, Hamilton, Ontario, Canada

Matri Patrique in gratitudine dedicatus

Contents

Foreword by Timothy George..xiii

Acknowledgements...xvii

Abbreviations..xix

Introduction
Preliminary General Assertions 1
Stating the Problem.. 3

Chapter 1: Keach in Context
Continuity within Church History 9
Biography and Literature Review 32
Benjamin Keach's Life and Controversies...32
Beginnings 33
A Life of Controversy...35
Residence in London..39
Final Stages 44
Literature Review...45
Tradition, Successionism and Scholasticism 50
Keach vs. Tradition..50
Consensual Tradition...50
Exegetical Tradition 51
Dogmatic Tradition..55
Keach vs. Successionism..58
Keach vs. Scholasticism...59
The Use of Syllogism..60
The Use of Quaestio or Objection 60
Metaphysical Speculation 61
Conclusion 62

Chapter 2: Keach's Federal Theology
Introduction..63

Seventeenth Century Setting..65
Antinomianism..66
Tobias Crisp (1600-1643)...67
John Saltmarsh (d. 1647)..67
Henry Denne (1605/6?-1666)...67
1st. CHRISTIAN PERFECTION: GOD NEITHER SEEING NOR PUNISHING SINS...69
2nd. WAR AGAINST THE FLESH: THE PLACE OF THE LAW............................70
3rd. CHRISTIANS ARE PASSIVE IN JUSTIFICATION: FAITH ONLY MAKES IT KNOWN..71
4th. FAITH IS STRICTLY TO PRECEDE JUSTIFICATION..............................71
5th. COVENANTS OF REDEMPTION AND GRACE NOT THE SAME..............72
Baxterianism..72
Richard Baxter (1615-1691)...73
Daniel Williams (1643-1716)..73
Samuel Clark (1626-1701)..73
Second Antinomian Controversy..75
John Owen (1616-1683)...77
Isaac Chauncy (1632-1712)..78
Samuel Rutherford (c. 1600-1661)..78
Patrick Gillespie (1617-1675)..78
Occasion of Keach's Writing..79
An Exposition of Keach's Federal Theology.....................................80
Method or General Outline of the Covenant's Exposition..................81
Explanatory Propositions...81
Presentation of the Main Exchanges that Brought about and Established the Pact of Peace..83
The Parties Consult, Confer or Discuss the Terms of Peace..............83
The Father and the Son Agree on the Terms Proposed.....................86
Selection of a Mediator and his Role in the Covenant......................86
On the Necessity of Christ the Mediator...87
On the Dual Nature of the Mediator...87
The Offices of Christ..89
Sacerdotal Office...90
Regal Office..91
Prophetic Office..91
The Suretyship of Christ..92
The Confirmation of the Covenant of Peace.....................................95
The Proclamation of Peace..97
The Proclamation of Peace Defined...97
The Heralds of the Proclamation of Peace.....................................100
The Conditions on which the Covenant of Peace is Proclaimed.....101
Commencement of the Covenant of Peace.....................................103
The Nature of the Covenant of Peace...103
THE UNITY OF THE COVENANT..103

THE CONVENANT OF PEACE IS EQUIVALENT TO THE PACT OF GRACE 104
THE ABSOLUTENESS OF THE COVENANT OF GRACE 106
Evaluation and Conclusion 107
The Place of the Law..108
Justification from Eternity 109

Chapter 3: Keach's Doctrine of Baptism
Introductory Considerations..111
Keach's Interlocutors and Antagonists 113
William Burkitt (1650-1703)..113
James Owen (1654-1706) 116
John Flavell (1630?-1691) 119
The Athenian Society (1690-?)..120
Gyles Shute (b.c. 1650) 120
William Smythies (d. 1715) 121
John Rothwell (d. 1661) 121
Joshua Exell (fl. 1690s) 121
Keach's Doctrine of Baptism..122
The Ecclesiological Implications of Keach's Doctrine of Baptism..................122
Baptism and the Defection of Christendom 122
Believer's Baptism and the Furthering of the Reformation 128
Keach's Debates with his Antagonists 133
Recipients of Baptism..133
The Abrahamic Covenant 133
Was the Abrahamic Pact a Covenant of Grace? 134
Is Circumcision Part of the Covenant of Grace? 142
Has Baptism Replaced Circumcision?.. 146
Is Circumcision a Seal of the Foedus Gratiae? 152
The Great Commission 155
Federal Holiness...160
Benefits Accrued by Pedobaptism..165
Incipient Faith as Basis for Pedobaptism 173
Suffer Little Children 176
John's Confession and Baptism 178
Households 181
Antiquity..184
Church Fathers 189
Mode of Execution..197
  Immersion vs. βαπτίζω: Linguistic Consideration 198
  Immersion vs. the Practice of the Early Church 201
  Immersion: Typical and Metaphorical 204
  Immersion: Objections to It 206
  Evaluation and Conclusion 215

Keach's View of Pedobaptism and his Covenantal Conception......................215
Immersion as the Only Mode of Baptism..218
Comments on Both Keach's Ecumenical Leaning and his Uncompromising Stance on the Need of Reformation..219

Conclusion..**222**

Bibliography..**225**

Index...**249**

Foreword

The age of the Reformation was a time of vitality and change which gave us the compass, the printing press, the telescope, gunpowder, a map of the "New World", widespread inflation, the rise of the modern nation-state, wars of religion—and a word to describe all of this, "revolution," from Nikolaus Copernicus's famous work, *De revolutionibus orbium coelestium* of 1543. The Protestant Reformation was a revolution in the original scientific sense of that word: the return of a body in orbit to its original position. It was never the desire of Luther to start a new church from scratch. He and the other reformers who followed in his tracks wanted to re-form the one, holy, catholic, and apostolic church on the basis of the Word of God and to do so by returning to the historic faith of the early church as found in the pure teachings of the Holy Scriptures. This led to a fundamental reorientation in Christian theology. Luther's rediscovery of justification by faith alone, Zwingli's insistence on the clarity and certainty of Holy Scripture, Calvin's emphasis on the glory and sovereignty of God, and the Anabaptist quest for a true visible church all found expression in numerous new confessions, commentaries, liturgies, hymns, martyrologies, and church orders.

Like monasticism in an earlier age and Methodism in a later one, the Reformation was a project of renewal through retrieval, a return to the rudiments, with consequences far beyond what was first intended. For the impact of the Reformation was not confined to the first generation of hearers who responded to the reformers' message. Like a great earthquake which continues to generate scismic aftereffects, the Reformation set in motion a revolution in religious life the effects of which were being felt well into the next century.

Out of this ferment, the Baptist tradition as we know it today emerged in the early seventeenth century. Modern historians have isolated two separable beginnings of the English Baptist movement: the General Baptists, who evolved out of a church planted by Thomas Helwys at Spitalfields near London in 1612, which was an offshoot of the re-baptized exiled congregation of John Smyth; and the Particular Baptists, who arose among the underground London congregations of the late 1630's. The Generals stressed the universal scope of the atonement, holding with the Dutch theologian Jacobus Arminius that Christ died for all persons. The Particulars were Calvinistic in soteriology holding with most other Reformed Christians to the five heads of doctrine propounded by the Synod of Dort (1618-19).

David Riker presents here a detailed and nuanced study of the thought of Benjamin Keach, the leading Baptist theologian of his era. When Keach was born in Buckinghamshire in 1640, the Baptist movement was in its infancy; when he died in 1704 no one could rival Keach as a formative shaper of Baptist worship and theology. His status as a writer was eclipsed by John Bunyan, and his work as a denominational organizer was overshadowed by William Kiffin, but Keach was the most respected Baptist pastor-theologian of his day and his influence extended to colonial America through the work of his son, Elias Keach.

Benjamin Keach entered the stream of Baptist life as a fifteen-year-old lad when he was baptized by John Russell, a General Baptist pastor, who encouraged his early preaching ministry. Exactly how and when he was converted to a more orthodox Reformed soteriology remains a mystery. But in 1668, when he was twenty-eight years old, he was ordained as pastor of the Particular Baptist Church of Horsleydown in Southwark, across from London Bridge. This congregation, which grew to one thousand members under his ministry, attracted a series of distinguished ministers including John Gill, John Rippon, and Charles Haddon Spurgeon.

Keach's pastoral labors and voluminous writings touched every aspect of Baptist life during the turbulent times between the Restoration and the accession of Queen Anne. He was a signatory to the Second London Confession, defended hymn singing in public worship, supported the laying on of hands as a Gospel ordinance, and wrote against Antinomianism, Arminianism, and Sabattarianism. He also published popular catechisms, championed believers' baptism by immersion and advocated strict congregational communion. He joined with other dissenters in opposing religious coercion and the establishment of a national church. The fact that Keach himself had suffered in prison and at the pillory for his religious convictions added a special warrant to his arguments.

Riker's careful analysis of Keach's covenantal theology places him in the mainstream of the Reformed Orthodoxy of the time and presents him as the most able Baptist representative of that theological tradition. However, Keach's concern for the invisible church, founded on God's covenant of grace, did not attenuate his interest in the visible congregation of regenerated believers, the gathered saints who through baptism professed repentance and faith in Jesus Christ. As Riker shows, one of Keach's major contributions as a theologian was to relate the doctrine of God's sovereignty in salvation to the understanding of the church as a covenanted community of baptized believers.

This study also rescues Keach from the confines of a narrow denominational perspective by uncovering the ecumenical interest at the heart of his many writings. This vision of the catholicity of Benjamin Keach points to deeper continuities than has often been recognized among the Reformation of the sixteenth century, the Great Tradition of Christian faith through the centuries, and the Particular Baptist movement. By placing Keach in this wider ecclesial and theological context, Dr. Riker helps us better to appropriate him today not only as a great pioneer of the Baptist way but also as a *doctor ecclesiae* from whom we still have much to learn.

Timothy George
Senior Editor of Christianity Today,
Dean of Beeson Divinity School of Samford University,
Birmingham,
Alabama, USA

Acknowledgements

This book is the end result of my Ph.D. project at the University of Aberdeen. I am grateful to the following institutions and individuals whose assistance made possible the completion of this work.

Studying in Scotland has allowed me to make many kind and generous friends. My church, Aberdeen Christian Fellowship, was a constant fountain of encouragement and hope at many dark hours. My prayer partner Billy Mail and my pastor Rev. Dr. Richard Taylor offered me practical and spiritual support more times than I could possibly number. In addition, our weekly prayer meetings at the "kennel," forged friendships of rare depth and love. The "dogs," a group of student-rogues who met at my flat, shall forever have a especial place in my heart.

It has been a privilege and a joy to research at the University of Aberdeen. The staff, particularly 'Special Collection,' were always helpful and, at times, relentless in the pursuit of difficult resources. The environment of Old Aberdeen, with its medieval aura, time and time again reminded me that I was part of an ancient and distinguished tradition of scholarship and learning—a tradition to which I am proud to belong and will always remember with great fondness. I extend my gratitude also to the archivists at the University of Oxford: both Mr. Russel Edwards at Bodleian Libray, and Mrs. Sue Mills at Regent's Park, were particularly patient and overly kind during my several visits to Oxford. Prior to moving to Scotland, I worked on a M.A. at King's College, University of London, and for two and a half years the British Library was my "home." Later, again in the course of my doctorate, I had to return to the capital and was once more well-served at the British Library: I am indebted to this institution!

I want to express genuine appreciation to the Rev. Dean Timothy George: teacher, friend, encourager and companion of many pilgrimages. His influence on my perception in general, and on my theology in particular, have been *gigantic*. Truly, "I thank my God every time I remember you!"

Finally, special recognition to my loving daughter, Dienny Riker, who had to pay the enormous price of the absence of her father in order for this project to be completed: I express my deep heartfelt gratitude to her. In this connection, my cousins, Elias and Simone Dias, were most helpful and deserve my recognition. I am indebted to my parents, Joe and Florinda Riker, who believed in me more than myself, provided spiritual, financial and emotional support, and encouraged me continuously. Without their help this project could never have come to light. To them this work is dedicated with *profound* gratitude.

"Non nobis, Domine, non nobis, sed nomini tuo da gloriam!"

D. B. Riker
Canis Ultimus
Belém (Amazon Valley),
Brazil,
November 2008.

Abbreviations

BDBR	*Biographical Dictionary of British Radicals in the Seventeenth Century*, R. L. Greaves and Robert Zaller, 2 vols. Brighton, Sussex: The Harvest Press, 1983.
BHH	*Baptist History and Heritage*
CBTEL	*Cyclopedia of Biblical, Theological and Ecclesiological Literature*, John McClintock and James Strong, eds. (Rio, WI.: Ages, 2000).
C.C.S.L.	Corpus Christianorum Scriptorum Latinorum
CCJC	*The Cambridge Companion to John Calvin*, Donald K. McKim, ed. Cambridge: Cambridge University Press, 2004.
C.S.E.L.	Corpus Scriptorum Ecclesiasticorum Latinorum
CH	*Church History*
CR	*Corpus Reformatorum*
CTJ	*Calvin Theological Journal*
DHT	*The Dictionary of Historical Theology*, Trevor Hart, gen. ed. Carlisle, Cumbria and Grand Rapids, Mi.: Paternoster and Eerdmans, 2000.
DNB	*Dictionary of National Biography*. London, Smith, Elder, & co., 1885-1901.
EvQ	*Evangelical Quarterly*
FBJHT	*Foundations: A Baptist Journal of History and Theology*
GCS	*Die Griechischen Christlichen Schriftsteller der ersten Drei Jahrhunderte* Leipzig: J. C. Hinrichs'sche Buchhandlung, 1925.
JEH	*Journal of Ecclesiastical History*
JETS	*Journal of the Evangelical Theological Society*
JHI	*Journal of the History of Ideas*
JRH	*Journal of Religious History*
NAK	*Nederlands Archief voor Kerkgeschiedenis*
NSHE	*New Schaff-Herzog Encyclopedia of Religion Knowledge*. New York and London: Funk and Wagnalls Co., 1911.
OCP	*The Oxford Companion of Philosophy*, Ted Honderich, ed. Oxford: Oxford University Press, 1995.
ODNB	*Oxford Dictionary of National Biography: In Association with the British Academy: From the Earliest Times to the Year 2000*, H.C.G. Matthew and Brian Harrison, eds. (Oxford: Oxford

	University Press, 2004).
PAO	*Patrum Apostolicorum Opera* (Lipsiae: J. C. Hinrichs, 1876).
P.G.	Migne's Patrologiae cursus completus—Series Graeca.
P.L.	Migne's Patrologiae cursus completus—Series Latina.
RR	*Reformed Review*
SBET	*Scottish Bulletin of Evangelical Theology*
SCJ	*Sixteenth Century Journal*
SJT	*Scottish Journal of Theology*
THis	*The Historian*
TJ	*Trinity Journal*
URM	*Ultimate Reality and Meaning. Interdisciplinary Studies in the Philosophy of Understanding*
WTJ	*Westminster Theological Journal*

Introduction

This book is introduced under two headings. Under the first, 'preliminary general assertions,' an attempt will be made to delineate broadly the reason for and the purpose of this work. The second, 'stating the problem,' delineates the charges *sectarianism*, in the form of biblicism and successionism in so far as they relate to Benjamin Keach. It also offers a definition of *Reformed Orthodoxy*. Benjamin Keach, we shall argue, is more correctly associated with the latter than the former.

Preliminary General Assertions

There has been a remarkable paucity of studies on Benjamin Keach (1640-1704).[1] This dearth is rather puzzling, given the fact that he was one of the most important early Fathers of the Reformed Baptists. John Bunyan's status as a Baptist has been rightly called into question, given that he did not defend believer's baptism as essential to church membership.[2] Keach, however, was a fierce defender of this Baptist principle, and thus, if Bunyan is excluded, Keach stands, unquestionably, as the most important Reformed Baptist of the seventeenth century.

On the other hand, in the last decade of the twentieth century, vigorous and fruitful researches have been undertaken on the Reformation. These studies have changed our view of this movement. It is no longer tenable to understand the sixteenth century Reform as a total break with the medieval church. Although significant changes occurred, the Reformation and Counter-Reformation movements were deeply influenced by preceding ideas, which both remained with and shaped the heirs of the Reform. Catholicity was sought by both the Roman and the Protestant churches.[3]

More recent research has also shown that post-Reformation Reformed Protestantism is better understood as a tradition shaped by many individuals,

---

[1] See infra pp. 32-45, for a full biography.
[2] Bunyan had a lenient view of baptism, accepting as valid both credo- and pedobaptism. See, e.g., John Bunyan's, *Differences in Judgement About Water-Baptism, No Bar to Communion: Or, To Communicate with Saints, as Saints, proved lawful. In Answer to a Book written by the Baptists and published by Mr. T. P. and Mr. W. K., entituled, 'Some serious Reflections on that parts of Mr. Bunyan's "Confession of Faith," touching Church-Communion with unbaptised Believers.' Wherein Their Objections and Arguments are Answered, and the Doctrine of Communion still Asserted and Vindicated* (London: Printed for John Wilkins, 1673).
[3] A detailed discussion of this scholarship will be shown infra, chapter one, section one, 'continuity within church history,' pp. 9-16.

rather than a single figurehead. It is argued that John Calvin exerted a massive influence on Reformed Orthodoxy, but that he was not the only builder. That is, it is claimed that not one but many writers and confessions—such as Dort, Helvetic and Westminster—are responsible for defining the contours of Orthodoxy.[4]

In light of these studies, there is a need to re-evaluate the Baptist tradition. This reappraisal has already begun, with Hong-Guy Park's study of John Gill (1697-1771).[5] Our work proposes to continue this re-evaluation, but on an earlier father of the Reformed Baptist churches, Benjamin Keach.

Concerning Keach, there is abundant evidence in his own statements that may lead us to think that he is not a catholic Christian, but rather a thorough sectarian. His potentially platitudinous appeal to *sola Scriptura* might suggest such sectarianism. In addition, the Baptist tradition to which Keach belongs has been repeatedly portrayed as one of a line of sects going back to the New Testament. In other words, the Baptists have, at several points in their history, advocated successionism.

The only two scholarly works on Keach have not considered him a proper theologian. William Spears claims that Keach "was not a theologian in the technical sense of the term."[6] Barry Vaughn purports that Keach was a "practical" theologian.[7] As a result, Keach's *loci* are superficially examined, and the common verdict is that the man is a moderate Calvinist.[8] For now, at least two points are to be said in response to this: first, given his acknowledged significance,[9] Keach deserves more than a superficial treatment of his theology; second, Keach does not quite fit, we contend, the Calvinistic mould.[10]

This book has two interrelated purposes. First, it tries to demonstrate that Benjamin Keach is neither a sectarian nor a Calvinist, but rather a catholic Reformed theologian. Second, it attempts to explore two of Keach's *loci*, his doctrines of covenant and baptism: such exploration has never been done

---

[4] We shall be using lower case 'orthodoxy' to allude to the conception of Christianity consonant with the early creeds, and capitalised 'Orthodoxy' to refer to post-Reformation Reformed Protestantism. See below pp. 17-32, for a discussion of this more recent research.

[5] Hong-Guy Park, 'Grace and Nature in the Theology of John Gill, 1697-1771' (Ph.D. diss., University of Aberdeen, 2001).

[6] William Spears, 'The Baptist Movement in England in the Late Seventeenth Century as Reflected in the Work and Thought of Benjamin Keach, 1640-1704' (Ph.D. diss., University of Edinburgh, 1953), 61.

[7] James Barry Vaughn, 'Public Worship and Practical Theology in the Work of Benjamin Keach (1640-1704),' (Ph.D. diss., University of St. Andrews, 1990), iv.

[8] Spears, 'The Baptist Movement in England,' 80; Vaughn, 'Public Worship and Practical Theology,' 260-262.

[9] See infra, p. 5, footnote 23.

[10] We shall deal more extensively with both Spears and Vaughn, under 'literature review,' pp. 45-50, infra.

before. It is, perhaps, excusable that no one has meticulously considered Keach's federalism, given that his scheme is not fundamentally different—we claim—from mainstream federalists. Nevertheless, the purpose of examining his concept of covenant is to show exactly where he belongs. On the other hand, it is remarkable that his doctrine of baptism has never been scrutinised. For the importance of the man in particular, and the doctrine in general is undisputed in the life of the Baptist tradition.[11] The purpose of considering this *locus* is to suggest that Keach is indeed a theologian—a theologian trying to recover the proper practice of baptism. His theological acumen is well demonstrated in his relentless and skilful attacks on both pedobaptism and sprinkling. In this he does not see himself as deviating from post-Reformation Reformed Protestantism, but rather as continuing the work of church Reformation.

Stating the Problem

Notwithstanding contrary opinions, Baptists have often perceived themselves to be discontinuous with the empirical church.[12] As a result, the Fathers, the Medievals, the councils of the church, etc. (simply put, the Tradition), are deemed to be at best unnecessary additions and at worse corrupted accretions to *Scriptura*.[13] President Abraham Lincoln, not affiliated to any denomination but

---

[11] See infra, chapter three, 'introductory considerations,' pp. 111-113.

[12] For continuity with the historical church, see e.g., W. Morgan Patterson, *Baptist Successionism: A Critical View* (Valley Forge, PA.: The Judson Press, 1969). For discontinuity, see footnote 20 infra. For a good summary of the history of the Baptist tradition, see William Henry Brackney, *The Baptists* (New York: Greewood Press, 1988), 3-121. For a more comprehensive history, see H. Leon McBeth, *The Baptist Heritage: Four Centuries of Baptist Witness* (Nashville: Broadman Press, 1987). For a contextualized presentation of the confessions of faith of Baptists in Europe, see G. Keith Parker, *Baptists In Europe: History & Confessions of Faith* (Nashville: Broadman Press, 1982).

[13] Tradition (*tradere*, 'to hand down' or 'to deliver') is the dogmatic body forged by the empirical church and 'handed down' to every succeeding generation. That is, 'Tradition,' up to early Medieval times, is the fundamental teaching of the church. The omnipresent plight of those who discard the Tradition seems to be twofold: in the first place, due to a naïve understanding of history, they ignore the impossibility of bypassing historical locatedness; that is, of leaping hundreds of years back into Bibleland as if nothing had occurred in the meantime. Second, perhaps as a result of that, they tend to fall into the same errors that the early church incurred. See the fine essay of Anthony Lane, '*Sola Scriptura*? Making Sense of a Post-Reformation Slogan,' in *A Pathway into the Holy Scriptures*, Philip E. Satterthwaite and David F. Wright, eds. (Grand Rapids: Eerdmans, 1994), 297-324. See also, Carl E. Braaten, 'The Problem of Authority in the Church,' in *The Catholicity of the Reformation*, Carl E. Braaten and Robert W. Jenson, eds. (Grand Rapids: Eerdmans, 1996), 62-63. We shall be using capitalised 'Tradition'

coming from a Baptist family, well illustrates the biblicism, "no Creed but the Bible," which has been so prevalent among free church Protestants.[14] More pointedly, Reformed Baptists have upheld the same biblical exclusivism: no institution or person has exclusive access to the truth, inveighed Elias Smith, a Baptist pastor at the turn of the 19th century. "I further protest," Smith avers, "against the unrighteous and ungodly pretence of making the writing of the Fathers, the decrees of councils and synods, or the sense of the church, the rule and standard of judging of the sense of Scriptures, as Popish, Anti-Christian and dangerous to the church of God."[15] The usual outcome of this type of biblicism is the rejection of dogmatic and traditional language.[16] It might appear that Benjamin Keach was inclined to agree with Elias Smith and thus show himself to be a typical biblicist.[17] For, in contending for doctrinal purity, he says that the truth relies not "upon the practice and custom of men, Fathers, General Councils, Protestant Reformers or churches; but upon the Word of God."[18]

Besides the appeal to *sola Scriptura*, there is further evidence that Baptists have perceived themselves to be separated from the historical church, viz., the recurring theme of successionism in Baptist historiography. According to this theory, Baptists derive their ancestry directly from the Apostolic church via the

---

to refer to the dogmatic body as a whole, and lower case 'tradition' to any part of the said body.

[14] Nathan O. Hatch, 'Sola Scriptura and Novus Ordo Seclorum,' in *The Bible in America: Essays in Cultural History*, Nathan O. Hatch and Mark A. Noll, eds. (Oxford: Oxford University Press, 1982), 59-60. Arguably, the best modern exemplars of this position are the so-called 'non-denominational' or 'independent' churches.

[15] Elias Smith, *The Lovingkindness of God Displayed in the Triumph of Republicanism in America: Being a Discourse Delievered at Tauton (Mass.) July Fourth, 1809; at the Celebration of American Independence* (S.l.: s.n., 1809), 26-27; quoted by Hatch, *The Bible in America*, 67. For similar examples of biblicism among free church Protestants, see ibid., pp. 67-71.

[16] For example, dogmatic terms like, 'Trinity,' 'Consubstantial,' 'Person,' etc.; and traditional terminology—i.e., expressions associated with the historical church—such as, 'Blessed Virgin,' 'Eucharist,' 'St. Paul,' etc.

[17] Biblicism is the rejection of everything that is not *explicitly* stated in the Bible, and the concomitant dismissal of all non-biblical witnesses (Fathers, creeds, Medieval doctors, councils, etc.). In summary, it is the upholding of *Scriptura nuda*. On the other hand, *sola Scriptura* holds the Bible as the bar against which all tradition is to be tested and, if necessary, re-formed. Cf. Timothy George, *Theology of the Reformers* (Nashville: Broadman Press, 1988), 79-86.

[18] Benjamin Keach, *Light Broke Forth in Wales, expelling darkness, or, The Englishman's love to the antient Britains being an answer to a book, intituled Children's baptism from Heaven, published in the Welsh tongue by Mr. James Owen* (London: Printed and sold by William Marshall at the Bible in Newgate-street, 1696), 226. See also ibid., p. 31; idem, *The Rector Rectified and Corrected, or, Infant-baptism unlawful* (London: Printed and sold by John Harris, 1692), 181. Seventeenth century spelling maintained, but punctuation and capitalisation modernised throughout this book.

"Montanists, the so-called 'Novations,' Donatists, St. Patrick, the Bogomils, the Albigenses, the Lollards, the Waldensians and, of course, the Anabaptists ..."[19] In other words, the precursors of the Baptists are a catena of sects/people outside the Great church (i.e., the Eastern Orthodox and Western Catholic churches). The title of a book reprinted as late as 1931 at Ashland Avenue Baptist Church summarises successionism: *The Trail of Blood Following Christians Down through the Centuries, or the History of Baptist Churches from the Time of Christ, Their Founder, to the Present Day.*[20] Again, it seems that Keach would be in full agreement with the 'fall-of-the-church theory.' The Constantinian conversion of the fourth century, Keach says, set the course for the initial departure of the church from the Apostolic faith. By the end of the reign of Theodosius, 395 A.D., and the ascension of "the Papal power and [the] Turkish Empire," the church had degenerated.[21]

Contrary to appearances, however, we shall argue that Keach does not fit the mould of a traditional biblicist. Neither does he belong to the usual Calvinist caricature which has been used to portray him.[22] Additionally, we shall see that a close reading of Keach reveals that he is not a successionist. In our judgement, this is the *Problemstellung*: the sporadic works studying this Baptist preacher have not *depicted* him well, nor have they properly *located* him.[23] Our

---

[19] D. H. Williams, *Retrieving the Tradition and Renewing Evangelicalism: A Primer for Suspicious Protestants* (Grand Rapids, Michigan/Cambridge, U.K.: Eerdmans Publishing Co., 1999), 118.

[20] Williams, *Retrieving the Tradition*, 116-117. For other historians advocating organic Baptist successionism, see Adam Taylor, *The History of the English General Baptists*, 2 vols. (London: T. Bore, 1818); G. H. Orchard, *A Concise History of the Baptists from the Time of Christ, Their Founder, to the Eighteenth Century* (Lexington: Ashland Avenue Baptist Church, 1838); J. R. Graves, *The Tri-Lemme; or Death by Three Horns* (Nashville: South-Western Pub. Co., 1869); J. M. Cramp, *Baptist History: From the Foundation of the Christian Church to the Close of the Eighteenth Century*, 2d. ed. unabrid. (Philadelphia: American Baptist Pub. Society, 1869); D. B. Ray, *Baptist Successionism: a Hand-Book of Baptist History* (S.l.: Geo. E. Stevens & Co., 1871); William Cathcart, ed., *The Baptist Encyclopedia*, single ed. (Philadelphia: Louis H. Everts, 1883), 74; J. T. Christian, *A History of the Baptists Together with Some Account of Their Principles and Practices* (Nashville: Sunday School Board of the Southern Baptist Convention, 1922).

[21] Benjamin Keach, *Antichrist Stormed: or, Mystery Babylon the Great Whore, and the great City, proved to be the present Church of Rome* (London: Printed for Nath. Crouch at the Bell in the Poultrey near Cheapside, 1689), [ii-iii].

[22] Under 'literature review,' pp. 57-62, we shall meet authors depicting Keach as a follower of the Genevan Reformer.

[23] A common complaint of the few who have studied Keach is the accurate allegation that despite his notoriety in the late 17th and early 18th centuries, little work has been done to bring his memory back. Spears wrote the first monograph on Keach 250 years after his death. He aimed at filling a gap "in the annals of Baptist history." Within "the sphere of public worship," Spears concluded, "Keach is significant for the whole of

study, as said before, will attempt to demonstrate that Benjamin Keach is not a sectarian but rather a catholic thinker[24] and, more specifically, that he is part of the Reformed Orthodox movement.

How then are we to define the Reformed Orthodox tradition? This scholastic expression of Protestantism "indicates both the confessionally defined teaching of the Reformed churches *and* the era, circa 1565 to circa 1725, during which Reformed theologians made their greatest effort in the definition and defence of that confessional teaching." This movement accepted, elaborated and defended both the so-called "five points of Calvinism" and "the doctrines of the Trinity, the two natures of Christ and infant baptism." All of these teachings were maintained and argued for by the Reformed Orthodox on account of the assumption that these doctrinal positions "are either taught directly by Scripture or follow as necessary or suitable conclusions from the work of exegesis."[25] Besides our first chapter, 'Keach in Context,' this book will have two other *loci*: in the second chapter, 'Keach's Federal Theology,' our protagonist stands firmly within Orthodoxy; in the third, 'Keach's Doctrine of Baptism,' he departs from it.[26]

England; however, most of his contributions were made by speaking to and for the Baptists. No serious study has ever been made of Keach, not even a biography; yet there is no dubiety concerning his widespread reputation during and immediately following the years of his work." 'The Baptist Movement in England,' 231. Over thirty years later, James Carnes made the same complaint *verbatim*. 'The Famous Mr. Keach: Benjamin Keach and his Influence on Congregational Singing in the Seventeenth Century England' (M.A. thesis, Denton, Texas: North Texas State University, 1984), 105. Vaughn, six years later, wrote another thesis to salvage Keach "from near oblivion and to show that he was the most important practical theologian among the Calvinistic Baptists of the seventeenth century." 'Public Worship and Practical Theology,' iii.

[24] Catholicity (κατά, 'according to;' ὅλος, 'whole') as a concept of 'universal,' 'whole' or 'total,' seems to first appear in Ignatius. "Ubi comparuerit episcopus, ibi et multitudo sit; quemadmodum, ubi fuerit Christus Jesus, ibi catholica est Ecclesia." *Epistola Ad Smyrnaeos*, VIII, 2. P.G.5. For a recent 850-page-attempt at the difficult appraisal of "who or what is a catholic?" see Diarmaid MacCulloch, *Reformation: Europe's House Divided 1490-1700* (London: Penguin Group, 2003).

[25] Richard A. Muller, *After Calvin: Studies in the Development of a Theological Tradition* (Oxford: Oxford University Press, 2003), 36. Cf. Idem, *Scholasticism and Orthodoxy in the Reformed Tradition: An Attempt at Definition* (Grand Rapids, MI.: Calvin Theological Seminary, 1995), 26.

[26] John Gill—one of Keach's successors, and of greater erudition—exhibits the same characteristic. The Particular Baptists are to be placed among the Reformed Orthodox, in spite of the complete difference of opinion "between Baptists and the Reformed confessional tradition over the doctrine of infant baptism: this one doctrine aside, their theology is primarily Reformed and what disagreements remain are nonetheless disagreements with and often within the Reformed tradition rather than indications of reliance on another theological or confessional model." Richard A. Muller, 'John Gill and the Reformed Tradition: A Study in the Reception of Protestant Orthodoxy in the

To return to the themes of biblicism and successionism, what are we to make of Keach's statements above? The first one—his dismissal of "the practice and custom of men, Fathers, General Councils, Protestant Reformers or churches"—was offered in the context of the dispute over pedo- vs. credobaptism. Evidently, whenever any tradition would conflict with what he understood to be the teaching of the Bible, no authority could overrule Holy Writ. On that score, needless to say, he, a Puritan,[27] was no different from other Protestants.[28] As to the second statement—that the church had fallen—it is correct to hold that Keach saw the ascension and domination of the Roman church as the degeneration of the Apostolic church. Even here, however, Keach is subtle in his ecclesiological approach: although the visible church suffered massive decline, there were *throughout all ages* Christians *within* her.[29] Moreover, as we shall see, Keach talks about the Fathers and Medievals favourably and calls upon them to support his points.[30]

Our procedure will be as follows: first, we shall introduce significant recent research on Reformation and post-Reformation historiography and then attempt to locate Keach in terms of its results. Second, Keach's doctrine of the covenant will be shown in order to demonstrate that he is a mainstream Reformed federalist. Third, an exhaustive study of Keach's doctrine of baptism will be presented in order to show that though in disagreement with Orthodoxy, he sees himself not as departing from it, but rather as a theologian carrying on the work of the Reformation. He believes that the Reformers dealt with the more fundamental issues, but left undone subsidiary points, which the Baptists are

---

Eighteenth Century,' in *The Life and Thought of John Gill (1697-1771): A Tercentennial Appreciation*, Michael A. G. Haykin, ed. (Leiden: E. J. Brill, 1997), 3.

[27] All that we mean by 'Puritan' is 'English Reformed.' On the whole, Puritanism stood within the bounds of the Reformed tradition. Robert A. Coughenour, 'The Shape and Vehicle of Puritan Hermeneutics,' in *RR* 30 (1976): 23-34, p. 24. On the difficulty of defining a Puritan, see Christopher Durston and Jacqueline Eales, 'The Puritan Ethos, 1560-1700,' in *The Culture of English Puritanism, 1560-1700*, Christopher Durston and Jacqueline Eales, eds (London: Macmillan Press, 1996), 1-31; William Lamond, *Puritanism and historical controversy* (London: UCL Press, 1996), 1-11; Harry Grant Plum, *Restoration Puritanism: A Study of the Growth of English Liberty* (Port Washington, N.Y.: Kennikat Press, 1972), 3, 5-6; Thomas D. Lea, 'The Hermeneutics of the Puritans,' in *JETS* 39/2 (June 1996): 271-284, pp. 271-272; Ian Breward, 'The Significance of William Perkins,' in *JRH* 4 (1966-67): 113-128, pp. 117-118.

[28] It "is a platitude of history" that Protestants appealed to Scripture as final arbiter in theological questions. The fact that the Reformed "were vehement asserters of its finality is also common knowledge." Perry Miller, *The New England Mind: The Seventeenth Century* (Cambridge, MA.: Harvard University Press, 1967), 19. On the emphasis laid on the authority of Scripture by Puritanism, see e.g., Lea, 'The Hermeneutics of the Puritans,' 271-284; Cougnenour, 'The Shape and Vehicle of Puritan Hermeneutics,' 23-34.

[29] Evidence to be presented infra, pp. 58-59.

[30] See, e.g., pp. 50-55, 58, 164, 209.

handling. The three points correspond to chapters one through three respectively.

CHAPTER ONE

Keach in Context

This chapter will be divided into three major sections. In the first one, we shall present some of the results of the so-called *Obermanschule*—a school of thought which did much to reverse the segmentation of church history.¹ In this connection our task will be to draw a line from the early church all the way to Keach, or, to state the converse, to place our protagonist along a continuum, which runs back through the Reformation, Medieval, Patristic and New Testament. Then, in Section II, a biography of this Baptist theologian will be offered and also a review of scholarly literature. Section III will look into Keach's relation to the issues of church tradition, successionism and scholasticism.

Continuity within Church History

The old historiographical paradigm representing the Middle Ages as a benighted period of decline or an era of complete *diastasis* or discontinuity with the Reformation has undergone a shift. Breaking down the segmentation between the Middle Ages and the Reformation, and showing that the roots of the latter period lay deep within the former, the works of Heiko Oberman and David Steinmetz, *inter alios*, have portrayed the period in a new light.²

---

¹ See Lyle D. Bierma's book review of, The Age of Reform, 1250-1550: An Intellectual and Religious History of Late Medieval and Reformation Europe, by Steven Ozment. *CTJ* 16 (1981): 100-103, p. 100.
² Heiko Augustinus Oberman, *Archbishop Thomas Bradwardine: A Fourteenth-century Augustinian. A Study of his Theology in its Historical Context* (Utrecht: Kemink en Zoon, 1957); idem, *The Harvest of Medieval Theology: Gabriel Biel and Late Nominalism* (Cambridge, Mass.: Harvard University Press, 1963); idem, *Forerunners of the Reformation* (New York: Holt, Rinehart, and Wilson, 1966); idem, *Masters of the Reformation: The Emergence of a New Intellectual Climate in Europe*, Dennis Martin, trans. (Cambridge: Cambridge University Press, 1981); idem, *The Dawn of the Reformation* (Edinburgh: T. & T. Clark, 1986); idem, *The Impact of the Reformation* (Grand Rapids: Eerdmans, 1994); idem, *The Reformation: Roots and Ramifications*, Andrew Gow, trans. (Edinburgh: T. & T. Clark, 1994). Charles E. Trinkaus and Heiko Oberman, eds., *The Pursuit of Holiness in Late Medieval and Renaissance Religion* (Leiden: Brill, 1974), see Trinkaus' foreword, xi, for a summary of Oberman's view of the transition from Middle Ages into the Reformation. David C. Steinmetz, *Misericordia*

Beginning with his 1957 doctorate on Thomas Bradwardine (†1349) and onwards, Oberman has demonstrated that the period was not one of declension and decay.³ Rather, the theology done in the Middle Ages was one of reaping and innovation, as illustrated by Gabriel Biel's creativity and interaction with the preceding theological tradition.⁴ Instead of singling out so-called "revolutionaries," such as Pierre de Bruys (a.c. 1106), John Wycliffe (c. 1330-1384) or John Huss (c. 1373-1415) and then proceeding to analyse how they dissent from the church, Oberman tried to trace trajectories, chains of thought or undercurrents within the church; that is, instead of locating *individuals* and showing how they disagreed with the church, he dealt with *ideas* shared by different traditions within the said institution. In so doing, Oberman was able to identify philosophical and theological concepts, which were part of the medieval church and which extended in different ways into the Reformation.

The concept of what Oberman calls "Tradition I and II" is a good illustration of the point: during the Middle Ages, there were two very different ways of understanding the relationship between the Bible and Tradition; both ways were acceptable and co-existed peaceably side by side. Tradition I held Scripture plus the exegetical tradition as authoritative, with the latter submitted to the former. Tradition II is exactly the same, but with the addition of oral tradition as a source of authority. The first tradition "represents the sufficiency of Holy Scripture as understood by the Fathers and doctors of the church. In the case of disagreement between these interpreters, Holy Scripture was the final

---

Dei: The Theology of Johannes von Staupitz in its Late Medieval Setting (Leiden: Brill, 1968); idem, *Luther in Context* (Bloomington: Indiana University Press, 1986); idem, 'The Scholastic Calvin,' in *Protestant Scholasticism: Essays in Reassessment*, Carl R. Trueman and R. Scott Clark, eds. (Carlisle, Cumbria: Paternoster Press, 1999). Steven Ozment, *The Age of Reform, 1250-1550: An Intellectual and Religious History of Late Medieval and Reformation Europe* (New Haven: Yale University Press, 1980).

³ For portrayals of the Middle Ages as an epoch of disintegration and/or declension, see e.g., Johan Huizinga, *The Waning of the Middle Ages: A Study of the Forms of Life, Thought and Art in France and the Netherlands in the XIVth and XVth Centuries*, F. Hopman, trans. (London: Edward Arnold & Co., 1924); Rudolf Sohm, *Outlines of Church History*, Sinclair May, trans. (London: Macmillan & Co., 1895), 135-145; Joseph Lortz, *The Reformation in Germany*, Ronald Walls, trans., 2 vols. (London: Darton, Longman & Todd, 1968), although very nuanced, the portraiture here is one in which Luther "discover[s] the Gospel" and thus stands discontinuous with the decadent preceding period, I: 194; idem, 'The Basic Elements of Luther's Intellectual Style,' in *Catholic Scholars Dialogue with Luther*, Jared Wicks, comp. (Chicago, 1970), 3-33; Erol Hulse, *An Introduction to the Baptists* (Haywards Heath, Sussex: Carey Publications, 1973), 5-23; Louis Bouyer, *The Spirit and Forms of Protestantism*, A. V. Littledale, trans. (London: The Harvill Press, 1956), 8-16, 161-164; Armand Maurer, *Medieval Philosophy* (New York: s.n., 1962), 265; Gordon Leff, *The Dissolution of the Medieval Outlook: An Essay on Intellectual and Spiritual Change in the Fourteenth Century* (New York: s.n., 1976), 91.

⁴ Oberman, *The Harvest of Medieval Theology*, 423-424.

authority." The exegetical tradition is an *integral* part of it and thus never to be disclaimed or repudiated; on the contrary, the exegetical tradition is to be "understood as the mode of reception of the *fides* or *veritas* contained in" the Bible. "Since the appeal to extra scriptural tradition is rejected, the validity of ecclesiastical traditions and *consuetudines* is not regarded 'self-supported' but depends on its relation to the faith handed down by God in Holy Scripture."[5] Thomas Bradwardine, John Wycliffe and Wessel Gansfort (†1489) would all be representatives of Tradition I. On the other hand, Tradition II encompasses the recorded and unrecorded "part of the apostolic message as approved by the church. Here it is not the function of the doctors of Holy Scripture but that of bishops which is relatively more stressed." These ecclesiastical authorities are deemed to possess a separate "oral tradition, to a certain undefined extent independent, not of the Apostles, but of what is recorded in the canonical books. Ecclesiastical traditions, including canon law, are invested with the same degree of authority as that of Holy Scripture." Representatives of this school would be William of Occam (†1349), Pierre d'Ally (†1420), Jean Charlier Gerson (†1429) and Gabriel Biel (†1495). By and large, theological formulations were made based on Tradition I until the early 1300s; with Tradition II employed on a supplementary basis.[6] With the advent of the Reformation and Counter-Reformation, the broad and somewhat loosely defined Western church bifurcated into two major blocks, sc., the Protestant and the Roman Catholic churches. The inheritors of Traditions I and II are respectively the former and the latter.[7] Understood in this light, the doctrine of *sola Scriptura* gains its proper context;[8] for, ultimately, the battle between the

---

[5] Oberman, *The Harvest of Medieval Theology*, 371-372. Cf. e.g., Idem, *The Dawn of the Reformation*, 280-288. Tradition I, to put it simply, is that which is opened or revealed by the biblical exegetical tradition. Ibid., 288. [As an interesting aside, we may add that this way of understanding Christianity's source of authority—especially Tradition II, but also Tradition I—makes this source a 'living' entity, so to say. Perhaps Chillingworth's famous motto, "the Bible and the Bible only is the religion of the Protestants," eventually came to destroy the dynamic concept of Tradition I among a large segment of Protestantism, as this is evidenced by the disappearance of the early creeds in many modern evangelical churches. William Chillingworth, The Religion of Protestants, A Safe Way to Salvation, in *The Works of William Chillingworth* (Oxford: s.n., 1838), I: 157-280.]

[6] Oberman, *The Harvest of Medieval*, 372-374. For the full discussion of Tradition I and II, see ibid., pp. 361-412. On the authority of church tradition, see Emil Brunner, *O Equívoco sobre a Igreja*, Paulo Arantes, trans. (São Paulo: Novo Século, 2000), 40-52, especially, 48-49.

[7] See the conclusions of the excellent essay, 'Quo vades Petre? Tradition from Ireneus to Humani Generis,' by Oberman, *The Dawn of the Reformation*, 280-289.

[8] *Sola Scriptura* does not mean the complete disregard for other authorities, sources or creeds: all these are rather subservient to *sacra pagina*. In other words, the Bible only "is the *norma normans non normata*, the norm or rule that rules but is not itself ruled."

Reformers and the Tridentines did *not* take place on the basis of a choice between Tradition and the Bible; rather their dispute represented a "clash of two radically different concepts of tradition: Tradition I and Tradition II."[9]

To what has been said, we may add two other evidences of continuity between the Reformation and the Great Tradition prior to the sixteenth century: one general, the use of the Fathers; the other particular, St. Augustine. The import of the *Patres* to the Reformers and their descendants was immense; for believing that the Protestant church was the true catholic ecclesia and, concomitantly, that the Roman church had departed from the faith, the Reformers and their successors deemed "the best of the tradition" theirs "by right." That this is the case can be seen by the new impetus employed by Protestants in the study of the Fathers, even coining a term such as "patrology" to describe their new style of appraising these authorities.[10] Augustinianism,[11] in particular, evinces also a linkage between the Reformation and the past.[12] Here

---

As faith is never alone, so also Scripture is not meant to be alone. For it is not possible to theologise without the aid of other sources or authorities; unless, that is, one wants to replace these authorities with his or her own adjudication. Nevertheless, the Bible alone is the final arbiter "to which one can appeal against all ecclesiastical authority. This was and remains the heart of the meaning of sola Scriptura." Lane, 'Sola Scriptura? Making Sense of a Post-Reformation Slogan,' 324, 327.

[9] Oberman, *The Dawn of the Reformation*, 283. Cf. D. H. Williams, 'The Search for Sola Scriptura in the Early Church', in *Interpretation: A Journal of Bible and Theology*, 52/4 (1998): 354-366, p. 357; Carl E. Braaten, 'The Problem of Authority in the Church,' 60-61.

[10] Muller, *After Calvin*, 52-53. Johann Gehard, a Lutheran Orthodox, composed the first modern study of the Fathers; that is, he put together a biographical account with the works and opinions of the doctors from the early church all the way to the Middle Ages. Robert L. Wilken, 'Lutheran Pietism and Catholic Piety,' in *The Catholicity of the Reformation*, 89.

[11] By it, we simply mean the soteriological monergism stressed by Augustine, with his emphasis on predestination, the irremediable nature of human sin, and God's utterly gratuitous forgiveness. For this and other less traditional understandings of 'Augustinianism,' see Frank A. James III, *Peter Martyr Vermigli and Predestination: The Augustinian Inheritance of an Italian Reformer* (Oxford: Claredon Press, 1998), 128-129; Steinmetz, *Luther and Staupitz*, 13-15.

[12] Obviously, there were other trajectories of thought, such as the Franciscan and Thomistic schools; nevertheless, the doctor gratiae was never absent. Oberman, *The Dawn of the Reformation*, 8-10. "There is probably no phase of medieval intellectual life," Oberman contends, "that could not be portrayed as having reassessed and redisgested the Augustinian legacy." It is striking that a medieval man like Bradwardine, when in need of finding the "intent of Scripture and of its expositors and [when] extolling the consensus of the church, Bradwarding could not escape the fact that his key informants (from Anselm, Bernard, Hugh of St Victor and Peter Lombard through Thomas and Scotus) had turned to Augustine when arriving at authentic and substantial assertions." Masters of the Reformation, 64-65. Cf. Willem J. van Asselt and Eef

we have a current of thought flowing from Patristic, through medieval, and into Reformation and post-Reformation theology.[13] Apart from the soteriological aspect of his thought, the *doctor catholicus* was a revered patristic authority, whose thought was often appealed to from different sides amidst controversy. It goes without saying that the Reformers and their descendants occasionally disagreed with Augustine and, sometimes, strongly criticised him.[14] Nevertheless, Augustine's authority is called upon by Luther,[15] Melanchthon,[16] Zwingli,[17] Calvin,[18] Bullinger,[19] and the Puritans across the board.[20]

Dekker, 'Introduction,' in *Reformation and Scholasticism: An Ecumenical Enterprise*, Willem J. van Asselt and Eef Dekker, eds. (Grand Rapids: Baker Academic, 2001), 36-37. For a summary of doctrinal developments as they relate to continuity within the medieval church (1100-1460s), see Oberman, *The Impact of the Reformation*, 35-37.

[13] The theology of the Reformers "stands in clear continuity with the Augustinian tradition of the later Middle Ages, just as the doctrine of the more synergistic thinkers of the ages has its clear medieval antecedents. Any comparison, therefore, between the teaching of Calvin and his contemporaries on the doctrine of predestination and the teaching of the later Reformed Orthodox theologians must take into consideration the fact that Calvin and other Reformers did not invent the doctrine and that their definitions and those of the Protestant Orthodox stand within and responsive to a long tradition of biblical interpretation and dogmatic formulation including such later medieval theologians as Thomas Bradwardine, Gregory of Rimini, and Johannes Staupitz." Richard A. Muller, 'Calvin and the "Calvinists": Assessing Continuities and Discontinuities Between the Reformation and Orthodoxy – Part I,' in *CTJ* 30 (1995): 345-375, pp. 362-363.

[14] "Ergo potest esse ecclesia, quae recte sentiat, cuius sit euangelion, etiam si non habeat Romanum pontificem; quo quid absurdus dici potest iuxta doctrinas et precepta hominum? Verum ne curramus extra oleas, videmini quantum nos divinare possumus, ad id Augustini respexisse, ad quo omnes ceu sub Telamonii scutum confugiunt, qui traditiones humanas supra euangelium evehunt: Euangelio non crederem, nisi ecclesia adprobasset euangelium. Hic aequitatem vestram imploro, ut libere dicatis, an non hoc Augustini dictum vidatur aequo esse audacius, aut imprudentius excidisse? Fingite enim Augustinum nunquam natum esse; adhuc tamen erat euagelium bonum gratiae dei nuncium, adhuc erat commercium, quod deus gratia sua cum deplorato hominum genere inierat idemque futurum erat, si posteaquam natus est, nunquam credidisset. Num qui ante Augustinum fuerunt, idem senserunt? Minime, nam nullis id literis proditum est ... At hoc esset impium, si quod deus ipse gerit, opus habere diceremus humana autoritate. Relinquitur ergo vel Augustinum fortius quam consultius id dicti pronunciasse, aut nunquam crediturum fuisse, si antequam scriptum esset euangelium, ipusum praedicari audivisset; nam nullus hominum tum adprobarat nedum totum aliquod concilium." Huldreich Zwingli, *Sämliche Werke* (Berlim: Verlag von C. A. Schwetschke and Sohn, 1905), I: 293. 1-28.

[15] Appeals to Augustine superabound in Luther's corpus. See e.g. how Luther relies on this Father to explain his understanding of God's 'rest' in Heb. 4.4, *D. Martin Luthers Werke: kritische Gesamtausgabe* (Weimar: Bohlau, 1883--), XXIX: 161-163. For several other positive citations of Augustine, see ibid. seqq.

Yet another evidence of continuity between the medieval and Reformation theology is the use of the scholastic method. That is, after an initial rejection of Aristotelianism, Melanchthon increasingly made use of "Aristotle's doctrine of matter and form, substance and accidents, and the rules of syllogistic thinking."[21] Scholasticism as a pedagogical tool, "flourished in Wittenberg under Melanchthonian leadership and was emulated by other Protestant universities, both Reformed and Lutheran."[22]

---

[16] "Postremo etiam si voti violatio reprehendi posset, tamen non videtur statim sequi, quod coniugia talium personarum, dissoluenda sint. Nam Augustinus negat debere dissolui 27. Quaest. 1 Cap. Nuptiarum, cuius non est leuis autoritas, etiamsi alij postea aliter senserunt." Philip Melachthon, *Confessio Augustana Ipsa*, s.v., 'De Votis Monachorum,' *CR*, 26.

[17] "Nam de me ipso coram deo testor, euangelii vim atque summam cum Joannis Augustinique tractatuum lectione didici, tum diligenti Graecanicarum Pauli epistolarum, quas hisce manibus ante undecim annos exscripsi, quum tu annis iam octo regnes." Zwingli, *Sämliche Werke*, V: 713-714.

[18] As dogmatic constructions were built, Augustine was claimed by both Protestants and Catholics: "'clearly Augustine is with us' [Calvin, *Institutes*, III.iv.33]. Indeed, the phrase could serve as a caption for an entire epoch endeavouring to come to terms with its scholastic past." Oberman, *The Masters of the Reformation*, 75. Although John Chrysostom was Calvin's most respected exegete, the Genevan Reformer was polite in his disagreements with Augustine. Anthony N. S. Lane, 'Calvin's Use of the Fathers and the Medievals', in *CTJ* 16 (1981): 149-205, pp. 172-173.

[19] "Quod si cui haec sententia nostra eiusque ex hisce Pauli locis confirmatio noua esse uidet, issciat D. Aur. August. ex hoc ipso Pauli ad Corinthios loco idem collegisse quod nos. Verba eius extant Tracta. in Ioan. XLV. in hanc ferme sententiam, ..." Heinrich Bullinger, *De Testamento seu Foedere Dei unico & aeterno Heinrychi Bullingeri breuis expositio* (Tigurini: In Aedibus Christ. Frosch. Mense Septemb. An., 1534), 26-27.

[20] William Haller, *The Rise of Puritanism: Or, the way to New Jerusalem as set forth in Pulpit and Press from Thomas Cartwright to John Lilburne and John Milton, 1570-1643* (New York: Columbia University Press, 1938), 85. For the general character of Puritanism, see Miller, *The New England Mind*. Second only to the Bible, Miller maintains, Augustine is Puritanism's greatest influence. Ibid., 4.

[21] John Patrick Donnelly, *Calvinism and Scholasticism in Vermigli's Doctrine of Man and Grace* (Leiden: Brill, 1976), 9. Donnelly concludes his fine study on Reformed scholasticism saying that "Jerome Zanchi was the most thorough-going and influential in pioneering Calvinistic scholasticism, Theodore Beza was the best known and most prolific, but Peter Martyr Vermigli was the first and the inspiration of all who came after." Ibid., 10. The scholastic method of the middle Ages and the one used by post-Reformation Protestants, by and large, share common features, such as, the use of *loci*, the truth expressed in propositional forms, the goal of complete dogmatic systems, the employment of natural theology, etc.

[22] Asselt and Dekker, 'Introduction,' 27. Cf. David Charles, 'Aristotelianism,' s.v., *OCP*. The Protestant *evangelium* has deep roots in the Western church prior to the Reformation. Among the Lutherans, the message of Luther represents fundamentally an evolution of the doctrine of penance, rather than the mere study of Paul or a

Therefore, the Reformation is not to be deemed a break from the medieval church.[23] To visit the past, to rearrange it, to try to come to terms with it, "even when the attempt succeeds, will never obliterate the archetypes that provide our perceptual and conceptual models."[24] Small wonder, then, that the greatest part of Christian doctrine was maintained and considered articles of faith by the Reformers. Thus, for example, the ecumenical creeds, the Chalcedonian definition, the doctrines of creation, providence, Trinity, etc. were embraced across the board by Protestantism.[25] To put it another way, although there were

---

Turmerlebnis. Just like the medieval Scotists had done, Luther encouraged the believer "to have faith in the word of the priest and be assured of his absolution, and developed the notions of faith and assurance in his Gospel out of those concepts." Additionally, Melanchthon was influenced by "Erasmus' *Novum Instrumentum* and worked ... within the matrix of the Franciscan and Nominalistic traditions" in his formulation of justification by imputation. Among the Reformed, Zwingli was influenced by humanism in his concept of the Eucharist as a memorial event. Other developments—such as lapsarian teleology, particular redemption and federalism—have deep roots in some streams of medieval scholasticism which emphasised "the freedom of divine will and its free acceptance in salvation. All of these doctrines—doctrines that are essential to Protestantism or, at least, characterised a part of its tradition—have their antecedents within the Catholic church and must be seen as a development of that tradition, even if developed in new directions." Stephen Strehle, *The Catholic Roots of the Protestant Gospel: Encounter Between the Middle Ages and the Reformation* (Leiden: E. J. Brill, 1995), 2-3.

[23] Incidentally, according to Routley, it is not accurate to refer to the medieval Western church as "the Roman Catholic Church," for this latter institution is the communion tied by the Tridentine resolutions. Erik Routley, *Creeds and Confessions: The Reformation and Its Modern Ecumenical Implications* (London: Gerald Duckworth & Co. Ltd., 1962), 34.

[24] Oberman, *The Reformation*, 3. The Reformation was not a movement which aimed at turning aside from catholicity; rather, it "was a turn toward the very heart of the catholic tradition." David S. Yeago, 'The Catholic Luther,' in *The Catholicity of the Reformation*, 26. His italics. See also, ibid., p. 29. "The Reformed churches have always understood the Reformation not as a cessation of the tradition of the church, but rather as a turning back to the wellspring of tradition." Jürgen Moltman, 'Theologia Reformata et Semper Reformanda,' in *Toward the Future of Reformed Theology: Tasks, Topics, Traditions*, David Willis and Michael Welker, eds. (Grand Rapids, MI./Cambridge, U.K.: Eerdmans Publishing Co., 1999), 124.

[25] Richard A. Muller, *Post-Reformation Reformed Dogmatics: Volume 1 Prolegomena to Theology* (Grand Rapids, MI.: Baker Book House, 1987), 17; idem, *God, Creation, and Providence in the Thought of Jacob Arminius: Sources and Directions of Scholastic Protestantism in the Era of Orthodoxy* (Grand Rapids, MI.: Baker Book House, 1991), 279; idem, *The Unaccommodated Calvin: Studies in the Formation of a Theological Tradition* (New York: Oxford University Press, 2000), 39. In the Anglo-American world, Oberman claims, the assumption that "Luther discovered the Gospel" is a given. Protestants should be embarrassed by such a triumphalistic arrogance. Did nobody know the *evangelium* prior to the Reformation, "did Luther not refer to innumerable faithful

obvious discontinuities between the medieval church and the churches that appeared after the debates (ecclesiological, soteriological, sacramental and other issues were called into question and underwent significant changes), the Reformers were concerned with re-forming, not creating *ex nihilo* a new church.[26] Likewise, the Counter-Reformed church maintained the bulk of the Tradition, but also modified it through the introduction of dogmatic definitions and normativity to that which had been a stream of thought among many. Trent illustrates the dogmatic definitions; a new vow for priests exemplifies normativity: in this priestly pledge, the ecclesiological concept of a gathering of believers around the Word and sacrament was rejected, and out of many "medieval concepts of the true church, one single strand was now to be followed as the unique delineation of orthodoxy."[27]

---

prophets and evangelists? Did he not always speak of the medieval church as our common Mother Church that handed down the treasures of the Gospel with such faithfulness? The medieval church passed the Apostles' Creed, the Lord's Prayer, the sacraments and Holy Scripture down from one generation to the next. Without these treasures and without the faithful perseverance of the medieval church no faith would be imaginable to later generations." *The Reformation*, 63. For Luther and Calvin on church Tradition, see David Steinmetz, *Luther and Staupitz: An Essay in the Intellectual Origins of the Protestant Reformation* (Durham, N.C.: Duke University Press, 1980), 85-97.

[26] A marked contrast between the Radical and Magisterial Reformers is a concern to maintain "continuity with the church's teaching" on the part of the latter. William, *Interpretaion*, 358. See also, Muller, *God, Creation, and Providence*, 279; Carl E. Braaten and Robert W. Jenson, eds., *The Catholicity of the Reformation*, vii-ix; Christian Link, 'The Notae Ecclesiae: A Reformed Perspective,' in *Toward the Future of Reformed Theology*, 258; Lane, 'Calvin's Use of the Fathers and Medievals,' 166; J. F. Peter, 'The Place of Tradition in Reformed Theology,' in *SJT* 18 (1965): 294-307, pp. 301-302.

[27] Oberman, *Masters of the Reformation*, 243. See the lengthy quotation of this 1523 priestly vow on the same page. Pelikan argues that the course set by the Reformers was more catholic than the one set by the Tridentines. In effect, he affirms, a Reformer such as Philip Melanchthon, with immense grasp of patristics and medieval scholasticism, could demonstrate that in rejecting the proposals of the Reformation, "Trent was also condemning a considerable portion of the very catholic tradition it claimed to be exalting." Jaroslav Pelikan, *Obedient Rebels: Catholic Substance and Protestant Principle in Luther's Reformation* (London: SCM Press, 1964), 49-51. Cf. Peter Toon, 'Introduction,' in *Puritans, the Millenium and the Future of Israel: Puritan Eschatology 1600-1660*, Peter Toon, ed. (Cambridge & London: James Clarke & Co. Ltd., 1970), 21. "Pode parecer paradoxal, mas é fato que a teologia Reformada nutre a noção mais estrita de tradição—uma noção que é idêntica àquela do cristianismo primitivo. *Os reformadores são os verdadeiros tradicionalistas*; eles tinham mais seriamente a idéia da tradição como preservação do Evangelho original." Brunner, *O Equívoco sobre a Igreja*, 51. His emphases.

The Western schism generated, besides the Roman church, two traditions within magisterial Protestantism: the Lutheran and the Reformed churches. Whereas the former had a single fountainhead, the latter had not one but several influences. John Calvin was indeed very influential, but he was not, emphatically not, the only builder.[28] Other theological minds were at work—such as Zwingli, Bullinger, Vermigli, Hyperius—whose contributions were significant.[29] Muller presents four characteristics of these two traditions, as each strove to promote 'orthodoxy' or 'precise teaching.' First, Orthodoxy, both Lutheran and Reformed, is a movement that proposes to present authentic Christianity in contradistinction to the doctrines of the many opponents challenged in polemical arguments. "Right teaching is for the edification of the church on both the positive and the polemical levels. Second, Orthodoxy indicates also a sense of catholicity, of continuity both with the revelation contained in the scriptural deposit and with the valid teaching of the church in past centuries." Third, Orthodoxy strongly connects

> systematic theology and church confessions, the confessions acting as subsidiary norm in the development and exposition of doctrinal systems: even at its most rigid and formal extreme, Orthodoxy, so-called, relates to the conviction that true doctrine can be stated fully and finally in a series of strict doctrinal determinations. In this sense, Orthodoxy involves an approach to scripture as the deposit of truth out of which correct definitions may be drawn. This assumption in itself entailed the

---

[28] Martin Bucer exerted great influence on Calvin's formulation of his "doctrine of predestination. Calvin found his commentary on Romans most inspiring." Hrsg. Von W. Neuser, *Calvinus Theologus* (Neukirchen-Vluyn: Neukirchener Verlag, 1976), 86-87, 103; cited by Strehle, *The Catholic Roots of the Protestant Gospel*, 35, n. 25. There were theological differences between Bullinger and Calvin and, at times, Bullinger's opinion proved more influential. "Musculus at Berne and Martyr at Strassburg were others who were by no means entirely overshadowed by the Genevan. Looking back on the scene, Calvin's figure may appear to tower over the others, but perspectives are sometimes deceiving, because history tends to concentrate on a few great names." Marshall M. Knappen, *Tudor Puritanism: A Chapter in the History of Idealism* (Gloucester, Mass.: Peter Smith, 1963), 137. Cf. James, *Peter Martyr Vermigli and Predestination*, 2. A writer has appropriately called Calvin *primus inter pares*. Robert Lethan, 'Faith and Assurance in Early Calvinism: A Model of Continuity and Diversity,' in *Later Calvinism*: International Perspectives. Sixteenth Century Essays & Studies, vol. 22 (Kirksville, MO.: Sixteenth Century Journal Publishers, 1994), 358.

[29] Richard A. Muller, *Christ and the Decree: Christology and Predestination in Reformed Theology from Calvin to Perkins* (Grand Rapids: Baker Book House, 1986), 39. For some of the distinctive contributions done by Bullinger, Calvin, Musculus and Vermigli to the development of Reformed thought, see ibid., 17-67. If England only is considered, Bullinger was more influential in his own lifetime than any other among the Reformed. Additionally, in the formative phase of the tradition, Bucer taught at Cambridge and Vermigli at Oxford. Steinmetz. *Calvin in Context*, 4-5.

development of a theological method more logical, more rigorous and more rationalist than that of the Reformation, though no less committed to the principle of *sola Scriptura*.[30]

This Protestant Orthodoxy (Reformation's second "step"), may be divided into three stages: early, high and late. Accordingly, these three phases "correspond with the initial framing and formulation of Orthodoxy, the large-scale elaboration of the theology, and the decline of the movement in the eighteenth century."[31] Keach lived during the high Orthodox period, but, like many other Reformed Orthodox, he did not produce entire scholastic systems or *loci communes*. Again, like other Puritans, Keach was primarily occupied with polemical, exegetical, homiletical and pedagogical works.[32]

We now leave aside the Lutheran and concentrate on the Reformed tradition.[33] The early theology of the fathers of the Reformed school and the theology of what later became post-Reformation Reformed Protestantism, or Reformed Orthodox, or simply Reformed, should not be seen as a shift from a biblical to a scholastic theology.[34] Rather, as the Reformed tradition felt the necessity to defend itself from outside and inside attacks, a greater need for precision and an ever more refined and subtle body of doctrine was developed.

---

[30] Muller, *Christ and the Decree*, 39, 12. Cf. Asselt and Dekker, *Reformation and Scholasticism*, 13.

[31] Muller, *After Calvin*, 4-5. For Lutheran Orthodoxy only, see Otto Webber, *Foundations of Dogmatics*, Darrel L. Gudder, trans. (Grand Rapids: Eerdmans, 1981), I: 120-122.

[32] By and large, Puritanism brought forth "fewer and less substantial systematic works than their continental brethren. Their theological reflection tended instead to take the form of sermon-cycles on issues of current pastoral or controversial importance which, when published became part of the theological literature." William K. B. Stoever, 'Nature, Grace and John Cotton: The Theological Dimension of the New England Antinomian Controversy,' in *CH* 44 (1975): 22-33, p. 24.

[33] On the development of Lutheran Orthodoxy, see Robert Preuss, *The Theology of Post-Reformation Lutheranism*, 2 vols. (St. Louis: Concordia, 1970-72).

[34] It is necessary to bear in mind, Muller affirms, "that the question of continuity or discontinuity of Protestant scholastic theology with the western theological tradition is highly complex and not at all to be reduced to the relationship of the doctrine of predestination developed by Beza or Zanchi to that of Calvin. Rather the question must be raised in terms of the influence of Calvin and his contemporaries upon the developing Augustinian theology the roots of which extend into the Middle Ages, indeed, back to Augustine; in terms also of methodological continuities and discontinuities both with the Reformers and with the medieval doctors; and finally in terms of the changes that occur in theological ideas as they developed systematically, recognising that continuity is found in developing traditions rather than in static reproduction of ideas from one generation to the next. *Christ and the Decree*, 13. On the rise of scholasticism amidst the Reformed, see Donald Sinnema, 'Antoine De Chandieu's Call for a Scholastic Reformed Theology (1580),' in *Later Calvinism*, 159-190.

Thus, the stream of thought from Zwingli, Bullinger, Calvin, Musculus and Vermigli; via Beza, Ursinus and Zanchi; down to Polanus, Perkins, Ames and Owen should be taken as an ever more elaborate *development* of doctrine and not as a descent into obtuse and unintelligible scholasticism.[35] A hostile attitude toward the scholastic method, Barth says, "is the mark of the false prophet. The true prophet would not shy away from submitting his message also to this test."[36] Although 'scholastic Orthodoxy' has been blackened by adjectives such as "sterile,"[37] "impersonal and rigid,"[38] "hard and fast,"[39] and similar derogatory terms, one may wonder if this has been the case on account of lack of familiarity with thought-patterns and rhetoric utilised by the scholastics.[40] In any event, these two terms, 'scholastic' and 'Orthodoxy', represent different things.[41] 'Orthodoxy' relates to the *content* of the faith and simply means correct teaching or accurate doctrine. The New Testament, Patristic, Medieval, Reformation and Post-Reformation church has always striven to articulate correct teaching. Whether or not the attempts have succeeded is something else. On the other hand, 'scholasticism' relates to *method*; i.e., it has to do with *how* the content of the faith is expressed. A method *qua* method is not necessarily good or bad. The scholastic method, variously used from the Middle Ages down to the Post-Reformation era, was a tool of great precision and thus very useful in polemics, especially elenctic ones.[42] Anselm, Aquinas, Beza, Cajetan,

---

[35] See Muller, *Christ and the Decree*, 175-182. A clear theological difference between Reformation and early Orthodoxy is that the latter is concerned with method. On the whole, the Reformers were not extremely concerned with structure and methodology. However, the first generation Orthodox wanted to present their theology in a cohesive and comprehensible fashion, which would be acceptable to church and—especially—to academia. Idem, *Post-Reformation Reformed Dogmatics*, 30-31.

[36] Karl Barth, *Kirchliche Dogmatik*, I/1, 296, quoted by Asselt and Dekker, *Reformation and Scholasticism*, 20.

[37] McBeth, *The Baptist Heritage*, 171.

[38] Richard Greaves, *John Bunyan* (Appleford, Berkshire: The Sutton Courtenay Press, 1969), 11, 71. Cf. Donald K. Mckim, 'John Owen's Doctrine of Scripture in Historical Perspective,' in *EvQ* 45 (1973): 195-207, passim.

[39] Dewey D. Wallace, *Puritans and Predestination: Grace in English Protestant Theology, 1525-1695* (Chapel Hill: The University of North Carolina Press, 1982), 55.

[40] Sometimes this lack of familiarity is blatantly obvious among those who are "evaluating" the Reformed Orthodox. Consider the following assertion: the two-fold covenant structure used by the federalists was invented by the "*obscure* theologians who followed Calvin." Holmes Rolston III, 'Responsible Man in Reformed Theology: Calvin versus the Westminster Confession,' in *SJT* 23/2 (May, 1970): 129-156, p. 129. Emphasis mine.

[41] See, Luco J. van Brom, 'Scholasticism and Contemporary Systematic Theology,' in *Prostestant Scholasticism*, 277-293.

[42] Generally, the term 'polemic' implies a mere attack; 'elenctic,' on the other hand, means to refute with the objective of constructing a positive stance. Richard A. Muller, *Dictionary of Latin and Greek Theological Terms: Drawn Principally from the*

Zanchi, Bellarmine, Arminius, Ames, Perkins, Owen and a vast multitude of others are all scholastics coming from different backgrounds and arriving at vastly different conclusions.[43] Whilst not a university man, Keach along with the whole sweep of Puritanism, was influenced by scholasticism.[44] This influence will be shown towards the end of this chapter, wherein we shall see Keach's employment of three scholastic tenets, sc., the use of syllogism, the use of *quaestio*, and metaphysical speculation.

Reformed Orthodoxy proper has its incipience in the publication of the second generation codifiers (Beza and Zanchi, for example). These early codifiers provided theological systems and confessions (Bullinger's *Second Helvetic*, for example), in which the particular characteristics and the spacious boundary lines of the movement were established. To put it differently, by the second half of the sixteenth century, the broad frontiers of Reformed theology were delimited, together with the distinguishing marks of the tradition.[45] Reformed theology, it should be noted, was not monolithic from its inception; there was space for diversity within its boundaries. It is therefore important to make a distinction between extra- and intraconfessional debates. The Reformed Orthodox disputed with those outside the family (Socinians, Papists, Anabaptists, Arminians,[46] etc.) and also with those within. Hence, whereas Bullinger presents God electing only to save (positive election), Calvin presents

---

Protestant Scholastic Theology (Grand Rapids, Baker Books / Carlisle, Paternoster Press, 1985), s.v., elenchticus.

[43] See Muller's fine essay, 'Scholasticism and Orthodoxy in the Reformed Tradition,' in *After Calvin*, 25-46. Cf. Idem, *Scholasticism and Orthodoxy in the Reformed Tradition*, 8; Asselt and Dekker, *Reformation and Scholasticism*, 11-14.

[44] Although "Puritan literature abounds with condemnations of scholasticism, almost no limits can be set to its actual influence." Miller, *The New England Mind*, 104.

[45] Muller, *After Calvin*, 34. Having a single figurehead (Luther) and one main confession from which to draw its doctrinal standards (Augsburg), Lutheran Orthodoxy was "narrower" or "tidier," so to speak, than the Reformed. See, Webber, *Foundations of Dogmatics*, I: 120-127.

[46] It is hardly conceivable to try to argue that Socinians, Papists and Anabaptists were in anyway part of the Reformed tradition. The possible exception would be the Arminians. However, it should be noted that in his *Declaration of Sentiments* (1608), Arminius rejects both supra- and infralapsarianism and presents his own theory. At this distinctive junction, he purposefully deviated from "the Reformed faith and its confessions—giving substance to his proposal that the Belgic Confession and the Heidelberg Catechism be emended. On purely historical grounds, therefore, we must reject the argument that Arminius was a 'Reformed theologian' and that his theology represented a type of Reformed thought somewhat out of style in the late sixteenth century. The view of predestination that Arminius presented in his *Declaration* opposed Reformed teaching, whether of Calvin or Bullinger, Beza or Zanchi, Gomar or Junius, and it opposed the unaltered Reformed confessions." Richard Muller, s.v., 'Arminius and Arminianism,' in *DHT*. See also, idem, 'The Federal Motif in Seventeenth Century Arminian Theology,' in *NAK* 62 (1982): 102-122.

a twofold election—to life and death (positive and negative election). Another example of familial difference would be the question: should the Adamic covenant be considered a *foedus operum* or a *foedus naturae*? Furthermore, there were disputes "between the Cocceian federalists and the Voetians,[47] between Amyraut and the opponents of hypothetical universalism[48] and between supra- [Beza, Zanchi, Daneu] and infralapsarianism [Polanus, Bucanus and the majority]."[49] In addition to all of these differences, there was a significant distinction between some thinkers, whose doctrine of predestination was crucial to "their theology (Zwingli, Buzer, Beza, Daneu, Polanus, Gomarus) and others who displayed a reticence to discuss it, whose formulation of the doctrine was open to question or who refused to adopt double predestination (Bullinger, ...Martinius)." Between these two extremes, other individuals could be found.[50]

All of these many currents were accommodated within the broad confines of the Reformed Orthodox stream. In the light of this diversity, it is hardly possible to confer an *autorité papale* to Calvin as if he were the rule against which the whole Reformed tradition were to be measured.[51] To belabour the

---

[47] They disputed whether or not the Sabbath was a perpetual moral principle; the status of believers under the Old and New Testaments; how remission of sin should be interpreted in both Testaments; etc. See the issues in Willem J. van Asselt, 'Amicitia Dei as Ultimate Reality: An Outline of the Covenant Theology of Johannes Cocceius (1603-1669),' in *URM* 21/1 (1998): 35-47. See also Olive M. Griffiths, *Religion and Learning: A Study in English Presbyterian Thought from the Bartholomew Ejections (1662) to the Foundation of the Unitarian Movement* (Cambridge: Cambridge University Press, 1935), 55-60.

[48] Instead of a straight-forward version of limited atonement, as the majority of the Orthodox held, Amyraut proposed "a universal design in God's will to save," and, concurrently, he taught that God freely limited his mercy to the elect. Brian G. Armstrong, *Calvinism and the Amyraut Heresy: Protestant Scholasticism and Humanism in the Seventeenth-Century France* (Madison and London: The University of Wisconsin Press, 1969), 266.

[49] Muller, *After Calvin*, 34; Robert Lethan, 'Faith and Assurance in Early Calvinism: A Model of Continuity and Diversity,' in *Later Calvinism*: International Perspectives. Sixteenth Century Essays & Studies. Vol. 22. (Kirksville, MO.: Sixteenth Century Journal Publishers, 1994), 364.

[50] Lethan, 'Continuity & Diversity in Early Calvinism', 364. To anticipate, we shall see that Keach fits the group who refuses to adopt double predestination.

[51] As we shall see shortly hereafter, this point tremendously underlines the notion that Calvin should not be used as the bar against which all Reformed theologians should be judged. Thus, it is far better to drop the term "Calvinism," and rather refer to the tradition as "Reformed." For the character of the Reformed tradition was forged by confessions—Helvetic, Belgic, Dort, Westminster, etc.—not by Calvin alone. See Carl R. Trueman, 'Calvin and Calvinism,' in *CCJC*, 225-226, 223. Additionally, unless very clearly defined, the notion that one practices "conservative Calvinism," the other, "extreme Calvinism," yet another, "evangelical Calvinism," still another, "moderate

point that there was latitude amidst the Reformed and that this remained the case among their descendants, consider the example of the sacraments: on the one hand, Calvin conceives "the sacraments as means and instruments of grace" and, on the other, Bullinger teaches "a conjoint and parallel action of grace with the administration of the sacraments. In the era of Orthodoxy, these differences of precise definition continue to be found among Reformed theologians:" instead of claiming "a shift from dynamic or fluid understanding of the faith to rigid and inflexible standards," Muller argues, "the far more accurate description of the contrast between the Reformation and Orthodoxy consists in a contrast between the movement toward confessional and institutional boundaries."[52]

An interesting aspect of the Reformed tradition was the development of the concept of covenant—a conception which came to have a massive influence on the theological Reformed systems of the seventeenth century Federalists.[53] Indeed, the federal theology of Coccceius, once its concept of covenant was perfected by Witsius and Burmann, eventually became the main guide for Reformed Orthodoxy.[54] This is particularly well represented by Puritanism in England.[55] As a matter of fact, "English Puritans shared both the doctrinal consensus and the theological individualism of Reformed Orthodoxy."[56]

Calvinism," the other "hyper Calvinism," yet another, "high Calvinism," still the other, "ultra Calvinistm," etc., tends to become confusing. See McBeth, *The Baptist Heritage*, 171, 172, 174, 176; and Wallace, *Puritans and Predestination*, 150.

[52] Muller, *After Calvin*, 34.

[53] Despite the difficulty of precisely locating the genesis of federalism, it is nevertheless tenable to affirm that "at least part of the doctrine of federal theology found its justification within the general Franciscan-Nominalistic tradition of *pactum*." Stephen Strehle, *Calvinism, Federalism, and Scholasticism: A Study of the Reformed Doctrine of Covenant* (Bern: Lang, 1988), 302-303.

[54] Muller, *Post-Reformation Reformed Dogmatics*, 37.

[55] "Most federalists were Puritans. Federal doctrine could be taken up by Anglicans, but a poll at any time would have given Puritans a healthy edge." Michael McGiffert, 'The Perkinsian Moment of Federal Theology,' in *CTJ* 29 (1994): 117-148, p. 124.

[56] William K. B. Stoever, *'A Faire and Easie Way to Heaven': Covenant Theology and Antinominanism in Early Massachusetts* (Middletown: Wesleyan University Press, 1978), 15. Cf. Haller, *The Rise of Puritanism*, 8-12. "The English Puritans were heirs of the Reformed tradition, ... Ulrich Zwingli and Heinrich Bullinger in Zurich, John Calvin and Theodore Beza in Geneva, John Oecolampadius in Basel and Martin Bucer in Strassburgh—these men laid the foundation for Puritan doctrine." E. Brooks Holifield, *The Covenant Sealed: The Development of Puritan Sacramental Theology in Old and New England, 1570-1720* (New Haven and London: Yale University Press, 1974), 1. Incidentally, though our focus of interest is English Puritanism, much of what we have said equally applies to New England. For example, seventeenth century Puritans in New and Old England, Stoever affirms, were part of the Reformed Orthodox movement—a movement "which was primarily concerned with defining Reformed doctrine and

Bullinger and Calvin wrote on covenant, with the former making more doctrinal contribution than the latter. Although these two Reformers had subtle differences in their covenantal notions, the two formulated covenant concepts whereby God takes the initiative in salvation and humanity is held accountable to relate responsibly with God. In other words, both of them conceived the covenant as monopleuric in its inception, but dipleuric in its maintenance. "The Reformed doctrine of the covenant is, therefore, neither opposed to nor in tension with the Reformed doctrine of predestination, which also declares a grace unilaterally bestowed by God and assumes human responsibility and obedience under and enabled by grace."[57] This is an important point, given the fact that several scholars have tried to drive a wedge, or make a disjunction, between Reformation and Reformed theology.[58] There have been, occasionally, major disjunctions or innovations in theological inquiry, as for example, "Augustine's linked vision of the doctrines of grace and the mixed church at the start of a distinctively and exclusively Latin theological tradition." However, this type of disjunction has not happened within Reformed theology.[59] That wedge is usually driven in such a way as to elevate Calvin to the status of "hero," and to down grade the "Calvinists" as mere followers or disciples of his: if they differ from the Genevan Reformer, then the "Calvinists" are labelled "deviators," "hyper-Calvinists," "betrayers" and the like. William Perkins,[60] John Owen[61] and many other theological giants, who never saw themselves as slavish imitators of Calvin, are directly compared to him and found wanting, regardless of the different context they faced and doctrinal *development* that

---

articulating it in the intellectual idiom of late scholasticism." Stoever, 'Nature, Grace and John Cotton,' 24.

[57] Muller, *After Calvin*, 12. See the fine article by Lyle D. Bierma, 'Federal Theology in the Sixteenth Century: Two Traditions?' in *WTJ* 45 (1983): 304-321. Contra, Strehle, *Catholic Roots of the Protestant Gospel*, 51.

[58] Among the many who attempted to drive such a wedge, note this following example: Federal theology "constituted a movement away from the older Scottish tradition of Knox, the Scots Confession, the pre-Westminster confessions as well as from the theology of Calvin himself." James B. Torrance, 'Covenant or Contract? A Study of the Theological Background of Worship in the Seventeenth-Century Scotland,' in *SJT* 23/1 (February, 1970): 51-76, p. 52. For other examples, see John S. Bray, *Theodore Beza's Doctrine of Predestination* (Nieuwkoop: De Graaf, 1975), 137-143; Møller, 'Beginnings of Puritan Covenant Theology,' passim; Armstrong, *Calvinism and the Amyraut Heresy*, 32, 37-42 et seqq.

[59] Stephen R. Holmes, *Listening to the Past: The Place of Tradition in Theology* (Carlisle, Cumbria / Grand Rapids, MI.: Paternoster / Baker Academic, 2002), 78.

[60] On Perkins, see Breward, 'The Significance of William Perkins,' 113-128.

[61] On Owen, see his profile, infra, 'Keach's Federalism,' pp. 77-78.

took place in the meanwhile.[62] Let us consider three examples of the theory "Calvin vs. 'Calvinists.'"

First example: R. T. Kendall argues that Calvin held in tension election and atonement, i.e., he advocated particular election but did not teach limited atonement. Amidst this purported tension, the French Reformer taught that assurance of salvation was integral to faith. Calvin's "followers," on the other hand, departed from him by teaching limited atonement, which resulted in lack of assurance.[63] Putting aside the issues of faith, election and assurance, let us confine our brief discussion to the matter of limited atonement.[64] To begin with, the question faced by later Reformed Orthodox—viz., did Christ die to *atone* for the sins of all or some?—was not the real issue in the sixteenth century. Rather, the debate was over *satisfaction*. Calvin, without any qualms, accepts the medieval scholastic distinction between the particular efficaciousness of Christ's work and its universal sufficiency. Commenting on 1 John 2.2 ("and not for ours only"), Calvin asserts,

> But here the question may be asked as to how the sins of the whole world have been expiated. I pass over the dreams of the fanatics, who made this a reason to extend salvation to all the reprobate and even to Satan himself. Such a monstrous idea is not worth refuting. Those who want to avoid this absurdity have said that Christ suffered sufficiently for the whole world but effectively only for the elect. This solution has

---

[62] Cf. Carl R. Trueman, *The Claims of Truth: John Owen's Trinitarian Theology* (Carlisle, U.K.: Paternoster Press, 1998, 10-11. Discussing the thesis 'Calvin vs. Calvinists,' Lethan makes an excellent summary of continental non-Calvinian Reformed influences on the Puritans, asserting, among other things, that William Tyndale and John Hooper had covenantal concepts strikingly similar to that of Bullinger, that the corpus of Ursinus was rendered "into English and the Heidelberg Catechism was used as a catechetical model by some Puritans," that Ramism had vast acceptance by the Puritans in Cambridge, that the *Sermonum decades quinque* of Bullinger was compulsory reading for Anglican priests, etc. Lethan, 'Continuity & Diversity in Early Calvinism,' 358-362.

[63] R. T. Kendall, *Calvin and English Calvinism to 1649* (Oxford: Oxford University Press, 1979). On the question of 'assurance' and how the supposed "disciples" of Calvin were led astray, see Torrance's agreement with Kendall: James Torrance, 'Covenant or Contract?' 66-67, 69. For another author advocating that the "Calvinists" departed from Calvin on the issue of limited atonement, see Armstrong, *Calvinism and Amyraut Heresy*, 137-138. See strictures to both Kendall and Torrance in Andrew McGowan, 'Federal Theology as a Theology of Grace,' *SBET* 2 (1984): 41-50; and in a more thorough form, see Paul Helm, *Calvin and the Calvinists*, 2nd ed. (Edinburgh: Banner of Truth, 1998).

[64] "The federal scheme thrust up the doctrine of a limited atonement, that Christ only died for the elect—a doctrine or conclusion unknown to Calvin." Torrance, 'Covenant or Contract?' 68. Cf. Bray, *Theodore Beza's Doctrine of Predestination*, 138-139; Strehle, *Catholic Roots of the Protestant Gospel*, 125.

commonly prevailed in the schools. Although *I allow the truth of this*, I deny it fits this passage.[65]

The distinction made by the Medievals between sufficiency and efficiency was maintained, or, to put it differently, it was accepted that Christ's death was enough to satisfy God for the sins of all humanity and that this satisfaction was effective only to those who would be saved.[66] The immediate question following from this was, what was the limiting factor in salvation, human or divine will? Given that Calvin taught that lasting faith is granted exclusively to the elect[67] and that—as we just saw—the work of Christ is efficacious to the same, it could be inferred that he *limited* Christ's work to the elect.[68] Later on, when the Reformed tradition faced the Arminian challenge, what had been a background issue came to the fore, what "Calvin and Bullinger hardly mentioned," became of major issue. Consequently, the Reformed Orthodox explicitly joined "the doctrine of election to the language of the limitation of the efficacy of Christ's death, arguing that the divine intention in decreeing the death of Christ was to save only the elect. This solution is presented in the Canons of Dort in concise formulae."[69] Therefore, Kendall's argument that the later Reformed tradition deviated or betrayed Calvin is hardly possible to maintain. It is far better to see the whole thing as a logical *development* of the tradition in the face of different challenges.

Second example: Basil Hall asserts that Perkins, Ames, Baxter and other Puritans present "an emphasis and a method quite different from Calvin." The French Reformer had a fine-tuned theological system, but his "followers" altered it, at times conspicuously not following his lead. For example, Perkin's modification of the doctrine of predestination may be seen in that "he does not

---

[65] John Calvin, *The Gospel According to St John 11-21 and The First Epistle of John*, T. H. L. Parker, trans., D. W. Torrance and T. F. Torrance, eds. (Grand Rapids: Eerdmands Publishing Co., 1959), 244. Emphasis mine. This quote is slightly different from the one offered by Holmes, *Listening to the Past*, 79. Cf. John Owen, *The Works of John Owen*, 16 vols. (Rio, WI.: Ages, 2000), X: 387ff.

[66] Incidentally, even when the focus of the controversy changed—i.e., when the issue became indeed limited atonement—the more subtle theologians remained aware of the distinction between sufficiency and efficiency. John Owen, arguably the greatest apologist of limited atonement, maintains that "the controversy about the death of Christ is not primarily about its extent, but its efficacy and fruits in respect of them for whom he died." Owen, *Works*, XIX: 68.

[67] Although the reprobate may have a taste of faith given them by God, "[o]nly his elect does he account worthy of receiving the living root of faith so that they may endure to the end." Calvin, *Institutes*, III.ii.11. Cf. Ibid, III.xxi.1.

[68] Contra, T. F. Torrance, 'The Distinctive Character of the Reformed Tradition,' in *RR* 54/1 (2000): 5-16, p. 9. For a discussion of 'Calvin on limited atonement,' see A. T. B. McGowan, *The Federal Theology of Thomas Boston* (Carlisle: Paternoster Press, 1997), 48-53.

[69] Muller, *After Calvin*, 14.

go to Calvin for this but to Beza ..."[70] The supralapsarian Beza scrutinised the purpose of God in election more precisely than Calvin. Furthermore, "Beza taught the imputation of Adam's sin to all mankind with precision, whereas Calvin, not finding this to be clear in Scripture, had avoided the point." In addition, "Beza taught explicitly that Christ did not die for all mankind but only for the elect (that is, the doctrine of limited atonement), whereas Calvin was not so explicit on this, rather he held that the Gospel is offered by God for all mankind, and that we should preach it to all men."[71]

As to the first point, it is not clear what is meant by Calvin's different "emphasis and ...method" to his supposed followers. The most likely possibility would be a reference to the scholastic method. Yes, both Renaissance humanism and Reformation severely criticised the overly intricate theological quibbles and hair-splitting niceties and speculations of the *scholastici*.[72] We are to keep in mind, though, that Calvin's attack on the scholastics is not to be taken as a renunciation *en bloc* of their method. His use of scholasticism is not as overt as it would be with the later Reformed scholastics. Nevertheless, much of Calvin's *Institutes'* underlying structure is palpably influenced by the scholastic method. His use of *quaestio*, his dialogue with the tradition amidst complex divisions and subdivisions—all testify to his debt to scholasticism. So, for example, in the *Institutes*, III.xxxii.1, he opens this chapter with two major objections and, after appealing to the tradition ("Augustine wisely notes ..."), he starts answering the first objection within the same paragraph. He then carries on the answer into §2, and in §3 he raises a minor objection to what he had said thus far and, then, proceeds to answer it. Half way through §4, he presents a counter-argument to what he has argued in this same paragraph and answers it. Paragraph 6 is opened with a question to which an immediate answer is given. About half way within §6, Calvin *finally* turns to the second major objection and addresses it. In addition to that, it is well worth noting that many of Calvin's fierce attacks on the *scholastici* are translated into French as *théologiens Sorbonniques*, which reveal that Calvin's main problem was not, on the whole, with the medieval scholastics, but rather with the tenacious resistance of the faculty of the University of Paris in accepting the Reformation. In sum, Calvin rejects some aspects of scholasticism, but he also *appropriates* it, occasionally explicitly, but most of

---

[70] Basil Hall, 'Calvin Against the Calvinists,' in *John Calvin*, Gervase Dunffield, ed. (Grand Rapids: Eerdmans, 1966): 19-37, p. 30

[71] Hall, 'Calvin Against the Calvinists,' 27. McGrath falls into the same pit: the Genevan Reformer "did not teach limited atonement, but affirmed that the Gospel was offered by God for all mankind." Alister E. McGrath, *Iustitia Dei: A History of the Christian Doctrine of Justification* (Cambridge: Cambridge University Press, 1986), II: 48.

[72] Muller, *After Calvin*, 29. We shall see a very brief example of that, as Keach classifies the goodness of God into two main types—communicable and incommunicable—and then subdivide each type into several subtypes of goodness: absolute, essential, infinite, unchangeable, unmixt, etc; infra, p. 61.

the time without acknowledging it.⁷³ "There is also parallels in method and intention, notably between Calvin's approach to system and commentary and the approach of Peter Lombard—moreover, there is the exegetical tradition to which Calvin became increasingly attentive and through which he received the insights both of the patristic and the medieval periods."⁷⁴

Concerning Hall's point that Perkins drew on Beza instead of Calvin, we may simply say that Perkins did not consider himself obliged to follow Calvin, and, what is more important, it is likely that Beza's more explicit and precise predestinarian scheme was more useful to Perkins than Calvin's. Beza and Perkins were contemporaries, both belonging to the same generation of codifiers, both working under pressure (from the Lutherans, e.g.) and distilling the full implications of the insights of the Reformation to the academy and to the pew.⁷⁵

Finally, having addressed the issue of limited atonement, we add that to hold this view does not necessarily entail the denial of universal and free offering of the Gospel, as Hall claims. Keach, for example, believed that Christ's work was limited to the elect on the one hand and, on the other (to contradict Hall using his own words), "he held that the Gospel is offered by God to all mankind, and that we should preach it to all men."⁷⁶ It is objected, Keach says, that "[i]f Christ died not for all, what grounds have I to believe he died for me? Answ. What doth it signify to believe Christ died for all, unless thou findest the effects of his death in thee?" Multitudes without number will "perish, notwithstanding Christ died for them in their judgement that make this objection, yea the generality of them for whom he died; therefore unless all were saved, what encouragement is there to believe from hence?" It is more coherent to think thus: anyone who "believes, shall be saved: if thou therefore believe, thou shalt

---

⁷³ Contra, Bray, *Theodore Beza's Doctrine of Predestination*, 138.

⁷⁴ Willem J. van Asselt and Eef Dekker, s.v., 'Scholasticism, Medieval,' in *DHT*; Muller, *The Unaccommodated Calvin*, 56-57. To overstress the point that Calvin used the scholastic method, see how he agrees with the Medievals in their diverse degree of necessity: *Institutes*, I.xvi.9. Cited by Muller, 'The Problem of Protestant Scholasticism—A Review and Definition,' *Reformation and Scholasticism*, 52. See also, idem, 'Scholasticism, Reformation, Orthodoxy, and the Persistence of Christian Aristotelianism,' in *TJ* 19/1 (1998): 81-96.

⁷⁵ See Béatrice Nicollier, s.v., 'Beza, Theodore (1519-1605),' in *DHT*. This article provides a good summary of Beza's influence and involvement in the development of Reformed Orthodoxy.

⁷⁶ Cf. Benjamin Keach, *The Display of Glorious Grace, or, The covenant of peace opened in fourteen sermons lately preached in which the errors of the present day about reconciliation and justification are detected* (London: Printed by S. Bridge and sold by Mary Fabian and Joseph Collier and Willam Marshall, 1698), 65. See also Owen, *Works*, X: 389.

be saved. Is not this a better ground of faith than that of Christ's dying for all."[77] In addition to that and to answer even more pointedly Hall's contention concerning the free offering and universal preaching of the Gospel, consider Keach's following assertion: "[i]f any soul believes in Christ, thirsteth for Christ, looketh to Christ, or cometh to Christ, and yet Christ rejecteth him, then charge him with injustice. But where lives that man, tho he was so vile and ungodly that did thus, but he found mercy? O see how free and universal the proclamation is!"[78] Yet again, on the objection that limited atonement curtails free Gospel offering, note how Keach finishes the following sermon. He invites unbelievers to receive the Gospel and raises possible objections or doubts they may have. He begins rhetorically: has the sacrifice of the Son

> such virtue in it, even to renew, quicken, regenerate all that believe in him? Is God through the death of his Son reconciled and shall all that take hold of him be justified? &c. O then, sinners, look up unto him and never cease looking, until you find the effects of his death in your souls. Object.1. But alas, Sir, I am a vile and abominable sinner. Answ. Well, notwithstanding that, yet there is virtue enough in Christ to save you ... Object.3. But I have been an old sinner. Answ. Well, let it be so, yet but a sinner, and Christ died for sinners, for the chief of sinners, therefore there is hope for you; nay if you believe and apply the virtue of Christ's blood, you shall find mercy. Object.4. But I fear Christ did not die for me. Answ.1. If he died for the chief of sinners, why not for thee? And if those that crucified him found mercy, why not thee? 2. Thou hast as much ground to believe that Christ died for thee as any ungodly person hath that dwells on the face of the whole earth ... 4. Did ever any sinner throw himself at his feet as a poor lost and undone creature, and take hold of him, that was rejected?[79]

Third example: James Torrance and Holmes Rolston portrayed Calvin's theology as gracious over against the supposedly legal theology of the

---

[77] Benjamim Keach, *A Golden Mine opened, or, The glory of God's rich grace displayed in the Mediator to believers, and his direful wrath against impenitent sinners* (London: For the author, 1694), 301. Keach defends limited atonement at several places within his corpus: the Son of God "died only to save some, and not all people in the world." *Exposition of the Parables*, 2 vols. (Grand Rapids: Kregel Publications, 1991), I: 264. See also, idem, *Christ alone the way to Heaven, or, Jacob's ladder improved containing four sermons lately preach'd on Genesis XXVIII, XII* (London: Printed and sold by Benja. Harris, 1698), 16-17; idem, *Display of Glorious Grace*, 158-164.
[78] Keach, *Display of Glorious Grace*, 166. Emphasis inverted. Quoted by Vaughn, 'Public Worship and Practical Theology,' 236. Cf. Keach, *Display of Glorious Grace*, 155-156.
[79] Keach, *Golden Mine*, 266-267.

Calvinists/Federalists.[80] In particular, whereas the Genevan Reformer knew only one covenant, the *foedus gratiae*, the Federalists conjured up a second pact, the legal or contractual *foedus naturae*, an invention of which Calvin would not have approved.[81] When God covenanted with us, Torrrance asserts, it was done unconditionally once for all. Nevertheless, a covenant requires a response, "a response of faith and gratitude and love. But here the distinction between a bilateral and a unilateral covenant is important." Obviously, when a covenant is bilateral, Torrance proceeds, it cannot take place apart from a reply. Such is the case, for instance, in marriage: both parties are in it by free consent; i.e., the future husband cannot covenant on behalf of the wife, she herself has to concur in order for the covenant to happen. On the other hand, a unilateral covenant is done on behalf of another—such is the case in the covenant of grace, Christ covenants with God on our behalf.[82]

How are we to reply to all of that? Both authors failed to see that the covenant of grace *includes* within it a bilateral aspect of human responsibility once the pact is implemented. Torrance and Rolston are correct in arguing that Calvin had envisaged a gracious and unconditional compact, a "freely given covenant, whereby God had adopted his elect" to belong to him, quite apart from anything they might or might not do.[83] However, that is not the end of the

---

[80] Torrance, 'Covenant or Contract?' 66. Holmes Rolston III, *John Calvin versus the Westminster Confession* (Richmond, Virginia: John Knox Press, 1972), 38. The picture painted by both authors is one in which the prelapsarian Adam has to deal with a very gracious and undemanding God according to Calvin, over against an ungracious and demanding deity according to the Federalists. See the strictures to these claims in Mark Karlberg, 'Reformed Interpretation of the Mosaic Covenant,' in *WTJ* 43 (Fall, 1980): 1-57.

[81] Torrance, 'Covenant or Contract?' 61-62. The twofold covenant scheme, Rolston claims, crafted by the Westminster divines "is not true to the Reformer himself." [Needless to say, Rolston considers the divines no more than Calvin's epigoni.] The Assembly started the confession, Rolston proceeds, "in the spirit of Calvin (if not borrowing from him) with a memorable answer to the opening question ... Such a beginning promises a close following of Calvin in answer to the question about the duty of man. But instead the Westminster divines made normative for all subsequent Presbyterians a concept of duty radically different from that which Calvin had given the Reformed church." Rolston, 'Responsible Man in Reformed Theology: Calvin versus the Westminster Confession,' in *SJT* 23/2 (May, 1970): 129-156, pp. 129, 144-145. Cf. Richard L. Greaves, 'John Bunyan and Covenant Thought in the Seventeenth Century,' in *CH* 36 (1967): 151-169, pp. 152, 158; idem, 'The Origin and Early Development of English Covenant Thought,' in *THis* 21 (1968): 21-35, passim; Møller, 'Beginning of Puritan Covenant Theology,' 64, 66; Alister E. McGrath, *A Life of John Calvin: A Study in the Shaping of Western Culture* (Oxford: Blackwell, 1990), passim.

[82] Torrance, 'Covenant or Contract?' 55. Cf. "The moderate Calvinists conceived the covenant more as a pact or contract ...For the strict Calvinists ...the covenant assumed more the character of a testament or promise." Greaves, *John Bunyan*, 105.

[83] Calvin, *Institutes*, II.vi.4.

story! Calvin, no less than the so-called "Calvinists," thought that within the covenant strict obedience and good works were integral to the God-humanity relationship. For what reason, Calvin rhetorically asks, has the Son of God taken "the person of the Mediator? He descended from the bosom of the Father and from incomprehensible glory that he might draw near to us. All the more reason, then, is there that we should one and all resolve to obey and to direct our obedience with the greatest eagerness to the divine will!"[84] In addition to that, Calvin explicitly comments on the duty of those included in God's compact:

> Indeed, in all covenants of his mercy the Lord requires of his servants in return uprightness and sanctity of life, lest his goodness be mocked or someone, puffed up with empty exultation on that account, bless his own soul, walking meanwhile in the wickedness of his own heart. Consequently, in this way he wills to keep in their duty those admitted to the fellowship of the covenant; nonetheless the covenant is at the outset drawn up as a free agreement and perpetually remains such.[85]

Let us turn to a federalist, let us see what Keach has to say about the issue at hand. Interpreting the trope which depicts the kingdom of heaven as a man that went to hire labourers into his vineyard (Mk.20.1), Keach discusses both sides of the covenant. On the one hand, the workers are—without any conditions whatsoever—freely admitted into the pact, i.e., the vineyard. On the other hand, once within the vineyard, they are expected to work.

> There is in hiring a mutual agreement between the Lord Christ and believers. Christ accepteth of them to be his servants, and believers accept of Christ to be their Lord. Every believer saith, 'I love my master,' and promises freely, heartily and sincerely to serve him. Christ says, I receive thee into my house, into my family and I will provide for thee, own and acknowledge thee to be my servant, ...and this mutual agreement passeth between Jesus Christ and every believer, before a believer is taken into the vineyard, and hath wrought or laboured there.[86]

In conclusion, to both Calvin and "Calvinists," God's covenant with believers is monopleuric in its commencement, but dipleuric in its continuance.[87]

---

[84] Calvin, *Institutes*, II.xv.5.
[85] Calvin, *Institutes*, III.xvii.5.
[86] Keach, *Exposition of the Parables*, II: 63-65. Cf. Idem, *Exposition of the Parables*, I: 405.
[87] Contra, Greaves, *John Bunyan*, 98; Stephen Strehle, 'Fides aut Foedus: Wittemberg and Zurich in conflict over the Gospel,' in *SCJ* 23/1 (1992): 3-20, p. 16; and, J. Wayne Baker, *Heinrich Bullinger and the Covenant: The Other Reformed Tradition* (Athens, Ohio: Ohio University Press, 1980), xxi-xxvi. Baker attempts to show that there were

English Puritanism is one of the many streams within the broad Reformed family;[88] with the Westminster Confession, its main doctrinal standard, representing a classic expression of covenant theology.[89] It is important to point out that, just like the Reformers, the Reformed Orthodox embraced the bulk of the Tradition, in addition to the previous work of codification done by earlier Protestants. Hence, for example, the work of the Westminster divines was sanctioned by the Parliament in Scotland "as the publick and avowed Confession of this church, containing the summe and substance of the doctrine of the Reformed churches." In saying that, the Parliament understood that the Westminster Confession contained the "substance of some thirty Reformed Confessions, including the Scots Confession and the First and Second Helvetic Confessions." All these documents explicitly approved "the ancient catholic creeds and conciliar statements of the church, the Apostle's Creed, the Nicene Creed, the formulations of Ephesus and Chalcedon and the so-called

---

two traditions within the Reformed from the very beginning. These supposedly different streams had different views of the covenant: Calvin saw it as a unilateral pledge, but Bullinger as a bilateral compact involving promise and responsibility. The root cause of these purportedly different traditions was the respective views of predestination espoused by the two Reformers: a *gemina predestinatio* followed by Calvin and a single one by Bullinger. Cf. supra, p. 18, footnote 34.

[88] The Puritans earnestly desired to have good relations with Continental Reformed churches. "The Westminster Assembly attempted to make a covenant with other Calvinist churches, and asked for advice on problems of organisation. Suggestions sent from Zealand, from Northern Holland, from the Synod of Utrecht and from a minister at Zürich were debated." Griffiths, *Religion and Learning*, 15. A suitable manner to see the general agreement between the English Reformed and Continental Reformed Orthodoxy is supplied by Dort's Canons. "A comparison of the Canons (1619) with Ussher's Irish Articles (1615) and the Westminster Confession (1647), reveals fundamental agreement on each of the famous 'five points,' although the two confessional documents inevitably cover far more theological ground than the more narrowly polemical Canons." Trueman, *The Claims of Truth*, 16-17.

[89] The Confession is the most important credal statement of federalism, a theological scheme so prominent among the Reformed that it became "the normative expression of Reformed Orthodoxy." A. T. B. McGowan, *The Federal Theology of Thomas Boston* (Carlisle, U.K.: Paternoster, 1997), 2. "The Federal structure of the Confession is by no means idiosyncratic, but rather is reflective of Reformed catholic doctrine ..." Karlberg, 'Reformed Interpretation of the Mosaic Covenant', 39. Incidentally, the divines crafted the famous Confession in such a way as to accommodate a great variety of currents (e.g., both infra- and supralapsarians) within the Reformed family. Muller, *Post Reformation Reformed Dogmatics*, I, 2nd. ed., 76-77. For a study of the Confession, see Robert Shaw, *An Exposition of the Confession of Faith of the Westminster Assembly of Divines* (Inverness, Scotland: Christian Focus Publication, first pub., 1845, new ed., 1973).

Athanasian Creed, and embodied all their main statements as essential articles of belief."[90] Keach is to be located among the Puritans; to him now we turn.

Biography and Literature Review

Benjamin Keach's Life and Controversies

The historian M. Mullet "has identified Benjamin Keach as the leading Baptist theologian of his era, similar in importance for his denomination as Richard Baxter was for the English Presbyterians, John Owen for the Congregationalists and Robert Barclay ...for the Quakers."[91] This biographical section aims at presenting a general picture of Keach and his importance.[92]

---

[90] Thomas Torrance, 'The Substance of Faith,' in *Toward the Future of Reformed Theology*, 167. To put it simply, although the Reformed churches crafted new confessions with distinctive forms, as the Westminster, they did not depart from the "catholic faith." Ibid. On the relationship between the Reformed Orthodox and the Tradition, see E. P. Meijering, 'The Fathers and Calvinist Orthodoxy: Systematic Theology,' vol. 2, in *The Reception of the Church Fathers in the West: From the Carolingians to the Maurists*, 2 vols. (Leiden: E. J. Brill, 1997).

[91] Michael Mullet, 'Radical Sects and Dissenting Churches, 1600-1750,' in *A History of Religion in Britain: Practice and Belief from Pre-Roman Times to the Present*, Sheridan Gilley and W. J. Sheils, eds. (Oxford: Basil Blackwell Ltd., 1994), 205; cited by Michael A. G. Haykin, *Kiffin, Knollys and Keach—Rediscovering our English Baptist Heritage* (Leeds: Reformation Today Trust, 1996), 83.

[92] For profiles of Keach, see Walter Wilson, *The History and Antiquities of Dissenting Churches and Meeting Houses in London, Westminster and Southwark*, 4 vols. (London: s.n., 1808-14), I: 241-250; Joseph Ivimey, *A History of the English Baptists*, vol. 1 (London: Printed for the author, 1811), 338-355, 384-385; Howard Marlcom, 'A Memoir of Keach's Life,' prefixed to Benjamin Keach, *The Travels of True Godliness*, rev. and improv. (Boston: Easingwold, Printed by Thomas Gill, 1845); W. R. Stevenson, 'Keach, Benjamin,' s.v., in *A Dictionary of Hymnology*, John Julian, ed., 2nd ed. (London: John Murray, Albemarle Street, 1907); A. C. Underwood, *A History of English Baptists* (London: Kings Gate Press, 1947), 111-112; Hugh Martin, *Benjamin Keach, 1640-1704: Pioneer of Congregational Hymn Singing* (London: Independent Press, 1961), 3-7, 17; Carnes, 'The Famous Mr. Keach,' 26-74; R. L. Greaves, s.v., 'Keach (or Keeche), Benjamin (1640-1704),' in *BDBR*; Humphrey Carpenter and Mari Prichard, eds. 'Keach, Benjamin (1640-1704),' s.v., *The Oxford Companion to Children's Literature* (Oxford: Oxford University Press, 1984); Kenneth Dix, *Benjamin Keach and a monument to liberty* (Dunstable, Beds.: The Fouconberg Press, 1985), 5-15; Haykin, *Kiffin, Knollys and Keach*, 84-87, 96-97; Spears, 'Baptist Movement in England,' 21-48; Vaughn, 'Public Worship and Practical Theology,' 5-25; idem, 'Benjamin Keach,' in Baptist Theologians, Timothy George and David Dockery, eds. (Nashville: Broadman & Holman Publishers, 1990), 49-56; Tom J. Nettles, 'Benjamin Keach (1640-1704),' in *British Particular Baptists*, Michael Haykin, ed., 2 vols. (Springfield, MO.: Particular Baptist Press, 1998), I: 95-100.

Beginnings

Son of John and Fedora Keach, Benjamin was born on 29 February 1640, at Stoke Hammond, northern Buckinghamshire. As it was customary, his parents had him christened on 6 March of the same year.[93] Thomas Crosby (c.1685-1752), the first Baptist historian, calls him a "genious" and laments that his parents could not provide an education befitting a future divine. Instead, "he was at first designed for a trade and employed in one a little while; but his capricious soul soon aspired after higher things."[94]

Studies of Holy Writ made him increasingly suspicious of the validity of his pedobaptism, to the extent that by 1655—as a fifteen-year-old—he had decided to be baptised upon his own profession of faith.[95] Those under whom Keach was influenced and catechised "held the Remonstrant scheme ...and went under the name of Arminians."[96] The General Baptists were the majority where Keach was living and, thus, it was merely circumstantial that he came under their care. It was not until he moved to London that the opportunity arose for him to consider carefully his position over against the Reformed view held by Particular Baptists.[97] In the meantime his growth in grace progressed unabated,

---

[93] BDBR, II: 150.

[94] Thomas Crosby, *The History of the English Baptists: From the Reformation to the Beginning of the Reign of King George I*, 4 vols. (London: Printed and sold by the author, 1738-1740), IV: 269, 209. There are two sections in Crosby dealing with Keach: a biographical account in IV: 268-314, and an account of some hardships Keach endured in II: 185-209. Keach seems to have been an avid reader from a very young age. Reminiscing, he says, "[w]hen I was a lad, I was greatly taken with a book, called *The Flowing of Christ's Blood freely to Sinners, as Sinners*." *The Marrow of Justification. Or Justification without Works* (London: Printed for Dorman Newman, at the King's Arms in the Poultrey, 1692), 8. For a collection of primary sources of documents that shaped the Baptist tradition, see H. Leon McBeth, *A Sourcebook for Baptist Heritage* (Nashville: Broadman Press, 1990).

[95] C. E. Whiting, *Studies in English Puritanism from the Restoration to the Revolution, 1660-1688* (London: Frank Cass & Co. Ltd., 1968), 84. Keach's association with the Congregationalists—to our knowledge, a fact thus far unnoticed in Keachean scholarship—must have ended at this time. He says that he was benefited by their teaching, but their practice of pedobaptism was not, as Keach understood it, a Christian verity. This is what he says: "I have as great reason to love and honour some of the Congregational way, as any man this day in England; it pleasing God to work upon my soul, I hope, effectually, when very young under the ministry of one of this persuasion ...whose name is dear to me and one I do honour and ever shall, as long as I live in this world. Yet nevertheless, my blessed Saviour and his truth lies nearer my heart." *Gold Refin'd; Or, Baptism in its Primitive Purity* (London: Printed for the Author, and are to be sold by Nathaniel Couch, at the sign of the Bell in the Poultry, 1689), 181.

[96] Crosby, *History of English Baptists*, IV: 209, 270.

[97] Crosby, *History of English Baptists*, IV: 270. Keach says, "I look upon my self bound to admire the riches of God's love and goodness to me, in opening my eyes to see those Arminians errors which when I was young, I had from some men of corrupt principles

to such an extent that those among whom he worshipped, soon asked him to minister to them. Thus, by 1660, Keach assumed a position of leadership in "the General Baptist congregation at Winslow,"[98] and, according to Crosby, he kept on preaching "publicly to the great comfort and edification of them that heard him."[99]

Given the fact that most Particular Baptists did not consider the laying on of hands an ordinance, arguably Keach thought differently as a result of his first involvement with the General Baptists.[100] Keach maintained and defended the ordinance of laying on of hands to the end of his life. On this issue, he published his *Darkeness Vanquished* as early as 1675, and twenty-two years later reprinted it altered as *Laying on of Hands upon Baptised Believers, as such, Proved an Ordinance of Christ.*[101]

In 1660, our protagonist married Jane (née Grove) of Winslow. The couple had five children, two of whom died at a young age. Additionally, with Jane, Keach endured trials and persecutions of all sorts: he "was often seized, when preaching, and committed to prison, sometimes bound, sometimes released upon bail, and sometimes his life was threatened."[102] An illustration of the type

---

sucked in; nay, and when I was about 23 years old, I wrote a little book for children, in which some of those errors were vindicated; which after my eyes were inlighted, I left out and now do declare my dislike of the first impressions and do disown what I there asserted: When I was a child, I thought as a child, I understood as a child, as the Apostle speaks. And let me intreat you to study the nature of the covenant of grace, for until I had that opened unto me, I was ignorant of the mysteries of the Gospel." *Golden Mine*, 314-315. The General and the Particular Baptists held, as the name suggest, to doctrines of general and particular redemption; i.e., the first was Arminian, the second Reformed. These two groups had different origins and separate lives. See B. R. White, *The English Baptists of the Seventeenth Century* (Oxford: The Baptist Historical Society, 1996), 9-11. Cf. Spears, 'Baptist Movement in England,' 5-14.

[98] *BDBR*, II: 150. There is still standing in Winslow a little chapel called 'Keach's Meeting House,' but considering that this place was constructed in the second half of the 1690s, it is not possible to know if "Keach himself ever worshipped or preached in the old chapel ..." Dix, *Benjamin Keach*, 22, 36.

[99] Crosby, *History of English Baptists*, IV: 270.

[100] Keach was inflexible, Spears affirms, on this ordinance as a condition for church membership. To uphold this position he had to contradict himself concerning what constitutes an "ordinance" (something that came out of Christ's lips). This is the result of Keach's previous membership with the General Baptists, who fought over this matter. 'Baptist Movement in England,' 184. See also Vaughn, 'Public Worship and Practical Theology,' 74-76.

[101] Cf. e.g., James Renihan, 'The Practical Ecclesiology of the English Particular Baptists, 1675-1705: the Doctrine of the Church in the Second London Confession' (Ph.D. diss., Trinity Evangelical Divinity School, 1997), 296-298.

[102] Crosby, *History of English Baptists*, II: 185.

of brutality Keach and the dissenters[103] in general were under may be seen in one particular episode, which almost cost him his life. To elaborate, troopers were sent to Buckinghamshire to suppress the dissenting movement and, discovering the place where Keach was preaching, "they came with great rage and violence upon the assembly and swore they would kill the preacher. Accordingly he was seiz'd and four of the troopers declared their resolution to trample him to death with their horses."[104] They then laid "him bound on the ground [and] prepared themselves for the fact. But the officer seeing their design, rode up towards them and just as they were going to spur their horses at once upon him, interposed and prevented them." Instead of trampling Keach, they decided to tie him across one of their horses and take him to jail. He was eventually released "after sometime of suffering great hardships and trouble."[105]

A Life of Controversy

In 1664 Keach wrote his first work, *The Child's Instructor*.[106] Here the author argued, among other things, that baptism should not be applied to children, that laymen could preach the Gospel, and that at the parousia, Christ would return to reign on earth. On those accounts, Keach was sent to goel, since his teaching was "contrary to the doctrines and ceremonies of the Church of England."[107]

During the judicious procedure, due to his chiliastic position, Keach was suspected of Fifth Monarchism.[108] As the exchanges between Keach and the

---

[103] By and large, dissenters would be Quakers, Baptists, Congregationalists (i.e., Independents). Under the reconstruction of the Old Regime (1661 onwards), dissenters would take in Presbyterians as well.

[104] Crosby, *History of English Baptists*, II: 186.

[105] Crosby, *History of English Baptists*, II: 186. Cf. Ivimey, *A History of English Baptists*, I: 338-339; B. Evans, *The Early English Baptists* (London: J. Heaton & Son, 1864), II: 307.

[106] *The Child's Instructor: or, a new and easie Primmer* (London: s.n., 1664). Original edition no longer extant. For a vivid description of the content of a re-written form of this book, see H. Wheeler Robinson, *The Life and Faith of the Baptists* (London: Methuen & Co., 1927), 37-40. See also, Whiting, *Studies in English Puritanism*, 570.

[107] Crosby, *History of English Baptists*, II: 187, 186. Keach thought that the saints would "reign with Christ on the earth a thousand years, even on Mount Zion, in the New Jerusalem, for there will Christ's throne be, on which we must sit down with him." Evans, *Early English Baptists*, II: 308.

[108] That Keach had sympathy with the movement is not disputed: Christ, he thought, shall receive all the kingdoms under heaven, and this will happen at the end "of the Forth Monarchy and upon the passing away of the Second Woe or Mahomitan power and downfall of the Beast and Mystery Babylon, which is now at the very door, when Christ will save his church from all her enemies." *Display of Glorious Grace*, 71. Incidentally, belief in a pacific Fifth Monarchy, like Keach had, was not restricted to the less learned and/or fanatics. An immensely educated man, like Owen, preaching on Daniel 7, proclaimed to the English Parliament that the Civil War was a battle "to

judge were coming to an end, it was becoming increasingly likely that the Baptist preacher could be sent to the gallows.[109]

We should keep in mind that almost from the very inception of the Restoration, dissent fell into great ignominy.[110] Thus, for example, in 1661, the Sabbatarian Baptist John James was arraigned on charges of calling Christ the sovereign of Britain. Despite evidence "in court that four witnesses had been coerced to testify falsely against him, he was convicted and hung, drawn and quartered on November 26." Additionally, "[t]he thirty members of his congregation were taken in groups to a justice of peace to take the oath of allegiance; as many as refused were committed to Newgate Prison."[111]

Keach did not receive a similar verdict, but, nonetheless, was sent to jail and made "to stand in the pillory at Ailsbury, in the open market, for the space of two hours, from eleven of the clock to one," sentenced the judge, "with a paper upon your head with this inscription: 'For writing, printing and publishing a schismatical book, intitled, *The Child's Instructor* ...'" Moreover, you are "to stand in the same manner and for the same period of time, in the market of Winslow; and there your book shall be openly burnt, before your face, by the common hangman, in disgrace of you and your doctrine." Additionally, the judged proceeded, "you shall forfeit to the King's Majesty the sum of twenty pounds and shall remain in jail, until you find sureties for your good behaviour, and appearance at the Assizes, there to renounce your doctrines and to make publick submission as shall be enjoined you. 'Take him away keeper.'"[112] As he was led out, Keach's deep convictions and great intrepidity were shown by his audible interjection: "I hope I shall never renounce those truths which I have written in that book."[113]

---

prepare for the kingdom" of Christ. John Owen, *Sermon...concerning the Kingdom of Christ and the Power of the Civil Magistrate*, preached Oct. 13, 1652; cited by Louise Fargo Brown, *The Political Activities of the Baptists and Fifth Monarchy Men in England During the Interregnum* (New York: Burt Franklin, 1911), 16.

[109] Crosby, *History of English Baptists*, II: 199.

[110] See White, *The English Baptists of the Seventeenth Century*, 95-133.

[111] Robert G. Torbert, *A History of the Baptists* (Philadelphia: The Judson Press, 1950), 80. For another example of judicial procedure against Baptists with death penalty as verdict, see J. Barry Vaughn, 'Benjamin Keach,' 50. Not only the authorities, but also sometimes the people displayed hatred towards the Baptists: "Robert Shalder, a Baptist who had been imprisoned [in 1666] for his beliefs, died shortly after he was set free and was buried in the churchyard. Some of the villagers took the man's body out of the grave, drew it on a sledge to the gate of his own house, and left it there." Whiting, *Studies in English Puritanism*, 144.

[112] Crosby, *History of English Baptists*, II: 202-203.

[113] Crosby, *History of English Baptists*, II: 203. Cf. Evans, *Early English Baptists*, 306-310; Whiting, *Studies in English Puritanism*, 114-118. See the complete account of Keach's trial in William Cobbett and Thomas Bayly Howell, *Cobbett's Complete Collection of state trials and proceedings for high treason and other crimes and*

Whilst in the pillory at Ailsbury, Keach preached to the crowd but was interrupted by a local parson who shouted that he was duly paying for his errors. The Baptist preacher, then, seizing the opportunity to start a debate, asked him to point out the said errors. Unable to do so and reminded by the people that he had been found drunk twice, the priest left demoralised.[114] Once out of jail, Keach re-wrote *The Child's Instructor* from memory; a book so successful that it had run through thirty editions by the second half of the eighteenth century, "including one at Boston, Mass., in 1685."[115]

While still living in Winslow, Keach wrote *Zion in Distress*.[116] In this and other works, he makes use of the most vituperative language he could muster to attack the Roman church.[117] It is not too much to say that our protagonist's entire life was one of disputations, polemics and controversies. Note the following strictures on Rome:

> Who in great pomp and royal state doth ride / Excelling haughty Jezebel in pride / Who in our modern times hath boasting been / That she rules all men as a mighty Queen / Trampling on kings and crowned potentates / Commanding kingdoms, common-wealths and states / Requiring subjects blindly to obey / Pressing the Beast and horns to kill and slay / At such a rate as that all Christendom / Like butchers bloody shambles are become / If by this mark she is not understood / Neither by garb, Beast, actions or by blood / To other waies of proof, I'le quickly come / And show this whore to be the church of Rome.[118]

---

misdemeanours, from the earliest period to the present time, 33 vols. (S.l.: Printed by T. C. Hansard, 1809-26), VI: 701-710.

[114] Crosby, *History of English Baptists*, II: 209.

[115] *BDBR*, II: 150.

[116] (London: s.n., 1666).

[117] As an important aside, it is noteworthy to say that one of the marks of the Reformed family was the great antipathy toward Rome. Even when furiously debating among themselves, as in the Amyraldian controversy, there was a proneness within the "Reformed to close ranks quickly if they envision their differences to be weakening their position vis-à-vis the Roman church." Armstrong, *Calvinism and the Amyraut Heresy*, 88.

[118] Benjamin Keach, *Sion in distress, or, The groans of the Prostestant church* (London: Printed by George Larkin, for Enoch Prosser, 1682), 109. Examples of this type could be given *ad nauseam*: There is a person which carries "a triple crown on his head and for a sceptre, a brace of keys in his hands; who I take to be the great king of Babylon; with a glorious retinue of cardinals, patriarchs, bishops, abbots, friars, monks, nuns, seminarians, Jesuits and a number more following him; with a great artillery, as, merit of works, limbus, purgatory, pardons, indulgences, vows, prayers to and for the dead, penance, holy water, pilgrims, auricular confession, extream unction, lamps, candles, torches, tapers, relicks, oyl, salt, spittle, crucifixes, beads, holy garments, signs, gestures, cannons, customs and the Lord knows what besides, as, blood, slaughter, massacres,

Besides gratuitous attacks, Keach blames Rome with creating state or national churches: she has "made void the laws and constitutions of the Gospel, forming whole nations into churches, though the greatest part shew themselves the worst of men."[119] (Anticipating our discussion on successionism, note that he did not say that all the individuals within these churches were not Christians.)

Another group which Benjamin Keach started to attack very early in his career was the Quakers.[120] There are countless assaults aimed at this group spread throughout his works.[121] His main complaint against the Quakers is that they deem the "internal light" or the "Spirit" as the ultimate source of authority: "those arch hereticks," Keach grumbles, who rely on the light within![122] Interestingly, Keach equates the Quakers with the Papists. They are on a par for submitting the Scripture to something other than itself: to the internal witness, on the case of the former; to Rome on the latter.[123] According to the Quaker's most important statement of faith, the Holy Scriptures "are not to be esteemed the principal ground of all truth and knowledge, nor yet the adequate primary rule of faith and manners ...they are and may be esteemed a secondary rule, subordinated to the Spirit..."[124] Keach asks the Quakers if the Indians in the

---

stake, fire and sword." *The progress of sin, or, The travels of ungodliness* (London: Printed for John Dunton, 1684), 188-189. Cf. Ibid., pp. 172 et seqq.; idem, *Marrow of Justification*, 9, 36; idem, *Light Broke Forth*, 210.

[119] Keach, *Sion in Distress*, 113. Cf. Idem, Antichrist Stormed, [i]. Rome is also blamed for poisoning many kings and noblemen, ibid., 95; for setting London ablazed in 1666, ibid., 101, 105; and for many other calamities. "The Chaldeans, who were the enemies of Israel of old, were said to be fiercer than the wolves: and so have the Papists been to the church of God, for many hundred years." Idem, *The Progress of Sin*, 136-137.

[120] *The Grand Impostor Discovered or the Quakers Doctrine weighed in the Balance and found wanting* (London: s.n., 1674). For a Quaker's counter-attack, see e.g., James Park, *False Fictions and Romances Rebuked: In Answer to Pretended Matter Charged against the Quaker in a book Intitled, The Progress of Sin, &c. Written by B. K. His Lies and Slanders therein returned back upon him and the Speakers of Yea and Nay in Truth Vindicated* (London: s.n., 1684).

[121] For example, *Jacob's Ladder*, 10, 27; *Marrow of Justification*, 8; *Display of Glorious Grace*, 56, 66, 135; *A Medium Betwixt two Extremes* (London: Printed for Andrew Bell, 1698), 37.

[122] Keach, *Display of Glorious Grace*, 128-129. Cf. Idem, *Golden Mine*, 87.

[123] Keach, *Progress of Sin*, 194, 246. Cf. Idem, *Golden Mine*, 80, 85. All through the "second half of the seventeenth century...the Quakers and the Puritans counted each other their bitterest" adversaries. Geoffrey Nuttal, *The Holy Spirit in Puritan Faith and Experience* (Oxford: Basil Blackwell, 1946), 151.

[124] Robert Barclay, *Theses Theologicae, or, Some Solid Positions of Sound Divinity Asserted* (Aberdeen: s.n., 1675), Thesis III. Cf. Again, the inward light of the Spirit is in agreement with the Bible and human reason, but the same Spirit is not "to be subjected to the examination, either of the outward testimony of the Scriptures, or of natural reason of man, as to a more noble or certain rule and touchstone ..." Ibid., Thesis II.

American Colonies or pagans in foreign countries can know "Christ or ... the Gospel" aided solely by the internal light. The revelation of Scriptures, Keach purports, are imperative to know and to evaluate all claims of faith.[125] Besides Roman Catholics and Quakers, Keach regularly lashes out against Arminians, Baxterians, Socinians and all whom he judges deviators from or non-adherents to Reformed Orthodoxy.[126]

Keach's disputations were not only via the printed word. He also engaged in *viva voce* disputes with the Arian Matthew Caffin,[127] Quakers and Pedobaptists. To illustrate, Keach was challenged to a public dispute on baptism by a group of ministers of the Church of England. On the appointed day, as Keach was travelling by boat to the place, one of the ministers overheard him conversing with his friends and immediately pre-engaged Keach. When the boat arrived at the destination, Gravesend, the said minister rushed out of the boat and told the Anglican party the arguments Keach intended to press against them. Upon hearing them, they decided not to dispute with the Baptist preacher any longer.[128] Although, Keach says, these ministers "had rendered us as odious as they well could (as if we had nothing to say for our practice, viz., for baptising men and women), yet when all came to all, none of them would appear to defend" their position.[129]

Residence in London

In 1668, Keach converted everything he owned into currency in order to move to London. On his way, his transportation was beset by highwaymen and he lost all he had, but his family (wife and three children) and their own clothing. Somehow he managed to get to the capital and due to his well-known probity

---

[125] Keach, *The Progress of Sin*, 247-249.

[126] For example, see against Arminianism, *Display of Glorious Grace*, 158-160; *Medium Betwixt two Extreams*, iv et seq.; *Golden Mine*, 240-241, 249; *Marrow of Justification*, 9-11 et seq. Against Baxterianism, *Exposition of the Parables*, I: 25 et seqq.; *Exposition of the Parables*, II: 156; Against Socinianism, *Beams of Divine Light: Or Some Brief Hints of the Being and Attributes of God, and of the Three Persons in the Godhead* (London: Printed by K. Astwood and Sold by William Marshall at the Bible in Newgate-street, 1700), 16-23 [it is deemed this work was written by Keach]; *Marrow of Justification*, 9 et seqq.; *Golden Mine*, 378-379. We "abhor the damnable heresies of the Socinians and Arrians and the detestable and damnable heresie of one Mathew Caffin" and his followers "who deny that Christ was God by nature, God of the essence of the Father, or man of the substance of the Blessed Virgin, or the seed of Abraham." *Beams of Divine Light*, 23.

[127] For an account of the antitrinitarianism of the General Baptist minister Caffin and the leniency with which his denomination treated him, see Ivemey, *History of English Baptists*, I: 548-555.

[128] Crosby, *History of the English Baptists*, IV: 302-303.

[129] Keach, *Gold Refin'd*, [i-ii].

and blameless character, the local Baptists soon came to his succour.[130] He was offered a position of leadership in a small group of people who met in houses south of the river Thames—house meetings were a way to avoid persecution, which was rampant during those days. Keach led this church from 1668 and remained with them for the rest of his life. At first, they met mainly at Tooly-street, but when dissenting was accorded tolerance, they built a church at Horsely-down. This facility would be enlarged several times in the years to come to the point of accommodating around a thousand individuals, an amazing feat for the time.[131]

Jane passed away in 1670, after only ten years of happy marriage. She had given Keach four girls and one boy. Taking the lead from Jacob (Gen.35.20), Keach made a tribute to his late wife, *A Pillar set up*.[132] Herein he praises Jane, especially for her encouragement during his incarcerations. After two years of widowhood, Keach married again to Susanna Partridge (née Skidmore), who outlived him by twenty years, gave him five girls and proved herself to be a woman of great character.[133]

The precise date of Keach's adherence to Reformed thought is unknown. However, the fact that Hanserd Knollys (c.1599-1691) officiated his second matrimony in 1672, indicates that he had already embraced the Reformed position.[134] It could be said that Keach's "conversion" occurred between 1668, when he moved to London, and 1672, when he remarried. His biographer asserts that once he was in the capital, aided by books and learned people, he carefully considered the distinctions between the two branches of the Baptist

---

[130] For an insight, in summary form, into the life of early Baptists in the capital—their building, burial grounds, services, organisation, etc.—see W. T. Whitley, *The Baptists of London 1612-1928* (London: The Kingsgate Press, 1928), 11-42.

[131] Crosby, *History of English Baptists*, III: 144, IV: 272-273. Crosby has a misprint (1688) concerning the date Keach assumed the leadership of the church in London. It seems that there was a split when the church moved to Horsely-down: Keach had embraced the Reformed position and taken people of the same persuasion with him to the new place of worship. Cf. Vaughn, 'Public Worship and Practical Theology,' 17-18. At Horsely-down Keach ministered from 1672 until his death in 1704. This congregation eventually became Spurgeon's tabernacle. Besides founding this one, Keach made a great contribution to the denomination by helping to establish places of worship in Essex, Southwark, White Street, Limehouse, Sheer's Alley and Rotherhithe. Spears, 'Baptist Movement in England,' 236, 125-126.

[132] *A Pillar set up, to Keep in Remembrance his first dear and beloved wife* (London: s.n., 1670).

[133] Crosby, *History of English Baptists*, IV: 273-275.

[134] On Knollys, see Benjamin Brooks, *The Lives of the Puritans* (Morgan: Soli Deo Gloria Publications, 1997), III: 491-500; and, Haykin, *Kiffin, Knollys and Keach*, 54-61.

tradition. Having made up his mind, Keach resolutely and full-heartedly subscribed to the Reformed scheme for the remainder of his days.[135]

Keach was harassed in London as he had been in the country.[136] At one point he was sought and found out by the authorities, who suspected him of reprinting *The Child's Instructor*. Through the support of a medical doctor, John Roberts, who stood bail, Keach was given manumission upon a twenty pounds fine. Curiously, this same doctor manufactured well-reputed pharmacological formulations and, one of them, "sugar-plums," was famous for its efficiency in bringing out of children "strange and monstrous worms." As he aged, Roberts found himself unable to produce his medicines. Thus, he contracted with Keach, his pastor, to teach one of his daughters how to do it, on the condition that the minister would provide a reasonable maintenance for the doctor and his wife, which Keach faithfully did.[137]

The demise of our protagonist looked certain in 1689. Although he had been a sick man for most of his life, this time no one doubted his departure. Hanserd Knollys was among those who came to say goodbye. Instead of bidding farewell, Knollys "betook himself to prayer and in an earnest and very extraordinary manner begged that God would spare him, and add to his days the time granted to his servant Hezekiah." At the end of his petition, Knollys pronounced: "Brother Keach, I shall be in heaven before you." What Knollys predicted came to pass to the letter: he died two years afterwards and Keach made a full recover and lived precisely fifteen years.[138] This would be Keach's most productive period because major political changes took place at the very end of the 1680s, which alleviated the situation of the dissenters. "In the election to the Convention Parliament in February 1689, the number of MPs who may have been dissenters increased to thirty, and on 28 February the Tory Earl of Nottingham introduced into the Lords the bill which three months later became law as the Toleration Act."[139] With the curtail of intolerance, Keach began to publish profusely: whereas before the Act, he had written about ten assorted pieces in the span of twenty two years (1666-1688); after it, he penned almost forty works in the short period of thirteen years (1689-1702).[140]

---

[135] Crosby, *History of English Baptists*, IV: 271. With the declaration of Indulgence of 1672, Spears says, Keach "led several of his adherents to leave the General Baptist church of which he was the pastor and found a new Particular Baptist church." 'Baptist Movement in England,' 60. Cf. Carnes, 'The Famous Mr. Keach,' 41.

[136] See several episodes of it in Crosby, *History of English Baptists*, III: 145-147.

[137] Crosby, *History of English Baptists*, III: 147.

[138] Crosby, *History of English Baptists*, IV: 307-308. See also Spears, 'The Baptist Movement in England,' 126.

[139] Michael Watts, *The Dissenters: From the Reformation to the French Revolution* (Oxford: Claredon Press, 1978), 259.

[140] See bibliography infra. Incidentally, Keach's *furor scribendi* is shown in that he is able to call a 230-page-book, a "small tract." *Antichrist Stormed*, i.

As the Baptist cause expanded, the need for trained and supported ministers became ever more acute.[141] On account of poverty, some churches were unable to maintain a pastor. More importantly, however, many congregations refused to support the minister as a matter of principle: they considered it unbecoming to pay a salary to the servants of God on the basis of certain passages of Scripture. This sentiment was reinforced by the opulent lifestyle of the Anglican clergy who harried the dissenters. Upon the request of the leadership of the Particular Baptists, Keach penned a tome attacking the general consensus of his fellow Baptists, *The Gospel Minister's Maintenance Vindicated* (1689). In the same year, the General Assembly debated and then fully endorsed Keach's viewpoint.[142] The said Assembly also asked Keach to tour the country to preach and help the churches—he did this with great success, launching several congregations.[143]

Education and ministry were two of Keach's main concerns and thus, despite the humble origin of the Baptists, he advocated a well informed and, as far as possible, well-trained ministry. Incidentally, in the 1690s, he was part of a group of revered ministers who assembled in a coffee shop in London to give counsel. "The group, which included Joseph Stennett, Hercules Collins and Richard Adams, was derisively referred to by Marlow," Keach's fierce opponent in the hymn singing controversy, "as the new kind of prerogative court."[144] Spears and Vaughn suggest that Keach's books were primarily concerned with instruction, especially religious education.[145] Puritanism put a great

---

[141] The most important "challenge to the ministry as perceived by the ministers at the General Assembly was the inadequate financial support given to so many of the pastors of the churches." Renihan, 'The Practical Ecclesiology of the English Particular Baptists,' 239.

[142] Crosby, *History of English Baptists*, IV: 294. For a summary of Keach's view on this matter see his, *The articles of the faith of the Church of Christ, or, Congregation meeting at Horsley-down; Benjamin Keach, pastor, as asserted this 10th of the 6th month, 1697* (London: s.n., 1697), s.v., 'Of Ministers and their Maintenance.' It is obvious that Keach had become a towering figure among the Particular Baptists. Hence, for example, he was one of the 6 signatories to the Convocation of the 1689 Assembly. Iviemy, *History of English Baptists*, I: 480.

[143] Spears, 'Public Worship and Practical Theology,' 177. It is indeed worth pointing out that, despite their commitment to congregational polity, the Particular Baptists had a very clear sense of catholicity. Novak's study shows that many Baptists were involved with preaching excursions and, at times, the General Association sent "messengers" to help and encourage congregations in different ways. Through these activities, they aimed at having a "uniform profession." Michael James Novak, 'Thy Will be done: the Theology of the English Particular Baptists, 1638-1660' (Ph.D. diss., Harvard University, 1979), 96. This same point is made by, e.g., Renihan, 'The Practical Ecclesiology of the English Particular Baptists,' 348-371.

[144] *BDBR*, II: 151.

[145] Spears, 'Baptist Movement in England,' 232-233; Vaughn, 'Baptist Theologians,' 65. Besides a general sense, Vaughn says, in which all books published by Keach may be

stress on education, especially pulpit education, as a means to attain true godliness, because "the common people will worship any dunghill god if preaching be neglected."[146]

It is very likely that the most important controversy Keach was involved with was the one dealing with corporate hymn singing. Inasmuch as the church sang during the Middle Ages, as the choral tradition attests, the laity did not participate in it; singing, that is, was restricted to those who were part of the ecclesiastical structures. With the advent of the Reformation, the Lutheran church, following Luther, came to practice the singing of hymns corporately. However, the Reformed churches, by and large, rejected "words of men" in God's worship and, thus, only the singing of biblical words was allowed. When the Protestant Elizabeth I acceded to the throne in 1558, zealous religious refugees returned to England bringing with them, *inter alia*, Reformed praxis: the Word of God alone—i.e., hymns contained in the Bible, like Miriam's (Ex.15) and, especially, the Psalter—was to be sung in the church. This practice became firmly entrenched.[147] Additionally, the Puritans argued that if the odious *Book of Common Prayer* were to be rejected on the basis that it contains— instead of spiritual—set forms of prayers, no less should any set form of singing be allowed. That is, if any singing were to take place, it had to be straight from the Spirit since the Bible commands "spiritual songs" to be sung.[148]

From his first publication, *The Child's Instructor*, in 1664, all the way to his *Spiritual Songs* in 1700, Keach wrote, in one form or another, about five hundred hymns. This last work, as a matter of fact, became the first hymn book

---

regarded instructional, there are particular books whose aim is purposefully catechetical. Although of contested authorship, the *Baptist Catechism,* Vaughn purports, should be deemed Keach's. Ibid., 66. For a discussion of the authorship of the said *Catechism* see Thomas Nettles, *Baptist Catechisms: 'To Make Thee Wise unto Salvation'* (Forth Worth: For the author, 1982), 76.

[146] Hugh Peter, *Mr. Peters Last Report of the English Wars* (London: Printed by M. S. for Henry Overton, 1646), 12-13; quoted by Christopher Hill, *Society and Puritanism in Pre-Revolutionary England* (London: Secker & Warburg, 1964), 57.

[147] See, Martin, *Benjamin Keach, 1640-1704: Pioneer of Congregational Hymn Singing*, 9-12; Whiting, *Studies in English Puritanism*, 97; Griffiths, *Religion and Learning*, 4-5; Copeland, *Benjamin Keach*, 111-116; Watts, *The Dissenters*, 308.

[148] See the arguments for and against singing fully discussed in, Murdina MacDonald, 'London Calvinistic Baptists, 1689-1727: Tensions within a Dissenting Community under Toleration' (Ph.D. diss., Regent's Park College, Oxford, 1983). See also, Spears, 'The Baptist Movement in England,' 126-143; Vaughn, 'Public Worship and Practical Theology,' 142-202. In a summary form, see idem, *Benjamin Keach*, 63-65; Haykin, *Kiffin, Knollys and Keach*, 91-96; Renihan, 'Practical Ecclesiology of the English Particular Baptists,' 298-312; Robinson, *Life and Faith of the Baptists*, 49-52. Another Puritan argument against congregational hymn-singing would be that it fostered unseeming brotherhood with non-believers.

widely accepted by the English Reformed. However, Keach's importance is not due to his originality or poetic prowess; neither of those was his forte. Rather, his contribution relates to the fact that he introduced corporate hymn singing on a regular basis and, in the teeth of fierce opposition, fought for the establishment of the practice.[149] On the whole, Puritanism owes to Keach's pioneering work, the "privilege of holding a hymnal in hand and sing forth praises and prayers" corporately.[150] "At the 1689 Assembly, the Particular Baptists gave cautious approval to singing or at least to the concept of each congregation deciding its own practices without censure from others."[151] As Vaughn concludes his examination of Keach's lasting impact, he asserts "that on 1 March 1691, when Keach's church voted to sing a hymn each Sunday following the sermon, the great tradition of English Protestant hymnody began."[152]

Final Stages

The general impression one gets from reading Keach's biographies is that, on the one side, he was a man with great zeal for the truths in which he believed—fighting indefatigably to maintain and propagate them. On the other side, Keach had a strong desire for a Protestant ecumenicity. The classical example to the former point is credobaptism: "I have my self baptised many hundred of men and women and some at all times of the year, yea in times of bitter frost and snow, when the ice was first broken, and persons of a weak sickly constitution, and women big with child, and others near seventy ...some near eighty years old ..." and none of them has had their health damaged by it.[153] To use again baptism to illustrate the latter point, amidst the pamphlet war with the Anglican's 'Athenian Society,' Keach says, "I wish that all bitterness of spirit was expelled; love and charity exercised towards all, tho in some things we differ from one another."[154]

---

[149] David Music, 'The Hymns of Benjamin Keach: An Introductory Study,' in *Hymn* 34 (July 1983): 147-154; Spears, 'The Baptist Movement in England,' 137. For the bitter exchange of books and pamphlets during the controversy of corporate hymn singing, see Carnes, 'The Famous Mr. Keach,' 82-88; Copeland, *Keach and the Development of Baptist Traditions*, 120-140; Vaughn, 'Public Worship and Practical Theology,' 145-156. Despite Keach's poor poetry, he nevertheless influenced Isaac Watts and Augustus Toplady, see Spears, 'Baptist Movement in England,' 139-142; Carnes, 'The Famous Mr. Keach,' 108.

[150] Hugh T. McElrath, 'Turning Points in the Story of Baptist Church Music,' in *BHH* 19 (January 1984): 4-16, p. 4. For an account of Keach's hymns published in the American Colonies, see Music, 'The Hymns of Keach,' 152-153.

[151] McBeth, *The Baptist Heritage*, 95.

[152] Vaughn, 'Public Worship and Practical Theology,' 379.

[153] Keach, *Light Broke Forth*, [257].

[154] Keach, *Pedobaptism Disproved*, 13.

From very humble origins, truly an unknown quantity, Keach became a distinguished figure in the latter part of his life. So, for example, his attack on Sabbatarianism[155] was so well regarded that he had the privilege to give a copy of it "into the hand of the Archbishop of Canterbury, who highly approved of his performance and received him into favour and conversation."[156] What a stark contrast to his days in Winslow when he, locked to the pillory, saw his *The Child's Instructor* burnt by the hangman—all of that for contradicting the teaching of the Anglican church!

Keach's son, Elias, successfully planted churches in Pennsylvania, but he eventually returned to England to pastor a Baptist church in Wapping, Middlesex, and "afterwards at Goodman's Field. He died in 1699, or, according to Ivimey, in 1701."[157] Another great distress to Keach, given the fact that he fought Quakerism all his life, must have been his daughter's conversion to this point of view. Hannah came to see her father at his deathbed. On that occasion, physically weak, Keach failed to talk to her despite his earnest attempts. Keach's ecumenical desire is seen once again by the selection of the Baptist Sabbatarian Joseph Stennett to officiate his funeral. Despite utter disagreement between the two, mutual respect prevailed. Keach's chosen text for the service was 2 Ti.1.12: "I know whom I have believed and am convinced that he is able to guard what I have entrusted to him for that day." At last, the Baptist preacher committed his wife "to a better husband, the Lord Jesus Christ and exhorted his children to love peace and unity, and a steadfast adherence to Christ and his ways."[158]

When Keach died, on 18 July 1704, the formative phase of the Particular Baptists came to a closure. "All of the key leaders who had helped to give shape and substance to this dynamic movement—among whom Kiffin, Knollys and Keach were pre-eminent—had entered into the reward for which they had laboured and longed."[159]

Literature Review

Given Keach's importance, as we have shown, it is nothing short of remarkable that there have been only two scholarly works on him.[160]

---

[155] *The Jewish Sabbath Abrogated: Or, the Saturday Sabbatarians confuted* (London: Printed and sold by John Marshall at the Bible in Grace-Church-street, 1700).

[156] Crosby, *History of English Baptists*, IV: 302. See the discussion of Keach's attack on Sabbatarianism in Spears, 'Baptist Movement in England,' 188-192.

[157] *DNB*, XII: 1143.

[158] Crosby, *History of English Baptists*, IV: 308.

[159] Haykin, *Kiffin, Knollys and Keach*, 99.

[160] A third work deals exclusively, as the title indicates, with Keach amidst the singing of hymns controversy: James Carnes, 'The Famous Mr. Keach: Benjamin Keach and his Influence on Congregational Singing in Seventeenth Century England' (M.A. diss., North Texas State University, 1984).

William Spears' 1953 thesis, 'The Baptist Movement in England in the Late Seventeenth Century as Reflected in the Work and Thought of Benjamin Keach, 1640-1704,' was the first scholarly study on this Puritan. Spears' fine work sets the life and writings of Keach over against the political and religious background of the seventeenth century. One of the fortes of this groundbreaking monograph was the demonstration of how influential Keach was during and after his lifetime. Making use of Harry Talon's extensive study of John Bunyan, Spears concludes that Keach was equal in popularity to the Bedford tinker in the late 17th and early 18th centuries. Each allegorist took cues from and influenced the other. It is noteworthy to point out that Keach's allegory *War with the Devil*, 1673, was published prior to Bunyan's *Pilgrim's Progress*, 1675.[161] Keach's imaginative work went through reprints as late as 1776[162] and became so famous that John Mason (fl. 1676-1683) wrote an introduction on how to read it.[163] Granting that both authors were translated into different languages and widely reprinted, why then has Bunyan remained a household name and Keach was eventually forgotten? Spears concludes that this is the case because Keach's characters are too abstract or lifeless, whereas Bunyan's are lively, i.e., full of unexpected reactions. Keach was also very influential across the ocean: his *Instruction for Children* morphed into *The New England Primer*, and turned out to be the most popular book in early America. Moreover, Keach's *Baptist Catechism* was employed by the Philadelphia Association and "widely used among early Baptists in the United States."[164]

However, there are several things which we deem inadequate in this thesis. Spears does not consider Keach "a theologian." These are his words: "In this entire study no attempt is made to draw out of his works a systematic theology because he was not a theologian in the technical sense of the term."[165] Perhaps on that account, secondly, Keach's doctrines are treated very superficially: one page is dedicated to "effectual calling," another to "saving faith," and between these two *loci*, Keach's doctrine of justification is dealt with in three pages.[166]

---

[161] Spears, 'The Baptist Movement in England,' 232, 70-74.

[162] Other allegories written by Keach had even greater fame and longer reprints: *The Progress of Sin*, 1684, and, *Travels of True Godliness*, also first printed in 1684, were reprinted until 1849.

[163] *Mentis Humane Metamorphis sive Conversio. The History of the Young Converted Galland or Directions to the Readers of that Divine Poem written by Benjamin Keach, Intittled Warre with the Devil* (London: B. Harris, 1676).

[164] Spears, 'The Baptist Movement in England,' 69, 72, 238, 233. Spears has an addendum to his dissertation, 'Appendix C: The Influence of Keach in the United States,' pp. 266-274, which is a useful guide to show Keach's impact in America. See also, Sandford Fleming, *Children & Puritanism: The Place of Children in the Life and Thought of the New England Churches, 1620-1847* (New Haven: Yale University Press, 1933), 80-82; McBeth, *The Baptist Heritage*, 251.

[165] Spears, 'The Baptist Movement in England,' 61. Cf. Ibid., 108.

[166] Spears, 'The Baptist Movement in England,' 208, 212, 208-211.

Third, Spears operates within the framework of Calvin vs. Calvinists: the Baptist preacher is compared to Calvin and regarded as a "moderate Calvinist;" in distinction to John Owen who is a hyper-Calvinist.[167] To be "moderate," according to Spears, is to stand "between Owen and Baxter;" alternatively, Spears says that his "study clearly indicates that among those in the Baptist tradition Keach was not so hyper-Calvinistic as John Gill nor so Arminian as Thomas Granthan, but that he stood between them and may accurately be termed a moderate Calvinist."[168]

In the first place, it is neither self-evident nor even vaguely clear what Spears means by the unexplained claim that Keach "is not a theologian in the technical sense of the term." What is clear, though, is that our protagonist dealt with certain doctrinal *loci*, such as baptism, in such way that their natures are microscopically analysed and scrutinised in every conceivable way—be it exegetical, homiletical or polemic. Indeed, in the case of baptism, Keach rigorously examines the subject with elenctic disposition, matched only by John Tombes (1603?-1676) before him. Surely, this fact alone would make Keach a theologian. Second, there is urgent need to re-evaluate Keach's theological *loci* in far greater depth. Third, the paradigm Calvin vs. Calvinists is unhelpful and even misleading.

Barry Vaughn's 1990 monograph, 'Public Worship and Practical Theology in the Work of Benjamin Keach (1640-1704),' aims at rescuing this champion "from near oblivion and [to] show that he was the most important practical theologian among the Calvinistic Baptists of the seventeenth century." As the title indicates, Vaughn's focus is twofold: Keach's contribution in the realm of worship, and the practical character of his theology. Vaughn concludes that Keach's views on corporate hymn singing were the most important gift he left to English Protestantism.[169] On the practical theology of Keach, among other things, Vaughn makes a fine contextual analysis and detailed examination of his "imaginative writings." Through the use of images, rhymes, metaphors and poetry, Keach wanted to teach piety or godliness to the church.[170]

The weakness of Vaughn's study is that Keach is treated as a *practical* theologian at best.[171] As a result, just like Spears, Vaughn makes no effort to dissect Keach's thoughts in a detailed manner. Hence, none of Keach's

---

[167] Spears, 'The Baptist Movement in England,' 80, 210, 211, 218, 47, 194, 193. See, for example, Trueman, *The Claims of Truth*, especially, 227-232, where the author argues that Owen is not a hyper-Calvinist, but rather a Reformed thinker working at the centre of Orthodoxy.

[168] Spears, 'The Baptist Movement in England,' 194.

[169] Vaughn, 'Public Worship and Practical Theology,' iii, 379.

[170] Vaughn, 'Public Worship and Practical Theology,' 297-344, 263-264.

[171] The theology of Keach was first and foremost practical. His works were shaped by two forces: a doctrine of justification utterly independent of human will and, secondly, a rich use of metaphors and images to convey this and other doctrines. Vaughn, 'Public Worship and Practical Theology,' iv-v.

theological *loci* is explored at length. For example, although the theme "covenant" is mentioned a few times in polemic form, Vaughn makes only one very superficial attempt to present Keach's covenant thought positively.[172] This is not adequate! Another problem—again, similar to Spears'—is that Vaughn operates along the lines of Calvin vs. Calvinists.[173] Two examples illustrate the point. First, John Gill, one of Keach's successors, is deemed a "hyper-Calvinist."[174] Second, and of far greater import, "Keach's recorded opinion verge on hyper-Calvinism;" he "departed substantially from the Calvinistic heritage in denying double predestination."[175]

What are we to make of Vaughn's definition of Keach as a "practical theologian?" First, Keach purports to have a method of his own regarding the relationship between the several covenants within the federal scheme. He says that conceivably someone has written more "excellently upon the covenant of grace, yet perhaps hardly any in the *method* here used, nor under the notion of a covenant of peace ..." Keach proceeds to explain what he means by a different method. He asserts, "in some things thou wilt find that I do differ from many learned men, who make the covenant of redemption, a distinct covenant from that of peace and reconciliation..."[176] In other words, Keach claims to have his own covenantal concept, one in which the eternal intertrinitarian covenant of redemption is not differentiated from God's historical covenant of peace with humanity. Obviously there are practical implications to this scheme (Keach is combating Baxterianism, as we shall see), *nevertheless*, if 'theory' had a scale, this type of musing (the collapse of the temporal into the eternal) would come very high on it.[177] Second, and of greater importance, Keach is a Reformer—as

---

[172] Vaughn, 'Public Worship and Practical Theology,' 247, 249, 252, 224-226.

[173] Vaughn seems to be aware of the debate about "Calvin and 'the Calvinists.'" He says that "English Protestant theology ...was too multiform to be characterised as the product of a single theologian, even a theologian as comprehensive and compelling as Calvin." However, Vaughn remarkably proceeds to present the views of Hall and Kendall without disagreeing with them. Additionally, the question of 'how faith relates to justification' in the Westminster Confession is briefly analysed and then Vaughn concludes that whether or not the Confession is "[a] betrayal of Calvinism or not," it did become a paradigm to Anglo-American Reformed thought. 'Public Worship and Practical Theology,' 205-207. Emphasis mine.

[174] Vaughn, 'Public Worship and Practical Theology,' 241. For yet another example deeming Gill a hyper-Calvinist, see Barry H. Howson, *Erroneus and Schismatical Opinions: The Question of Orthodoxy Regarding the Theology of Hanserd Knollys (c.1599-1691)* (Leiden: Brill, 2001), 14, 24. For arguments that Gill is not a hyper-Calvinist, but rather a Reformed thinker working within the parameters of Orthodoxy, see Hong-Gyu Park, 'Grace and Nature in the Theology of John Gill (1697-1771)' (Ph.D. diss., University of Aberdeen, 2001).

[175] Vaughn, 'Public Worship and Practical Theology,' 19, 238.

[176] Keach, *Display of Glorious Grace*, iv-v. His emphasis.

[177] We shall deal with Keach's concept of 'covenant' in the next chapter.

we shall see in the third chapter—and as such he is a theologian. This contention will be underpinned by his skilful confrontations with his pedobatist opponents. Third, the doctrine of justification involves much 'theory,' and Keach wrote no less than five books dealing with this theme, not to mention his many references to it sprinkled throughout his other works.[178] Concerning Keach's alleged "Calvinism," as Vaughn sees it, one in which Keach's position "verge[s] on hyper-Calvinism," one in which he "departed substantially from the Calvinistic heritage in denying double predestination"—this is tenable only if the whole Reformed school is defined by strict agreement with the French Reformer.[179] That is to say, Vaughn's conclusion can only stand if Keach is seen as a follower of Calvin. However, as we have already shown, the Reformed tradition is more than Calvin. Vaughn is correct in saying that Keach did not hold double predestination. We add to what Vaughn said, on account of precision, that Keach maintained a single or positive decree only, and "preterition" or "passing by" as corollary.[180]

A segment of the Reformed also either (1) ignores reprobation or (2) understands it as preterition. Of the first kind, neither *reprobatio* nor *gemina predestinatio* is mentioned in the *Confession of Faith of Geneva*, the *First* and the *Second Helvetic Confession*, the *Heidelberg Catechism*, and the *Genevan Catechism*.[181] Of the second type, *reprobatio* is not understood as decreed but merely as passing by in the *French Confession of Faith*, the *Scots Confession*, the *Belgic Confession*, etc.[182] Ergo, a correct understanding of the Reformed

---

[178] *Marrow of Justification* (1692), *The Everlasting Covenant* (1693), *Christ Alone the Way to Heaven* (1698), *The Display of Glorious Grace* (1698), and *A Medium betwixt Two Extremes* (1698).

[179] Calvin, *Institutes*, III.xxiii.7.

[180] "Question. Did God pass an eternal decree of reprobation on angels or men, as a simple act of his sovereignty, without any respect had to their sin or disobedience? Answ. Some are bold to affirm he did, but I am not of that opinion..." *Exposition of the Parables*, I: 93. See the full discussion of reprobation in ibid., 93-98. Keach's understanding of positive and negative election may be illustrated by the following assertion: While salvation is accomplished by God alone, in the end God will show that humanity's "destruction is of themselves, tho their help is only in God." *Display of Glorious Grace*, 168-169.

[181] See, http://www.creeds.net/reformed, *Confession of Faith of Geneva*, 1536, 'Article IV: Natural Man;' http://www.creeds.net/reformed, *First Helvetic Confession*, 1536, 'Article XVIII: Election;' http://www.ccel.org/creeds, *Second Helvetic Confession*, 1566, 'Chapter X: Of the Predestination of God and the Election of the Saints;' http:www.reformed.org/documents, *The Heidelberg Catechism*, 1563, 'Answer 20;' ibid., *Genevan Catechism*, 1545, 'Answer [95].'

[182] See, http://www.creeds.net/reformed, *The French Confession of Faith*, 1559, 'Article XII;' ibid., *The Scots Confession*, 1560, 'Chapter VIII: Election;' http:www.reformed.org/documents, *The Belgic Confession*, 1618, 'Article XVI: the Doctrine of Election.'

tradition allows us to aver that Keach unquestionably remained within the pale of Reformed Orthodoxy. Mark it well, therefore, Keach, as suggested by our thesis, is not to be deemed a Calvinist, but rather as a Reformed thinker.[183]

Tradition, Successionism and Scholasticism

Keach vs. Tradition

At several places within his corpus, Keach denies an authoritative role to Tradition: "...know, noble Britains, that we build not our faith ...upon the practice and custom of men, Fathers, General Councils, Protestant Reformers or churches; but upon the Word of God."[184]

Contrary to all appearances, however, Keach's aforesaid protestation does not obliterate the Tradition. In other words, Keach's commitment to the Bible does not drive him to embrace *Scriptura nuda*. We shall argue that this is the case on the basis of three pieces of evidence. First, Keach thought that the Tradition itself would consent to or agree with his view of sole Scripture authority. Second, he makes positive use of the exegetical tradition to argue his cases. Third, Keach employs the dogmatic tradition and, in doing so, makes it normative. For the sake of clarity, let us divide this heading, 'Tradition,' into three sub-headings, 'consensual,' 'exegetical,' and 'dogmatic.'

Consensual Tradition

In the first place, then, Keach envisaged—whether rightly or wrongly is immaterial to our argument—that his view of *sola Scriptura* was shared by the Tradition itself: the Holy Scriptures, he affirms, are the complete and perfect rule for all that is required for faith and practice, as "*all* the ancient Fathers and modern divines" testify.[185]

The following are some of the authorities Keach presents to substantiate his point. See how Athanasius (c. 296-373) speaks about it: the Scriptures, "being inspirations of God, are sufficient to all instructions of truth."[186] Likewise, Basil

---

[183] On this point, we may add that even though Keach's opponents refer to him as a 'Calvinist,' Keach himself never does so. See, e.g., Gyles Shute, *A Replication to a Late Book written by Mr Benjamin Keach Against Infant-Baptism, Intituled A Counter-Antidote* (London: Printed for the author, 1694), 6.

[184] Keach, *Light Broke Forth*, 226. The Gospel of Christ is our guide, "not cunning devised fables, not the traditions of men, not decrees and canons of general counsels..." Idem, *Exposition of the Parables*, I: 122. Cf. Ibid., 262; idem, *Rector Rectified*, 129, 138-139.

[185] Keach, *Light Broke Forth*, [325]. Emphasis mine. Cf. Idem, *Counter-Antidote to purge out the malignant effects of a late counterfeit, prepared by Mr. Gyles Shute* (London: Printed for H. Bernard, 1694), postscript, 3.

[186] Athanasius, *Oratio Contra Gentes*, I. A. P.G.25; in Keach, *Light Broke Forth*, [325]; *Gold Refin'd*, 93; *Counter-Antidote*, postscript, 3.

the Great (c. 330-379) said that it "would be an argument of infidelity and a most certain sign of pride, if any man should reject any thing written and should introduce things not written."[187] John Chrysostom (c. 349-407) asserts that "all things be plain and clear in the Scriptures and whatsoever are needful are manifest there."[188] In the same manner, Augustine (354-430) affirmed that within the Bible "are found all things which contain faith, manner of living, hope, love, &c. Let us seek no further than what is written of God and Saviour, lest a man should know more than the Scriptures witness."[189]

Exegetical Tradition

Here we are to note that despite Keach's apparent dismissal of all authorities save Scripture, he actually relies on past and contemporary figures. Obviously, at times he disagrees with them (and does so strongly). Should we not blame some of the Fathers, Keach asks, for admitting infants to the Eucharist "without censuring and condemning" such a practice? "Besides, did not the same Fathers hold to other errors?"[190] In doing so, he is no different from other Reformed Orthodox.[191]

Although disagreements do occur, Keach does talk about the Fathers highly and reverently. Consider how he praises Nazianzus and the Apostle in the same breath. "Gregory Nazianzen, a man of *prodigious wit and learning*, when he came to take to the study of this sacred philosophy, vilifies all other ornaments of literature amongst the Greek philosophers. And not only Nazianzen did so,

---

[187] Cf. e.g., Basil, *De Fide*, (224-225), P.G.31; in Keach, *Light Broke Forth*, [325]; *Gold Refin'd*, 94; *Counter-Antidote*, postscript, 3.

[188] John Chrysostom, *In Epistolam Secundam Ad Thessalonicenses Commentarius*, Homilia III, 4. P.G.62; in Keach, *Light Broke Forth*, [309]; *Gold Refin'd*, 94; *Counter-Antidote*, postscript, 3.

[189] Augustine, *Epistola CXLVIII: Ad Fortunatianum*, IV (15). P.L.33; in Keach, *Light Broke Forth*, [325]; *Gold Refin'd*, 94; *Counter-Antidote*, postscript, 3. For other authorities, see e.g., *Light Broke Forth*, [325] et seqq. For Protestant agreement with Keach's position, see, for example, Calvin, *Institutes*, II.v.17: At times, the advocates of free will call upon "Origen and Jerome in support of their position. I could in turn oppose Augustine to these. But what these hold makes no difference to us, provided we understand what Paul means." This statement should not lead us astray; the respect Calvin nurtured for the Fathers, especially Augustine, is well known. See, e.g., ibid., III.xxii.8; ibid., Prefatory Address to King Francis.

[190] Keach, *Rector Rectified*, 138. Cf. Idem, *The Ax Laid to the Root, or, One blow more at the foundation of infant baptism, and church-membership, containing an exposition of that metaphorical text of Holy Scripture, Mat. 3. 10*. 2 vols. (London: Printed for the author, and are to be sold by John Harris, 1693), I: 30.

[191] For example, Perkins blames the Fathers for having "error, yea, and sometimes gross ones." *William Perkins: His Probleme of the Forged Catholicisme, or Uniuersalitie of the Romish Religion* (London: Iohn Legatt, Printer to the University of Cambridge, 1613), 549.

but the learned Paul also." Keach adds that he does not devalue the proper use of all "human learning, for it is excellent in its place," nevertheless, "Justin Martyr excellently says, *Infelix est sapientia extra verbum Dei sapere.*"[192]

As to Protestants, the Reformed Orthodox John Owen was Keach's darling: truly, his most cherished and positively mentioned author. Myriads of references to Owen are to be found throughout Keach's corpus. For example, in a booklet of 54 pages, Owen is referred to no less than twelve times.[193] Keach compared great Christians to "lights" or "stars," with various degrees of luminosity: some dim, others of gigantic splendour. Curiously and significantly, Calvin is not mentioned in this context.[194] Keach speaks about the Apostle "Paul, who was a glorious light and outshone many of Christ's ministers; moreover, we have had in latter days some that have been like stars of the first or greatest magnitude." Keach proceeds, remarkably, to put Owen on a par with Luther. "What a light was blessed Luther in the last age. And what great lights have we had in this age? Though none shone more splendidly (in my judgement) in our days, than renown Dr. Owen ..."[195]

Keach makes use of the exegetical tradition not only in the polemic context, but also positively. That is, he uses the tradition to build, reinforce and prove his points. Not surprisingly, he is highly selective in his use of it. This selectivity is illustrated by the following blunt example. Amidst the several authorities Keach uses to show that baptism is the rite of entrance into the church, he quotes William Ames: "Baptism is a sacrament of initiation."[196] Upon consulting the original, however, one discovers that the totality of what Ames says is, *Baptismus est sacramentum initiationis aut regenerationis.*[197] Disagreeing with the opinion that baptism regenerates, Keach cuts the last two

---

[192] Keach, *Preaching from the Types of the Bible* (Grand Rapids: Kregel, 1972), henceforth, *Tropologia*, xi, ix. Gregory, cf. e.g., *Oratio XXVII: Theologia Prima*, I (488), P.G.36. Unable to locate Justin.

[193] Keach, *Counter-Antidote*, 17, 18, 19, 22, 26, 28, 46, 47, 48, 49, 50, 51. No author is cited as much as Owen throughout Keach's corpus. See, for example, *Display of Glorious Grace*, 86, 88, 203; *Marrow of Justification*, 31, 33; *Golden Mine*, 91, 207, 221, 226, 239; *Exposition of the Parables*, I: 189, 190, 191; II: iii, 16, 19, 20, 21; *Tropologia*, xxvii, etc. However, it should be emphasised that despite Keach's immense admiration of Owen, he is not a slave imitator. See him disagreeing with Owen in *Exposition of the Parables*, II: 222.

[194] John Calvin is rather conspicuous for his absence. There are about only half a dozen quotes of the Genevan Reformer sprinkled throughout Keach's corpus.

[195] Keach, *Exposition of the Parables*, II: 58. In light of Keach's view of Scripture, it is obvious that Paul would be in a category of his own. Nevertheless, it is rather striking that in this passage the Apostle has had similar "stars of the first or greatest magnitude" in the persons of Luther and Owen.

[196] Keach, *Gold Refin'd*, 178.

[197] William Ames, *Medulla Theologica* (Amsterdam: Apud Ioannem Ianssonium, 1648), s.v., 'De Baptismo & Coena Domini.'

words and translates only what fits his purposes. He may not be accused of distorting Ames, since the argument he is building has nothing to do with the sacramentality of the rite; i.e., when Keach presents Ames agreeing with him, all he wants to do is to demonstrate that the unbaptised is not to be part of the church.[198]

In order to incite the "just odium" of England against Rome, Keach argues that the Roman church is the Antichristian Beast or Scarlet Whore of the book of Revelation.[199] He makes his case relying heavily on the Protestant exegetical tradition (in its apocalyptic mode), from which Keach requests the aid of the Fathers and other witnesses.[200] The book is presented as a court case: Sion is the Protestant church; several countries (Bohemia, Germany, Poland, England, etc.) are the witnesses, and Keach is the prosecutor. The final verdict of the work is a sentence passed on Rome as "guilty of ...horrid and prodigious crimes..."[201] Of our particular interest is the way Keach uses the tradition positively to build his case. Let us consider three examples. In the first place, the general declension of the primitive church marks the first stage of the rise of the Beast, as Keach understands it. That is, there would have to be a wide spread apostasy, 2Thes.2.3, before this antichristian force would come to usurp the place of Christ. This declension is witnessed by, *inter alios*, Jerome, who asserts that around "the year 390, the law perished from the priest and the vision from the prophet, avarice and corruption crept into the church; they condemned meats and marriage and yet gave themselves up to luxurious banquets and uncleanness."[202] Augustine likewise says that Christianity at the end of the fourth century "was corrupted with traditions and humane rites, that the condition of the Jews under the law was easier than that of Christians under the

---

[198] See infra, 'Baptism and the defection of Christendom,' pp. 122-128.

[199] Keach, *Sion in Distress*, [i], [iii].

[200] Among others, Keach refers to John Jewel, *A Viewe of a Seditious Bul sent to Englande from Pius Quintus Bishop of Rome, Anno 1569* (London: Printed by R. Newberie & H. Bynneman, 1582); William Hughes, *The Man of Sin: Or a Discourse of Popery* (London: Printed by J. D. for Robert Boulter, at the Turks-Head in Cornhil, over against the Royal-Exchange, 1677); Thomas Brightman, *A Revelation of the Revelation* (Amsterdam: s.n., 1615); Joseph Mede, *The Key of the Revelation searched and demonstrated out of the Naturall and proper Characters of the Visions*, Richard More, trans. (Printed in London by R. B. for Phil. Stephens at his shop in Pauls Church-yard at the sign of the guilded Lion, 1643); John Tillinghast, *Generation-Worke: Or, An Exposition of the Prophecies of the Two Witnesses* (London: Printed for Livewell Chapman, at the Crown in Popes-head-Alley, 1654); Peter Du Moulin, *The Accomplishment of the Prophecies, Or the Third Booke in defence of the Catholicke faith* (Printed at Oxford by Ioseph Barnes and are to be sold by Iohn Barnes dwelling neere Holborne Conduit, 1613).

[201] Keach, *Sion in Distress*, 113.

[202] Jerome, *Epistola LII: Ad Nepotianum, De Vita Clericorum* (255-270), P.L.22; in Keach, *Sion in Distress*, 46.

Gospel."²⁰³ In the same way, Dionysius complains that "they were burdened with ceremonies and traditions that were obtruded and laid upon Christians, and that the sacraments both of Baptism and the Lord's Supper, suffered great mutations and were grievously corrupted."²⁰⁴ Additionally, Keach continues, John Chrysostom allegedly decries the primacy of the pope and the concept of purgatory.²⁰⁵ These distortions were augmented by the introduction of the worship of images, which thing is preached against by the Bishop of Iconium, Amphilocus, as well as by Epiphanius. The latter asserts, "be mindful, my beloved children, that ye bring not images into the church, but bear about God in your hearts."²⁰⁶ In the second place, Keach proceeds, the next stage or the second mark of the Beast is represented by the weakening of the Roman empire. Keach sees the political Roman empire as the restraining force, 2Thes.2.6, and its fall marks another step of the church's decline—a decisive step for the appearing of the "Son of Perdition." This interpretation, he alleges, is shared by Tertullian, John Chrysostom, Augustine and others.²⁰⁷ In the third and final place, discussing the fifth mark of the Beast, Keach asserts that the Man of Sin would sit in the temple of God, i.e., the Christian church. Herein Keach negates any reference to the temple in Jerusalem; and to do so, he

---

²⁰³ Cf. e.g., Augustine, *Ad Inquisitiones Januarii Liber Secundus, seu Epistola LV*, XIX (35), P.L.33; in Keach, *Sion in Distress*, 46.

²⁰⁴ Cf. e.g., A letter from Dionysius bishop of Corinth to Pynitus bishop of Knossos, quoted in Eusebius, *Ecclesiasticae Historiae*, L. IV, c. xxii (144), P.G.20; Keach, *Sion in Distress*, 46.

²⁰⁵ Keach, *Sion in Distress*, 46. We were unable to track down to the original: Keach borrows the idea from Woffius, "Chrysostom de prioritate, quam Pontifex Romanus iam tum sibi arrogabat, sic sentit: Inter servos Christi computari non posse, qui de primatu tractaverint; & qui desideraverint primatum in terram, mereri confusionem in coelo. Et de libertione ex purgatorio per communicationem bonorum operum qualis est illa iustitia, ait, munerare mortuos, & exspoliare vivos? Cur promitis pecuniam redemptionem defuncto & acceptam eam, illum in inferno reliquis? Iohannis Woffius, *Lectionum Memorabilium et Reconditarum Centenarii XVI* (Palatinus: Impressit Leong. Reinmichel, 1660), 121.

²⁰⁶ Keach, *Sion in Distress*, 46-47. Unable to locate Amphilocus' reference. Again, Keach relies on Woffius, who has the bishop of Iconium saying, "Non enim nobis sanctorum corporales vultus in tabulis coloribus effigiate curae est, quoniam his opus non habemus, sed illorum vertutum memores esse debemus. Clarè hoc dicto imaginum cultum damnavit." Woffinus, *Lectionum Memorabilium*, 121. Epiphanius' criticism of the worship of images, in *Adversus Haereses*, L. II, Tom. 2 (1061), P.G.42. Epiphanius' citation, "Estote memores, dilecti filij, ne in Ecclesiam imagines inferatis, neque in sanctorum caemeterijs eas statuatis, sed perpetuò circumferte Deum in cordibus vestris," in Woffius, *Lectionum Memorabilium*, 122.

²⁰⁷ Keach, *Sion in Distress*, 47-48. Tertullian, *De Carnis Resurrectione*, XXIV, C.S.E.L.47; Chrysostom, *In Epistolam Secundam Ad Thessalonicenses Commentarius*, Homilia IV, P.G.62; Augustine, *De Civitate Dei*, XX, 19, C.C.S.L.48; Du Mollin, *The Accoomplishment of Prophecies*, 119, 157.

appeals to Chrysostom who unequivocally "expresses τὸν ἐν Ἱεροσυλύμοις ἀλλὰ καὶ τὰς ἐκκλησίας, that is, not in Jerusalem but in the church."[208]

This illustrates an occasion in which Keach is not simply responding to an adversary by using the tradition negatively. Rather, here he is making a lengthy and concatenated argument to demonstrate his view of the Roman church, and he constructs it using the positive authority of the tradition.

Dogmatic Tradition

At this point we come to what, arguably, is the most important use of the tradition. At the risk of boring repetition, we have observed Keach denying authority to anything save the Bible, but notice hereafter his use of counciliar parlance—a use which normatizes it. It is as if what Keach takes with one hand, he gives with the other. Observe the following example:[209] on the same page of one of his works, Keach says that a true Christian is not guided by the decisions of "General Councils," but characterised by, among other things, a firm belief on "the doctrine of the Blessed Trinity ...One in essence, yet three Persons or Subsistences." As to Christology, a Christian ought to believe that Christ

> is God by nature, the most high God, *coeternal and coequal with the Father and the Holy Ghost*; abominating the doctrine of Arius, who asserted he was not of the substance of the Father ...And the doctrine of the Socinians, who affirmed, he is meer man and had no pre-existence ... [and] the doctrine of Eutyches, who maintains that the matter of Christ's flesh was from heaven, or that it was a conversion of the deity of the second Person of the Trinity into flesh and that he partook not of the nature of the Virgin.[210]

Note this attack on Monophysitism: it is an abomination, Keach asserts, to believe "that Christ doth consist of one Nature only ..."[211] This is not by any

---

[208] Chrysostom, *In Epistolam Secundam Ad Thessalonicenses Commentarius*, Homilia III, 2, P.G.62; in Keach, *Sion in Distress*, 52. Besides Chrysostom, Keach requests the support of Ambrose, Anselm and others, see ibid.

[209] In the following paragraphs, note the heavy use of creedal, dogmatic and traditional language.

[210] Keach, *Golden Mine*, 85. His emphasis. "Christ is co-equal, co-eternal and co-essential with the Father ...[thus] the most high God." He is indeed, "man, and so man as well as God in one Person; God of the substance of the Father and man of the substance of the Blessed Virgin ...Born of her and sucked her breast." Idem, *Beams of Divine Light*, 18, 19.

[211] Keach, *Golden Mine*, 85. It is indeed worth pointing out that one of the main goals of Keach's Articles, was to show to other Protestants that his church did not dissent from other denominations "in any fundamental point" of doctrine. For example, Christ, "the Second Person of the Trinity ...according to that holy covenant and compact that was between them both, became man and continueth to be God and man in two distinct

means the only instance of such dogmatism in Keach's work. A few pages later, he again avers that it is not possible to know "the Essence and eternal generation of the Son ..." The Son who took "our nature into mystical union with his deity, being made like unto us in all things, sin only excepted; and thus God and man in one Person."[212]

What of the Holy Spirit? Note the echoes of the Athanasian Creed conspicuously used to describe him: He "is an eternal, divine, existing substance, or the same God or essence with the Father and the Son; or an intelligent, ordinary, divine agent, he knoweth, he maketh, he willeth and is therefore an intelligent agent or Personal subsistence." Furthermore, the Holy Spirit "subsisteth of himself, as doth the Father and Son so subsist."[213] Keach closes this treatise on the Trinity by making differentiations within the Godhead. The Father, the Son and the Holy Spirit, he affirms, "are Three Hypostasis or Persons, distinctly subsisting in the same Divine Essence; upon the account of an especial property, [each Person] subsisting in a special manner." Thus, "in the Person of the Father, there is a Divine Essence and Being, with the Property of begetting a Son, subsisting in a especial manner as the Father." The same thing happens to the other two Persons: like the Father, they share the same Essence but subsist in a particular way; "so that each Person hath the whole Divine Nature or Godhead in that the wisdom of God, the understanding of God, the will of God, the immensity of God, &c. is in each Person ...as that Person is God." This is much "more to be adored than comprehended."[214]

In addition to all of that dogmatism, observe how Keach unashamedly uses sequential segments and verbatim language of the Nicene Creed to describe the several steps taken by the Son in his soteriogical work: Christ "came down from heaven to fix his foot in our Nature ...He was incarnate, born of the

---

Natures in one Person for ever." *The Articles of the Faith*, 9. For another example, see Keach's doctrine of "Original Sin." Ibid., 6-7.

[212] Keach, *Golden Mine*, 91, 93. Emphasis inverted. Cf. Idem, *Beams of Divine Light*, 21.

[213] Keach, *Beams of Divine Light*, 23, 25.

[214] Keach, *Beams of Divine Light*, 26. Keach is quoting John Owen, but in an abbreviated and elliptical manner; see *Works*, II: 497-498. The Holy Spirit, Keach affirms, has a "distinct personality from the Person of the Father and the Son, i.e., that he is an eternal divine existing substance or essence with the Father and the Son, or an intelligent voluntary divine agent; he knoweth, worketh, he willeth, &c., and therefore is an intelligent agent." The fact that he operates as "a distinct Person from the Father and the Son, and yet the same God in essence, set forth the glory of the Holy Ghost." The Spirit was conferred equal dignity with the other Persons in the baptismal command (Mt.28)—among other passages—and so "we are thereby obliged to worship him and live to him." Keach, *Exposition of the Parables*, I: 34. See also the *Second London Confession*, 1689, II:1-3 (subscribed by Keach).

Virgin, ...He died, ...He rose again from the dead, ...He ascended up into heaven ..."[215]

Pelikan's verdict on Luther could equally be applied to Keach. This Baptist theologian rejected the authority of councils; but, nonetheless, interpreted the Bible "in conformity with the dogmas of the councils and in this sense made the councils normative."[216]

As a typical Puritan, Keach saw Christianity not only as a cerebral assent to propositions, but as a hearty internalisation of the articles of faith.[217] The first indispensable article was the doctrine of the Trinity. Then, after listing seven other articles, Keach adds that belief in Christ entails a deep commitment of the heart to love and obey God: not an external "morality, nor an historical, notional or dogmatical knowledge of the sacred Gospel and its precepts." Rather, to be a Christian is to hate sin above all things and cling to God, saying with Augustine, "he loves not Christ at all, that loves him not above all."[218]

To sum up this section, Keach disclaims any authority to the Tradition and places it rather on the Scriptures. This fact, however, does not make him a biblicist, for (1) he conceives the Tradition itself as sharing his view of

---

[215] Keach, *Jacob's Ladder*, 19. Cf. Idem, *Travels of True Godliness*, 23-24. For other instances of Keach's use of dogmatic language, see *Golden Mine*, 91-94, 377; *The Everlasting Covenant*, 22; *Jacob's Ladder*, 65, 75; *Keach's Catechism*, passim.

[216] Pelikan, *Obedient Rebels*, 76. "As a Protestant, he [Luther] subjected the authority of church councils to the authority of the word of God; as a Catholic he interpreted the word of God in conformity with the dogmas of the councils and in this sense made the councils normative. This attitude was an inconsistency according to both the traditionalists and the iconoclasts; for neither of them could see that Catholic substance and Protestant principle belong together, not only in Luther's Reformation, but in the life of the church and indeed in the very message of the New Testament." Ibid.

[217] Cf. Holifield, *The Covenant Sealed*, 1-2. With their emphasis on *praxis pietatis*, the Puritans had a minute and complex "schedule of devotions, introspections, meditations, preparations for conversion, spiritual diaries, fastdays and other 'spiritual exercises,'" which aimed at forming godly character. The elect, the Puritans taught, "are exactly surveyed and wholly transparent. Held thus instantly accountable for every mis-step (including each 'wandering thought'), a saint must move and act with 'that precisenesse, which is commended ...in Gods pure and holy Word;' and that Word, stipulating the saint's duty within the covenant of grace to obey the Lord's commandments, lays down an exact script for saintly precision." T. D. Bozeman, 'The Glory of the Third Time': John Eaton as Contra-Puritan,' in *JEH* 47/4 (October 1996): 638-654, pp. 638-639.

[218] Keach, *Travels of True Godliness*, 26. Cf. e.g., Augustine, *Confessionum Libri XIII*, L. VI, c. vi (9), P.L.32. This very tight connection made by Keach between sound doctrine and deep personal piety is, according to Moltmann, a mark of the Reformed catholic faith. "This had been the understanding of Reformed Christianity since Zwingli and Calvin." Jürgen Molmann, 'Theologia Reformata et Semper Reformanda,' in *Toward the Future of Reformed Theology*, 122. Cf. Willem J. van Asselt, *The Federal Theology of Johannes Coccejus (1603-1669)*, Raymond A. Blacketer, trans. (Leiden: Brill, 2001), 1.

authority, (2) he relies positively on the same Tradition to construct arguments, and (3) he makes the Tradition normative through appropriation. Under this light—whatever his claims—Keach turns out to be a *catholic* thinker.

Keach vs. Successionism

There are reasons to interpret Keach as a successionist. He affirms that Christendom is comprised of only two segments: the Roman church "and those who dissent from her, ...whether Waldenses, Albigenses, Hogenots or other Protestants ..."[219] Moreover, all the churches in the world, Keach deems, have been contaminated by Rome for more than twelve hundred years and, as a consequence, a general apostasy came to pass. The result of that was that the true church went into hiding on account of Rome.[220] What would be a likely conclusion? The visible church fell around the fifth century but was always represented by a succession of several sects.

There are many reasons, however, to deny this conclusion. First, Keach never makes a catena of sects from the New Testament to the Reformation. Discussing his apocalyptic views, Keach says that God's final vial was poured "about the time of Luther's Reformation wrought by his preaching above others, who go as high as Waldo, nay, Jurieu, to the tenth age, since there was some worthy men in *every century* that bare testimony against" popish "idolatry and wounded the papistry very sorely, tho' 'tis granted not to such a degree as in the last age."[221] In other words, Keach does not attempt to go further back beyond Jurieu to the early church forming an unbroken succession of alternative churches. Second, as the italics of the first point showed, Keach explicitly asserts that there has been a Christian presence at all times: "In every age I had some sons of light ..."[222] Third, Medieval doctors, St. Anselm (1033-1153), St. Bernard (1090-1153), St. Thomas Aquinas, etc., are admired by Keach and favourably quoted to support his points.[223] The logical conclusion would be that Keach deems them true Christians, though part and parcel of the great Western church. Fourth, note that Keach seems to use the twelve hundred

---

[219] Keach, *Antichrist Stormed*, 54-55. Cf. Ibid., 77.

[220] Keach, *Antichrist Stormed*, 54-55. See infra, 'Ecclesiological Considerations,' pp. 142ff.

[221] Keach, *Antichrist Stormed*, 205. Emphasis added. The tenth century is also mentioned as a time of persecution of believers within the medieval church. Keach affirms that the Roman church had given Christians much pain and, in countries such as "Bohemia, Poland and Lituania," believers had suffered from "about 977," when a great multitude of the faithful were killed by the Whore. Ibid., 93.

[222] Keach, *Sion in Distress*, 100.

[223] For quotes of Anselm within Keach's corpus, see, e.g., *Marrow of Justification*, 29; *Rector Rectified*, 118; *Sion in Distress*, 52. For Bernard, *Rector Rectified*, 182; *Antichrist Stormed*, 74. For Thomas Aquinas, *Jacob's Ladder*, 93; *Rector Rectified*, 118, 185; *Exposition of the Parables*, I: 236.

years of Rome's influence not only to say that the church went into hiding, as above mentioned, but also to tell of Rome's persecution within her: what is the origin, Keach asks rhetorically, of "the murthers, massacres and martyrdom of all the religious professors of Christianity that have died by violence in the Christian world, for the space of twelve hundred years past? ...Came these unparallel'd degree of impiety from the Turks?"[224] Again note what Keach says: "...there were faithful preachers who bore their testimony against the Beast from his first rise,[225] and so downward all along, and it had much like effect with Waldo's [and] Luther's preaching, &c."[226]

In addition to all of that, the Second London Confession,[227] subscribed to by Keach, implicitly denies it and explicitly affirms the continuity of believers across the ages. "The purest churches under heaven are subject to mixture and error, and some have so degenerated as to become no churches of Christ, but Synagogues of Satan; nevertheless Christ always hath had, and ever shall have a Kingdome in this world, to the end thereof, of such as believe in him and make profession of his name." Art. 27, § 3.

Finally, Keach agrees with Tombes that Christ's promise that the gates of hell would not prevail against the church refers to the visible ecclesia. The church, to put it as clearly as possible, would never fall *totaliter et finaliter*; the church, to use Keach's words, would never "err *finally* to damnation," that is, she would never completely fall.[228]

Summing up this section, Keach, as we just saw, is not a successionist. Although this fact does not in and of itself prove that he is a catholic, it nevertheless *supports* our claim to his catholicity.

Keach vs. Scholasticism

We said that Puritanism was influenced by scholasticism.[229] We shall see Keach

---

[224] Keach, *Antichrist Stormed*, 17, 18. Many pious believers have been "most unhumanly butchered by the bloody Papists, children born of their own body, ...to allay the thirst of this bloudy Whore." Ibid., 88-89. Cf. Ibid., 22.

[225] Keach claims that the majority of the authors agree "that the rise of the Beast" took place around A.D.450. *Antichrist Stormed*, 188.

[226] Keach, *Antichrist Stormed*, 176.

[227] This highly influential 1689 standard is the recension of the 1677 confession.

[228] John Tombes, *Anti-Paedobaptism: or the Third Part. Being a full review of the dispute concerning infant-baptism. In which the Arguments for infant-baptism from the Covenant and initial seal, infants visible church-membership, antiquity of infant-baptism are referred* (London: Printed by E. Aisop, 1657), 758; cited by Keach, *Rector Rectified*, 140. Cf. Calvin, *Institutes*, 'Prefatory Address to King Francis I,' 24-25.

[229] See supra, p. 29. On scholasticism, see 'Scholastic Method,' s.v., in *New Catholic Encyclopedia* (New York: McGraw-Hill Books Co., 1967); 'Scholastic Method,' s.v., and 'Scholastic Theology,' s.v., in *Encyclopedic Dictionary of Religion* (Washington,

using three common scholastic features: first, the use of syllogism, that "relic of scholastic disputes...;"[230] second, the use of *quaestio*, that important medieval method of study;[231] and third, metaphysical speculation, which—though attacked by the Reformers—was never completely dropped by Protestants.[232] The examples are extremely brief and simple, but sufficient to illustrate the point.

The Use of Syllogism

Keach sees the prescribed manner of justification under the Law ('do this and live') and the Gospel ('believe in the Lord...'), as totally incompatible with each other. Hence, as he attacks Baxterianism's principle of 'sincere obedience,' he argues,

> That doctrine which confoundeth the terms of the Law and Gospel together in point of justification, is a false and corrupt doctrine: But the doctrine that mixeth sincere obedience, or works of any kind done by us, with faith in point of justification, counfoundeth the terms of the Law and the Gospel together in point of justification; therefore that doctrine is false and a corrupt doctrine.[233]

The Use of Quaestio or Objection

Let us see an example of a question, in which the answer is divided into four replies, with the first one subdivided into three. Interpreting Lk.14:28-30, "For which of you intending to build a tower..." Keach posits, "Quest. Why should he sit down and count the cost?" Firstly, the builder should sit down for "it will be a very costly building to him. (1) He must give up all his cursed sins and lusts, though as dear to him in times past, as a right hand or a right eye. (2) He must expect it will cost him the loss of" whatever "he once accounted gain. (3) He must part with all his former companions and expect they will mock and deride him..." Secondly, considering that "great storms may rise and floods come and beat upon his high tower: and he should count the damage he may sustain in such storms." Thirdly, on account of his lack of power and skill, "he will never be able to finish, and then men will mock him and say, 'this man

---

D.C.: Corpus Publications, 1979); 'Scholasticism,' s.v., in *The Encyclopedia of Religion* (New York: Macmillan Publishing Co., 1987); 'Scholasticism,' s.v., in *NSHE*.

[230] Fraser W. Mitchell, *English Pulpit Oratory From Andrewes to Tillotson: A Study of Its Literary Aspects* (London: Society for Promoting Christian Knowledge, 1932), 78.

[231] Erik Per Persson, *Sacra Doctrina: Reason and Revelation in Aquinas*, Ross MacKenzie, trans. (Oxford: Basil Blackwell, 1970), 9.

[232] Trueman, 'Calvin and Calvinism,' 235. Cf. Miller, *The New England Mind*, 13.

[233] Keach, *Marrow of Justification*, 21.

began to build, but was not able to finish.'" Fourthly, the builder must rely on Christ, whose power and justice is the man's materials; "and if he depends wholly, constantly, he needs not fear, but he shall have wherewith to finish this famous tower, i.e., the salvation of his precious soul."[234]

Metaphysical Speculation

Keach affirms that God's holy attributes are, among others, wisdom, justice, unchangeableness.[235] He claims that divine goodness, "of all the attributes of God, seems to be the sweetest, it is one of the choice perfection of his nature..." There are two aspects under which God's goodness may be examined. First, it is to be considered "[t]he perfection and excellency of the Being of God, I mean his *essential goodness*, this cannot be imparted to creatures." Second, God's "*communicative goodness*, or that which God hath wrought out, laid up and which he lets forth to believers..." Under the non-communicable goodness, Keach lists and comments on six types of goodness. The deity (1) "is *absolutely good* in the perfection of his being, he is independently good, there is nothing wanting in him, no defection, he subsisteth in and of himself...and there can be no addition made to his goodness to make it more than it is."[236] Moreover, the Creator (2) "is *originally and essentially good*, not only good, but goodness it self; goodness in creatures is an accessary quality, or a created or superadded gift, but goodness in God is not a quality, but 'tis his essence..." God also (3) "is *infinitely good*...(4) *immutably and unchangeably good*, as goodness in God cannot be augmented, so it cannot be diminished, he cannot change or loose his goodness, no not the least degree thereof..." The Lord is also (5) "*universally good*...[and] (6) *unmixt good*..." Under the second aspect, viz., the communicable goodness, there are five kinds of goodness. God, Keach proceeds his claims and comments, (1) "is *soul-inriching good*...There is enough in God to satisfie the Holy Angels, much more smaller vessels..." He (2) "is *soul-ravishing good*, he is an eternal spring of joy and delight..." Additionally, the deity (3) "is a *superlative good*...he is a man's only *summum bonum*...(4) God is a *communicative good*, this crowns all. Why did he enter into a covenant of peace, and provide such a Mediator, but to let out, as through a conduit pipe, his infinite goodness to us?" Finally, (5) "God is an *eternal good*...His love, mercy and goodness to his people is not fading or inconstant, but everlasting and unchangeable..."[237]

---

[234] Keach, *Exposition of the Parables*, I: 99.
[235] See *Display of Glorious Grace*, 229-237.
[236] Keach, *Display of Glorious Grace*, 229-230. His emphasis.
[237] Keach, *Display of Glorious Grace*, 231-234. His emphasis.

Conclusion

The definition presented of Reformed Orthodoxy—that scholastic expression of Protestantism—is comprised of adherence to the so-called five points of Calvinism, Trinitarian orthodoxy, the dual nature of Christ and pedobaptism. As a Particular Baptist, it is hardly necessary to show Keach's agreement with the TULIP.[238] Concerning the doctrine of the Trinity and Christ's dual nature, we saw Keach's orthodoxy under the heading 'dogmatic tradition' supra. In chapter 3, we shall deal with the last characteristic of Orthodoxy, viz., pedobaptism, the only feature in which there is departure from the traditional Reformed position. Now, however, we turn to Keach's federal theology, wherein we shall encounter him not only as an adherent to, but also as an entrenched defender of Orthodoxy.

---

[238] Nevertheless, for 'Total depravity,' see *Golden Mine*, 82, 233; *Exposition of the Parables*, I: 222, 224. For 'Unconditional election,' see *Display of Glorious Grace*, 123, 243; *Golden Mine*, 76 et seqq; *Exposition of the Parables*, I: 221-222. For 'Limited atonement,' see *Exposition of the Parables*, II: 264; *Golden Mine*, 56, 98, 125, 161; *Display of Glorious Grace*, 120, 167. For 'Irresistible grace,' see *Golden Mine*, 70, 80, 151, 158; *Display of Glorious Grace*, 116-117, 242, 245, 275. For 'Perseverance of the saints,' see *Exposition of the Parables*, II: 233, *Golden Mine*, 14 et seqq; *Display of Glorious Grace*, 257, 277-278.

CHAPTER TWO

Keach's Federal Theology

Introduction

In its classical expression, 'covenant'[1] is a voluntary agreement between two parties in which both become bound to perform certain conditions. Federal theologians superimposed this concept on the relationship between the deity and humanity. It is incumbent upon humanity to believe and in doing so it is saved. To put it another way, God has freely bound himself to save where belief is shown. Thus, when one believes, one is saved.[2]

More specifically, covenant or federal theology is a Reformed scheme in which the relations between humanity and God are expressed *per modum foederis*. Here the 'covenant' is the architectonic principle or blueprint guiding the whole theological edifice. There are two main divisions to this scheme: the Adamic 'covenant of works' (with perfect obedience as the condition to life), and the 'covenant of grace' made with the elect (with Christ performing obedience and the believer exercising faith). Very often, the intertrinitarian 'covenant of redemption' is added, in which the pretemporal transactions between the Father and the Son are spelt out.[3]

---

[1] Throughout this chapter the words 'pact,' 'covenant,' '*foedus*' and 'compact' are used interchangeably.
[2] Perry Miller, *The New England Mind: The Seventeenth Century* (Cambridge, MA.: Harvard University Press, 1967), 375-377. See also, Donald Macleod, 'Covenant Theology,' in *Dictionary of Scottish Church History and Theology*, Nigel Cameron, David Wright, David Lachman, and Donald Meek, eds. (Edinburgh: T&T Clark, 1993), s.v.
[3] Operating within the framework of the Augustinian tradition, Puritanism conceived the world as God's good creation, but since the fall irreparably marred by sin. As such, creation can only be renewed by God's intervention and yet human beings, once renewed, freely participate with God in the process of regeneration. Federalism is an effort to couch this process in covenantal language. To elaborate, when God made the first covenant with humanity and promised "blessedness on condition of perfect obedience to the moral law, God was held to have bound himself to a moral order that defined mankind's relationship with him thereafter. Adam's failure to obey did not alter the significance of the law as the standard of human conduct, nor did it alter the terms of blessedness, which remain contingent upon obedience to the law." Christ obeyed the law in the place of believers and, on the other hand, believers once regenerated are enabled

The Salvation of the elect or ingress into the covenant, as the Reformed Orthodox saw it, was entirely an act of God's will. Although God uses several means—e.g., the words of the preacher—ultimately, the process is completely dependent on him who calls. Salvation is connected to faith "only because God has arbitrarily established such a relationship. Faith does not merit justification; and the act of faith springs from a gracious power, added beyond man's natural endowment."[4] The covenant of grace thus has faith as a promised *condition*, or so the majority of the Puritans thought.[5] In other words, justification is inextricably connected to faith.

Yet, how does God's unconditional election interact with a genuine and real faith on the part of believers? The Reformed had conceived an *ordo salutis* within which predestination was part of a greater whole. This conception envisaged "actual justification coming only when a person is effectually called and actually believed, that calling and believing being also the beginning of a holy life..." Hence, this scheme lent a reality to the temporal aspect of justification, thus safeguarding sanctification.[6] All that we just saw represents the thought of mainstream Orthodoxy, a school in which both extremes of Arminianism and Antinomianism were on the whole rejected.[7]

This chapter aims to show that Keach saw himself as part of the mainstream Reformed Orthodox movement, and that this was in fact the case. It does this by comparing his chief doctrinal points with those of other mainline Reformed thinkers (Owen, Chauncy, Rutherford and Gillespie). As we examine Keach's

---

by grace to exercise faith. Federalism attempted to take seriously the aspects of God's grace and human participation and, through the concept of covenant, tried to articulate "the mechanism of redemption in terms set by the dialectic of nature and grace." Stoever, *A Fair and Easie Way to Heaven*, 8-9. See also the fine definition of 'covenant theology,' in David A. Weir, *The Origins of the Federal Theology in Sixteenth Century Reformation Thought* (Oxford: Clarendon Press, 1990), 5. Cf. Peter A. Lillback, *The Binding of God: Calvin's Role in the Development of Covenant Theology* (Grand Rapids, Michigan and Carlisle, Cumbria: Baker Academic and Paternoster Press, 2001), 26-28; M. Eugene Osterhaven, 'Covenant,' in *Encyclopedia of the Reformed Faith*, Donald K. Mckin, ed. (Louisville, Kentucky and Edinburgh: Westminster/John Knox Press and Saint Andrew Press, 1992), 85; Vernon Joseph Ruland, 'Covenant Theology,' in *New Catholic Encyclopedia*, vol. 4, William McDonald, gen. ed. (New York: McGraw-Hill Book Co., 1967), s.v.; Robert G. Close, 'Covenant Theology,' in *The International Dictionary of the Christian Church*, J. D. Douglas, ed. (Exeter, Devon: Paternoster Press, 1974), s.v.

[4] Stoever, 'Nature, Grace and John Cotton,' 26.
[5] Von Rohr, *The Covenant of Grace*, 64.
[6] Wallace, *Puritanism and Predestination*, 118-119. God justifies entirely by his will and, on the other hand, he bestows grace in such way that the human will is not violated, but rather actively concurs in the process of salvation. Thus, Reformed thought ascribed an actual participation, a real response to humanity in the process of salvation. Von Rohr, *The Covenant of Grace*, 136.
[7] Cf. Miller, *The New England Mind*, 367, 373.

federal scheme, we shall encounter him, on the one hand, repeatedly attacking Baxterianism, which he considers a very dangerous departure from Reformed thought. As a matter of fact, Keach sees little or no difference between Arminianism and Baxterianism.[8] On the other hand, Keach rejects the Antinomian extreme. Our procedure will be as follows: (I) the debate is situated in a broader historical context—i.e., the seventeenth century setting; (II) Antinomianism and its characteristics are examined; (III) Baxterianism is summarised; (IV) the second Antinomian controversy is considered briefly; (V) the occasion of Keach's writing on covenant is examined; (VI) and finally the exposition of Keach's federalism is presented.

Seventeenth Century Setting

Although many changes took place during the second half of the seventeenth century, none was more remarkable than the downfall of Reformed thought in the English church. During the last decades of the previous century and the first part of the seventeenth, Reformed theology had been dominant in Britain, however. "The return of Charles II was at once the overthrow of the Puritan party and the defeat of the Puritan theology."[9] The hellish upheaval caused by the civil war (which threw the whole nation into chaos), the regicide, the Protectorate (as an unsuccessful project) and finally a degree of apparent stability with the Restoration—all of this made England recoil from doctrines that could possibly lead to anarchy and disorder. As a result, "Arminianism" gained the upper hand within the Church of England and the government. This new situation was propitious for a latitudinarian or moralistic theology, which was hostile to solafideism and absolute imputation of righteousness to the elect: Both principles in former times had been consonant with Anglicanism. As the tidal wave of moralism gained momentum, Antinomianism was increasingly viewed with distrust, regardless its close affinity with soteriological precepts of the Reformation.[10] Baxter, for example, was ready to exonerate soteriological

---

[8] "Let those who are tainted with the errors of Arminianism or Baxterianism, think of this, who strive to mix the King's wine with their muddy water, or mix their polluted works with God's free grace." Keach, *Exposition of the Parables*, 1: 151.

[9] G. R. Cragg, *From Puritanism to the Age of Reason: A Study of changes in Religious thought within the Church of England, 1660 to 1700* (Cambridge: Cambridge University Press, 1950), 13. Cf. Wallace, *Puritanism and Predestination*, 158. Obviously, Arminianism had been around since 1630s under the aegis of Charles I and William Laud. See Howson, *Erroneous and Schismatical Opinions*, 19.

[10] Richard Baxter attacked justification by mere imputation of Christ's righteousness as that which "setteth up and introduceth all Antinomianism or libertinism and ungodliness, and subverteth the Gospel and true religion and morality." *A Treatise of Justifying Righteousness* (London: Nevil Simons and Johath Robinson, 1676), 91. The primary preoccupation of Baxter was the *consequences* of Antinomianism; i.e., where this theological view would lead the people.

aspects of Romanism, but unwilling to make similar concessions to Antinomianism.[11] For, he thought, faulty theology was one of the main reasons why the civil war brought such confusion and anarchy upon English society, and thus, men like Saltmarsh and other Antinomians were to be blamed for the havoc of the 1640s.[12] Besides the omnipresent menace of libertinism on a personal level, Antinomianism also threatened to tear the fabric of society on the collective level. For, if the Antinomians were "one" with God; if they were God's conduit or vessel, why should they listen to the less illumined men of the state to obey its laws?[13] What, however, is Antinomianism?

Antinomianism

There was never an Antinomian 'movement' as such. Antinomian ideas—and they varied—lived and died in the lives of their exponents.[14] These men were fundamentally Reformed Orthodox divines, but with some emphasis in their theology which led them in an Antinomian direction.[15] That is, contrary to appearances, Anti-nomians (against-law) sprung directly from the very heart "of evangelical piety, spoke much the same theological tongue as mainstream Puritans, experienced similar impulsions toward spiritual clarity and purity, and addressed the same broad file of doctrinal problems, with quite similar priorities."[16] Antinomianism may be represented by Tobias Crisp, John Saltmarsh and Henry Denne.

---

[11] Tim Cooper, *Fear and Polemic in Seventeenth-Century England: Richard Baxter and Antinomianism* (Aldershot: Ashgate, 2001), 153, 193.

[12] William Lamont, *Puritanism and Historical Controversy* (London: UCL Press, 1996), 47.

[13] Gertrude Huehns, *Antinomianism in English History: With special reference to the period 1640-1660* (London: The Cresset Press, 1951), 94; Miller, *The New England Mind*, 370.

[14] Huehns, *Antinomianism in English History*, 85. In a nutshell, the Antinomians believed that they were so in sync with the Spirit or received such an immediate direction from Christ that, as a result, they did not need the Law. In no way were they immoral, like, say, the Ranters; but on the contrary, they were recognized by virtually all to be upright men.

[15] Trueman, *Claims of Truth*, 207. As a result, there never was a definite set of Antinomian beliefs—sometimes two or three Antinomians would have the same position on, say, 'God does not punish sins' (infra, Crisp, Saltmarsh and Denne), but then Saltmarsh would disagree with 'passivity in justification' (*Free-Grace*, 163-164), over against Crisp and Denne, infra.

[16] Michael McGiffert, 'The Perkinsian Moment of Federal Theology,' in *CTJ* 29 (1994): 117-148, p. 131.

Tobias Crisp (1600-1643)

Crisp studied at Cambridge and then Oxford, getting an M.A. and a D.D. He worked as a pastor in Brinkworth and London. A man of wealth, he was generous with the needy and lived a life of great piety and holiness. He began his career as a strong advocate of Arminianism, but swung rather forcefully to the other extreme and became an Antinomian. Crisp's only published work, his sermons, came to light posthumously in 1643-46. The Westminster divines discussed the possibility of having them burned for their Antinomian content.[17]

John Saltmarsh (d.1647)

This Church of England minister was educated at Cambridge, from which he earned a B.A. and an M.A. As a chaplain in the Parliamentary army, he scandalised Baxter as a preacher of a so-called "free grace." This "free grace is an extension of Orthodox Reformed doctrines on the supremacy of grace over law, while, in Saltmarsh's version, departing from Calvinist election in the direction of universalism, 'the law is now in the Spirit,' is a representative phrase." Saltmarsh could be described, *avant la lettre*, as a Pentecostal or charismatic believer.[18]

Henry Denne (1605/6?-1666)

Denne went to Cambridge where he earned a B.A. and an M.A. In 1630, he became a minister in the Church of England, but by 1643 he had come to embrace Baptist views. Denne himself proclaimed that "the Lord hath sent me as a man of contention,"—an epithet rightly befitting him. He became notorious as both a promoter of controversies and agitation. As a controversialist, his *Seven Arguments*, 1643, drew criticism from Samuel Rutherford, who accused him of Antinomianism. As an agitator, his involvement in a mutiny in 1649 almost cost him his life.[19]

It is to be stressed that Antinomians were no libertines. Samuel Rutherford was rather unfair to Saltmarsh, Crisp, Denne, and others, as he brushed them all with libertarian tar.[20] Crisp, for example, says that "sanctification of life is an

---

[17] NSHE, III: 306; CBTEL, II: 10; Brooks, *Lives of the Puritans*, II: 472-475.

[18] ODNB, 48: 770-771. CBTEL, IX: 266; Brooks, *The Lives of the Puritans*, III: 70-74. On Saltmarsh, see Leo F. Solt, 'John Saltmarsh: New Model Army Chaplain,' in *JEH* 2 (1951): 69-80.

[19] DNB, XV: 804-805. See also, Brooks, *The Lives of the Puritans*, III: 376-380; J. Wayne Baker, '*Sola Fide, Sola Gratia*: The Battle for Luther in Seventeenth Century England,' in *SCJ* 16 (1/1985): 115-133, p. 120; Huehns, *Antinomianism in English History*, 85.

[20] Samuel Rutherford, *A Survey of the Spiritual Antichrist. Opening the secrets of Familisme and Antinomianisme in the Antichristian Doctrine of John Saltmarsh, and*

inseparable companion with the justification of a person..." Also, "God requires your obedience to glorifie him, to be the manifestation of your thankfulness, for the good of your brethren, for the manifesting and accomplishing his gifts in the use of ordinances; but that these should be a price is a gross mistake."[21] Nevertheless, Puritan emphasis on fasting, obedience to the moral law, church attendance, self-examination, strict devotional life and piety, ended up creating a sense of insecurity in the believer. That is, if one did not perform these things to perfection, one tended to feel that he or she was failing God. The backlash against this insecurity was Antinomianism. Its central tenet was an *evangelion* of "free justification."[22]

What then are some of the characteristics of this Gospel of free justification? In the anonymous work, *A Declaration Against the Antinomians*, various supposed characteristics of their doctrinal position are presented.[23] They may be reduced to four: 1. God neither chastens nor notices sins in the lives of believers. 2. The pursuit of sanctification is worthless. 3. War with the flesh is an illusion. 4. The elect are capable of seeing who does and who does not belong to God.

In addition to that, Baxter claimed that "faith procuring but the knowledge of pardon and justifying in *foro conscientiae*," was one of the main Antinomian

---

Will. Del, the present Preachers of the Army now in England, and of Robert Town, Tob. Crisp, H. Denne, Eaton, and others (London: Printed by J. D. & R. I. for Andrew Crooke, 1647), 2-6.

[21] Tobias Crisp, *Christ Alone Exalted, being the compleat works of Tobias Crisp, D.D., containing XLII sermons* (London: Printed for William Marshal, at the Bible in Newgate-street, 1690), 46, 183. Cf.e.g, Henry Denne, *The Man of Sin discovered whom the Lord shall destroy with the brightnesse of his coming: the root and foundation of antichrist laid open in doctrine* (London: Printed for John Sweeting, 1646), 5.

[22] T. D. Bozeman, 'The Glory of the "Third Time:" John Eaton as Contra-Puritan,' in *JEH* 47/4 (October 1996): 638-654, pp. 638-640. Cf. Keith L. Sprunger, 'Technometria: A Prologue to Puritan Theology,' in *JHI* 29 (1968): 115-122, p. 122. Antinomians rejected "self-referential schemes of self-examination that seemed, in effect, to make man the measure of spiritual things." McGiffert, 'The Perkinsian Moment of Federal Theology,' 130-131. See, Crisp, *Christ Alone Exalted*, 150-151; John Saltmarsh, *Free-grace or, the flowings of Christ's blood freely to sinners* (London: Printed for Giles Calvert, dwelling at the black Spred-Eagle at the West-end of Pauls, 1645), 39, 60-63.

[23] They are, "I. That God doth never inflict punishment upon the Elect for their sins. II. That God is never angry with his children. III. That God sees no sin in those that are his. IV. That such as are elected are at all times beloved of God, in what condition soever they be, be they never so great sinners, yea, in the very act of sinne it selfe. V. That sanctification of life in duties of piety is nothing at all esteemed of God. VI. That the godly finde no difficulties in the way to heaven, but live in much pleasure and delight in this world. VII. That those who belong to God are able in this world presently to distinguish betwixt Gods people and the wicked." *A Declaration Against Antinomians...* (London: Printed for Iohn Iones, 1644), cover page.

features.[24] To combat Antinomianism, Baxter offered a twofold argument. First, he claimed that faith ought to *precede* justification; otherwise the distinction between God's legislative and decretive wills is obliterated. Second, in order to give a role to humanity in the process of salvation, he carefully distinguished the eternal pact made between the Father and the Son (the covenant of redemption), from the temporal one made between God and believers (the covenant of grace): they were different covenants, Baxter suggested.[25]

If we were to combine the claims of the *Declaration* with Baxter's, we would have five main points: 1. Believers are perfect—God neither sees nor punishes faults in their lives. 2. Christians are not to concern themselves with sanctification, for the battle against the flesh is illusive, and thus the law has no place in their lives. 3. As faith is a mere awareness (in *foro conscientiae*, as Baxter says) of one's justified state, believers are passive in the process of justification. 4. Faith is strictly to precede justification 5. The covenant of redemption and the covenant of grace are distinct.[26] Let us briefly look into each one of them in turn and, as we do, we shall see that Keach does not fit the Antinomian mould.

1st. CHRISTIAN PERFECTION: GOD NEITHER SEEING NOR PUNISHING SINS[27]

A person can only be deemed justified, Crisp claims, if no sin is to be found in him. He must be totally pure, for "[i]t is a contradiction for a man to say, that a man is innocent, and yet nocent." Additionally, God has no reason "to be offended with a believer, because he doth not find the sin of the believer to be the believers own sin, but he finds it the sin of Christ."[28]

Keach, on the other hand, asserts that "whilst we are in this world, there is much sin and corruption remaining in the best of saints." What is more, the

---

[24] Richard Baxter, *Plain Scripture proof of infants church-membership and baptism* (London: Printed for Robert White, 1653), 124.

[25] Richard Baxter, *Rich: Baxter's confession of his faith* (London: Printed by R.W. for Tho. Underhil, and Fra. Tyton, and are to be sold at the Anchor and Bible in Pauls Church-yard, and at the three Daggers in Fleetstreet, 1655), 290. On God's legislative and decretive wills, see infra pp. 89-90.

[26] In our amalgamation of the *Declaration* with Baxter, it is to be noted that we have not included the last point of the *Declaration* (i.e., that believers are capable of knowing who is and who is not a Christian). Neither the main Antinomians (e.g., Crisp) nor their adversaries (e.g., Baxter) make much of it. In our reading of the material, we have not found a single reference to it. For another synthesis of Antinomian tenets, see Howson, *Erroneous and Schismatical Opinions*, 114.

[27] Cf. Bozeman, 'The Glory of the "Third Time,"' 642; Wallace, *Puritanism and Predestination*, 118.

[28] Crisp, *Christ Alone Exalted*, 9, 15. Cf. Saltmarsh, *Free-Grace*, 74, 129, 141, 142; Denne, *The Man of Sin*, 32.

Lord does "not, will not spare to correct his own elect when they sin, or do unjustly."[29]

2nd. WAR AGAINST THE FLESH: THE PLACE OF THE LAW[30]

Antinomians tended to deem the body a shell for the soul, with the body being seen as being of little or no significance when contrasted with the soul. As a result, the traditional Puritan metaphor of life as a war, in which the soul and body are involved in conflict with the Devil, is without significance to them.[31] The conflict is rather conspicuous for its absence in Antinomianism. Whenever "you fall upon humiliation, fasting, prayer, weeping, and self-denial, what do you look for?" Crisp asks. Among several possible answers, he includes: "'I get this by it: prevention of many great evils hanging over my head.' Another saith, 'peace of conscience, joy in the Holy Ghost, assurance of the pardon of sin, assurance of reconciliation with God; these things would I get by attending upon Ordinances, by serving God day and night in that way, he calls me out unto.'" Crisp's verdict, however, is as follows: "I tell you plainly, there is none of all these things that you do that conduce a jot towards the obtaining of any of these ends you propose to your selves; all you do gets not a jot; nay, doth not concur in it."[32] As to the Law, the Holy Spirit, "sets a beleever as free from Hell, the Law and bondage here on earth, as if he were in heaven; nor wants he any thing to make him so, but to make him beleeve that he is so; for Satan, sin, sinful flesh and the Law, are all so neer and about him in this life, that he cannot so walk by sight, ...but the just do live by faith..."[33]

Keach stands in diametrical opposition to all of that. First, he maintains that "Christ loves not the souls of believers only, but their bodies also: yea, and he loves their graces, and all the holy and spiritual duties and services they perform to his glory..." Second, that being the case, "...let us all strive after holiness, because it was the design of God in this work, to magnify his own holiness; all the acts of God's doings, in and about Christ, and our salvation, lay us under the highest obligation to oppose sin and all ungodliness." Third, concerning the place of the Law, Keach maintains that as a matter of fact, "the law of perfect obedience remains the same in Christ's hand as firm as ever,

---

[29] Keach, *Exposition of the Parables*, I: 67, II: 97.

[30] An author has said rather well that there were three streams of Puritan thought concerning the law. The coming of Christ was understood by the mainstream as *establishing* the law, the Antinomians deemed it as *abolishing* it, and the Baxterians as *modifying* the law. Ernest Frederick Kevan, *The Grace of the Law: A Study in Puritan Theology* (London: Carey Kingsgate Press, 1964), 137. On the importance of the place of the law in the Antinomian debate, see Mark Karlberg, 'Reformed Interpretation of the Mosaic Covenant,' in *WTJ* 43 (1980): 1-57, pp. 25-41.

[31] Huehns, *Antinomianism in English History*, 102.

[32] Crisp, *Christ Alone Exalted*, 150.

[33] Saltmarsh, *Free-Grace*, 140.

though it is abrogated as a covenant of work; yet it abides as a perfect rule of obedience. For it is still our duty to love God with all our hearts, souls and strength, and our neighbour as ourselves; yea, to be perfect as our Father in heaven is perfect."[34]

3rd. CHRISTIANS ARE PASSIVE IN JUSTIFICATION: FAITH ONLY MAKES IT KNOWN[35]

"A passive receiving of Christ," Crisp says, "is such a receiving of him as when a froward patient takes a purge or some bitter physick; he shuts his teeth against it, but the physician forceth his mouth open and pours it down his throat and so it works against his will, by the overruling power of the one over him, that knows it is good for him." Therefore, when the Son is to be given to an individual, "the Father doth force open the spirit of that person and pours in his Son in spite of the receiver." Faith does not "effect any thing to the good of man, but only to be the witness of that good to the spirit of that man, and so give light to that which was hidden and secret before."[36]

Note, again, how differently Keach speaks. The meaning of irresistible grace is "not that he forces the will, for that is to destroy the nature of that noble faculty; but he sweetly inclines it, overpowers it, and makes the unwilling will, (that was so naturally) to be willing in the day of this his power." Additionally, faith is that which Keach calls "the condition of connection." All covenant conditions were executed by the Son, still one may concede "a condition by way of connection; and thus, if you will have union with Christ, you must receive the Holy Spirit, or if you will put on the new man, you must put off the old man; and if you will be justified, you must believe in Christ..."[37]

4th. FAITH IS STRICTLY TO PRECEDE JUSTIFICATION[38]

Note the opposite with the Antinomians: Denne affirms that "[a]ll the elect of God are justified before God, but some of the elect of God doe not yet beleeve. Therefore some that doe not beleeve, are justified before God..."[39]

Keach, on the other hand, understands faith as concurrent with justification. "What noise is there of late, of sinners being justified and united with Christ before faith, nay without faith?...no man is personally justified, i.e., acquitted

---

[34] Keach, *The Exposition of the Parables*, I: 423, II: 45, I: 26.
[35] Cf. Stoever, *A Fair and Easie Way to Heaven*, 140; Rohr, *The Covenant of Grace*, 135.
[36] Crisp, *Christ Alone Exalted*, 98-99, 326. Cf. Denne, *The Man of Sin*, 35; idem, *Seven Arguments to prove, that in order of working God doth justifie his elect, before they doe actually beleeve* (London: s.n., 1643), 12.
[37] Keach, *Exposition of the Parables*, I: 349, 241.
[38] Cf. Trueman, *Claims of Truth*, 207-208; Wallace, *Puritanism and Predestination*, 118.
[39] Denne, *Seven Arguments*, 4. Cf. Crisp, *Christ Alone Exalted*, 85.

and pronounced a just and righteous person, unless he obtains a vital union with Christ..."[40]

5th. COVENANTS OF REDEMPTION AND GRACE NOT THE SAME[41]

Antinomians tended to make no distinction between the eternal and the temporal as touching the covenant. They were thus bent on amalgamating the covenants of redemption and grace in its covenantal schema: this is the case with both Saltmarsh and Crisp.[42]

This is the only place in which there is same meeting of minds between Keach and the Antinomians. However, we may add that there were many who opposed Antinomianism and, like Keach, made no distinction between the eternal pact and the temporal one.[43] At this juncture, a point ought to be made: it is clear that Keach would rather lean towards Antinomianism, than move towards the Baxterian side.[44] The fact that he identifies the temporal and the eternal covenants is a symptom of that. Keach abhorred any hint of human participation in the process of salvation.

Baxterianism

Before the civil war, Antinomians in England were a non-quantity, but this changed with the belligerence of the 1640s. Within the New Model army, Antinomianism gained a good number of sympathisers.[45] Working as chaplain in the Army, Baxter witnessed first hand the consequences of a "non-moral" or "libertine" theology. As a result, he pushed Reformed thought in the direction of Arminianism, to the point of his being characterised as "neonomian"—that is, as one who holds that one is justified by obeying an evangelical "new law."[46] Criticising Baxterianism, Keach affirms that its main tenet maintains that when Christ fulfilled the Law he made amends to God on our behalf; however, our

---

[40] Keach, *Exposition of the Parables*, I: 417.

[41] "Distinguish carefully between that Decree, Law or Covenant, call it which you will, whereby the Father did, as it were, appoint his Son both his work and reward; and [on the other hand] that Law or Covenant by which both Father and Son do govern the church, and make over to us the parts of our salvation. Confounding these hath lost the Antinomians in their theology, so that so much of Gods covenants as they do take notice of, is little more than the promise of the Father to the Son, and the absolute discovery of his Decree. They reduce almost all the covenants to this, and denominate all from this." Baxter, *Baxter's Confession*, 290.

[42] Saltmarsh, *Free-Grace*, 125-127; Crisp, *Christ Alone Exalted*, 74-110, 241-259.

[43] Isaac Chauncy (*Neonomianism*, 27) would be one of them. For other examples, see infra p. 126.

[44] See infra, pp. 79-80.

[45] Cooper, *Fear and Polemic*, 67; Huehns, *Antinomianism in English History*, 72, 79.

[46] Von Rohr, *The Covenant of Grace*, 98.

compliance to the new law of sincere obedience "is our evangelical righteousness whereby we fulfil the Gospel, and that our obedience is the condition of our justification before God. Thus Mr. Baxter, Mr. Williams, Mr. Clark, and many others."[47] These are the main representatives of Baxterianism. Let us acquaint ourselves with them, and then attempt to summarise the movement.

Richard Baxter (1615-1691)

Although not a university man, "through omnivorous reading Baxter became one of the most learned of seventeenth-century divines." A prolific writer, he composed over 130 volumes and an array of unpublished treatises and missives.[48] In addition to his massive output, Baxter worked as a preacher, chaplain, lecturer and pastor.[49] Alarmed by the number of sects in the Parliamentary Army, most of which, he claimed, had Antinomian tendencies, Baxter felt the need to emphasise steady "moral commitment, growth in grace and the conditionality of justification." With its accent on free grace and unconditional justification, the Antinomians—as Baxter understood them—were espousing a theology that was detrimental to the pursuit of righteousness in this life. Baxter's 1649 *Aphorismes of Justification*, was an attempt to argue for salvation as a synergistic act of God's grace coupled with human co-operation. This presumable departure "from predestinarian orthodoxy embroiled Baxter in prolonged controversy, with Owen among others, but he would maintain his position throughout his life, repeatedly drawing upon himself charges of Arminianism, popery, and even Pelagianism."[50]

Daniel Williams (1643-1716)

Baxterian in his theology, the Presbyterian minister Daniel Williams—the Bishop of the Dissenters—worked as a pastor in Ireland for about twenty years, before returning to England. In London, he led several churches, held the distinguished position of lecturer at Pinner's Hall from 1691 to 1694, and followed Richard Baxter as a preacher to the merchants of the city. Among many other books, Williams wrote a five volume *Practical Discourses*.[51]

Samuel Clark (1626-1701)

First son of a minister, this Puritan received education at Oxford and

---

[47] Keach, *Display of Glorious Grace*, 77.
[48] ODNB, IV: 419, 430. This is a fine article. See also DNB, I: 1349-1355.
[49] Paul Lim, 'Baxter, Richard,' in *DHT*, s.v.
[50] ODNB, IV: 422.
[51] Cooper, *Fear & Polemic*, 173; NSHE, XII: 365-366; CBTEL, X: 485-486.

Cambridge, and was given a fellowship from the latter in 1644. Although Clark only penned eight tomes, his commentary on the whole Bible or *Annotations*, 1690, was highly acclaimed for its thoroughness and conciseness. Clark's theological sympathies may be seen in that "Baxter had expressed a wish" to see his *Scripture Justification*, 1698, published.[52]

Having seen the representatives of this "school", let us briefly look into its main teaching. In broad outline, Baxterianism may be summarised as follows: God's will is to be understood in a twofold manner. Firstly, God has a decretive or purposing will, by which he determines all things: "what shall be and what shall not be *de facto*; secondly," God has "a legislative or preceptive will, for the government of the rational creature, whereby he determineth what shall be and what shall not be *de Jure* or in point of duty, and in order thereto concludeth of rewards and punishments."[53] God's will of purpose is *absolute* and it includes his decree or the covenant of redemption, election, reprobation, etc. God's legislative will, on the other hand, is *relative*, and mediated by the covenant of grace, whereby benefits and punishments are attached to the performance of certain conditions. Christ bore the punishment of Adam's violation of the covenant of works and, because of that, God partially removed the curse of the law and now offers everyone a "new law." This new law or covenant of grace stipulates that anyone who repents, believes and perseveres "to the end, shall be justified..." In other words, the covenant of grace is conditional.[54]

Christ's obedience is of two types, active and passive. His active obedience fulfilled the condition of the covenant of works and is not communicable to us. Christ's passive obedience is his sacrifice, which is our imputed legal righteousness.[55] Thus, first, Christ has removed the barrier between God and us (satisfaction to the law) by his passive obedience, which is imputed to us. That

---

[52] Samuel Clark, *Scripture Justification: Or, A Discourse of Justification, According to the Evidence of Scripture-Light. Wherein the Nature of Justification is fully open'd; the Great Point of Justification by Works, both of the Law and Gospel, is clearly Stated* (London: Printed by S. Bridge, for Tho. Parkhust at the Bible and Tree Crowns in Cheapside, near Mercers Chapel, 1698), 114.

[53] Richard Baxter, *Aphorismes of Justification, with their explication annexed wherein also is opened the nature of the covenants, satisfaction, righteousnesse, faith, works, &c.* (Hague: Printed by Abraham Brown, 1655), 1.

[54] Baxter, *Aphorismes*, 5-8, 13, 43-48, 56-58.

[55] Note carefully that this point is a departure from mainline Reformed Orthodox, for nearly all Orthodox authors deemed both Christ's active obedience (fulfilling of the Law) and passive obedience (receiving the penalty thereof) as necessary to justification. See, Stoever, *A Fair and Easie Way to Heaven*, 94, 218. Cf. e.g., Owen, *Works*, V: 217ff; Patrick Gillespie, *The Ark of the Covenant Opened: Or, A Treatise of the Covenant of Redemption Between God and Christ, as the Foundation of the Covenant of Grace* (London: Printed for Tho. Parkhurst at the Bible and three Crowns, in Cheapside, near Mercers Chappel, 1677), 92; Keach, infra, p. 79, footnote 79.

done, God has set the rule that sincere faith and obedience are the conditions by which humankind is justified. The active obedience of these conditions by each individual comprises his own evangelical righteousness, for Christ did not personally obey—or did not actively stand—in our place. The legal and the evangelical righteousness correspond to the pacts of works and grace respectively. Baxter puts it thus: "Legall righteousness, which is our conformity or satisfaction to the law. And Evangelicall righteousness, which is our conformity to the new covenant." Three things are to be noted, as explanation: "1. Every Christian must have both these. 2. That our legall righteousness is onely that of satisfaction: but our evangelicall is only that of obedience or performance of the condition. 3. That our legall righteousness is all without us in Christ, the other in our selves." To conclude, our salvation "may be said to be imperfect and by degrees toward our full and perfect Iustification at the last Iudgment."[56]

All of that is to be contrasted with mainstream Reformed Orthodoxy which conceived of the law as immutable, satisfied by Christ in the stead of believers and imputed to them.[57] Baxter, as we just saw, deemed the law as mutable (not in its essence but in that which God requires), that Christ stood not in the place of believers and that the imputation of the righteousness of Christ is restricted to satisfaction only.

Second Antinomian Controversy

In the mid seventeenth century, the English Reformed fought over the thought of Luther. What is remarkable is that the so-called Antinomians seem closer to the German Reformer than their foes; for, more than anybody else, the Antinomians were strictly solafideists, whereas their opponents, mainline and Baxterians, tended to include "conditions" (faith, obedience, etc) for justification.[58] An utterly unconditional Gospel is seen in Tobias Crisp's *Christ Alone Exalted*, published in 1643 and republished in 1690, which provoked the first and second Antinomian controversies. The furore of the controversies may be illustrated by the Westminster Assembly's condemnation of Crisp and, say, Henry Denne as exemplars of Antinomianism.[59] Baxter deemed Crisp's works worse than Popish teaching.[60] Between the first and the second controversies,

---

[56] Baxter, *Aphorismes*, 62-104, [215-221], 124.
[57] Von Rohr, *The Covenant of Grace*, 99. See, e.g., Owen, *Works*, I: 182-185; Gillespie, *Ark of the Covenant*, 82; Isaac Chauncy, *Neonomianism Unmask'd: or the Ancient Gospel Pleaded, Against the Other, Called A New Law or Gospel* (London: Printed for J. Harris, 1692), 17.
[58] J. Wayne Baker, 'Sola Fide, Sola Gratia: The Battle for Luther in Seventeenth Century England,' in *SCJ* 16 (1/1985): 115-133, p. 129.
[59] Vaughn, 'Public Worship and Practical Theology,' 214, 209-210.
[60] Griffiths, *Redeem the Time*, 99. Cf. Wallace, *Puritanism and Predestination*, 182.

Baxter thought that Antinomianism had subsided, but the 1690 republication made matters even more difficult to him since it included a refutation of Baxterian imputation. Additionally, and annoyingly to Baxter, several well-known divines, including Hanserd Knollys, endorsed the reprint.[61]

The said republication elicited a printing battle between those who opposed them, such as Daniel Williams, and those in favour, such as Isaac Chauncy. Generally, the Congregationalists tended to support and the Presbyterians to disapprove of "Crispianism." When the controversy was over, about seven years later, the Arminian position was all but embraced by the Presbyterians, and the Reformed by the Congregationalists.[62] Bearing in mind that, apart from baptism, there was no essential difference between the Congregationalists and the Particular Baptists,[63] it is easy to imagine in which trench Keach would fight.

Mainline Reformed Federalists include John Owen, Isaac Chauncy, Samuel Rutherford and Patrick Gillespie.[64] Keach's federalism is distinct from that of the Antinomians and Baxterians and, on the other hand, is similar—as we shall see—to that of the mainstream Orthodox. We have already seen how influential Owen was to Keach.[65] Chauncy's *Neonomianism* and Gillespie's *The Ark of the Covenant* were frequently cited by our protagonist.[66] Although Keach does not quote Rutherford, we included him as a representative of the Westminster Assembly.[67] All of them purposefully avoided both Antinomianism and Baxterianism, thus pursuing a midway within Orthodoxy.[68] We shall compare

---

[61] Baker, 'The Battle for Luther,' 62. Incidentally, the eruption of the second Antinomian controversy "caused such agitation because the whole debate had wider implications. This was not simply a battle between Baxter and his familiar foes; much more was at stake. The Presbyterians and the Independents were about to attempt a 'Happy Union,' but they were divided over just these soteriological issues." Cooper, *Fear and Polemic*, 173. In the search for holiness and doctrinal purity, the Dissenters fought both the established church and each other. "The Pinner's Hall lecture in London was intended as a common platform for Presbyterian and Independents, but by 1674, Baxter was being attacked by Independents for his 'Arminian' theology and he, in turn, portrayed their Calvinism as Antinomian and anti-rational." John Spurr, 'From Puritanism to Dissent, 1660-1700,' in *The Culture of English Puritanism*, 256.

[62] Griffiths, *Redeem the Time*, 100. Cf. Cooper, *Fear and Polemic*, 178-179.

[63] Tulloch, *English Puritanism*, 320.

[64] See their biographical sketch shortly.

[65] See supra, p. 52.

[66] See, for example, Keach's *Display of Glorious Grace*, 208-211, 219.

[67] The Federalism produced by the Assembly was "the normative expression of Reformed Orthodoxy." See chapter one, p. 31, footnote 89.

[68] Owen, *Works*, XXII: 121; X: 561ff; Chauncy, *Neonomianism*, 21, iii- v; Gillespie, *The Ark of the Covenant*, 1-2, 380-385; Samuel Rutherford, *The Covenant of Life Opened: Or, A Treatise of the Covenant of Grace* (Edinburgh: Printed by Andro. Anderson, for Robert Broun, and are to be sold at his shop, at the Sign of the Sun, 1654), 346, 156-157.

Keach's federalism with that of Owen, as he is a recognised standard of Orthodoxy. The parallels between Keach and Owen will be shown mainly in the body of the text. In the footnotes, Chauncy, Rutherford and Gillespie will be used in order to demonstrate further Keach's Orthodoxy.

Before considering the 'occasion of Keach's writing,' let us briefly acquaint ourselves with the aforementioned mainline Reformed Federalists: A short profile of these men follows.

John Owen (1616-1683)

Son of a Church of England minister, Owen was educated at Oxford. He would eventually become Dean of Christ's Church and Vice-Chancellor there under Cromwell's Chancellorship. By any standard, Owen was an intellectual giant, "an Aristotle among the Puritans."[69] Indeed, he is considered by many to be the best British theologian of all time.[70] A bastion of Reformed Orthodoxy,[71] the man himself averred, "I have no singular opinion of my own, but embrace the common known doctrine of the Reformed churches."[72] As a matter of fact, with

---

[69] CBTEL, VII:291; Geoffrey Nuttal, *The Holy Spirit in Puritan Faith and Experience* (Oxford: Basil Blackwell, 1946), 11. Even the great Richard Baxter admitted that "he had 'meddled too forwardly with Dr Owen.'" Reliquae Baxteriana, Pt. 1, 107, cited by Wallace, *Puritanism and Predestination*, 138

[70] Toon, *God's Statesman*, 171. See, Sinclair B. Ferguson, *John Owen on the Christian Life* (Edinburgh: Banner of Truth, 1987), 16, 19; Carl Trueman, *John Owen: The Man and His Theology*, Robert Oliver, ed. (Darlington: Evangelical Press, 2002), 43; Hernandes Dias Lopes, *A Importância da Pregação Expositiva para o Crescimento da Igreja* (São Paulo: Editora Candeia, 2004), 53; Steve Griffiths, *Redeem the Time: Sin in the Writings of John Owen* (Fern: Mentor, 2001), 7; Thomas D. Lea, 'The Hermeneutics of the Puritans,' in *JETS* 39/2 (June 1996): 271-284, p. 277; John Tulloch, *English Puritanism and its Leaders: Cromwell, Milton, Baxter, Bunyan* (Edinburgh: William Blackwood and Sons, 1861), 283

[71] "Owen's theology stands well within the broad contours of continental Reformed Orthodoxy and would have provided a first-class way of keeping the Catholic threat at bay, being as intolerant of any hints of papal sympathies as of any other perceived error. Nevertheless, Owen's theology was self-consciously developed in part in sharp opposition to Arminianism, and, indeed, to any who deviated to any degree from strict Reformed Orthodoxy." 61 Carl R. Trueman, 'Richard Baxter on Christian Unity: A Chapter in the Enlightening of English Reformed Orthodoxy,' in *WTJ* 61 (1999): 53-71, p. 61.

[72] Owen, *Works*, XII: 753. There are many references wherein Owen champions the Reformed cause: "I own no religion, no article of faith, but what is taught expressly in the Scripture, mostly confirmed by the ancient general councils of the primitive church, and the writings of the most learned Fathers, against all sorts of heretics, especially the Gnostics, Photinians, and Pelagians, consonant to the articles of the Church of England, and the doctrine of all the Reformed Churches of Europe." Ibid., II: 380. Cf. Ibid., 381, 427; III: 281, 301; IV: 274; VII: 19; X: 21-22; XII: 84; XV: 126; etc.

the Restoration of the Church of England in the 1660s, the vast swathe of non-Anglicans—Presbyterians, Congregationalists, non-conformist of all colours (Baptists included)—fell into great disfavour. Owen, "a national figure," was expected to offer invaluable direction at that critical juncture: "Thousands looked to him for an example and for guidance: the eyes of the Reformed churches abroad were on him. So in his home at Stadhampton he consulted with, and provided hospitality for, some of his former Oxford colleges, who had lost or were losing their posts."[73]

Isaac Chauncy (1632-1712)

Early in Chauncy's life, his father—an Anglican minister—left for Massachusetts, eventually becoming president of Harvard. In this institution, Chauncy pursued studies in medicine and theology, obtaining an M.A. in 1654. It seems that on his return to England, he also studied at Oxford. After his ejection in 1660, Chauncy became a staunch Congregationalist, pastoring several churches, including one that had been led by John Owen. When the second Antinomian controversy erupted, Chauncy launched a concerted attack on Baxterianism through his *Neonomianism Unmask'd*—published in three sections during 1692-93—and also his *Rejoynder to Mr. D. Williams* in 1693.[74]

Samuel Rutherford (c.1600-1661)

Rutherford was an academic, political theorist and massively influential in the life of both church and state. He was educated at the University of Edinburgh, and offered posts at the Universities of Harderwyck and twice from Utrecht, but turned them all down, only accepting positions at St Andrews and Edinburgh. As champion of Presbyterianism, he was Scottish commissioner to the Westminster Assembly, where he sat from 1643 through 1647. Staunchly Reformed, Rutherford "engaged in disputations with the 'Aberdeen doctors,' whose moderate Calvinism he regarded as sheer Arminianism."[75]

Patrick Gillespie (1617-1675)

Another Scottish Puritan, Gillespie was the son of a Church of Scotland minister. He went to St Andrews University, where he earned an M.A. in 1635. Under the Protectorate, the competent and powerful Gillespie became Principal of the University of Glasgow. His work on federalism was prefaced "by his old friend John Owen."[76] The praise of the Congregationalist leaves no doubt of his

---

[73] Toon, *God's Statesman*, 123.
[74] ODNB XI: 266; DNB IV: 171-172. Cf. CBTEL, II: 123; NSHE, III: 22.
[75] ODNB, XLVIII: 392-394.
[76] ODNB, XXII: 259-260.

approval of Gillespie's efforts. Owen says, concerning "order, method, perspicuity in treating, and solidity of argument, the ensuing discourse exceedeth whatsoever single treatise I have seen written with the same design; as it also is entirely compliant with the Doctrine of the Gospel, in what is asserted in it."[77]

Occasion of Keach's Writing

Keach constructs his covenantal scheme in the context of the second Antinomian controversy. As he introduces his *Display of Glorious Grace*, he makes one central point: he envisages the covenants of redemption and grace (or, as he calls the second, the covenant of "peace and reconciliation") as one and the same. This type of covenantal system obstructed all human effort in the process of justification. As a result of constructing his covenantal doctrine this way, Keach says that he expects the Baxterians to call him "an Antinomian, for that hath been their artifice of late, to expose the true ancient Protestant doctrine about justification, &c."[78] He denies Antinomianism, but also rejects—rather vehemently—all type of moralism. Taking into account the heretical situation of the times, he urges that all orthodox Protestants were "to cement together in love and union, and to pass by small matters of difference, considering what a grand design is carrying on by the great enemies of the true Christian religion." The main menace, he continues, is Baxterianism lately revived by Samuel Clark's *Scripture Justification*. The traditional doctrine of justification had not been under such sustained attack "since blessed Luther's days..."[79] That traditional doctrine, Keach purports to share with "Luther, Melanchthon, Calvin, Zanchy, Perkins, Ames, Dr Ussher, Dr Goodwin, Dr Owen, Dr Sibbs, Dr Preston, Norton, Burroughs, Caryl, Pemble, the [Westminster] Assembly, and indeed all other antient and modern writers generally."[80] The times are such, Keach complains, that the mere defence of that which Protestants had always believed was now deemed Antinomianism. He affirms that writers such as Tobias Crisp were being misrepresented on this issue. Although Keach does not agree with Crisp in some points, he would

---

[77] Gillespie, *The Ark of the Covenant*, [iv].
[78] Keach, *Display of Glorious Grace*, iv-v.
[79] Keach, *Medium Betwixt Two Extremes*, 35-36. By traditional doctrine, Keach means "justification by the imputed righteousness of Jesus Christ, or by his active and passive obedience alone, according to the Scripture, and as maintained by most of the ancient Fathers, and all our worthy Protestant divines." Ibid., 35.
[80] Keach, *Medium Betwixt Two Extremes*, 36. In the Postscript of this book, Keach promised to write more—but never did—on justification by imputation, in order to show that he preached no "new doctrine, but the very same that all good men and Orthodox Christians in every age have maintained." To substantiate it, Keach says, "I shall produce the testimony of the ancient Fathers, and a multitude of our faithful modern divines and worthy writers." Ibid., 39

prefer to be mistaken with those "who strive to exalt wholly the free grace of God, than...[with those] who seek to darken it and magnifie the power of the creature..."[81] The opposition to the traditional doctrine of justification, Keach concedes, relates to a worthy concern with holiness or good works. Nevertheless, holiness is not to be considered a prerequisite to entrance into God's covenant: "Now because we say sanctification is not necessary, as antecedent to justification, but is the fruit or product of union with Christ...must we be look'd upon as promoters of a licentious doctrine?" Despite abhorring licentiousness, Keach wants to leave justification entirely dependent on monergistic free grace, through the mediation of human faith.[82]

Orthodox concurrence with Keach on that previous paragraph is not difficult to find. Owen affirms that those who denied "the necessity of universal obedience or good works," and defended the traditional doctrine of justification by faith alone, are to be deemed "solifidians, Antinomians, and I know not what...If by solifidians they mean those who believe that faith alone is on our part the means, instrument or condition...of our justification, all the prophets and apostles were so, and were so taught to be by Jesus Christ..."[83]

An Exposition of Keach's Federal Theology

The key text used by Keach to ground his covenant theology is Isa.54.10: "For the mountains shall depart and the hills be removed, but my kindness shall not depart from thee, neither shall the covenant of my peace be removed, saith the Lord that hath mercy on thee."[84] He opens this passage by dint of five key points. First, God is making a promise about a covenant. Second, this promise was made prophetically to the Gentiles, not to the Jews. There are promises in the Old Testament, Keach claims, that are pertinent only to the natural seed, the Jews; and there are others which pertain only to the engrafted branch (Rom.11). Third, the substance of the promise is peace with God. Fourth, the mercy of God is what caused the covenant to happen. This shows that the covenant of peace was made after the fall, when humanity was in a state of misery.[85] "Man

---

[81] Keach, *Marrow of Justification*, [i-ii]. It is not an easy thing, Keach affirms, to maintain a proper balance between Antinomianism and Baxterianism. "My main design in all my preaching," he asserts, "is wholly to advance the free grace of God, through the redemption which is in Jesus Christ, and utterly abase the creature, tho it may seem a hard thing to keep in an even line, and not to fall into either extream." *Display of Glorious Grace*, v.

[82] Keach, *Marrow of Justification*, [ii]; *Medium Betwixt Two Extremes*, 23-24.

[83] Owen, *Works*, V: 105.

[84] All biblical quotations are Keach's, unless noted. At times he seems to be using the Authorised Version (not the Geneva Bible), but often, on account of very small differences, the citations appear to be from memory.

[85] This point is important, as Keach is attempting to take seriously that which happens within time. That is, his covenantal scheme does not distinguish the intertrinitarian pact

before his Fall needed not Gods mercy, he was the object of Gods love and favour, but not of his mercy. For mercy extended to any person, denotes he was in a forlorn and miserable condition before..." Fifth, this promise is more stable than the hills and mountains; i.e., the pledge of the covenant of peace was sworn by God and nothing can change it. All of that said, Keach infers from the text a proposition which summarizes his entire covenantal concept: "That there is a covenant of peace made or agreed upon, and it stands firm in the behalf of all Gods elect."[86]

Method or General Outline of the Covenant's Exposition

The proposition above is developed in six parts; or, to put it differently, the covenant of peace is explained using the following method: 1. Keach presents eight explanatory propositions by way of premise; 2. he delineates the principal transactions concerning the establishing of the compact; 3. next, he opens the nature of the treaty; 4. then, he presents the content of this concert; 5. Keach briefly deals with the nature of peace embodied in the covenant; 6. finally, a conclusion is made.

Explanatory Propositions

The first and second propositions state that the Fall and its awful consequences were foreseen by God, hence Father and Son established an eternal covenant to salvage the situation (2Tim.1.9).[87] The third proposition declares that the Adamic rebellion would create an immense separation (enmity) between the Creator and the creature; it would instil a permanent state of hostility in the human heart—a state that only God himself could overturn (Col.1.21). As a result, the entire race was put under a curse, even God's chosen ones, Keach affirms, are under this curse in their carnal state. Thus, all humanity is already damned, "tho the sentence is not presently executed."[88] Next, the Fall was a federal event; that is, Adam represented the whole human race in a compact of works.[89] Fifth, God required complete satisfaction for the breach—a payment

---

from the temporal one; *nevertheless*, Keach speaks rather forcefully on the reality of human history. Another evidence of this attempt to balance time and eternity is seen when Keach affirms that salvation is not by decree, but by faith. *Golden Mine*, 175-176.

[86] Keach, *Display of Glorious Grace*, 4-9.

[87] Keach, *Display of Glorious Grace*, 9-10. Cf. Chauncy, *Neonomianism*, 19; Gillespie, *The Ark of the Covenant*, 6, 7.

[88] Keach, *Display of Glorious Grace*, 10-14. Cf. Owen, *Works*, XXII: 69.

[89] Keach, *Display of Glorious Grace*, 14. Heppe presents the whole Reformed tradition supporting this point. "Dogmaticians usually insist that as representing the human race Adam was a *persona publica*, and therefore entered as such into a covenant with God along with all who were represented in him." Heinrich Heppe, *Reformed Dogmatics*, G. T. Thompson, trans. (London: George Allen & Unwin Ltd., 1950), 291.

that could not be borne by any creature. Sixth, the Lord, nevertheless, chose to show himself appeasable; and, in doing so, he demonstrated that he is not only just but also merciful.[90] The seventh proposition asserts that the eternal covenant and the temporal one are equivalents, that is, the compacts of redemption and grace are indistinguishable.[91] Lastly, the merciful covenant God made with Christ was done in such a way that through the Son, God entered "into covenant with his elect, viz., it was with them in Christ, and what of this is actually accomplished on us in time, in our persons, is but the execution of all that grace, pity and mercy manifested to us in Christ from eternity; he then shewed his eternal purpose of compassion towards his chosen," making them his possession in his Son.[92]

---

[90] Keach, *Display of Glorious Grace*, 17. God's nature, Keach affirms, is comprised of not only justice and equity, but also mercy and grace. It is important to know, though, that God does not have to be merciful—that is, he is not compelled or forced to be merciful. Accordingly, he has shown no mercy to the falling angels. On the other hand, God is not less righteous in showing mercy to the elect and not showing it to the reprobate. Merely out of his free will, the Lord has decided to redeem none of the wicked angels and only a part of the mass of humanity. The existence of the cosmos and all that occurs in it flows from God's sovereign will. All happens, as Keach understands, "according to his absolute decree and purpose from everlasting; and according to his absolute sovereignty he governs and disposes of all things, and may do what he will with his own." Keach then points out that God has chosen to make a pact with Abram and not with somebody else. Equally, he covenanted with Israel and left a multitude of nations in the dark. When Christ came, he chose to show the truth to a few ignorant peasants and bypass the sage and religious literate leaving them enthralled to the Devil. The examples could be multiplied: why is the Gospel preached in certain nations and not in others? Even within these nations, some respond but others do not. "Now from whence is all this? but meerely from the sovereignty of God, or good pleasure of his will, for 'it is not of him that willeth, nor of him that runneth, but of God that sheweth mercy'" (Rom.9.16). Ibid., 17-19. Cf. Owen, *Works*, XVIII: 105; Gillespie, *The Ark of the Covenant*, 58, 260; Rutherford, *The Covenant of Life*, 15, 244, 246.

[91] Keach, *Display of Glorious Grace*, 20. Cf. Chauncy, *Neonomianism*, 27, 119. However, we may add that many Reformed Orthodox made a distinction between these two covenants: "we must distinguish between the covenant that God made *with men concerning Christ*, and the covenant that he made *with his Son concerning men*." The eternal compact concerns only that which was transacted within the Trinity. The temporal concert, on the other hand, "is a transcript and effect of that" eternal pact. Owen, *Works*, XVIII: 95, XXIII: 599. Cf. Rutherford, *The Covenant of Life*, 290-302; Gillespie, *The Ark of the Covenant*, 74, 380ff.

[92] Keach, *Display of Glorious Grace*, 21, 42. Elsewhere, Keach makes a direct contrast between the concerts of works and grace in this manner: The covenant of works was established with the first man as our head and representative. Adam himself was obligated to fulfil the requirements of that covenant. The covenant of grace, on the other hand, was eternally established among the Persons of the Trinity, with the Son as our head and representative. Ibid., 177. Cf. Owen, *Works*, X: 309-311.

Presentation of the Main Exchanges that Brought about and Established the Pact of Peace

There are six points to be considered in establishing this treaty of peace: a. the parties consult with each other on the terms of peace; b. the parties agree on the terms proposed; c. selection of a mediator and his role in the compact; d. validation or confirmation of the covenant; e. publication or annunciation of the pact; f. its inauguration, who is to be partaker thereof and what are the prerequisites for possessing this concert.

The Parties Consult, Confer or Discuss the Terms of Peace

Benjamin Keach was not a naïve anthropomorphist. This Baptist preacher and writer composed a four-volume work covering all biblical metaphors[93] and thus, he had a excellent knowledge of figures speech. When he compares divine and human activity, he does so in a 'God-ward' not 'man-ward' direction. That is to say, Keach postulates that God's activities do not resemble ours; rather, ours resemble God's. With that firmly in mind, let us present what our author has to say. First of all, he wants to draw parallels between the everlasting covenant of peace and a mundane human covenant. He starts off asserting that, in an earthly covenant of peace, kings send representatives on their behalf to discuss the terms of the covenant. However, in the divine covenant there were no messengers or representatives, for the agreement was eternally intra-trinitarian. A human covenant has ambassadors on behalf of the chief of state, for "they do not treat about it in their own persons; but the treaty of peace in this covenant was only between God the Father and God the Son, sinners then had no actual being, or did not exist, and therefore could not send any plenipotentiary to agitate matters on their behalf." Although Scripture calls Christ "the messenger of the covenant" (Mal.3.1), and indeed he is our representative and fiduciary, yet we did not appoint him as such—the Father has appointed him for this task.[94] The point Keach is putting forth is standard Reformed: Owen asserts: Indeed, the Son "was designed and appointed by the Father unto this office" of mediator.[95]

The eternal character of the discussion of the covenant is shown in a fourfold manner. First, king David is used as a figure of Christ: "I have made a covenant with my chosen" (Psa.89.3). Keach interprets, "[i]t is said to be made with David but no otherwise than as he was a type of Christ. It is Jesus Christ who is the true David." This Davidic covenant is a shadow of the eternal covenant

---

[93] *Tropologia: A Key to Open Scripture Metaphors* (London: s.n., 1681).
[94] Keach, *Display of Glorious Grace*, 24-25. Cf. There was no mediator provided for the covenant of works, our first parents had perfectly to obey God and thus live. In contradistinction, a mediator was appointed to the covenant of grace, whose obedience and sacrifice granted us life and peace. Ibid, 177-178.
[95] Owen, *Works*, XXII: 68

made by the Father with the Son—the Son being covenanted to represent and act as trustee of God's chosen ones.[96]

Second, the final part of Zac.6.3, "...the covenant of peace is between them both," is allegorically applied to a pact between the persons of the Trinity. Moreover, Wisdom, as traditionally interpreted, is identified with Christ, "I was set up from everlasting..." (Pro.8.23). In that verse and those that follow it, is implicit that Christ is the one set up "as the covenant-head of all God's elect, or as mediator and peace-maker between God and them, and this setting-up...clearly implies a covenant or holy compact that was between them both."[97] Owen likewise maintains that the transactions within the Trinity were done "by the way of 'counsel,' for the accomplishment of the end designed in a-covenant: Zachariah 6:13... The counsel about peace-making between God and man was 'between them both;' that is, the two persons spoken of, —namely, the Lord Jehova, and he who was to be צמח, 'The Branch.'" Owen proceeds by saying that in this passage the Son is to be deemed "eternal Wisdom, only with respect unto his future incarnation; for therein he was to be both the 'Branch of the Lord' and 'the fruit of the earth,' Isaiah 4:2."[98]

Third, having established that, Keach thinks that one party, the Father, proposed to the other, the Son, who accepted it.[99] It is as if a transaction within the Trinity took place, where the Son obediently accepts the will of the Father, and the Father shows "him what he will have him do, if ever our peace succeed and is made."[100] Along the same lines, Owen affirms that God the Father is to be deemed "the proposer both of the duty and of the reward of the mediator,...the Son accepts of his terms and proposals..."[101]

Fouth, the Father gave promises to the Son and to those he would redeem. The Son would earn this redemption, which the redeemed would receive freely by grace. Thus, Christ said that he had come to do the will of his Father which involved laying down his life for redemption. God the Son did know that what he came to do on earth was in accordance with the everlasting covenant, "purpose and decree of the Father, unto which he consented; God the Father agreed to prepare the Son a body, the Son consented to assume our nature, or to take the body" (Heb.10.9). The prophet Isaiah, Keach claims, mentions the intertrinitarian "federal" agreement: "He shall make his soul an offering for sin" (53.10), and "I will give thee (that is, thee my Son) for a covenant to the

---

[96] To further support his point, Keach adds and comments on Psa.89.28 and Act.2.23; *Display of Glorious Grace*, 26.
[97] Keach, *Display of Glorious Grace*, 26-27.
[98] Owen, *Works*, XVIII: 104.
[99] This point is fully dealt with under the next heading: 'The Father and the Son agree on the terms proposed,' pp. 86ff.
[100] Keach, *Display of Glorious Grace*, 27.
[101] Owen, *Works*, XIX: 464-465.

people" (42.6, interpolation by Keach).[102] Clearly, Keach says, the Father is appointing the Son to be the internuncius or mediator of the covenant of peace. The Scriptures witness not only the appointment of the Son but also his response to it: "The Lord hath opened mine ears, and I was not rebellious, I gave my back to the smiters, and my cheek to them that plucked off the hair; I hid not my face from shame and spitting" (Isa.50:5,6). Thus, the Son submitted to the will of the Father though he knew the implications thereof; for he had been given unfailing and marvellous promises. These promises were that a group of people would be justified, that he would have an inheritance, "that the pleasure of the Lord shall prosper in his hand; he shall have them all united to himself, pardoned and saved for ever."[103]

To support even further the current heading, Keach adds a famous covenantal text, viz., Psa.2.7. He personifies this passage as follows: "I will declare the decree" (i.e., the pact or agreement) made between my Father and me. That which was eternal and unknown to humanity, I, Christ, will make known. However, this shall be known only to my people; "[t]he secrets of the Lord is with them that fear him, and he will shew them his covenant" (Psa.25.14). The words for "decree" (קח) and "covenant" (תירב)[104] may be used as synonyms and may be understood literally or metaphorically. If understood literally, it means a bilateral pact, i.e., both parties have obligations. This is the way the covenant of peace agreed by the divine Persons should be understood. On the other hand, pact may be taken metaphorically as is the case with, say, Noah and Abraham: both received a promise. This is the way that "covenant," when applied to humanity, should be understood. Old and New Testament saints receive free grace as a result of God's promised union between them and his Son. To put it differently, the covenant is a promise because there are no conditions whatsoever insofar as believers are concerned; "for we receive no covenant-blessings upon any mutual stipulation betwixt God and us, upon or from the merit of our work, but all upon the account of free grace and of Christ's covenant with God, and by virtue of that federal union we had then with him." This is the case because everything we are given in the temporal order "was promised to us in Christ from eternity."[105]

Concerning the circumstances of the concert between God and humanity, John Owen likewise affirms that "...the condition of the covenant is not said to be required, but it is absolutely promised."[106]

---

[102] Keach, *Display of Glorious Grace*, 27-28.

[103] Keach, *Display of Glorious Grace*, 28. Cf. Rutherford, *The Covenant of Life*, 293, 296-297.

[104] Both words are misspelled in the book. For "decree" it has חק and for "covenant" הירב.

[105] Keach, *Display of Glorious Grace*, 28-29. Cf. Gillespie, *The Ark of the Covenant*, 10-12.

[106] Owen, *Works*, X: 310.

The Father and the Son Agree on the Terms Proposed

Keach presents several passages to suggest that the covenant was proposed by the Father to the Son, on one side (e.g., Isa.49:5-6); and, on the other, that the Son accepted the proposal (Heb.10:5-7).[107] In the same way, Owen suggests that God is to be deemed "as the proposer both of the duty and of the reward of the mediator, the Son incarnate, as the Son accepts of his terms and proposals, Heb. 10:5-9."[108]

There are a few things, Keach proceeds, to be considered under the transactions of the covenant and the agreement of the parties thereof. 1. Two persons were involved in this transaction: the Father, whose righteousness required complete satisfaction, and the Son, who pledges to grant it; and in so doing provided peace. 2. The content of the transaction was the remission of the elect, though they did not yet exist. 3. This transaction was made *per modum foederis*: the honour of the Father had been challenged by us, but the Son as our *representative* uplifts his honour again. "I have glorified thee on earth, I have finished the work thou gavest me to do. And now Father, glorifie me with thy own self" (Joh.17.4-5). Keach elaborates, it is as if Christ were saying, "the terms agreed upon, or thy demands are done, therefore let me have my reward, and let mine elect 'be made one in us,' let me not only personally be one with thee, but also mystically one, and so be glorified, as it is due to me, as the hire or reward of my work." 4. Eternity was the ambit of the transaction, which leads us to the next point. 5. This transaction had a mediator, somewhat like a treaty done by human beings.[109]

Selection of a Mediator and his Role in the Covenant

Keach makes further considerations on the transactions of the covenant in so far as it relates to Christ, the mediator. Firstly, he points to 1Tim.2.5, "[t]here is one mediator between God and man, even the man Christ Jesus," and affirms that without an internuncius there could not be a covenant, for, secondly, God's honour had been challenged and as a just sovereign he cannot disregard his own law. Thus, our intermediary had to satisfy God's law, otherwise "there could be no covenant of peace concluded..." Since, therefore, God had decided to engage us in a covenant, it was *necessary* to have the Son as our intermediary.[110] On this and the following point, Owen affirms that it was indispensable that the Son of God would assume our nature as mediator. "The

---

[107] Keach, *Display of Glorious Grace*, 30-31.

[108] Owen, *Works*, XIX: 464-465.

[109] Keach, *Display of Glorious Grace*, 32-33. God the Father and the Son agreed on the terms of the covenant, with the Son having to satisfy "offended justice on the behalf of the elect," so as to make satisfaction to the Father. Chauncy, *Neonomianism*, 114. Cf. Owen, *Works*, XVIII: 95.

[110] Keach, *Display of Glorious Grace*, 34-35.

nature of angels being not taken, those that sinned in that nature must perish for ever; and they that fancy a possibility of saving sinners any other way but by satisfaction made *in the nature that had sinned*, seem not to have considered aright the nature of sin and the justice of God." Owen proceeds, "[h]ad any other way been possible, why doth the perishing of angels so inevitably follow the non-assumption of their nature? This way alone, then, could it be wrought."[111]

On the Necessity of Christ the Mediator

The Father did not compel the Son to underwrite the covenant, but once it was done, "there was a necessity for Christ to be the mediator and surety of it; I say, necessity, so far as we can, or are able to conceive, in respect to this matter."[112] Keach seems to be somewhat reticent on this issue, nonetheless he adds the following observations on the necessity of Christ's mediatorship: this manner— as opposed to another—was the way it was *revealed* to us. Moreover, the size of the offence left a gap that only God himself could bridge. The seriousness of offences against God is illustrated by Old Testament sacrifices, which are shadows of Christ's mediatory sacrifice. Hence, in due time God sacrificed his Son, whom he would have spared, "if he had foresaw that our peace might have been made from some other way." In other words, why would God make his Son "a curse for us, or suffer the cursed death of the cross, to make our peace, if peace could be made any other way, without least injury to the justice, law and holiness of God?" All of this, Keach claims, implies that without the mediatorship of Christ, the covenant could not be set in place.[113]

Note how similarly Owen talks about it. The Lord granted "that there should be a mediator, a sponsor, an undertaker, with whom he would treat about a new covenant, and so establish it." Indeed, "it was absolutely necessary that in this covenant there should be a surety, to undertake for our answering and firm standing unto the terms of it."[114]

On the Dual Nature of the Mediator

The ladder of Jacob is used by Keach to provide a picture of heaven and earth coming together in the dual nature of Christ. The Son, Keach claims, had a body prepared for him, human and divine, to reach both heaven and earth. Concerning his human side, "which is the foot of the ladder, this stands as it were upon the earth." As to the divine side, "which is the top of the ladder, this reacheth unto heaven; and in these two natures in the person of Christ, we have

---

[111] Owen, *Works*, XIX: 565-566.
[112] Keach, *Display of Glorious Grace*, 35.
[113] Keach, *Display of Glorious Grace*, 35-37.
[114] Owen, *Works*, XXII: 186, 187.

what is represented by Jacob's ladder..."[115] It was essential that Christ would have both natures, Keach maintains, for only God himself fully knew how offended he was with humanity's offence. On the other hand, only a human being can fully sympathise with the frailties and infirmities of human nature. Christ is the middle person between the two parties, "he is at an equal distance, and equally drawing near to and like related" to both, God and man. On the one side, he is the divine Son of God and on the other, he is our human brother. In him, the two natures became one person.[116] Owen concurrs by saying that "[a] mediator must be a middle person between both parties entering into covenant; and if they be of different natures, a perfect, complete mediator ought to partake of each of their natures in the same person."[117]

Keach further expands on the need of Christ to be both God and human. In the first place, the mediator had to be God because (1) only God could earn infinite merit to countervail infinite injury. Our sins had dishonoured an infinite God and thus infinite compensation had to be made. (2) Christ had to be God to bear the burden of wrath that was due to sin, for, Keach says, "if the guilt of one sin were laid on any meer man, it would sink him down to the lowest hell; much more then would the weight of all the sins of God's elect have sunk down" the Son "when laid upon him, had he not been God but meer man" (Mar.14.33-34).[118] Besides compensating for the infinite insult we had done to God's majesty; (3) only Christ as God could earn for us an eternal inheritance and infinite benefits. That is, only Christ as God could—negatively—pull us out from hell, and—positively—lift us to the heavenly places. In addition, (4) Christ had to be God, for otherwise he could not have conquered his and our mighty enemies, viz., death and Satan (Hos.13.14). Lastly, (5) Christ had to be God because only God can give life, and Christ had to enliven his chosen ones "who in the first Adam 'were dead in sins and trespasses.'" In sum, a mere human figure could not do all these things; therefore Christ is God.[119] In the same way, Owen maintains that pertaining to "satisfaction unto justice, by way of compensation for injuries and crimes, there must be a proportion between the injury and the reparation of it, that justice may be as much exalted and glorified in the one as it was depressed and debased in the other."[120]

In the second place, Keach continues, the Son had to share humanity with us (1) in order to make our unrighteous nature righteous. The same essence or being that disobeyed had to produce obedience. Humanity was under the obligation to comply with God's law and God cannot merely dispense with it.

---

[115] Keach, *Jacob's Ladder*, 12-13.
[116] Keach, *Display of Glorious Grace*, 38-39, 44-46. Cf. Gillespie, *The Ark of the Covenant*, 146, 230.
[117] Owen, *Works*, XXII: 68.
[118] Keach, *Display of Glorious Grace*, 39-40.
[119] Keach, *Display of Glorious Grace*, 40-41.
[120] Owen, *Works*, XXII: 549.

Thus, man himself—the flesh—had to fulfil the law. Accordingly, Jesus the man fulfilled it on behalf of his chosen ones in the covenant of peace. Keach then contrasts Adam and Christ: "For as we were all made sinners by one man, as the head and representative of all his seed, so we became righteous by the complete and perfect obedience of one man, as the head and representative of all his seed." He further clarifies, "for as the law being broken by one man, is imputed to all his seed, so the law being completely kept by one man, Jesus Christ, is imputed to all his seed" (Rom.5.18-19).[121] Moreover, Christ had to be man (2) because the law stipulated death for any who broke it. Consequently, the Son, though divine and hence immortal, had to suffer death in order to satisfy divine justice. Furthermore, (3) Christ had to share our nature in order to bestow on that nature his merits. Additionally, (4) Christ as our high priest had to become human so as to sympathise with our frailties and infirmities. For these reasons, Christ as man became (5) a source or spring of grace, and (6) we can trust in one who has the same nature as ours, as opposed to an animal or angel. Thus, Christ is man.[122]

The Offices of Christ

As mediator, Christ has sacerdotal, regal and prophetic offices.[123] Here, Keach's statement is another Reformed commonplace: "There are (as is out of controversy) three offices which the Lord Christ, as the mediator and surety of the new covenant, beareth and exerciseth towards the church, namely, those of king, prophet, and priest."[124] The intermediary does "not atone for our sins as a king," Keach affirms, "but as a priest, so he doth not give forth laws as a priest, but as a king; nor doth he teach, instruct, or reveal God and salvation to us simply as a priest or king, but as a prophet."[125] Let us briefly consider these three classical offices.

---

[121] Keach, *Display of Glorious Grace*, 41-42. Cf. The first covenant, Keach says, threatened with ire and vengence all who might disobey it. In the second compact, this wrath was unleashed upon the Son, and by it we received everlasting pardon. Ibid., 179-180.

[122] Keach, *Display of Glorious Grace*, 42-44. Christ had human "nature which offended, and so being fit therein to safisfie wrath;...there is [thus] a most full and reall compensation made to offended justice..." Rutherford, *The Covenant of Life*, 283. See also, Owen, *Works*, XIX: 575; Gillespie, *The Ark of the Covenant*, 406.

[123] Keach, *Jacob's Ladder*, 41.

[124] Owen, *Works*, XVIII: 179. Cf. Chauncy, *Neonomianism*, 48; Gillespie, *The Ark of the Covenant*, [210] et seq.

[125] Keach, *Display of Glorious Grace*, 73.

Sacerdotal Office

Christ as a priest is superior to Old Testament high priests, for he is "the substance and antitype of all those priests; he is both priest, altar and sacrifice."[126] That is, the sacrifices presented by Old Testament priests were only symbolic of the great sacrifice Christ was to present. Besides, the priesthood of Christ surpasses the Levitical one on account of permanency and appointment; his is eternal and with an oath,[127] while the Levitical priesthood is temporal without an oath. No human priesthood could achieve what Christ's achieved, namely, the reconciliation of two antagonistic poles, justice and mercy. By presenting himself at the altar as priest and sacrifice, he appeased the wrath of God that was due to humankind and concomitantly earned mercy to be applied unto the elect. Through this sacrifice, heaven and earth were connected, as we said before. It is by Christ that the high and exalted "God comes down to us, as well as we go up to God; it is by Christ that God comes down to us in a way of mercy, peace and reconciliation; and it is by Christ we go up to God in a way of faith and dependence... [In Christ] God and sinners meet together on this sacred ladder..."[128] All of that relates to Christ's atoning sacrifice. On the other hand, Christ as a living priest is the advocate (1Joh.2.1) and intercessor (Heb.7.25) of the elect before the Father (Heb.7.24). He asks the Father that the elect may have his merits "applied to their souls...[and that they] may have all that grace which they need bestowed upon them, to help them to resist temptation and to be supported under all trials and afflictions, and be enabled to perform all holy duties, and have all their sins pardoned."[129] However, the living priesthood of Christ is not only effective in that which he does for us, but also in that which he does through us: we have our requests granted *via* the intercession at work in us. That is, through the Spirit of the Son "we have free access unto God, which is the effect of Christ's priestly office" (Heb.4.14).[130] Finally, despite his eminent kingship, it is as priest, not as king, that Christ

---

[126] Keach, *Jacob's Ladder*, 42.

[127] A full discussion of this point under the heading, 'The confirmation of the covenant of peace,' infra, pp. 95-97.

[128] Keach, *Jacob's Ladder*, 42-43. Truly, "by bringing down God to man, and bringing up man to God, and thrusting both to meet in a mediator, wonderful did the wisdom of God appear in reconciling justice and mercy, and making them meet together in this business; in punishing sin, and setting the sinner free; in making a covenant with us through a mediator, when there could be none without a mediator..." Gillespie, *The Ark of the Covenant*, 154. Cf. Rutherford, *The Covenant of Life*, 303.

[129] Keach, *Display of Glorious Grace*, 67. "Through him are all the blessings of the covenant applied to us, and the fruit of his purchase is drawn forth by his intercession as a priest for ever, which he doth as a mediator..." Gillespie, *The Ark of the Covenant*, 150.

[130] Keach, *Jacob's Ladder*, 43-44.

reconciles us to God, i.e., reconciliation "is not done by what he works in us, but by what he hath done for us."[131]

Regal Office

As mediator, Christ is endowed with kingly jurisdiction; "yet have I set my king upon my holy hill of Sion" (Psa.2.6). His domain "is not *regnum naturale*, which he hath as God, co-essential with the Father, but *regnum oeconomicum*, which he hath by donation and unction from his Father..." As king, Christ reigns over Satan, his angels as well as the holy angels; over countries and over his church whose head he is (Mat.28.18).[132] As king, Christ has crushed under his feet Satan, sin and death. However, he not only destroys, he also builds and guides. That is, as kingly legislator he gives us precepts and laws, not in order that we may gain acceptance with God, but rather that, having been accepted, we may be built up and guided along as worthy and free children of the Father. These laws and precepts provide all necessary guidance for the government, order, conduct and correction of his church. As king, Christ overcomes the hostile will of the elect and draws them to God. He pours grace, that is, into the hearts of his chosen ones, and so overcomes Satanic influence and sinful enmity. Thus, Christ takes over the elect "as king and supream ruler, whom as priest he purchased by his blood."[133] Although Christ holds all power and authority, his kingdom is presently being halted, Keach claims, by the Papists and the Turks. Soon, however, Christ will defeat these adversaries and the entire world will be handed over to him. The coming of the kingdom shall be seen with the demise of "the Fourth-Monarchy and upon the passing away of the second Woe, or Mahomitan power, and downfall of the Beast, and the mystery Babylon, which is now at the very door, when Christ will save his church from all her enemies."[134]

Prophetic Office

The prophetic office of Christ may be seen in several ways. To begin with, he revealed the plans and intentions of God to his elect; for humanity without Christ could never discover the mind of the creator (Mat.11.25). Next, these revelations were not his own but the Father's (Joh.12.49). Moreover, Christ's

---

[131] Keach, *Display of Glorious Grace*, 68-69. "Christ wrought out our forgiveness by way of atonement as a priest, and God was atoned and appeased thereby..." Chauncy, *Neonomianism*, 48.

[132] Keach, *Display of Glorious Grace*, 69. Keach's concept is taken strait from Chauncy, see *Neonomianism*, 207. Cf. Owen, *Works*, VIII: 312.

[133] Keach, *Display of Glorious Grace*, 70. As "a king, [Christ] conquers and subdues the hearts of sinners to himself..." Chauncy, *Neonomianism*, 48.

[134] Keach, *Display of Glorious Grace*, 71.

prophetic office is superior to all other prophets, for they received their inspiration from him: they had only a limited measure of the Spirit, and they could only address the exterior of their hearers; whereas Christ knew the hearts of his listeners, had a limitless measure of the Spirit, and himself gave instructions to those prophets which came before him.[135]

The Suretyship of Christ

Keach proposes to open the nature of, and the type of covenantal relation involved in, suretyship by eight points.

First, one who offers himself as surety works in the place of "others, wherein they are defective...*sponsor fide jussor*, a surety is one that engages" on behalf of another to satisfy a condition. We see illustrations of sureties in the lives of Judah and Paul. The first put himself in the condition of surety to restore his brother Benjamin to his father (Gen.43.9). The latter became a surety to sponsor Onesimus (Phm.18-19). Those two relationships may serve to illustrate Christ's suretyship. However, this does not exhaust the nature of suretyship, for it also entails the giving of a pledge (2Kin.18.23), and hand-striking (Pro.22.16). Equally, in the covenant of peace, Christ has shaken "hands with God for us." Keach attempts an overarching definition: "a surety is one that undertakes for one or more persons whose credit is gone, or is not good; one not to be trusted, or whose faithfulness or ability is suspected." Because we had proven unfaithful to our maker, he would not covenant with us, but graciously provided for us "a sponsor or surety; 'by so much was Jesus made a surety of a better covenant'" (Heb.7.22).[136] This first point is again standard Reformed. "Ἔγγυος, or ἐγγυητής, a 'surety,' is one that undertaketh for another wherein he is *defective*, really or in reputation...Such an one is sponsor, or 'fidejussor,' in all good authors and common use of speech."[137]

Second, Christ became our testator, for he gives us gifts. We understand "testator" as one whose death triggers a legacy to somebody else. The suretyship of Christ, that is, involves more than guaranteeing the faithfulness of the covenant; it also involves the bestowing of an inheritance upon those he has elected.[138] In dying, Owen maintains, the Son bought "all good things for the church; and as a testator bequeathed them unto it."[139]

---

[135] Keach, *Display of Glorious Grace*, 72 and, idem, *Jacob's Ladder*, 45-46.

[136] Keach, *Display of Glorious Grace*, 86-87. "The Lord the Creditour and Christ the Cautioner did strike hands together: Christ put himself in our room, as an hostage, pledge and surety to die for us, and payed the first and second death, the summe that we were owing, according to a paction between the Lord and Christ..." Rutherford, *The Covenant of Life*, 248. Cf. Ibid., 197, 321; Owen, *Works*, XXII: 66-67; Gillespie, *The Ark of the Covenant*, 138, 149.

[137] Owen, *Works*, XXI: 613. His emphasis.

[138] Keach, *Display of Glorious Grace*, 87. "The testator by his Will and Testament, bequeaths, disposes, and leaves in legacy the very same mercies and covenant-blessings

Before moving on to the next point, Keach indicates that some people were objecting to the suretyship of Christ on the basis of two separate covenants. They were saying that Christ was a surety for the covenant of grace, but not to the covenant of redemption.[140] Keach, as we saw, considers the two pacts one and the same and states that if Christ had not "engaged in this covenant of peace and redemption for us, there had been no covenant nor peace for us at all, because all dependeth on Christ's obligation to the Father for us..."[141]

Third, the suretyship of Christ was unilateral, i.e., he was a surety for us to God, not for God to us. God does not need a surety on his behalf, for "he never failed any of his creatures, he broke not his covenant with man, but man with him."[142] Combating Socinianism and agreeing with the bulk of Orthodoxy, Owen affirms that the mediator "was properly a surety or undertaker unto God for us, and not a surety or undertaker unto us for God."[143]

Fourth, as in human covenants a surety provides stability, so also in the covenant of peace Christ is the agent of security and stability—the assurance that it will never fail. Keach underpins his claim with Psa.89.28. "My covenant shall stand fast in him."[144] The Son, Owen similarly affirms, was the guaranty of the pact, in such a way that "the covenant on every side might be firm and stable, and the ends of it fulfilled."[145]

Fifth, it was out of free will that the Son covenanted with the Father on our behalf. This was an act of his free grace and gratuitous love toward us, since there is nothing in the law that would compel someone else to take our place. God's holy law, which we disobeyed in Adam and daily continue to disregard, "laid no obligation on him, nor was he under any necessity of nature" to fulfil it in our place. Christ did it so freely, and did it "for man, and not for angels, and

---

that were his at the first-hand, and all treasured up in the mediator and testator, as in a store-house...when Christ hath made his Will, he laid down his life, and by his death he opens a way, and gives legal access to his people, to have his testament executed and his will therein actually fulfilled." Gillespie, *The Ark of the Covenant*, 449. Cf. Owen, *Works*, XXII: 109, XI: 288-289; Chauncy, *Neonomianism*, 112; Rutherford, *The Covenant of Life*, 318.

[139] Owen, *Works*, XXII: 109.
[140] Cf. e.g., Baxter, *Aphorismes*, [215-221].
[141] Keach, *Display of Glorious Grace*, 87.
[142] Keach, *Display of Glorious Grace*, 88.
[143] Owen, *Works*, XXI: 612. "Christ was not a surety for God, nor did God need any, having confirmed his promise with an oath, swearing by himself, because he had no greater to swear by." Idem, *Works*, XXII: 70.
[144] Keach, *Display of Glorious Grace*, 88-89.
[145] Owen, *Works*, XVIII: 96. "Through him is the covenant held fast with those who are once really engaged in it, that it crumble not away as the first covenant did, but it may stand firm and stable, Psa.89.34,35." Gillespie, *The Ark of the Covenant*, 152. Cf. Rutherford, *The Covenant of Life*, 337.

also only for some of the lost sons of Adam, and not for all" (Joh.10.5).[146] That point is consistent with Orthodoxy: God "was at liberty to have left all mankind under sin and the curse, as he did all the fallen angels that fell; he was at a liberty utterly to have destroyed the race of mankind." Therefore, it is not to be thought "that this work of entering into covenant about the salvation of mankind was any way necessary unto God, or that it was required by virtue of any of the essential properties of his nature, so that he must have done against them in doing otherwise. God was therein absolutely free…"[147]

Sixth, a surety is at one with the debtor. He or she is united to the one for whom suretyship was underwritten. "In a law sense it denotes a foederal, or law union, the surety and the debtor are but one party…[thus] it is the surety that pays; it is his money and not the debtors."[148] Christ not only became a debtor on our behalf, but he also became consubstantial with us. An objection is raised at this point: if indeed Christ has become one with us, if his justice has become ours by imputation, then it follows that we can save ourselves, we became mediators. However, the conclusion, Keach claims, does not follow, otherwise, "they may as well argue the debtor is the surety, because his surety's payment is accepted for him." A similar objection is raised along the same lines: if we are actually one with Christ and his justice is ours, then we are as just as he is.[149] Keach bluntly retorts that it may well be said that, "the bankrupt is as rich as his surety, because his surety pays his debts."[150]

Seventh, there are times when sureties go beyond the paying of debts, and pay rather for lives. This is the case with Christ; he took the place not only for debts but also for crimes. Keach has "work-mongers" and Socinians in mind here. They were claiming that the Son had died *nostro bono*, for our good and profit."[151] Keach denies it and affirms that he rather died "*nostra vice*, in our

---

[146] Keach, *Display of Glorious Grace*, 89.

[147] Owen, *Works*, XVIII: 105

[148] Keach, *Display of Glorious Grace*, 89-90.

[149] Cf. Christ's "righteousness is not subjectively in them, nor is there a change of person betwixt them and Christ, neither are they as righteous as he, but there remain spots and blemishes in them, until Christ by his Spirit perfect that holiness begun in all true believers, which he will effect before he bring them to heaven." Williams, *Gospel Truth*, 31.

[150] Keach, *Display of Glorious Grace*, 90. "Imputation of Christ's righteousness in redemption for justification or forgiveness, doth not denominate us saviours or redeemers…" Chauncy, *Neonomianism*, 90

[151] Cf. To say that Christ died in the actual place of the elect, Baxter claims, "is the very turning point of Antinomianism and the very *Primum vivens & ultimum moriens*, the heart of the whole system of their doctrine." *Of Justification*, 382. See also, *Racovian Catechisme* (Amsterdam: Brooer Janz, 1652), 134.

room, he died for his church, for his elect..."[152] Once again, Keach's position is in agreement with Owen's. The latter affirms that "in dying for us Christ did not only aim at our good, but also directly died in our stead."[153]

Eighth and finally, once the surety has paid the debt, the injured party cannot claim anything from the debtor. Once satisfaction is achieved, the criminal—as point of justice—must be "discharged and acquitted according to the time and terms agreed on between the creditor and the surety." There is now no condemnation, Keach continues, for those Christ, the surety, has replaced.[154] The point Keach is making is congruous with Reformed thought. The work of Christ, Owen says, merited the salvation of the elect to the extent that God, as it were, became a debtor to the mediator. Thus, "[m]erit is such an adjunct of obedience as whereon a reward is reckoned of debt. Now, there was in the nature of things themselves a proportion between the obedience of Christ the mediator and the salvation of believers."[155] Even more pointedly: "Where merit intercedes, the effect is reckoned as of debt...The fruits of the death of Christ are the issues of merit, bottomed on God's free acceptation and reckoned as of debt. He for whom a ransom is paid hath a right unto his liberty by virtue of that payment."[156]

The Confirmation of the Covenant of Peace

Keach thinks that the covenant of peace was confirmed by the Father with an oath. This oath he made to the Son—and his seed in him—from eternity, and in time it is typified by David (Psa.89.3). This oath is also shown in the book of Hebrews, Keach alleges, where the Father has made the Son a priest not in the temporal Aaronic line, but in the eternal line of Melchizedek, (Heb.7.14-17, 20-22).[157]

---

[152] Keach, *Display of Glorious Grace*, 90-91. "Christ the surety of the New Testament died, not only *nostro bono*, for our good and profit, as Socinians say; but he died also in our stead and room, *nostra vice*." Gillespie, *The Ark of the Covenant*, 380.

[153] Owen, *Works*, X: 225.

[154] Keach, *Display of Glorious Grace*, 91-92. "How sweet and comfortable is this to the believer, that by the suretyship of Christ, not only favour and grace is for him, but justice also? That satisfied justice is the sinful believers friend, stands on his side; and if God be righteous and just, he will, he must, he cannot but forgive the confessing believer, and save him upon Christs account, who suffered and satisfied punitive justice and merited by a condign price, holding proportion with the thing which he bought, that commutative and remunerative justice should give this reward for his work." Gillespie, *The Ark of the Covenant*, 140. Cf. Rutherford, *The Covenant of Life*, 212.

[155] Owen, *Works*, XVIII: 114

[156] Owen, *Works*, X: 623.

[157] Keach, *Display of Glorious Grace*, 110. Cf. Owen, *Works*, XVIII: 174; Rutherford, *The Covenant of Life*, 300.

In response to the Father's oath, Keach claims, the Son everlastingly struck hands with him for us. In the temporal order, Jesus ratified this pact by his death (Heb.9.16-17). In addition, Keach says that the temporal ratification (i.e., Christ's death), made the compact irrevocable: "...no man disanulleth or addeth thereunto" (Gal.3.15).[158]

The covenant of peace, Keach affirms, has always been the instrument through which God has dealt with humanity: "all God's elect who lived under the Old Testament dispensation, received the grace and blessings thereof, through faith in Christ's death, who they knew would come in the fullness of time, and by his blood confirm his covenant." In the fullness of time, God laid the responsibilities of the pact on Christ's shoulders and his death "is the great and sure ratification and confirmation of the covenant of peace."[159] The continuity of the covenant under both Testaments is a platitudinous feature of Reformed Orthodoxy: "The judgment of most Reformed divines is, that the church under the Old Testament had the same promise of Christ, the same interest in him by faith, remission of sins, reconciliation with God, justification and salvation by the same way and means, that believers have under the New." Owen goes on, "[a]nd whereas the essence and the substance of the covenant consists in these things, they are not to be said to be under *another covenant*, but only a *different administration* of it."[160]

Following this, Keach asks: for what end did Christ die? Besides dying to ratify the eternal covenant, he also "took away the [old], that he might establish the [new]" (Heb.10.9). That is, the Old Testament rules and regulations were set aside by Christ's death. Although old dispensation saints were saved by the sacrifice of Christ, they nevertheless were still under the law-obligation of

---

[158] Keach, *Display of Glorious Grace*, 109-113. Cf. Owen, *Works*, XI: 288, XIX: 578.

[159] Keach, *Display of Glorious Grace*, 127. In order to argue for the unity of the covenant throughout the Testaments—i.e., that from Adam all the way to Christ the covenant is basically the same—Keach points to Eph.2.12, "...at that time ye were without Christ, being aliens from the commonwealth of Israel, and strangers from the covenants of promise, having no hope, and without God in the world." He argues that Paul uses the plural, 'covenants,' concerning the many "revelations, or declarations of it, as to Adam, Abraham, David, &c. and as revealed in the Gospel, tho it is but one and the same covenant." Truly, "it may differ in some accidents, but in substance it was the same, viz., Jesus Christ promised and free justification through him." Does not the Apostle affirm the unity of it? "Is the law against the promises? That is, is the law, as given on Mount Sinai, against the covenant of grace? No, but given in subserviency thereunto; or as leading to it by discovering the evil of sin and the absolute necessity of Christ's perfect obedience thereunto in our stead." Ibid., 181.

[160] Owen, *Works*, XXII: 86. His emphasis. Old Testament believers were redeemed by faith in the Messiah, just as we are. The saints before Christ had only a promise which God made "the great foundation of the covenant of grace; and afterward declared, confirmed, and ratified by his oath, that covenant wherein all the means of bringing the elect unto glory are contained..." Idem, *Works*, I: 220, XIX: 465.

'works' or 'do this and live.' This obligation was transferred to the Son who complied with all legal requirements, and consequently broke the condemning power of the law upon believers. The saints,

> who lived under the Old Testament were saved by the covenant of grace Christ was to establish, as I said before; yet was not the old covenant actually taken away till Christ died, the latter covenant is called an everlasting covenant; not, I say again, that the first, as to righteousness, is ceased or disannulled; no, but as a covenant of works, requiring perfect righteousness of us in our own persons, if ever we are justified in God's sight; but that the perfect obedience, which the law required of us is transmitted to another head, i.e., Christ Jesus, who having answered all its demands in point of obedience and righteousness, so that 'He is the end of the law, as touching righteousness, to every one that believeth;' insomuch that the law cannot *curse* or *condemn* them that are in Christ Jesus (Rom.10.4).[161]

The Proclamation of Peace

As usual, Keach compares human proclamations of peace with God's. This proclamation is thus presented: i. The proclamation of peace defined; ii. The heralds of the proclamation; iii. The conditions on which it is proclaimed.

The Proclamation of Peace Defined

"The proclamation of the covenant of peace is the Gospel of Jesus Christ. Hence the Gospel is called the word of reconciliation, and the Gospel of peace" (2Cor.5.19; Eph.6.15). How can we know that the Gospel is this proclamation? First and foremost, herein, and nowhere else, is found the reconciling mechanism between an offended God and an offending humanity. In other words, through the Gospel, God is "declared to be reconciled or pacified toward sinners, even in Jesus Christ; 'to wit, that God was in Christ, reconciling the world to himself, not imputing their trespasses unto them'" (2Cor.5.19).[162] On the basis of this reconciliation, many were claiming that all were reconciled.[163] As a result, Keach briefly defends limited atonement. He maintains that if all were reconciled, salvation would then be unavoidable to all. In other words, if the death of Jesus brought about reconciliation to all, so much more would his life bring salvation to all; "for so Paul argues in respect of all them that God by the death of his Son, was reconciled to: 'for if when we were enemies, we were reconciled to God by the death of his Son, much more

---

[161] Keach, *Display of Glorious Grace*, 114.

[162] Keach, *Display of Glorious Grace*, 120.

[163] Cf. e.g., The General Baptist's *An Orthodox Creed, or, A Protestant Confession of Faith* (London: s.n., 1679), s.v., 'Article XVIII: Of Christ Dying for All Mankind.'

being reconciled, we shall be saved by his life'" (Rom.5.10). Keach proceeds, it is irrational to conceive of God giving a large gift to us and denying a small one. Would God save a person and let him fall from his hands? Would God reconcile a sinner and then deny him perseverance? Furthermore, "if he had reconciled the whole world to God, he would have prayed for the whole world, but that he saith he did not, yet he prayed for all he died for" (Joh.17.9).[164] Needless to say, limited atonement is standard Reformed Orthodox: "For whose offences he died, for their justification he rose—and therefore, if he died for all, all must be justified, or the Lord failed in his aim and design, both in the death and resurrection of his Son; which though some have boldly affirmed, yet for my part I cannot but abhor the owing of so blasphemous a fancy."[165]

Next, this Gospel, which proclaims the reconciliation of God to sinners, also announces the reconciliation of sinners to God. By dint of it, a bilateral peace is established. First, peace is established between God and the elect; then, in time, it is established between the elect and God, as our hostility is taken away and union with God takes place.[166] It follows that the Gospel reveals a power to remove the above hostility, hence it is called 'the power of God' (Rom.1.16). It is this power brought about by the sacrifice of Christ—not our faith, sanctity or any other thing—that enables us to be reconciled to God. In effect, peace, on God's part, precedes our faith—our faith only apprehends or grabs hold of our temporal justification. In other words, "justification is the effect of reconciliation."[167] It is noteworthy that Keach stresses that faith *qua* faith does not justify. Faith, he maintains, is not "a quality or habit...as the papists teach; *ipsa fides*, saith Bellarmine, *censetur esse justitia*, faith it self is counted to be a justice, and it self is imputed unto righteousness."[168] Rather, faith only seizes the substance of justification, viz., the work of Christ. That is, faith is merely "a hand to take hold of, or receive, or apply Christ and his righteousness." Alternatively, "*Manus accipientis*...the hand of the receiver is grace of justifying faith. 'Tis not faith, but the object and righteousness faith apprehends or takes hold of, that justifies the ungodly."[169]

---

[164] Keach, *Display of Glorious Grace*, 120.

[165] Owen, *Works*, X: 240. Cf. Idem, *Works*, XIX: 464; Gillespie, *The Ark of the Covenant*, 80-81.

[166] Keach, *Display of Glorious Grace*, 121. Yet again we see Keach's balance of eternity and time. The covenant is absolute, but history is nonetheless meaningful.

[167] Keach, *Display of Glorious Grace*, 121-122.

[168] Cf. e.g., Robert Bellarmine, *Disputationum Roberti Bellarmini, de Controversiis Christianae Fidei, adversus huius Temporis Haereticos, Quatuor Tomis Comprehensarum* (Coloniae Agrippinae: Sumptibus Ioannis Gymnici, sub Monocerote, 1628), s.v., 'De Justificatione,' Tom. 4, Lib. II, cap. iv, col. f-g.

[169] Keach, *Marrow of Justification*, 6. Justification by faith does not mean "any moral or physical causality in faith as qualification, but only by virtue of its object." Chauncy, *Neonomianism*, 238. Baxter, on the other hand, ultimately rejects objectivity to faith, and calls it "darkness, and either non-sense or false doctrine." *Of Justification*, 310.

The role of faith is an important point of divergence between Baxterians and mainline Orthodoxy, Keach claims. Clark, for example, is compared to Bellarmine in that he asserts that faith is to be understood subjectively.[170] Clark affirms,

> I would avoid many figurative expositions of Scripture, which others are feign to make use of to salve their phenomena, as when we are said to be justified by faith, they take it metonimically for the object of faith, viz., the righteousness of Christ; which what is it else than to make the Scripture a meer nose of wax, and a laden rule, and to comply with our fancies.[171]

Keach reacts to Clark's statement asking, "[w]hat is now become of that doctrine Paul preached and all our worthy Reformers? How will this make the Papists and Quakers smile."[172] However, how exactly does faith function according to Baxterians? It "is not, according to Clark, the object of faith, not Jesus Christ that faith apprehends and we alone trust in, but it is faith that justifieth us comprehensively taken; that is, faith, love, charity, good works and sincere obedience that is imputed to us, to our justification in the sight of God." As a result justification is partial or incomplete, i.e., "so far as you act in faith, holiness and sincere obedience, so far are you justified."[173] This "erroneous" view of partial justification, as Keach sees it, stems from a confusion between justification and sanctification, for whenever these two are mixed or confused, justification becomes incomplete since nobody can be completely holy.[174] A consequence of this Baxterianism, Keach claims, it to make the Roman Church right in affirming that on this life we cannot be completely certain of our salvation.[175]

> If famous Luther and other worthy Reformers had wrought no better Reformation than this, the church of God would have received but little benefit from them, but the notion of Mr Clark and his abettors certainly tends to raze and root out that antient doctrine which the Apostles preached, and those worthy men laboured to restore about justification. Did Bellarmine ever deny that their good works and inherent holiness,

---

[170] Keach, *Medium Betwixt Two Extremes*, 37. Subjective faith (*fides 'qua' creditur*) is the faith 'by which' one believes, i.e., the belief itself. Objective faith (*fides 'quae' creditur*) is the faith 'which' is believed, i.e., the matter, content, or substance of faith.
[171] Clark, *Scripture Justification*, 85. Cf. Baxter, *Aphorismes*, 202-335.
[172] Keach, *Medium Betwixt Two Extremes*, 37.
[173] Keach, *Medium Betwixt Two Extremes*, 37 and Clark, *Scripture Justification*, 18.
[174] Keach, *Marrow of Justification*, 12. All three—Baxter, Williams and Clark—deemed justification as gradual or incomplete: *Aphorismes*, 149; *Gospel Truth*, 55; *Scripture Justification*, 18.
[175] Keach, *Medium Betwixt Two Extremes*, 37-38. Cf. e.g., Bellarmine, *De Controversiis Christianae Fidei*, s.v., 'De Justificatione,' Tom. 4, Lib. II, cap. vii, col. b.

which they made the matter of justification before God, were performed by the grace of God and the assistance of the Holy Spirit?[176]

That Keach sees himself as mainstream Reformed, can be seen by both the claims he makes and the supports he seeks. He avers that, "all Orthodox divines agree with us that faith, neither as a habit, or grace, or as an act, much less in respect of the fruits thereof, justifies us: when therefore 'tis said we are justified by faith, it intends not any moral or physical causality in faith as qualification, but only by virtue of the object it apprehends." To substantiate his position, Keach appeals to Zanchi and the Westminster Assembly, among others.[177]

The Heralds of the Proclamation of Peace

The greatest and most important herald of the covenant of peace is the Son himself, "hence he is called the messenger of the covenant. 'The Lord whom ye seek, shall suddenly come to his temple, even the messenger of the covenant'" (Mal.3.1). "Messenger," says Keach, means "an ambassador, מלאכי."[178]

Several reasons are presented as to why Christ is the main ambassador of peace. To start with, the Son was given power to finish the transactions they had eternally treated, "I was set up from everlasting" (Pro.8.23). Next, only the Son knew the implications of humanity's sin and affront to God sufficiently well to announce them to us properly. Moreover, he is called the messenger because he was appointed or commissioned to be such: "the Father that sent me, is with me" (Mat.11.27). Finally, since only God knew the covenant, only

---

[176] Keach, *Medium Betwixt Two Extremes*, 38. Cf. e.g., Bellarmine, *De Controversiis Christianae Fidei*, s.v., 'De Poenitentia,' Tom. 3, Lib. II, cap. xii, col. c-d.

[177] Keach, *Medium Betwixt Two Extremes*, 22-23: "Nam neque actione fidei nostrae iustificamur: sed ea re tantum, quae per fidem apprehenditur, quae est Christus cum sua obediencia, iusti censemur. Et sic illud intelligo, *Credidit Abraham Deo & imputatum est illi ad iustitiam*. Quid reputatum ad iustitiam? Non actio qua: sed id quod credidit, seu, ut alij loquuntur, ipsa fides, non fui apprehendentis, sed obiecti apprehensi respectu." Jerome Zanchius, *Hieronymi Zanchii Theologi clarissimi in D. Pauli Apostoli Epistolas ad Philippenses, Colossenses, Thessalonicenses, Et Duo priora capita primae Epistolae D. Iohanni Commentarii, in quibus et textus Apostoli accurate explicatur: & multi loci communes Theologiae solide pertractantur* Editio altera recognita et aucta (Neustadii Palatinorum: Apud haeredes Wilhelmi Harnisij, 1601), s.v., 'Ad Philippenses,' III:9. "How doth faith justifie a sinner in the sight of God? Faith justifies a sinner in the sight of God, not because of those other graces that do always accompany it, or good works, which are the fruits thereof, nor as if the grace of faith, or any act thereof were imputed to him for justification; but only as instrument by which he receiveth and applieth Christ and his righteousness." *The Confession of Faith, the Larger & Shorter Catechism*, (S.l.: s.n., 1688 ed.), 143. Keach also refers to the *Second Helvetic Confession* and to John Bradford (1510?-1550), ibid. Cf. Rutherford, *The Covenant of Life*, 170; Chauncy, *Neonomianism*, 238.

[178] Keach, *Display of Glorious Grace*, 131-132.

he in the Son could reveal all to humanity, "...I have given them the words that thou gavest me" (Joh.17.8).[179] That Christ deems himself a messenger, Owen maintains, is testified by the Scripture which says "'I will declare it'—recount it in order, number the particulars that belong unto it, and so distinctly and evidently make it known. Ἀπαλλελῶ, 'I will make it known as a messenger, sent from thee and by thee.'"[180]

Although Christ is the chief ambassador, he has commissioned others to be heralds of the Gospel, namely, ministers of his church. However, not all ministers are included herein, for there are many heretics who preach a law-Gospel or an adulterated and false message. With Baxterians in mind, Keach attacks those promoting a new law Christ had bought for us, a new law of "imperfect faith and sincere obedience, as the matter and condition of justification before God."[181] Such a position, Keach maintains, understands Christ's sacrifice buying this new law and under this new jurisdiction human imperfections are "not proper sins. *Praeter, non contra legem*, as the Papists say." Which law is this, Keach asks. All sin against God is damnable whether committed before or after the sacrifice of Christ. If obedience of any kind is to be introduced in point of justification, Keach hypothetically argues, it must be perfect. For thus it was with the *foedus operum*.[182] This Baxterian principle of sincere obedience is flawed, Keach claims, on the mere grounds of conscience, not to mention the Scriptures. Which person would rely on his own obedience, however sincere, when he stands before the judgement seat of Christ? Surely he would "say with Anselm, *Terret me vita mea*...My life doth terrifie me. Alas, what man is fully able to say he is perfect or that he sincerely has done all his duty in respect of that milder law of obedience which they talk of?"[183] Owen, a relentless enemy of Baxterianism, also states that "the Gospel is no new law" and Jesus no "new law giver; yea, he declares the contrary—that he came to confirm the old, Mat.5.17."[184]

The Conditions on which the Covenant of Peace is Proclaimed

All the terms and conditions rest on faith. The proclamation is thus announced:

---

[179] Keach, *Display of Glorious Grace*, 132-134. Cf. Gillespie, *The Ark of the Covenant*, 21.

[180] Owen, *Works*, XIX: 519. Cf. Ibid. 617.

[181] Keach, *Display of Glorious Grace*, 135. "I say," Clark avers, "what else can be the plain meaning of it, but that, as perfect obedience to the law was law-righteousness, so faith or sincere obedience to the Gospel, is Gospel-righteousness?" *Scripture Justification*, 64. Cf. Williams, *Gospel Truth*, 102.

[182] Keach, *Marrow of Justification*, 27.

[183] Keach, *Marrow of Justification*, 29. Anselm, *Sancti Anselmi ex Beccensi Abbate Canturiensis Archiepiscopi Opera* (Parisiis: Sumptib. Ludovici Billaine et Joannis Du Puis, 1675), s.v., 'Meditatio II.'

[184] Owen, *Works*, I: 183.

"whosoever believeth shall be saved."[185] However, we cannot produce faith ourselves, Keach claims, God is the one who works out faith in our hearts. "Faith draws virtue from Christ, but the branch cannot draw sap from the root, until it is grafted into the stock; faith is the fruit of the Spirit, therefore the seed must be first sown in our hearts." What is then the genesis of faith in our hearts? Keach's answer seems to have two dimensions: one eternal, and the other the outwork of it in time. He claims that, firstly, faith "proceeds from our foederal union with Christ, in the covenant of peace. And secondly, by our mystical union with him by the Spirit; for it is hereby faith is wrought."[186] We have already shown Keach's balance between human faith and God's initiative.[187] This mysterious tension between real and proper human belief on the one hand, and, on the other, the action of God is a common feature of Reformed Orthodoxy:

> Unto a full and complete interest in all the promises of the covenant, faith on our part, from which evangelical repentance is inseparable, is required. But whereas these also are wrought in us by virtue of that promise and grace of the covenant which is absolute, it is a mere strife about words to contend whether they may call conditions or not. Let it be granted on the one hand, that we cannot have an actual participation of the relative grace of this covenant in adoption and justification, without faith or believing; and on the other, that this faith is wrought in us, given unto us, bestowed upon us, by that grace of the covenant which depends on no condition in us as unto its discriminating administration, and I shall not concern myself what men will call it.[188]

The proclamation of the covenant announces that the creator is "our Father, and we his sons and daughters, upon receiving Jesus Christ." No sin is excluded from this proclamation—sins committed in the past and present as well as sins to be committed, all of them are freely proclaimed, "pardoned!" Furthermore, enough grace is provided to keep us within the covenant until the end. Moreover, in whichever city or nation the elect are found, this message will be proclaimed with the chosen ones brought into the fold of the covenant. Finally,

---

[185] At this junction, it is worth mentioning the contrast Keach makes between the pacts of works and grace. He says that the *foedus operum* is based on deeds, "do this and live;" the *foedus gratiae* is based on faith, "believe on the Lord Jesus Christ and thou shalt be saved" (Joh.3.16). Keach puts it rather neatly: the first "puts men upon working or doing *for* life; the other puts them upon believing and working *from* life." *Display of Glorious Grace*, 180.

[186] Keach, *Display of Glorious Grace*, 164-165.

[187] See supra p. 71. For futher support, see infra p. 183.

[188] Owen, *Works*, XXII: 166-167. Cf. Gillespie, *The Ark of the Covenant*, 88; Rutherford, *The Covenant of Life*, 12-13, 16.

though salvation is accomplished by God alone, in the end God will show that humanity's "destruction is of themselves, tho their help is only in God."[189]

Commencement of the Covenant of Peace

Although the covenant of peace is eternal, it had a commencement in time. It was first put partially in place when Adam broke the first covenant, viz., the *foedus operum*. Afterwards, the unfolding of the covenant of peace is increasingly clearer, as seen in Abraham, Sinai, David, and finally in Christ, wherein the treaty of peace was fully implemented: "He took away the first, that he might establish the second." Inclusion in the covenant is restricted to the elect alone, though the entire race benefits from it; for if this covenant with its mediator had not been in place when we fell, "the whole visible fabrick doubtless had been dissolved, and the whole race of mankind lost for ever."[190]

The Nature of the Covenant of Peace

Concerning the nature of the covenant, there are three aspects to be shown: its unity, equivalence and absoluteness.

THE UNITY OF THE COVENANT

In the seventeenth century the number of covenants was a bone of contention. For example, Baxterians, among others, were advocating that besides the covenant of works, God had made two other pacts: the eternal *ad intra* covenant of redemption; and, the temporal *ad extra* covenant of grace or reconciliation. Keach asks, if the covenant, whichever name it might receive, was graciously done through the suretyship of Christ, why is there this dichotomy between redemption and grace? The Apostle is pressed into service, "...how is it Paul saith, 'God was in Christ reconciling the world to himself?' Indeed, as far as I can see," Keach contends, "this notion or two distinct covenants of redemption and grace," appears to substantiate the mistaken claims of those who say that "in the covenant of redemption...Christ made God amends for our breach of the law of perfect obedience, by himself alone and for himself only," in order that "he might be a fit mediator and merit a new law of faith and sincere obedience...which law or covenant he confirmed by his death."[191]

According to this scheme, Keach continues, God establishes a covenant of grace with human beings on the basis of their performance of "the conditions of it, or so far as they do, so far they shall be justified, and shall have eternal life,

---

[189] Keach, *Display of Glorious Grace*, 168-169.
[190] Keach, *Display of Glorious Grace*, 181, 170-171. Cf. Owen, *Works*, XVIII: 105.
[191] Keach, *Display of Glorious Grace*, 212.

provided they continue unto the end;" for "Christ is our legal righteousness in the covenant of redemption, he fulfilled the law of works, or the strict law of perfect obedience; but our faith, inherent-righteousness, Gospel-holiness and sincere obedience, is our evangelical righteousness; or that which justifies us at Gods bar or in his sight."[192] Keach exclaims, "...this dangerous error, I say, seems to follow the allowing two distinct covenants!"[193] Although there are two aspects under which the covenant should be considered, as we shall see hereafter, there is no need to infer from it two different covenants, Keach alleges. That is, the temporal and the eternal aspects of the covenant are theoretical explanations drawn from the biblical material. The grace that the elect receive upon their calling was eternally given to the federal head: "Who hath saved us and called us, not according to our works but according to his own purpose and grace which was given us in Christ before the world began" (2Tim.1.9). In other words, the eternal covenant of peace *includes* reconciliation with the elect; for they are not only made righteous but also freed from sin (Zac.9.11). To support his point that there is no separate covenant of redemption, but rather only two pacts, grace and works, Keach quotes the Westminster catechism,

> Q. 30. 'Doth God leave mankind to perish in a state of sin and misery? Answ. God doth not leave all mankind to perish in a state of sin and misery, into which they fell by the breach of the first covenant, called the covenant of works; but of his meer love and mercy delivereth his elect out of it, and bringeth them into a state of salvation, by the second covenant, commonly called the covenant of grace.'
> Q. 31. 'With whom was the covenant of grace made? Answ. The covenant of grace was made with Christ as the second Adam, and in him with all the elect as his seed.' Thus [Keach says] that learned Assembly.[194]

THE COVENANT OF PEACE IS EQUIVALENT TO THE PACT OF GRACE

The argument against the equivalence of the two covenants is usually made in order to give a role to human beings. Otherwise, it was thought, Antinomianism would always try to rear its ugly head. Nevertheless, Keach warns about preaching a "conditional covenant." What is meant by this, he explains, is that "repentance, faith, regeneration and obedience" are turned into conditions of entry into the covenant. These conditions are impossible to perform, and more importantly, if that were the case, the graceful covenant would rather be a

---

[192] This is a summary of Baxterianism. Cf. Baxter, *Aphorismes*, 82-83; Williams, *Gospel Truth*, 86-87; Clark, *Scripture Justification*, 26-30. Cf. also with our own outline, supra, pp. 74-75.
[193] Keach, *Display of Glorious Grace*, 212-213.
[194] Keach, *Display of Glorious Grace*, 216.

foedus operum, for one would have to work to have peace with God.[195] Keach is adamant that entrance into the covenant is by gracious *promise* and not by obedience to any law (Rom.1.14; Gal.3.8). However, why is it that human beings play no part? Keach claims that it is so because the honour of salvation ought not to be ours but God's. Additionally, it must be by grace alone in order to make it sure—to make it certain that all the elect would be saved; else it would depend upon some human performance and, consequently, be not certain.[196]

To make the covenants of redemption and grace equivalent, or to make a single covenant out of these two pacts, entails seeing the covenant under two aspects. On the side of Christ, Keach purports, this covenant is *conditional*, for it is based on his sacrifice and the worth of his works. He acquired all that would be given to us. On our side, the compact is absolute, for all the benefits we receive are freely given.[197] Such favour, Keach affirms, is incomprehensible: "It was the free grace of God the Father to vouchsafe us a substitute, a saviour, a mediator of this peace, and to choose, ordain, and appoint his Son to be the person and to accept him in our stead." Not only the goodness of the Father, but also the goodness of the Son is magnificently displayed.

> See how the mediator prevails with God, for instead of God's demanding an inherent righteousness, a righteousness wrought out in our own persons; he accepts of an imputed righteousness wrought out in the person of his Son in our nature as mediator, 'who of God is made unto us, wisdom and righteousness, and sanctification, and redemption'—in the Lord, shall one say, have I righteousness and strength [1Cor.1.30][198]

Therefore, the Bible bears witness, Keach claims, to both the gratuitousness and everlasting character of the covenant, (2Tim.1.9); as well as to its temporal nature. They interact, as seen in that all the grace we are given in time is the consequence of the "covenant of peace made with us in Christ before all time."

---

[195] Cf. The first pact was made *conditionally* with our parents. The same covenant had a "second addition" made with the Hebrews—made with the same condition of obedience (Exo. 19.5-6). The covenant of grace, on the other hand, is *unconditional*. Keach, *Display of Glorious Grace*, 178.

[196] Keach, *Display of Glorious Grace*, 175-176. The *foedus operum* was made up of ordinances, commands and precepts; some of them moral and others ceremonial. The *foedus gratiae* was, as far as humanity is concerned, made up of promises. "Hence the elect are called, 'the children of promise'" (Rom.9.8). Ibid., 181.

[197] Cf. The *conditions* of work and obedience were imposed on Christ to fulfil them; however, "they are ours freely for no price or hire." Rutherford, *The Covenant of Life*, 314.

[198] Keach, *Display of Glorious Grace*, 20-21, 59.

What an inconceivable grace, Keach marvels, that a king would provide his own son as mediator, surety and sacrifice for his enemies.[199]

THE ABSOLUTENESS OF THE COVENANT OF GRACE

Everything God has promised to accomplish in us is irrevocable and not subject to contingencies. It is so because it does not depend on us. All the work, including the terms or conditions of peace, is done by grace which is provided for us by God himself. In other words, ultimately, it is God who performs the work in and through us, it is he, "who works in us to will and to do of his own good pleasure" (Phili.2.3).[200]

In a systematic way, Keach puts this heading as follows: first, the absolute character of the pact is shown by the fact that nothing is earned by humanity: salvation and all the benefits thereof come about through the *absolute will* of the Father, who placed the conditions of the covenant upon the federal shoulders of the Son. Second, in the temporal realm, the power to bring the elect within the sphere of the covenant—i.e., the power to resurrect the elect—is unconditionally done by God. That this is so can be seen in, third, the absoluteness of the promises. "Thus it was to Adam, to Abraham, to David and to us; 'I will be your God and you shall be my people.' It is not that you shall have peace," pardon and salvation if you perform this, that or the other. On the contrary, "...he that worketh not, but believeth on him that justifieth the ungodly" (Rom.4.5). Duty, obedience, love or any other work are all excluded.[201] However, one may object that the covenant is not absolute since it

---

[199] Keach, *Display of Glorious Grace*, 19-21. Arguably more than any other tradition, the Reformed has tended to make the gap between God and humanity unbridgeable, thus stressing salvation's monergism. Calvin states "that God's making a covenant with man is as great an evidence of his favour as if an earthly king would make a covenant with a swineherd." 'Sermon on Deut. 26.16-19,' cited by Lillbeck, *The Binding of God*, 138. Along the same lines, Owen declares, unfathomable "condescention it is in God, that he will enter into covenant with dust and ashes, with poor worms of the earth." Owen, *Works*, XXII: 82. See also, Ibid., 447; XIX: 514-516; Rutherford, *The Covenant of Life*, 15-16, 300.

[200] Keach, *Display of Glorious Grace*, 167. The *foedus operum* imposed personal obedience, yet provided no power to accomplish it. The *foedus gratiae* had, on one side, the Son—and his seed in him—performing all the conditions required by it. Here Christ and the elect are presented as a unit, that is, what we are said to have performed, we did so in him; "that the righteousness of the law might be fulfilled in us" (Rom.8.3). On the other side, God has provided the Holy Spirit to accomplish in us all that we must perform. For example, if faith is required, faith is given (Eph. 2.8); if a new heart is needed, "he hath promised to give us a new heart and to put a new Spirit into us" (Eze.36.26)...Ibid., 178.

[201] Cf. the whole heading so far with Chauncy, *Neonomianism*, 116: the *foedus gratiae* is freely and absolutely given, as seen in its revelation "to Adam, Abraham, David, and in

requires faith. Keach has a prompt answer. "True, there are in the covenant, conditions of connexion; if a man believes, he shall be saved. But who gives that faith? Is it not God? Pray observe that Jesus Christ hath made our peace, and faith to receive the atonement is given as an absolute promise." Hence, the Spirit is freely granted. "And pray, doth not God give the Spirit before faith can be exerted by us? Is not faith 'the fruit of the Spirit?' And doth not the fruit proceed from the seed, and the act flow from the habit?"[202] That said, it is important to note yet again that Keach gives faith an *active* role in justification. The Holy Spirit regenerates the elect—which is a passive process—but as a result of regeneration, people actively put their faith in, or receive, Christ.[203] Likewise, Owen affirms "that our *own wills*, or the free actings of them, are required in our faith and obedience; whence it is promised that we shall 'be willing in the day of his power.'"[204]

Evaluation and Conclusion

One should treat with a certain amount of scepticism Keach's claim that his covenantal scheme had been used by almost nobody.[205] Contrary to what he purports, many individuals within the Reformed tradition joined the covenant of grace with the covenant of redemption: for example, Tobias Crisp, Isaac Chauncy, John Saltmarsh, William Perkins, William Ames *et alii*, did just that, and did so before him.[206] Thus Keach's pretention to virtual uniqueness does not

---

the Gospel-Dispensation since Christ...The absoluteness of this covenant appears to us in that all the federal entitling conditions contained in it, is to be found in another, and not in us, nor wrought in us; for whatever is wrought in us is from free gift and of promise, and must have some condition performed by another as Federal, before we can partake of it."

[202] Keach, *Display of Glorious Grace*, 182-184. The absoluteness of the pact with faith as *promised* condition is standard Reformed Orthodox. "...faith here is to believe that the condition it self is promised, as well as the reward." Rutherford, *The Covenant of Life*, 16. Cf. Owen, *Works*, XXII: 83, 166-168; Chauncy, *Neonomianism*, 117, 150; Gillespie, *The Ark of the Covenant*, 88.

[203] Keach, *Medium Betwixt Two Extremes*, 23-24. It is impossible, Keach affirms, to be united "to Christ without a hearty consent: for as no person must have a true knowledge of Christ, so he must yield to accept of him; for a marriage ought to be a voluntary transaction of both persons, Jesus Christ accepteth of the sinner, embraces the sinner, and the sinner accepteth of Christ, they give themselves to each other: as Christ first chose us, so we chose him, it is a free and ready act of the will." Idem, *Exposition of the Parables*, I: 405.

[204] Owen, *Works*, XXII: 166-167. Cf. Gillespie, *The Ark of the Covenant*, 88; Rutherford, *The Covenant of Life*, 12-13, 16.

[205] Supra pp. 48-49.

[206] Crisp, *Christ Alone Exalted*, 74-110, 241-259; Chauncy, *Neonomianism*, 27; Saltmarsh, *Free-Grace*, 125-127; for references to Perkins, Ames and others, see

stand scrutiny. Why, then, does he adopt this kind of covenant theology?

The reason why Keach makes the eternal pact of redemption and the temporal covenant of grace one and the same is to disallow any hint of human participation in the process of justification. The threat he faced, Baxterianism, granted humanity a part in the said process. It is worth repeating that Baxterians understood justification as incomplete on this side of eternity.[207] This fact, we believe, explains Keach's leaning towards the Antinomian side of the spectrum, though not as far as actually embracing Antinomianism. What about his claims to pursue a middle ground between the extremes of Baxterianism and Antinomianism? Keach himself avers that there were many who had given up "the true Orthodox faith, as to some of the main fundamental principles thereof; and either sucking in Socinian errors, or Baxterian errors, or some as bad as they; being sadly corrupted in and about the doctrine of justification..." On the other hand, "some of them [i.e., the Antinomians], as at this day assert, that unbelievers and vile ungodly sinners, may be actually justified and in a good state."[208] Given what we presented throughout this chapter, there is no need to supply further proof of Keach's repudiation of Baxterianism: *Display of Glorious Grace* was an attack on it. Concerning Keach's rejection of Antinomianism, we may add two things: 1. A further comment on a point briefly mentioned, viz., the place of the Law;[209] and, 2. a new piece of evidence, namely, justification from eternity.

The Place of the Law

The tension between obedience to the Law on the one hand and, on the other, the grace of God was a problem for Puritanism. The Antinomians rejected the combination of the two; mainline Orthodoxy saw this combination as essential.[210] A way to reconcile these two poles was to make the Law as a rule of life for believers—a position usually embraced by mainstream Reformed.[211] Indeed, on this point we find a general agreement by the majority in the Orthodox tradition.[212] The moral law, as encapsulated in the Ten Commandments, is binding upon all humanity, and Christians are to be directed by it concerning their duty and God's will for their lives. Keach's position is

---

Richard Muller, 'The Spirit and the Covenant: John Gill's Critique of the *Pactum Salutis*,' in *FBJHT* 24/1 (January-March, 1981): 4-14, p. 5.

[207] See supra p. 99, footnote 174.
[208] Keach, *Exposition of the Parables*, I: 145.
[209] See supra pp. 70-71.
[210] McGiffert, 'Perkinsian Moment of Federal Theology,' 134.
[211] Karlberg, 'Reformed Interpretation of the Mosaic Covenant,' 40. Cf. Møller, *The Beginnings of Puritan Covenant Theology*, 63.
[212] Owen, *Works*, V: 193, 316; Rutherford, *The Covenant of Life*, 199; Gillespie, *The Ark of the Covenant*, 406, 412; Chauncy, *Neonomianism*, 111; *The Westminster Confession of Faith*, XIX: 2.

standard: "When the Apostle saith, 'by the works of the Law no flesh shall be justified', he doth not mean only the Law as in the hands of Moses, but also as it is anew given forth by Jesus Christ; for we are still under obedience to the Moral Law..." It is worth paying attention to the way in which Keach makes the point explicitly as he continues: "By the Law is meant that rule of life God hath given, whether as written in the heart, or given by Moses, or as given anew by Christ as a rule of life to us. Lust is a breach of Christ's Law...as well as it was given by Moses."[213]

Justification from Eternity

It was not uncommon to see Baxterians accusing their adversaries of holding 'justification from eternity.' Richard Baxter, for example, challenges the "Antinomians" to show a single passage of "Scripture which speaks of justification from eternity."[214] Eternal justification is the concept that faith plays no real part in one's salvation; that one is not only elected but also justified eternally; that the historical event of justification is a mere awareness of one's eternal state. The three Antinomians we studied—Crisp, Denne and Saltmarsh—described justification as preceeding faith.[215] On the whole, mainline Reformed denied justification from eternity. Owen emphatically rejects the idea: "I do not believe that any man is *actually justified from eternity*..."[216] Keach is also very clear on his refusal of eternal justification: The elect, he maintains, were not made righteous at the moment when the Father and the Son agreed the terms of peace. It is the prerogative of the creditor to say at what time the debtor has been acquitted, since the terms were laid down by him. Furthermore, it is obvious that we did not exist "when Christ struck hands for us; besides, it was for such that he foresaw would fall under sin, wrath and condemnation, and Christ did not become a surety to keep the elect from falling under wrath and the sentence of death, but to recover them out of that state..." Additionally, he affirms that "justification presupposeth we were once charged and condemned."[217]

A final feature of Keach's covenantal scheme worth highlighting is his balance between eternity and time. Frequently, we have seen how, on the one hand, he stresses the unconditional nature of the pact, with all the elect eternally

---

[213] Keach, *Marrow of Justification*, 24.

[214] Baxter, *Aphorismes*, 60.

[215] See Crisp, Christ Alone Exalted, 100; Denne, *Seven Arguments*, 4; John Saltmarsh, *Sparkles of glory, or Some beams of the morning-star. Wherein are many discoveries as to truth, and peace. To the establishment, and pure enlargement of a Christian in spirit and truth*, 2nd ed. (London: Printed for Giles Calvert, and are to be sold at the Black-spred-Eagle, at the West end of Pauls, 1647), 191-192.

[216] Owen, *Works*, XII: 791. His italics. See also, ibid., 792; II: 221. Cf. Rutherford, *The Covenant of Life*, 209; Chauncy, *Neonomianism*, 52, 230.

[217] Keach, *Display of Glorius Grace*, 102.

included in Christ; and, on the other hand, how he emphasises the actuality of human history, the reality of union between the elect and the Holy Spirit within the temporal realm. To put the point in a different way, Keach's covenantal scheme correctly leaves in tension the eternal nature of election, and the temporal conversion of the same elect. A final illustration may be put forth: Keach cites Act.18.10 thus. "'I have much people in this city;' they were his people *decretively*, though not *actually* his at that time."[218]

To sum up our thoughts, we may close this chapter with a comment concerning Keach's place within the Reformed Orthodox tradition. His covenantal scheme shows abundant parallels with those of other mainstream Reformed thinkers. In addition to that, we have him acting as if he were a defender of the tradition. On the one hand he sees Baxterianism—or any form of moralism which may impinge on the absoluteness of the covenant—as a threat to the utter gratuitous nature of salvation. On the other hand, he avoids Antinomianism. We may say, therefore, that our author makes a genuine attempt to pursue a middle way within Orthodoxy.

---

[218] Keach, *Display of Glorious Grace*, 243. His emphasis.

CHAPTER THREE

Keach's Doctrine of Baptism

Introductory Considerations

It is not possible to overemphasise the role of baptism in the early decades of the life of 'Baptists'.[1] After all, they placed so much importance on this rite as expressed by their overt denominational label. However, we are going to see in this chapter that the fundamental issue is not baptism *qua* baptism, but rather baptism as an element of the properly constituted, visible church. That is, the seventeenth century Baptists deemed that a defective baptism, as they saw it, affected the order or constitution of the said ecclesia.[2] We shall see herein that Keach desires to rid the visible church of pedobaptism by sprinkling, so as to give her what he believes to be an adequate organisation.

This chapter aims to show that Keach is a *theologian*. Our protagonist sees himself as a Reformer—a Reformer captive by his conscience over against the platitudinous principle of *sola Scriptura*. The first Reformers dealt with weightier doctrinal maters; the Baptists, Keach purports, are finalising the less important issues of church organisation. In other words, Keach does not perceive himself as an innovator, but rather as working—or theologising—to remove the remaining obstacles to the Reform of the church—i.e., to *restore* it to the biblical pattern.[3] Thus, as a Reformer, we argue, he is a theologian. This claim will be substantiated by the relentless and skilful interaction Keach makes with every argument levelled against credobaptism by immersion. For the sake of clarity, this chapter will be divided into three main sections. In the first one, we shall meet Keach's interlocutors; in the second section, we shall present his views of baptism, and in the last, we shall make an evaluation of

---

[1] As Vaughn concludes his investigation of Keach, he accurately affirms that nobody among the Baptists of Keach's "generation defended the Baptist understanding of baptism at greater length or with more passion" than our protagonist. Vaughn, 'Public Worship and Practical Theology,' 379.

[2] Cf. "The most fundamental contribution which Baptists made to Christian theology was a new vision for the visible church ...From this vision of the church has proceeded a particular view of the sacraments, church membership, denominational organisation beyond the local congregation, and of the ministry." Brackney, *The Baptists*, 37.

[3] For a general view of the Baptists on this issue, cf. e.g., the conclusion of Renihan's study, 'Practical Ecclesiology of the English Particular Baptists,' 372-379, especially, 378.

Keach's baptismal views.

Before we begin section one, two important points ought to be made. First, the reader will encounter Keach responding in a repetitive manner, to different objections with the same answer. One reason for this repetition is the simple fact that Keach thinks that the same answer addresses different objections from his antagonists. Another reason for this repetition on Keach's part is his attempt to expose an inconsistency in his opponent's views on baptism over against the Eucharist. A succinct example of this is seen when a complaining Keach is forced to reiterate his replies on account of Burkitt's[4] arguments for pedobaptism, which also "tend to prove infants ought to receive the Lord's Supper."[5] Both authors are against pedocommunion per se; Burkitt, however, argues that the reasons for admission to the Eucharist are different from those for baptism and, therefore, an infant can be baptised but cannot receive communion.[6] Keach denies that by saying that consistency demands that the two sacraments require confession of "faith and repentance as well as actual examination..."[7] The reader will see, reading on, other instances of Keach dealing with this type of supposed incongruity again and again.

The second point relates to Keach's indiscriminate use of authorities to support his arguments against both infant baptism and sprinkling. Hence, we shall see him citing Martin Luther, the high Anglican Jeremy Taylor, the Reformed Jerome Zanchi and a vast array of other authors—all of them to back his points. Obviously the broader context of the arguments of these men are at times ignored, but this fact per se does not diminish Keach as a thinker, because the very same arguments are presented by Keach's adversaries. To illustrate, Keach affirms that "Calvin saith, Baptismus esse sepulturam in quam nulli nisi jam mortui tradenti sunt; i.e., that Baptism is a form or way of burial and none but such as already dead to sin or have repented from dead works are to be buried."[8] Two conclusions follow Calvin's statement, Keach claims: first, "...sprinkling is not the form of baptism, because not the form of burial." Second, babies cannot be candidates for baptism, for they cannot die to sin nor repent of their faults, and "as they are not able, they are not required so to do by Christ."[9] As to the first claim against sprinkling, Calvin affirms that the mode is *adiaphoron*.[10] However, we shall see below, under the heading 'mode of execution,' Keach rather presenting a host of arguments for the necessity of immersion. Concerning the second claim against pedobaptism, all arguments

---

[4] We shall be introduced to William Burkitt shortly hereafter.

[5] Keach, *Rector Rectified*, [vi].

[6] William Burkitt, *An Argumentative and Practical Discourse of infant-baptism* (London: Printed by T.M. for Tho. Parkhurst, 1695), 23.

[7] Keach, *Rector Rectified*, 105.

[8] Keach, *Gold Refin'd*, 52.

[9] Keach, *Light Broke Forth*, 41.

[10] Calvin, *Institutes*, IV.xv.19.

used by Calvin—circumcision, federal holiness, benefits accrued by pedobaptism, etc[11]—are faced also head on below, 'Keach's Debates with his antagonists.' We reiterate that, to our knowledge, all the arguments used by pedobaptists in the sixteenth and seventeenth centuries were energetically confronted by Keach.

Having given this word of warning we turn to the first section, which, as said before, will introduce Keach's opponents.

Keach's Interlocutors and Antagonists

During the protracted baptismal controversy of the seventeenth century, Keach clashed with no less than eight opponents. They are introduced here in descending order of importance with just enough information to give a basic idea of who they were and what motivated them to write. There is almost nothing available on the lives of the more obscure individuals.

William Burkitt (1650-1703)

Son of a minister, Burkitt was educated at Cambridge University, receiving a B.A. in 1668 and an M.A. in 1672. Following his academic years, he worked briefly as chaplain in Bildeston Hall and, then, received ordination at the young age of 21 or 22. For the next twenty years (1672-92), Burkitt served as a curate and then as a rector in Milden, Suffolk. Devoted to his duties, he usually preached three times a week and laboured on catechising his parishioners and helping the poor and refugees from France. His last post was in Dedham, Essex, where he worked as vicar and lecturer for the last ten years of his life.[12]

During Burkitt's rectorship in Milden, a Baptist congregation was formed under the leadership of John Tredwell. The rector, according to Tredwell, preached a sermon casting "most odious reflection ...on the people falsely called Anabaptists." In response to a letter Tredwell had written him, Burkitt and a crowd walked into the Baptist congregation, lectured them and departed. "I thought," Tredwell says to Burkitt, "you would have come in a Christian manner to me in private and not to have an uproar and disturbance in our meeting-place (which is entered according to the law in that case provided) ...and take up an hour or two, and not to suffer me to give you a sober reply."[13] The controversy escalated when Burkitt published a book in which the "Anabaptists" were portrayed as furtively attracting his parishioners into rebaptism, in order to join their community. What is more, this baptism, Burkitt wrote, was done "in a nasty horse-pond into which the filth of the adjacent stable occasionally flows and out of which" Tredwell's followers "come forth

---

[11] Calvin, *Institutes*, IV.xv.
[12] DNB, III: 371-372.
[13] John Tredwell's Epistle to Mr. Burkitt, in Keach, *Rector Rectified*, [i].

with as much mud and filthiness upon them that they rather resemble creatures arising out of the bottomless-pit, than candidates to holy baptism; and all this before a promiscuous multitude in the face of the sun."[14] In response, Tredwell published a certificate with the signatures of eleven persons refuting these claims. Of the subscribers, five were Baptists and six otherwise. Burkitt's book was answered by Keach, whom Tredwell considered a man he "knew could do it better than my self."[15] This fact shows how highly regarded Keach was by the Baptist community in England. Although quick to stand for what he considered an important constitutive element of the church, viz., baptism, Keach was yet concerned with the lack of peace among fellow Christians. "It grieves and afflicts my very soul to see such strives, animosities and bitterness of spirit among Christians, because of that difference [i.e., pedobaptism] there is among us in respect of some truths of Jesus Christ, in a time when we are all threatened by a common enemy."[16] Nonetheless, Keach asserts, Burkitt's "allegations, objections, base reflections and false calumnies cast upon Mr. Tredwell and indeed the Baptists in general" cannot be ignored: a full answer ought to be given.[17]

Burkitt claims that he feels sorry for Tredwell, a man who lacks linguistic skills and, moreover, attempts to pastor a church—a duty for which he is disqualified and is doing just to earn his bread. As to the Baptists in general, they "creep out of darkness and private corners and in the face of the country, scandalously dip their deluded proselytes at noon-day ..." These practices must be opposed, "lest God justly permit the enemies of the truth to prevail," Burkitt maintains, "as to force us into corners when we would not."[18]

As far as Tredwell is concerned, Keach says, he has a legitimate call to preach and is a capable teacher, though not well acquainted with biblical languages. This fact, however, does not disqualify him.[19] Arguing against the fact that often people's opinion of baptism is based on the fame of the teachers

---

[14] Burkitt, *Argumentative Discourse*, [i].

[15] Tredwell's Epistle, in Keach, *Rector Rectified*, iii-iv.

[16] Keach, *Rector Rectified*, [v]. The "enemy" referred to is the Roman church: "Why cannot Christians with each other bear? / Among the Apostles some dissentions were; / But did they therefore persecute each other? / These mortal conflicts, brother against brother, / Destroy our safety, for they set a gap, / Open for Rome, that would us all intrap, / In fatal snares: their maxim is, we know, / Divide and rule, distract and overthrow. / Their crafty agent do creep in among, / Our heedless parties, and divide the throng, / That with more ease they may all devour, / Destroy our nation, and subvert our power. / Why therefore do not Protestants agree, / As One, against the common enemy." Idem, *Sion in Distress*, 31-32.

[17] Keach, *Rector Rectified*, 158.

[18] Burkitt, *Argumentative Discourse*, 67, 63. The issues of lay preaching and baptism kept the Baptists in constant battles with theologians of other denominations. Brown, *The Political Activities of the Baptists*, 7.

[19] Keach, *Rector Rectified*, 211.

of it, Keach affirms several things. First, God might decide to veil "this and some truths from some of his faithful servants...as a rebuke to them for their over-valuing of humane learning..." Nevertheless, Keach says, "the knowledge of the tongues I esteem in its place and could wish, if the Lord saw it good, all the Gospel ministers had the knowledge of the original languages..."[20] Second, as to earning a living, a Church of England minister has "the least reason of any man to talk as you do about preaching for bread, for that will not serve your turn, you must have fat benefits."[21] Third, as touching the Baptists, there is nothing dark practised by us; on the contrary, the Lord has taken "us out of the darkness you are in and hath given us...knowledge and light of his Word ...and we are not ashamed to show our heads on the house-top; not do we 'scandalously dip our deluded proselytes,' as you with envy and prejudice enough say," rather through the Baptists the rite of baptism is restored to its original perfection.[22]

The animosity between Burkitt and the Baptists reached fever pitch. One example will suffice. "The Anabaptists," Burkitt claims, say that pedobaptism is not lawful "because it is unuseful: children, say they, understand no more than brute-beasts what is done to them."[23] Keach retorts that there is simply no Scriptural authorisation for pedobaptism. As for the unbecoming correlation between a beast and a child, Keach asks, "who of the Anabaptists ever said such words as you here mentioned? [D]are you accuse your neighbors falsly?" Small wonder we are calumniously accused of "baptising naked. God will judge between us and you in his due time."[24]

---

[20] Keach, *Ax Laid to the Root*, I: [i]. The Baptists did not negate the importance of education; they only considered it non-essential to the pastorate. "I doubt not," Keach avers, "our call from God to the ministry is as good as others have, tho may be not every way so well qualified as we ought; yet humane learning is no qualification left by the Holy Spirit." *Counter-Antidote*, 53.

[21] Keach, *Rector Rectified*, 211.

[22] Keach, *Rector Rectified*, 210-211.

[23] Burkitt, *Argumentative Discourse*, 34. Cf. John Rothwell, *Paedobaptismus Vindicatus, or, Infant-baptism stated in an essay to evidence its lawfulness from the testimony of the Holy Scripture* (London: Printed for John Dunton at the Raven in the Poultrey, 1693), 14; John Bridgewater, *The Athenian Oracle: being an entire collection of all the valuable questions and answers in the old athenian mercuries. Intermix'd with many cases in divinity, history, philosophy, mathematicks, love, poetry, never before publish'd. To which is prefix'd, the History of the Athenian Society and an essay upon learning*, 3rd ed., 4 vols. (London: Printed for J. and J. Knapton, et. al., 1728), I: 307-308.

[24] Keach, *Rector Rectified*, 141-142. The place and accusation of naked baptism will be dealt with infra, p. 118, footnote 36. The enemies of the Baptists attempted at various points to associate them with the scandalous episodes, as, e.g., the one led by Hendricks Snyder, who at a nocturnal meeting, threw his clothes into the fire and told his Anabaptists followers to do likewise. Then the group ran naked through the streets of Amsterdam shouting, "woe, woe, woe; the vengeance of God". The band was seized,

Despite all the heat, Keach's ecumenical spirit can be seen when he asks Burkitt: "Should we not all unite together in love and affection and strive to promote peace and concord and not tear one another in pieces after this manner? I am sure this cannot tend to the honour of God ...not to the service of the church or state."²⁵ Why not peace instead of contention, seeing that "in all the articles of religion, we are acknowledged to be sound and orthodox," and this acknowledgement is done, Keach affirms, by our enemies. Our only important disagreement relates to the fact that "believers only are the true subjects of baptism, and that baptising is dipping and not rantizing..."²⁶

James Owen (1654-1706)

Polemicist, Presbyterian minister (Keach mistakenly thought he was a Congregationalist) and translator of the Westminster's Shorter Catechism into Welsh, Owen wrote on ordination, conformity, baptism, etc. His 1693 publication of *Bedydd Plant or Nefoedd*²⁷ inaugurated the pedobaptist controversy in Wales.²⁸ The thrust of this book is the perceived legitimacy and right of infants to baptism. The Anabaptists, Owen claims, were trying to steal this ancient right from children, which their guardians must not allow.

> We are shepherds and it is our duty to care for the lambs of the flock so that no one drives them out of the sheepfold as prey for wild lions. We are builders and soldiers and we must build the walls of Jerusalem, with one hand at work and the other holding a weapon, we must not reject those small stones which the Father accepted into the old building, and which the Son accepted into the new building, and which the Holy Spirit

---

"the men beheaded, the women drowned, except one who escaped." Abraham Kuyper, *Lectures on Calvinism*: The Stone Lectures of 1898. See, http://www.igmarshall.org/Reformed/kuyper_lecturescalvinism.html.

²⁵ Keach, *Rector Rectified*, [v].

²⁶ Keach, *Rector Rectified*, [vi]. We will deal with $\rho\alpha\nu\tau\iota\zeta\omega$ (i.e., sprinkling) under *modus applicanti* infra, pp. 197ff.

²⁷ James Owen, *Bedydd Plant or Nefoedd: Neu Draethawd Am Natur a Diben Bedydd. Yn profi, Trwy ddeuddeg o Resymmau Scrythuraidd dylid bedyddio plant y ffyddloniaid* (Printiedic yn Llundain gan F. Collins, 1693). That is, *Children's Baptism from Heaven: Or a Thesis about the Nature and Purpose of Baptism. Proving, through twenty Scriptural Reasons that the children of the faithful should be baptised* (Printed in London by F. Collins, 1693). I am grateful for the assistance of Timothy and Ruth Kelso in translating new passages and also thoroughly revising the English translation of the Welsh original presented by Keach. No Welsh translation of James Owen's book was published. Given the fact that Keach could not read the Welsh, somebody must have produced a manuscript, which he read and to which he replied. See infra footnote 32.

²⁸ DNB, XIV: 1313-1314.

accepts—the One who makes them into living stones from the Jerusalem above.[29]

Additionally, Owen accuses those who dismiss their own infant baptism and embrace the adult rite as fallen and ensnared by Satan;[30] which, for Keach, is equivalent to what the Roman Church used to do with "the Protestants that disowned the human traditions and the vain fopperies of their rotten Church, and thunder'd out their bulls against them."[31] Keach's reply to Owen aims to show to the Welsh people "the main arguments that other pedobaptists have brought for infant-baptism fully answered."[32]

An important point must be made at this juncture: the label "Anabaptist," which has appeared a few times already, is loaded with negative connotations; it is a word associated with the rebaptisms done by John Smyth and, more importantly, with the Münster episode.[33] When used against the Baptists, the word is intended as a term of mockery or derision and there were frequent attempts to tarnish all credobaptists with *re*-baptising or *ana*-baptism. Note, for example, the following assertions of James Owen, the "Athenians" and Richard Baxter. As he attacks the Baptists, Owen says that "[t]he first to baptise some for the second time in England was John Smyth, minister of the Church of England, who went to Holland and united with the church of one Mr. Ainsworth and, in the end, after he was thrown out of the church for error, he baptised himself and then rebaptised others."[34] The "Athenians"—whom we

---

[29] "Bugeiliaid ydym a'n ddyledswydd yw gofalu am wyn y praidd, rhag i neb eu bwrw allan or gorlan, ai gwneuthur yn ysclyfaeth ir llew rhuadwy. Adeiladwyr, a milwyr ydym, a rhaid i ni adeiladu muriau Caersalem, gan weithio âg un llaw yn y gwaith, ac â'r llaw yn dal arf, ac nid oes i ni wrthod y meini bychain hynny, a dderbyniodd y Tad ir hên adeiliad, a dderbyniodd y mab ir adeiliad neydd, ac adderbynnir gan yr yspryd glan, yr hwn sydd yn eu gwnethur yn feini bywiol or Gaersalem uchod." Owen, *Bedydd Pland or Nefoedd*, [iii-iv].

[30] Owen, *Bedydd Pland or Nefoedd*, 163.

[31] Keach, *Light Broke Forth*, [254-255].

[32] Keach, *Light Broke Forth*, xxii. Incidentally, Keach says that he hopes the translation into Welsh of his work will be faithful to his intended meaning. Ibid., xxi.

[33] For a short introduction on Smith, see Zaqueu Moreira de Oliveira, *Liberdade e Exclusivismo: Ensaios Sobre os Batistas Ingleses* (Rio de Janeiro: Horizontal Editora, 1997), 78-84. For a full treatment, see Jason Kenneth Lee, 'The Theology of John Smith' (Ph.D. diss., University of Aberdeen, 1999). For a summary of the Anabaptist "kingdom" in Münster 1534-35, see George, *Theology of the Reformers*, 257. For a treatment of the excesses, see Darrent Williamson, '"For the Honor of God and to Fulfill His Will": The Role of Polygamy in Anabaptist Münster', in *Restoration Quarterly* 42/1 (2000): 27-38.

[34] "Y cyntaf a fedyddiodd rai yr ailwaith yn Lloegr oedd John Smyth, gwenidog o eglwys Loegr, yr hwn a aeth i Holland, ac a unodd gydâg, Eglwys Mr. Ainsworth, yn y diwedd wedi ei fwrw ef allan or Eglwys honno am amryfusedd, efe ai bedyddiodd ei hun, ac yna efe a ail-fedyddiodd erail." Owen, *Bedydd Plant or Nefoedd*, 157.

shall meet soon hereafter—affirm that whenever pedobaptism was objected, "it was by such as were glossly erroneous in other things" as well; it is among other heretics that the Münster leaders are to be found.[35] The Anabaptists, Baxter says, immerse "persons naked ...or next to naked;" an unclean practice performed by the most modest of them. How can such wickedness be tolerated?[36]

Even if, Keach conjectures, the Münster episode were accurate (i.e., that some of the Anabaptists were doctrinally corrupt and guilty of immorality), is it fair to conclude that all who adhere to believer's baptism are likewise guilty of the same faults? This kind of reasoning would disqualify both the Jewish and the New Testament churches, for "in the first there were very ill persons, as Chora, Dathan, Abiran and many others; and in the last a Judas, a Diastrophes and an incestuous person," as Paul testifies.[37] What is more, the accounts of Münster were penned by either Romanists, who hated the Anabaptists, or by begrudged Protestants who were ready to accept false reports in order to stain the reputation of those who disagree with pedobaptism. "Alas," Keach interjects, "I could here soon recite some writings of inveterate spirits, who have in as base a manner vilified and calumniated the Episcopals, nay and the Presbyterians and Independents also, giving instances both in respect of their vile principles and practices." Unquestionably, it would be a disgrace "for any good man to take up a charge against so great a party of godly Christians from the venemous pens of such shameless persons."[38] In the light of the *sola Scriptura* principle, credobaptists should not be criticised, Keach purports, but

---

[35] Bridgewater, *Athenian Oracle*, I: 311, IV: 162. The Baptists, Keach protests, are no different "from other orthodox Christians in any essentials of salvation, no, nor in fundamentals of church-constitutions," with the exception of the baptismal rite. *Pedobaptism Disproved*, 13.

[36] Baxter, *Plain Scripture Proof*, 136. Besides Baxter, Keach complains (*Gold Refin'd*, 158) that Featley also calumniously accuses the Baptists of baptising naked. Daniel Featley, *The Dippers dipt: or the Anabaptist Duck'd and Plung'd over Head and Ears, at a Disputation in Southwark* (London: Printed for N. B. and Richard Royston at the Angel in Ivy-Lane, 1647), 38. Cf. Shute, *Replication to Benjamin Keach*, 7.

[37] Keach, *Gold Refin'd*, 159.

[38] Keach, *Gold Refin'd*, 158-159. Although we shall soon deal with Keach's ecclesiology, it is worth asking him, at this point, the following query: having affirmed what he just said about the Episcopalians, Presbyterians and Independents, does he consider them true churches? On the basis of what he says to the Independents, we would have to answer affirmatively. Yes, he says, "they are true churches, as well as we, they being godly Christians, tho I do believe they are less compleat churches, than those who are baptised upon the profession of faith, or not so orderly in their constitution; besides they receive, as we judge, a tradition of man in the stead of Christ's institution." *Counter-Antidote*, 54. Cf. Idem, *Light Broke Forth*, 227. Contrast with Shute, *Antidote to Anabaptism*, 190-192. For further information on Keach's views of what constitutes a true complete church, see his syllogisms in *Counter-Antidote*, 34.

rather emulated. "Is it not a foolish thing to cry out against traditions and all inventions of men, and yet strive to uphold and maintain them? And doth not these things hinder that glorious Reformation we all long for, and encourage Papists?"[39] If infant rantism were discarded, "what a glorious Reformation in point of church-constitution and discipline would there be! And what a sweet harmony and union would follow amongst us!" Undoubtedly, nothing has caused as much trouble lately in the church, Keach claims, as the Christening of babies. "If our brethren would but lay this seriously to heart, I can't think it would put them to a stand or pause about it." Since baptism is part of the constitution or foundation of the church, it is not possible to accept unlawful practices, as they would jeopardise the whole edifice.[40]

John Flavell (1630?-1691)

Flavell was educated at Oxford and published voluminously on many subjects. When writing against the "Anabaptists," he has a twofold objective: he, on the one hand, alleges to be combating their pernicious error of believer's baptism and, on the other hand, he seeks to confirm "many great and weighty points of religion."[41] Flavell warns that because error suspects its own feebleness, it is the stauncher in its defence, often taking refuge under the auspices of "antiquity, reason, Scripture and high pretentions to Reformation and piety."[42] In effect, once an erroneous opinion takes hold of one's mind, a string of other errors follows in its footsteps in order to justify the initial mistake. A case in point is the controversy of baptism: if it were not for the defence of credobaptism, who would have tried to negate that the Abrahamic pact was "a covenant of grace, or to assert the ceremonial law—so full of Christ—to be an Adam's covenant of works; and circumcision —expressly called the seal of righteousness of faith—to be the condition of" the Adamic compact? The enemies of pedobaptism, Flavell concludes, are "forced into these errors and absurdities by

---

[39] Keach, *Gold Refin'd*, 169.
[40] Keach, *Gold Refin'd*, [iii].
[41] John Flavell, ΠΛΑΝΗΛΟΓΙΑ, *A Succinct and Seasonable Discourse of the Occasions, Causes, Nature, Rise, Growth and Remedies of Mental Errors. Written some months since, and now publick, both for the healing and prevention of Sins and Calamities which have broken in this way upon the Churches of Christ, to the great scandal of Religion, hardening of the wicked and obstruction of Reformation. Whereunto are subjoined by way of appendix: I. Vindiciarum Vindex, being a succinct but full answer to Mr. Philip Cary's weak and impertinent exceptions to my Vindiciae legis & foederis. II. A Synopsis of Ancient and Modern Antinomian Errors, with Scriptural Arguments and Reasons against them. III. A Sermon composed for the preventing and healing of Rents and Divisions in the Churches of Christ* (London: Printed by R. Roberts for Tho. Cockrill, 1691), 172. Cf. Wallace, *Puritans & Predestination*, 187.
[42] Flavell, *Vindiciarum Vindex*, 22-23.

dint of argument in defence of their darling opinion."[43]

The Athenian Society (1690-?)

This organisation has as its aim the spreading of knowledge to as many people as possible. "England has the glory," an anonymous writer says, "of giving rise to two of the noblest designs that the wit of man is capable of inventing, and they are the Royal Society, for the experimental improvement of natural knowledge, and the Athenian Society, for communicating not only that, but all other sciences to all men ..."[44] People from all over Britain and beyond wrote questions to which the Athenians replied. These questions covered a broad gamut of subjects[45] as well as all aspects of life: from the most mundane ("Why we commonly fart in pissing?"[46]), to the most arcane ("Is evil *quid positivum*, or has it any positive real being?"[47]). The dispute with the "Anabaptists" seemed to have been a particularly heated one, for it is said that it contributed to "the promotion of printing," which likely means that there was a great interest in it.[48]

Gyles Shute (b.c. 1650)

According to Keach, Shute is a Congregationalist.[49] This author wrote six books only. Beside the "error" of believer's baptism, Shute accuses the Baptists of several other heretical points and warns his readers to avoid them. Beware of following sects, Shute affirms, for "some of the Anabaptists are Arminians, and some [have] gone back to Judaism, ...another sort ...are soul-sleepers, and some of them deny the deity of Christ ..."[50]

---

[43] Flavell, *Vindiciarum Vindex*, 31.

[44] Anonymous, *The History of the Athenian Society: For the Resolving of all Nice and Curious Questions. By a Gentleman who got Secret Intelligence of their Whole Proceedings* (London: Printed for James Dowley and are to be sold by the Booksellers on London and Westminster, n.d.), 3. See also ibid., 10.

[45] As the title of their work witnesses: Bridgwater, *The Athenian Oracle: being an entire collection of all the valuable questions and answers in the old athenian mercuries. Intermix'd with many cases in divinity, history, philosophy, mathematicks, love, poetry, never before publish'd. To which is prefix'd, the History of the Athenian Society and an essay upon learning*, 3rd ed., 4 vols. (London: Printed for J. and J. Knapton, et. al., 1728).

[46] Bridgewater, *Athenian Oracle*, IV: 215.

[47] Bridgewater, *Athenian Oracle*, II: 15.

[48] Anonymous, *History of the Athenian Society*, 3.

[49] Keach, *Counter-Antidote*, 16, 42.

[50] Gyles Shute, *An Antidote to prevent the prevalency of anabaptism clearly vindicated from that foul aspersion of being a counterfeit, and the aspersors totally confuted, or, Another broad-side against anabaptism* (London: Printed by J.R., and are to be sold by Nathaniel Hiller et. al., 1694), 48.

William Smythies (d. 1715)

Writer of half a dozen works, Smythies was university educated, lecturer at St. Michael Cornhill in London and apologist for the Church of England.[51] His only work referred to by Keach, deals mainly with the Eucharist.[52] "It is not only great haughtiness of mind," Smythies maintains, "by which men think themselves wiser than the most holy and learned men in all ages of the world, but ignorance through length of time that makes an Anabaptist."[53]

John Rothwell (d. 1661)

A Church of England minister, Rothwell produced only two books. The first one[54] is a compilation of works that he deems orthodox and profitable to his parishioners.[55] In his second tome,[56] Rothwell claims that the "Anabaptists" are to blame for disturbing the peace and leading people astray. "[T]here is a sect of men called Antipaedobaptists that have set up a meeting in this parish to seduce men from the ancient truth, I think it my duty" to protect, by vindicating infant baptism which has been the practice of the Church of England to this day. Rothwell purports that he has no animosity toward the "Anabaptists," whom he only considers prone to "novel opinions against the primitive Canons and Ecclesiastical Establishments."[57]

Joshua Exell (fl. 1690s)

Like Rothwell, Exell authored just two works.[58] Exell claims that pedobatism

---

[51] William Smythies, *The Spirit of Meekness, Recommended for the Reducing of the Erroneous and Such as have Dissented from the Church of England* (London: s.n., 1684), Epistle Dedicatory, ii-iv.

[52] William Smythies, *The Unworthy Non-Communicant. A Treatise Shewing the Danger of Neglecting the Blessed Sacrament of the Lords Supper, and Rectifying the Mistakes of many in This Age Concerning it*, 2nd impression corrected (London: Printed by T. Milbourn for Samuel Lee at the Feathers in Lumbard Street, 1683).

[53] Smythies, *The Non-Communicant*, 90-91.

[54] John Rothwell, *A Catalogue of Approved Divinity Books which have been printed or reprinted about twenty years past, and continue down to this present year, 1657, mensis Junii 18* (London: Printed for John Rothwell, 1657).

[55] With titles such as, *The Leper Cleansed or an Anabaptist Reduced*; see Rothwell's *Catalogue*, 84.

[56] *Paedobaptismus Vindicatus*.

[57] Rothwell, *Paedobaptismus Vindicatus*, xviii, xxxv, ii.

[58] Joshua Exell, *A Serious Enquiry into, and containing plain and express Scripture-proofs, that John the Baptist did as certainly Baptise Infants, as the Adult* (London: Printed for R. Man, and are to be sold by many booksellers in London, 1693). And, *Plain and Exquisite Scripture Proof that St. John the Baptist and the blessed Apostles and all the Primitive Baptizers, did baptise by sprinkling or pouring water upon the*

has been practised by "men of renown, both for parts and piety; and this at all times and in divers manners," and therefore this tradition cannot be wrong. In other words, the antiquity of the rite and the nobility of the characters who have practised it authenticate the certainty of infant's right to baptism.[59]

Keach's Doctrine of Baptism

Having met Keach's adversaries, we move on to our second section. The material will be dealt with under two main sub-sections. In the first, we shall see the ecclesiological implications of his doctrine of baptism, and in the second, Keach's polemical interactions with his antagonists.

The Ecclesiological Implications of Keach's Doctrine of Baptism

We shall consider two ecclesiological issues as they relate to baptism. First, the defection of Christendom and, second, the furthering of the Reformation.

Baptism and the Defection of Christendom

Keach's understanding of ecclesiology is paramount in his discussion of baptism. In exchanges with Burkitt and others, he says that baptism is important to the proper constitution of the visible church; that is, the church can only be correctly established if her members are admitted upon profession of faith. Otherwise, admission to the church by pedobaptism effaces her nature.[60]

A quote by William Burkitt will be used as a starting point to show Keach's ecclesiological opinions and his alleged need for the continuance of the work initiated by Luther and his associates. Relying on universality, Burkitt asserts that "the Anabaptists can believe that Almighty God has suffered all his churches, ancient and modern, ...in all parts of the world, to fall into one and the same church-destroying practice," namely, infant baptism.[61]

In answer to the above, Keach says the following: firstly, Burkitt assumes that all pedobaptist churches are true complete churches. However, it should be borne in mind that Paul foresaw a great backsliding after his departure (2The.2.3).[62] In other words, as the Apostolic era came to an end, errors began to creep into the church and so she did not remain "a pure virgin to Christ much

---

person or persons they baptised and not by dipping the person into the water (London: Printed for the author, to be sold by Thomas Parkhurst and William Langford, 1693).
[59] Exell, *Serious Enquiry*, [i].
[60] Keach, *Rector Rectified*, 141. For a fine discussion of several theological issues (soteriological, ecclesiological, etc.) as they relate to baptism among the Puritans, see the chapter 'Baptismal Debate in England,' in Holifield, *The Covenant Sealed*, 75-108.
[61] Burkitt, *Argumentative Discourse*, 34.
[62] Keach, *Rector Rectified*, 139-140.

longer than one hundred years after his death..."[63] This backsliding came to pass by means of the Roman Church. Has "not the Church of Rome ...made all the earth drunk with her cup for near 1200 years or more, and corrupted all those churches, more or less, with her poisonous errors and false doctrines, rites and ceremonies; and yet Almighty God hath suffered her for a long time?" In addition to that, Keach maintains that there have been "many other errors among Protestants."[64] Though using the expression "pure virgin," he does not believe that the church has ever been free of error. Moreover, there has always been a remnant of Christians on the earth throughout all the ages. For although the genuine church was hidden for a long period of time and into "the desert she fled from the face of the Romish Beast...[yet] I must confess that infant-baptism hath in part been a means to keep up the name of the Christian religion in the church ever since the apostasy..."[65]

Secondly, Keach thinks that the promise that the gates of Hell would not prevail against the church should be interpreted to mean that she will never *completely* fall. In other words, when it comes to errors in the church, it is better to think of degree, rather than the absence of them. Indeed, "the churches nearer the Apostles had more means to keep them from error than other ages, yet they err'd in doctrine and discipline..."[66]

Thirdly, the Church of England as well as other Reformed Churches—Keach continues to address Burkitt—possess many flaws, "yet God suffers you and them to continue at present in those errors, for reasons best known to himself; nor do we say we are without any error, or any church on earth, we pretend to no infallibility. But in point of baptism, we are right...I mean, as to the baptising of believers."[67]

Fourthly, the practice of pedobaptism, past and present, has continually undermined and wrecked the church, yet it has not destroyed her. "We do not say this error of yours about infant-baptism is a soul-damning error, God forbid." Nonetheless, pedobaptism tends to ravage "the nature of the holy Sacrament, and so also a right Gospel-church according to the Apostolic

---

[63] Keach, *Gold Refin'd*, 75.

[64] Keach, *Rector Rectified*, 140.

[65] Keach, *Light Broke Forth*, 234. Cf. Calvin, *Institutes*, 'Prefatory Address to King Francis I,' 24-25.

[66] Keach, *Rector Rectified*, 140. Keach is quoting John Tombes, *Anti-Paedobaptism*, 758. In our first chapter, 'Keach in Context,' we saw the same point made to argue against successionism. In this chapter, however, we are interested in the fact that since all churches throughout all ages have had error, continuing Reformation, Keach argues, is to be sought.

[67] Keach, *Rector Rectified*, 140. Somewhere else, Keach reinforces this point: the Baptists may have erred in the past and still, perhaps, err now; error is common to all denominations. *Pedobaptism Disproved*, 22. See also, idem, *The Glory of the True Church and its Discipline display'd* (London: s.n., 1697), 38.

constitution, making your church national, when the Gospel-churches planted by Christ and the Apostles were congregational."[68]

Keach asks the following questions to the advocates of national or parish churches: if pedobaptism makes their children part of the church, in that case "I would know whether they have their names in their church-book or register, as members?" Second, Keach wonders if "they ever excommunicate (or bring under any church censure) such of their children who fall into scandalous sins or actually transgressions or not?" Third, "[i]f not, what kind of polluted churches must thir's [theirs] be, who have not purged out such corrupted members?"[69]

Therefore, the need to continue the work of the Reformers, Keach maintains, is now incumbent upon those who want to see the church as pure as possible, which thing can only be achieved in a gathered or converted community.[70] Otherwise, the adulteration of Christianity by national churches will not come to an end. "I look upon infant-baptism," Keach bemoans, as "one of the chief pillars of the Romish Church and of all national Churches and Constitutions in the European world; this is that Christendom that is so cried up, and the way of making and continuing the pretended Christian-Name."[71] Pedobaptism serves this pretence, for by it every person becomes a so-called Christian. Consequently, either pedobaptism is dismissed (together with the nominalism it creates), or "there will never be a thorough Reformation: I mean," Keach insists, there must be a rejection of the invented and meaningless Christening

---

[68] Keach, *Rector Rectified*, 140-141. Cf. Idem, *Gold Refin'd*, 168; idem, *Counter-Antidote*, 16. Analysing the whole sweep of Particular Baptists, Renihan asserts that they understood their churches to come into being as the result of a personal encounter with God. The true church, then, would become visible wherever believers were to convene, and their catholicity is shown by the fact that they considered pedobaptists assemblies as authentic churches, though defective. The true catholic church, additionally, "had no human authority or power centre, could not be national or incorporate the political subjects of an empire, but gathered at the feet of its present 'head,' Jesus Christ. None of the assemblies of Christians were perfect, but they nevertheless showed the characteristics of the work of God and so demonstrated to those who would notice the reality and validity of their claim to be true churches." Reniham, 'The Practical Ecclesiology of the English Particular Baptists,' 124-126.

[69] Keach, *Ax Laid to the Root*, II: 34. Cf. Idem, *Gold Refin'd*, 167-168. For church discipline among Particular Baptists, see Renihan, 'Practical Ecclesiology of the Particular Baptists', 126. A church, Keach claims, may be properly constructed in both matter and form, "yet without regular and orderly discipline, it will soon lose its beauty, and be polluted." *The Glory of the True Church*, iii-iv.

[70] Keach, *Light Broke Forth*, 234. "The beauty and glory" of a local church reside in having members who are "all converted persons or lively stones, being by the Holy Spirit united to Jesus Christ the precious corner-stone and only foundation of every particular congregation, and of the whole catholick church." Idem, *The Glory of the True Church*, 6.

[71] Keach, *Light Broke Forth*, 234.

on the one hand and, on the other, there ought to be a personal appropriation of the faith (viz., trusting in Christ followed by baptism) by those who want to be Christians as it was done in the New Testament.[72]

In order to implement this Reformation, proper baptism (immersion of believers) must be reinstituted, for without baptism there is no admission to the visible church.[73] This is the consensus "of worthy writers,...howsoever in other things they may differ from us, and one from another; nor will those of the Church of England, Presbyterians or Independents admit any as members into their communions, as to take the Lord's Supper, except they have been baptised" by whichever way they do it.[74] Among these worthy writers the following was said by "Cyprian and other eminent Fathers,...'No unbaptised persons were admitted to the communion of the church.'"[75] This is reiterated by another authority. "'Let them, saith Austin (that is, the catechumens) pass through the Red Sea; that is, be baptised; and let them eat manna, that is, the body and blood of Christ.' This shews the practice of the church in his days."[76] The Protestant Ursinus, Keach proceeds, asserts that "[b]aptism is a sacrament of entrance into the church, whence it cometh that the Supper is presented to

---

[72] Keach, *Light Broke Forth*, 234. "Every house or building consisteth both of matter and form; and so doth the church of Christ, or house of the living God. The matter or material with which it is built are lively stones, i.e., converted persons. Also the matter and form must be according to the rule and pattern shewed in the mount, I mean Christ's institution [Mt.28.19],...and not after men's inventions." Idem, *The Glory of the True Church*, iii.

[73] As an aside, it is worth mentioning that Keach makes a clear distinction between the visible and the invisible church. Lot, for example, belongs only to the latter, as seeing in the following case: comparing the necessity of baptism with the necessity of circumcision, as to entrance into the church, Keach asks, "[i]f Lot should have offered himself to come to Abraham's family (which was then God's church), do you think Abraham would have admitted him (though he was a righteous man), unless he would first consent to be circumcised (which was the initiating ordinance at that time)?" Obviously, Keach expects a negative response and, with it, the agreement that if the *properly constituted* Old Testament church required the appointed rite of initiation, no less ought to be expected from the Gospel church. *Gold Refin'd*, 179. As to the mystical or "invisible church, [it] is but one and the same in every age, that consisteth only of the elect;...but the visible church is not the same now as it was under the law." *Counter-Antidote*, 17.

[74] Keach, *Gold Refin'd*, 178-179. Cf. Smythies, *The Non-Communicant*, 84.

[75] Keach, *Gold Refin'd*, 177. Cf. e.g., Cyprian, *Cyprianus Iubaiano Fratri S.*, Epistula LXXIII. c.13. C.S.E.L.3. See also, Augustine, *De Baptismo Contra Donatistas*, Liber Secundus, XIV, P.L. 43; and Justin Martyr, *Apologia Prima pro Christianis*, 61-62, P.G.6.

[76] Keach, *Gold Refin'd*, 177. Augustine, *In Johannis Evangelium*, Tractatus XI, 4, P.L.35.

none except first baptised."[77] Ames maintains that "baptism is a sacrament of initiation."[78] The Westminster Assembly affirms that "baptism is a sacrament of the New Testament, ordained by Jesus Christ—for the *solemn admission* of the party baptised into the visible church..."[79] Granting therefore that baptism is the proper way to enter the church and that the immersion of believers is the correct way to baptise (as Keach claims and expects to demonstrate below), why not return, he queries, to the Apostolic practice? During the New Testament times, baptism was found "in its beauty and primitive purity," truly "in its virgin glory, and it was soon after the Apostles times corrupted, as well as other truths were. We are to go to the original copy, to the primitive, or first institution and practice ...Were not the Saints 'to keep the ordinances (and commanded so to do) as they were first delivered to them?'" (1Cor.11.2)[80] Thus, the Baptists, Keach alleges, are reinstituting the baptismal rite to its pristine practice. He avers, "...we built not our faith about baptism upon the practice and custom of men, Fathers, General Councils, Protestant Reformers or Churches; but upon the Word of God."[81]

While this Reformation is being implemented, Keach declares, all types of interaction with pedobaptists are permissible except church membership, for they have not been made members of the visible church. "We have so much charity to all godly Christians that are pedobaptists, that we own them to be our brethren and members of the mystical body of Christ and have like love to them as to those who are of our own persuasion in the point of baptism, even to all where we see the image of God." Concerning communion at the Table, however, "we believe we are limited and bounded therein by the rule of God's Word, and 'tis not for want of charity to your churches we cannot have communion with you...but 'tis because we would walk orderly as" ordained in the New Testament. Keach concludes, "I am for Catholick communion and charity with all Saints, tho not for church communion with any unbaptized, as I believe you all are that have only had infants rantism."[82]

An imaginary interlocutor is brought in by Keach with the following objection. "But there are many very holy and pious men, yea, pastors of

---

[77] Keach, *Gold Refin'd*, 177. Zacharias Ursinus, *Catechesis Religionis Christianae*, s.v., 'De Baptismo,' Quaest. LXIX, (3), in *Opera Theologica*, tomus primus (Heildelberge: Typis Johannis Lancelloti, 1613).

[78] Keach, *Gold Refin'd*, 178. Ames, *Medulla Theologica*, s.v., 'De Baptismo & Coena Domini.'

[79] Keach, *Gold Refin'd*, 178. His emphasis. Westminster Assembly, 'Chapter XXVIII: Of Baptism,' in *The Confession of Faith, And the Larger and Shorter Catechisme* (London: Company of the Stationers, 1651).

[80] Keach, *Rector Rectified*, 203. For church admission, see also idem, *Answer unto two Athenian Mercuries*, syllogism # 24, p. 7.

[81] Keach, *Light Broke Forth*, 226. See also, ibid., 31-32; and, *Rector Rectified*, 180-181. Cf. Luther's statements in Pelikan, *Obedient Rebels*, 62-65.

[82] Keach, *Light Broke Forth*, [308].

churches that are for the baptising of little infants. Nay, and why should so few learned men be of your way if it were a truth, for most speak against those of your persuasion?"[83] This is simply lamentable, Keach exclaims! However, the Scriptures, not human beings, are to be our guide. For history witness that "some godly men who have had great light and were glorious Reformers too in their day, yet lay short of some great things and duties; as Jehosapht, &c. who 'did not removed nor pull down the high places'" (1Kin.22.43). Moreover, "[l]ight and knowledg of divine truths have broken forth *gradually*. When [the 16th century] Reformation first began, those godly men laboured to restore the doctrinal part of the Gospel and yet great corruptions remained in point of discipline (which errors God hath since by degrees discovered)."[84] At this junction, Keach clearly includes himself as a Reformer, saying,

> [h]ad the best and late Reformers (for such you will find at last the Baptists to be in point of the administrations of God's house and holy temple) been generally learned men, 'tis very like this truth would have been more readily received among such (I mean learned persons) than we see now it is, so hard a thing is self-denial.[85]

The point Keach has just made is critical to our thesis that he only departed from the earlier established Reformed Orthodox thought where necessary to continue the work of the Reformation. Let us consider this matter as summarised by Miller as he interacts with a pedobaptist, a front rank Puritan among "Reformed divines," viz., William Ames.[86] Note how *strikingly* similar is Keach's point with the following one: the first Reformers, Miller affirms, endeavoured with all their might to re-establish the fundamental Christian doctrines, which in their view had been corrupted. "The 'captaines' had not descended to particulars, William Ames said, because they 'were necessarily inforced to fight awaies in the front against the enemies to defend the faith, and to purge the floore of the church.'" However, in the initial decade "of the seventeenth century this work was done; confessions were formulated, Protestant armies had gained a degree of security and leisure for theologians, universities had been established and scholars were ready for settling the yet unfinished business of Protestant theology."[87] Therefore, our claim that Keach is a theologian, working as a Reformer, to restore the church to what he perceives to be the biblical pattern, is not at all farfetched. Keach is not deviating from post-Reformation Reformed Protestantism, but rather calling his

---

[83] Keach, *Gold Refin'd*, 154-155.
[84] Keach, *Gold Refin'd*, 155. His emphasis.
[85] Keach, *Gold Refin'd*, 155.
[86] Stoever, *A Fair and Easie Way to Heaven*, 15. Cf. Karlberg, 'Reformed Interpretation of the Mosaic Covenant,' 24; Ong, *Ramus, Method and the Decay of Dialogue*, 304; Sprunger, 'Ames, Ramus and Method,' 151.
[87] Miller, *The New England Mind*, 94.

brethren to join him in this continuing Reformation.

As an aside, it is worth pointing out that Keach had a very high view of his country (and likely of himself as well) amidst other Reformed nations: Great Britain is the place where God will establish his fortress (Dan.11) before the final attack on the Beast, since this land is "so eminent above all other places of the churches Reformed,...[a country] God hath made the eminent seat of the church in these latter days and which he hath loved above all the inhabitants of Jacob."[88]

Believer's Baptism and the Furthering of the Reformation

Under this heading, we will present some important aspects of baptism in a positive or non-controversial form. Here Keach deals, first, with the foundation or first institution of this doctrine; second, he examines the purpose, subjects and mode of baptism; third, Keach considers the interconnectedness of baptism and the Eucharist and how this interconnectedness impacts these ordinances. This is followed by, forth, an objection to the Reform of baptism and the justification of such Reformation based on the New Testament practice; and, finally, Keach concludes this section by conceding his willingness to embrace pedobaptism if proved wrong.

First, the controversial status of baptism tends to shape the manner in which Keach writes about it. Hence, his writings are for the most part conducted either in an argumentative way or in a negative fashion; that is, Keach is often to be found striving to show the rightness of his stance, or, alternatively, he is trying to point out the wrongfulness of somebody else's position. Seldom does Keach positively presents his views of baptism, as we shall see hereafter. How then, did he understand this ceremony? Christian baptism, Keach affirms, as to its origins, is a divine rite and a dominical command, since it was given by Christ himself. The giving of baptism is found within what is commonly known as the Great Commission (Mat.28.18-19). In this charter, Christ firstly asserts "his power and authority. Secondly, he delegates a power to his disciples. Thirdly, he subjoyns a gracious promise to them."[89] Let us briefly look at these three points in turn, as they are the foundation and reason why Keach deems baptism so important. Firstly, then, this authority and power given to Christ encompasses the whole universe. Although he already had these attributes before coming into the world, after his resurrection, Christ received confirmation that such power and authority were his. On this account, he gives everlasting life to those he wishes, establishes laws, changes ordinances, directs

---

[88] Keach, *Antichrist Stormed*, 185. For the rise of nationalism among the Puritans, see Nuttall, *The Holy Spirit in Puritan Faith*, 121.

[89] Keach, *Gold Refin'd*, 2. Elsewhere Keach reaffirms that the principle and grounds of baptism is not the Abrahamic covenant (or circumcision), but rather the Great Commission. *Counter-Antidote*, 32. *Contra*, Shute, *Antidote to Anabaptism*, 186.

his church, etc. Secondly, on the basis of this authority, he delegates to his followers power to teach and baptise or, more simply put, to disciple the world as the "word μαθητεύσατε, make disciples," indicates. Thirdly, to this command a promise of companionship is attached, which reads, "go ye therefore and teach all nations, baptising them...and lo, I am with you always to the end of the world." This Great Commission belongs to Christ's "last will and testament ...wherein baptism is found and expressly given forth, and with as great and in as solemn a manner as ever was any precept or ordinance that we read of in all the Book of God."[90]

Second, concerning the aim or purpose of baptism, this rite was instituted in order to be a visible sign of an invisible grace already effected in the life of the believer, i.e., it is a sign that new life was given.[91] The Church of England, Keach proceeds, correctly phrases it as she calls baptism "an outward sign of an inward grace."[92] Moreover, baptism is to be a sign of union with Christ, as Baxter says, "baptism is the solemnising of our marriage with Christ."[93] Another objective of this rite is that it is a token, as Perkins notes, "of the covenant on God's part of the washing of our sins in the blood of Christ..."[94] Baptism has yet another purpose, namely, to assert faith in the resurrection of Christ. Hence, baptism is designated, "an answer of a good conscience, by the resurrection of Christ..." (1Pet.3.21).[95] Again, Keach claims, Perkins concurs saying that what saves "...is not the baptism of water, but the stipulation of a good conscience by the resurrection...The outward baptism without the inward is no mark of God's child, but the mark of a fool that makes a vow and afterwards breaks it."[96] Lastly, baptism is the appropriate means to induct believers into the "visible church," and it allows them church privileges, such

---

[90] Keach, *Gold Refin'd*, 3.

[91] Keach, *Gold Refin'd*, 81.

[92] Keach, *Gold Refin'd*, 149. See, e.g., *The Anglican Catechism*, 1549, in Philip Schaff, *The Creeds of the Evangelical Protestant Churches* (London: Hodder & Stoughton, 1877), 521.

[93] Keach, *Gold Refin'd*, 81. Richard Baxter, *Confirmation and Restauration, the necessary means of Reformation and Reconciliation* (London: Printed by A. M. for Nevil Simmons Bookseller in Kederminster, and are to be sold by Joseph Cranford, at the Kings-Head in Pauls Church-yard, 1658), 32.

[94] Keach, *Gold Refin'd*, 82. Cf. e.g., William Perkins, *A Commentarie or Exposition upon the Five First Chapters of the Epistle to the Galatians: penned by the godly, learned and iudicial Diuine, M. W. Perkins. Now Published for the Benefite of the Church, and Continued with a Supplement upon the Sixth Chapter* (London: Iohn Legatt, Printer to the University of Cambridge, 1613), 256. Keach also quotes Bullinger in support of his argument: *In Acta Apostolorum Heinrychi Bullingeri Commentariorum Libri VI: ab authore recogniti ac denuo iam recusi* (Tiguri: Excudebat Christophorus Froschoverus, 1583), s.v., Cap. II, [38].

[95] Keach, *Gold Refin'd*, 82.

[96] Keach, *Rector Rectified*, 152-153. Perkins, *A Commentarie upon Galatians*, 256.

as the Lord's Supper.⁹⁷ Therefore, the importance of baptism is unquestionable; in fact, though not essential to salvation, virtually all denominations agree that baptism is cardinal to a properly constituted church. Consequently, it is imperative that the baptismal rite be clearly presented "in the Word of God, and so it is."⁹⁸ The Scriptures depict this rite, Keach purports, as the representation of Jesus' death, burial and resurrection as metaphorically experienced by a believer, viz., death to sin and resurrection to newness of life. That is, besides representing the burying and resurrecting of Christ, baptism "also signifies our death to sin or that blessed work of mortification of the body of sin and death; by which means believers who enter into baptismal covenant are put into a gracious and meet capacity" to live a pious life.⁹⁹ Since infants can neither die to sin nor be born to new life, and since babies can neither be converted nor profess faith, adult believers alone—Keach concludes—are the proper subjects of baptism.¹⁰⁰ Without any compulsion, the Christian is to consider carefully and weigh "with all seriousness and deliberation imaginable, the nature of this covenant before he signs it."¹⁰¹ Regarding the mode of execution, immersion—not sprinkling—is the proper way, since only immersion conveys to the senses, the image of death and resurrection and spurs the candidate to bury the sinful nature and live a holy life.¹⁰² As if baffled and frustrated, Keach asks, "why will not our brethren keep to the great institution and exact rule of the primitive church?" Should the church be satisfied "with that light which the church had in respect of this and other Gospel-truths at the beginning of the Reformation, since God hath brought forth greater ...[light] in our days?" What is more, "why should a tradition of the antichristian state be so zealously defended? The church will never certainly appear in its primitive glory, till this rubbish be remov'd; which is nothing less than to take a stone of Babylon and lay it in Sion for a foundation."¹⁰³

---

⁹⁷ Keach, *Gold Refin'd*, 84-85.
⁹⁸ Keach, *Light Broke Forth*, xi. Cf. Idem, *Pedobaptism Disproved*, 2.
⁹⁹ Keach, *Rector Rectified*, 149. Cf. Idem, *Answer unto two Athenian Mercuries*, syllogism # 25, p. 7; and *Counter-Antidote*, 4-5.
¹⁰⁰ Keach, *Gold Refin'd*, 81. Extensive discussion of 'recipients of baptism' infra, pp. 133ff.
¹⁰¹ Keach, *Rector Rectified*, 149.
¹⁰² Keach, *Gold Refin'd*, 81. Again, extensive discussion of 'modus aplicanti' infra. The "recovery" of what Baptists understood to be the primitive practice of baptism took place by degrees. Influenced by Anabaptists, General Baptists were practising credobaptism around 1609 and Particular Baptists in the 1630s. Later on, 1640-41, the Particular Baptists introduced the practice of immersion, which the General Baptists came to adopt a decade or so later. McBeth, *The Baptist Heritage*, 44.
¹⁰³ Keach, *Gold Refin'd*, iv-v. See Keach's very similar but far lengthier plea for Reformation at the end of the same book, p. 157. See also, idem, *Light Broke Forth*, [310]. Contrast with Shute, *Antidote to Anabaptism*, 188-189.

Third, the Lord's Supper and baptism are irreducibly connected in that both sacraments represent core events in salvation history.[104] Whilst secondary things may be portrayed by the Eucharist, the primary ones are "Christ crucified, and our feeding on him by faith, or the breaking of his body and the pouring forth of his blood;" these things indeed "are most lively set forth and represented to our visible sight. So in baptism likewise, the main and more immediate significations, which are the death, burial and resurrection of our blessed Saviour, with our death unto sin and vivification to new life, are clearly resembled..."[105] This resemblance, Keach proceeds, is not secondary or incidental to baptism, rather it is of fundamental import if a proper baptism is to occur. Thus, as the candidate is immersed, her burial to a former way of life is presented; as she stays awhile under the water, the entrance "into a state of death or mortification" is shown; and, as she raises out of the water, a new state of life is portrayed. "This, saith Augustine, speaking of these things, is by a sacramental metonymy, and the meaning of it is, not that one thing is changed really into another, but because the sign doth so lively resemble the thing signified."[106] Therefore, Keach continues, it is clear that men of erudition are in agreement with our position, namely, that the Bible presents the rite of baptism as a "resemblance of Christ's death, burial and resurrection and not of the spiritual things signified only, viz., our mortification of sin and rising to holiness in a way of likeness to Christ's death and resurrection; but also," mark it, "the outward rite or form of administration of the sign it self—to be done in a way of likeness or lively resemblance of them both..."[107] Alluding to baptism as a sign and the mystery of regeneration which baptism represents, Taylor says, "[t]his indeed is truly to be baptised, when it is both in the symbol and in the mystery; whatsoever is less than this, is but the symbol only, a meer ceremony, an *opus operatum*, a dead letter, an empty shadow, an instrument without the agent to manage or force to actuate it."[108]

---

[104] There is a deep relationship, Keach thinks, between the two ordinances in that both witness covenant realities to the senses: baptism declares the entrance into a covenanted life and the Lord's Supper communicates nourishment of the same life. In other words, the former relates to *access* to and the latter relates to *maintenance* into the covenant. For the view of Keach's antagonists concerning the relationship between the sacraments, see, for example, Smythies, *The Non-Communicant*, 84, 85.

[105] Keach, *Gold Refin'd*, 52. See also ibid., 43. Cf. Idem, *Counter-Antidote*, 9.

[106] Keach, *Gold Refin'd*, 54. Cf. e.g., Augustine, *De Doctrina Christiana*, Liber Tertius, IX-X (13-14), P.L.34.

[107] Keach, *Gold Refin'd*, 54-55. Cf. Idem, *Counter-Antidote*, 8.

[108] Keach, *Gold Refin'd*, 55. Jeremy Taylor, ΘΕΟΛΟΓΙΑ ἘΚΛΕΤΙΚΗ: *A Discourse of the Liberty of Prophesying, with its Just Limits and Temper. Showing the Unreasonableness of Prescribing to Other Men's Faith, and the Iniquity of Persecuting Differing Opinions*, new ed. (London: Printed for Gale and Fenner, Paternoster Row, 1817), 347.

Fourth, since the practice of immersion of adults was lost during the apostasy, it may be objected that it cannot be restored without a new commission. Keach replies that not only baptism but also many other ordinances lost their perfection and simplicity during the apostasy. However, just as the Israelites lost the festival of tabernacles, "yet by reading in the Book of the Law there was such a thing required, they immediately revived it and did as they found it written without any new mission or extraordinary prophet to authorise them so to do; even so ought we to act," the Bible "being a warrant sufficient to justify us in so doing."[109]

In order that such Reformation should be justifiable, an important question would be, how did the Apostolic churches baptise as they develop? After the Apostles preached, the Scripture testifies that the hearers asked, "...what shall we do? Then said Peter, *repent and be baptised...*and then they that gladly received the word were baptised..." (Act.2.38, 41; Keach's emphasis). "Pray observe the footsteps of this flock," Keach says, "I mean, the manner of the constitution of this church, it being the first church that was planted in the Gospel-days, it was the church at Jerusalem," the spring from which all churches derive.[110] In the second place, still very early on, Philip proclaimed the word in Samaria, "and when they believed...they were baptised both men and women" (Act.8.12). It is important to note that in the Samaritan church the sequence is the same, sc., faith first, then baptism. Moreover, the text speaks about adults, not infants, being baptised. Third, slightly later, after the Eunuch received the word and asked for baptism, Philip said, "if thou believest...thou mayst" (Act.8.37).[111] Fourth, the same pattern is seen with Cornelius (Act.10.45-48), Lydia (Act.16.14-15), the Philipian jailor (Act.16.30-33) and Crispus (Act.18.8): they believed and then received baptism.[112] Owing to all of this, it is to be inferred that the practice of the early church was to baptise only after faith. "Luther saith that in times past, the Sacrament of baptism was administered to none except it were to those that acknowledged and confessed their faith and knew how to rehearse the same..."[113]

In conclusion to this part, it is worth mentioning that, as to pedobaptism, Keach claims to be willing to follow his fellow Protestants if they can prove him wrong. One example will suffice: James Owen says, "[w]hy despise Christ's ordinance of water baptism? Beware of following in the path of the Pharisees, those who ignored God's counsel and refused the baptism of John the Baptist. You are not rejecting John's baptism but rather the baptism of

---

[109] Keach, *Gold Refin'd*, 23-24. He does not give reference, but Keach may have based this on Neh.8.14-15.

[110] Keach, *Gold Refin'd*, 71. *Contra*, Bridgewater, *Athenian Oracle*, I: 308.

[111] Keach, *Gold Refin'd*, 72.

[112] Keach, *Gold Refin'd*, 73. Contrast e.g., Bridgewater, *Athenian Oracle*, I: 308.

[113] Keach, *Gold Refin'd*, 73. Cf. e.g., Luther, *Luthers Werke*, XXXV: 57.

Christ and are therefore guilty of a greater sin than they."[114] Keach responds that those who "despise and slight the baptism of infants, despise neither the baptism of John nor Christ; because neither John nor our blessed Saviour commanded infants to be baptised, nor did ever baptised one child as we read of; if you can prove they did do it, we will say no more, but will soon baptise our children."[115]

Having set the stage for the baptismal controversy proper, we now turn to it.

Keach's Debates with his Antagonists

This section has two main headings. The first deals with the proper subjects of baptism, that is, *who* Keach believes to be the legitimate recipients of this rite. The second discusses what Keach thinks is the form of baptism's administration, that is, *how* the baptismal rite is to be dispensed.

Recipients of Baptism

The grounds or basis for infant baptism will be considered under ten main headings: (a) the covenant made with Abraham (or simply, circumcision), (b) the Great Commission, (c) federal holiness, (d) the benefits accrued by pedobaptism, (e) incipient faith, (f) the invitation to all children, (g) the inclusiveness of John's confession and baptism, (h) the baptism of households, (i) the antiquity of pedobaptism, and (j) the testimony of the Fathers. Although these headings have varying degrees of importance, Keach nevertheless exhaustively and minutely examines each of them. At times, we shall see that after claiming to have answered the argument at hand, Keach proceeds to raise a further barrage of reasons why the said argument is invalid. Let us turn to the first argument.

The Abrahamic Covenant

Undoubtedly the most important argument for pedobaptism is derived from God's covenant with Abraham. This argument may be stated in an overarching manner as follows: as Abraham and his descendants were at that time in covenant with God, likewise Christians and their descendants are now in covenant. Otherwise, God's people before Christ would have had benefits superior to God's people now. This single argument bifurcates thus: first, it asserts that the Abrahamic pact was a *covenant of grace*, which received a seal,

---

[114] "Pa ham y dirmygi Ordinhad Christ am fedydd dwfr? Gochel lwybrau yr hen Phariseai, y rhai yn eu herbyn eu hunain a ddisystyrasan gyngor Duw, heb eu bedyddio, gan Joan Fedyddiwr. Yr wyt ti yn diystyru, nid bedydd Joan, eithr bedydd Christ, ac am hynny mwy dy bechod di nai pechod hwy." Owen, *Bedydd Plant or Nefoedd*, 21.
[115] Keach, *Light Broke Forth*, 9.

namely, circumcision. Second, as Jewish descendants were in covenant with God and were given circumcision as a seal, so also the descendants of Christians are in covenant with baptism as seal. To put this second prong simply: baptism has replaced circumcision. The first part *establishes* the basis of the continuity between Jewish and Christian parents, viz., the Abrahamic pact was a covenant of grace. The second identifies the seals as a specific locus of continuity. Keach articulates all of this in the following manner: the pact "made with Abraham was the covenant of grace or Gospel covenant, to which the seal of circumcision was annexed; and as circumcision belonged to the children of the faithful under the law, so baptism belongs to the children of the faithful under the Gospel," otherwise "the privileges under the Gospel would be less than those were under the law."[116]

The ensuing debate between Keach and his opponents will be guided by four questions: (i) was the Abrahamic compact a covenant of grace? (ii) is circumcision part of the covenant of grace? (iii) has baptism replaced circumcision? (iv) is circumcision a seal of the pact of grace?[117]

Was the Abrahamic Pact a Covenant of Grace?

"I affirm," Burkitt claims, "that the covenant which God made with Abraham, Gen.17, was most certainly a covenant of grace."[118] That is, the pact that "God makes with believers now under the Gospel is the very same for substance with that which he made with Abraham under the Old Testament." This is the case because of at least three factors: first, the way it was framed or expressed;

---

[116] Keach, *Gold Refin'd*, 100.

[117] This fourfold division is done on account of clarification only. The four queries are interconnected and could be compressed in a Procrustean way ultimately to a single one, namely, does baptism stand in the place of circumcision?

[118] Burkitt, *Argumentative Discourse*, 11. Flavell avers that "the right of believers infants to baptism is secured" on the basis of the Abrahamic covenant. *Vindiciarum Vindex*, 176. See also, ibid., pp. 191, 222-223. Similarly Shute says that "the foundation of our baptism is in Abraham's covenant." *Antidote to Anabaptism*, 191. See also ibid., 53; idem, *Replication to Benjamin Keach*, 36, 186. Cf. Exell, *Serious Enquiry*, 66, 68, 69; Bridgewater, *Athenian Oracle*, IV: 167; Rothwell, *Paedobaptismus Vindicatus*, xv, 12-13, 102-104. Although the Puritans used other arguments to underpin pedobaptism, this is by far the most important one. Virtually the entire sweep of Puritanism asserts that the *foedus gratiae* was for Christians and their children and, consequently, "the seal of the covenant must extend to the latter as well. In the earlier times of Israel that seal was circumcision. Now it is baptism, under the prescriptions of the New Covenant." Von Rohr, *Covenant of Grace*, 91. Herein and henceforth, we are going to provide extensive cross-referencing to both Keach and his opponents in order to enable the reader to follow the arguments consulting other sources.

second, its' length; and third, on account of its' benefits.[119] As to how it was couched, Scripture affirms, "I will be a God unto thee and to thy seed after thee" (Gen.7.7). Burkitt rhetorically asks, "is not this a pure Gospel-phrase and shews it to be a covenant made with Abraham in Christ?" Could it be possible that "God (who upon the breach of the covenant of works made with us in Adam became our enraged enemy) to be a God unto fallen man, any other ways than by a mediator..."[120]

Keach agrees that the covenant with Abraham is gracious or a Gospel-pact, but that is only *part* of the story. For this covenant has a double nature or a twofold character: on the one hand, the *foedus gratiae* "made with Christ was promised to Abraham, which takes in only the true spiritual seed..." On the other hand, the fact that the Almighty promised to be a God unto Abraham and his seed does not necessarily make it a covenant of grace. This is illustrated by the Sinaitic covenant, wherein God explicitly promised to be a God to the Israelites (Exo.20.2), yet Paul calls this pact "a ministration of death and condemnation" (2Cor.3.7).[121]

Burkitt's second argument relates to the length of the compact. This agreement is said to be eternal or "an everlasting covenant" (Gen.17.7).[122] Keach replies by saying that the word "everlasting" in this context means "a long continuance of time." This same term is used to express the everlasting character of Jewish rites and ceremonies, which were all abolished by the coming of Jesus.[123]

Lastly, Burkitt affirms that the pact with Abraham is a Gospel covenant on the basis of the advantages or benefits it provides, that is, that God would give himself to Abraham and to his seed. He elaborates by saying that in this covenant, "God gives a person an interest in all he is and all that he has, so far as can be communicated to a creature." The advantages provided by this

---

[119] Burkitt, *Argumentative Discourse*, 11-13. Cf. Exell, *Serious Enquiry*, [43], [44]; Shute, *Replication to Benjamin Keach*, 37, 48; idem, *Antidote to Anabaptism*, 184-185; Flavell, *Vindiciarum Vindex*, [xxiii].

[120] Burkitt, *Argumentative Discourse*, 11-12. Cf. Flavell, *Vindiciarum Vindex*, 222-223; Exell, *Serious Enquiry*, 69, 71.

[121] Keach, *Rector Rectified*, 70-71. See also ibid., 42. Keach's *Ax Laid to the Root*, Part I, which we shall present below it is almost exclusively dedicated to demonstrating that the Abrahamic covenant is not monolithic. Against this view stand, *inter alios*, John Flavell and the Athenians. See, for example, *Vindiciarum Vindex*, 178ff.; *Athenian Oracle*, IV: 194.

[122] Burkitt, *Argumentative Discourse*, 12. Cf. Shute, *Antidote to Anabaptism*, 116-117.

[123] Keach, *Rector Rectified*, 71. Cf. Idem, *Counter-Antidote*, 28. Elsewhere Keach illustrates the meaning of the word "everlasting:" Canaan was to be an everlasting possession to the Israelites (Gen.17.8), but they were eventually disinherited. The Levites were to exercise an everlasting priesthood (Num.25.13), but it came to an end with the advent of Christ. Several other abrogated ordinances are said to be everlasting, as e.g., the day of atonement (Lev.16.34). *Ax Laid to the Root*, II: 13-14.

compact, Burkitt claims, include "Christ, grace, holiness here, and glory and happiness hereafter."[124] Keach points out that God gave himself to Abraham *prior* to the covenant of circumcision. That is, Abraham received God's approval through faith before circumcision was instituted (Rom.9.10). Furthermore, not all the descendants of Abraham and not all the descendants of Christians have interest in God. In both cases, only the spiritual seed or the elect have regard for godliness. Hence, "a multitude of Abraham's natural offspring and the natural offspring of believers have neither Christ, nor grace, nor shall be saved, but perish eternally." Given that circumcision was given to the elect and to the reprobate, "I may from hence," Keach declares, "with the greatest boldness imaginable affirm, that in the covenant of circumcision," the Lord did not give himself to Abraham to be his God and the God of his seed.[125]

Against the claim made by pedobaptists that their practice is appropriately grounded in the Abrahamic covenant, Keach has yet much to say. One of the key texts used by him is Mat.3.10, "...now the ax is laid to the root of the trees, every tree therefore that bringeth not forth fruit is hewn down and cast into the fire." The recipients of this message, Keach purports, are mainly the religious authorities (v.7), whom John is casting out "from the external and legal covenant God made with Abraham and his fleshly seed or offspring."[126] All Jews—especially zealous ones—saw themselves as God's covenanted people on the basis of the Abrahamic concert. However, John, Keach claims, dismisses their assumption saying, "...think not to say within your selves, we have Abraham to our father..." (v.7). What they had failed to grasp was "that there were two covenants made with Abraham and also a two-fold seed, viz., a carnal or natural, and a spiritual seed." These Jews had too closely associated the promise made to Abraham with their right to that promise regardless of their faith or behaviour. The promise here refers to the statement that in Abraham's seed, "all the nations of the world shall be blessed" (Gen.12.3). To fulfil this promise, God would turn stones into children that would have the faith of Abraham and bless the world.[127] To make sure that the Jews understood that, without faith, natural lineage was useless, John says that fruitless trees are "cast into the fire" (v.10). On hearing this, the Jews would have argued that, as descendants of Abraham, they all had the right to both church membership and the benefits of the covenant. This was the case, Keach continues, before the "ax" cut these external benefits. That is to say, the expression "...*now* the ax" refers to a new thing God is doing, namely, putting an end to exclusive Jewish

---

[124] Burkitt, *Argumentative Discourse*, 12. Cf. Exell, *Serious Enquiry*, 69, 70, 71; Flavell, *Vindiciarum Vindex*, 222-223.
[125] Keach, *Rector Rectified*, 72. Cf. Idem, *Ax Laid to the Root*, II: 5-6.
[126] Keach, *Ax Laid to the Root*, I: 1.
[127] Keach, *Ax Laid to the Root*, I: 3-4. Cf. Idem, *Ax Laid to the Root*, II: 40; and, *Counter-Antidote*, 23.

privileges.[128] In effect, Keach adds, after cutting the Jewish Church, this ax will eventually cut "the bloody idolatrous Church of Rome, when the Beast 1260 years are expired;" and also, in God's time, "all other corrupt and national churches" shall have their end.[129] The point of the passage, Keach maintains, is that heritage is useless. You who have Jewish ancestry or who have Christian parents—this shall "stand you now in no steed, this will give you no right to Gospel ordinances, nor particularly to Gospel baptism; tho it did to circumcision and legal ordinances and Jewish church membership."[130] The situation has changed because God is reiterating the administration of the Gospel and under this dispensation the Jewish legal covenant is put aside together with the children of *circumcised* Abraham. In its' place, God wants to "raise up children unto *believing* Abraham and so make good the covenant of grace or Gospel covenant made with him."[131] Thus, in this Gospel dispensation, God destroys the ceremonial and legal root and, concomitantly, confirms the pact made with uncircumcised Abraham and his faithful children. It should be stressed that what has changed was "the old covenant; [for] the covenant of grace is but one and that never changeth."[132] One of the main effects of this change was church association: the children of Christians have no right to church membership.[133]

Keach introduces another text (Gal.4.22-23) to demonstrate the double nature of the Abrahamic pact; "...he who was born of the bond-woman was born after the flesh, but he of the free woman was by promise." Both sons correspond to covenants: Ishmael to the *foedus operum* and Israel to the *foedus gratiae*. This allegorical interpretation is justified, Keach claims, by Paul, who affirms that Hagar and Sarah "are an allegory for these two covenants" (v.24). What is more, the first covenant is to be discarded, as the context shows: "Cast out the bond-woman and her son, for the son of the bond-woman shall not be heir with the son of the free woman" (v.30).[134] At least three things may be said

---

[128] Keach, *Ax Laid to the Root*, I: 4, emphasis mine. Cf. Idem, *Pedobaptism Disproved*, 19; *Light Broke Forth*, 233; *Ax Laid to the Root*, II: 43-44. *Contra*, Shute, *Antidote to Anabaptism*, 98-99, 104-113; Exell, *Serious Enquiry*, 26, 38, 72, 75; Bridgewater, *Athenian Oracle*, IV: 160.

[129] Keach, *Ax Laid to the Root*, I: 7. Far more is said on the metaphors 'root,' 'tree,' 'ax,' 'fire,' in ibid., pp. 4-8. For an extensive treatment of metaphors, see Keach's *Tropologia*: 'root,' 79, 132, 424-426; 'tree,' 134, 431, 680; 'ax,' 186; 'fire,' 85, 109, 157, 297-301, 306, 501, 577-582.

[130] Keach, *Ax Laid to the Root*, I: 10.

[131] Keach, *Ax Laid to the Root*, I: 11. Emphasis mine.

[132] Keach, *Ax Laid to the Root*, I: 11. Cf. Idem, *Counter-Antidote*, 17, 25. Keach also says that there has been only one *foedus operum*, though it has had many additions and administrations. *Counter-Antidote*, 25.

[133] *Contra*, Exell, *Serious Enquiry*, 26, 41, 56, 75; Flavell, *Vindiciarum Vindex*, 280; Shute, *Antidote to Anabaptism*, 34-35.

[134] Keach, *Ax Laid to the Root*, I: 13-14.

by way of summary. In the first place, Galatians 4 reveals that God made a two-fold covenant with the patriarch: one with Abraham's natural descendants, the other with his spiritual heirs; not all of his natural descendants were spiritual heirs.[135] This is supported, Keach continues, by Rom.9.7-9, where Ishmael is said to be outside the covenant of grace, whereas his brother is part of it. Consequently, the two pacts are not equivalent.[136] In the second place, the repudiation of Hagar and her son implies the abolition of the carnal covenant with its benefits and "the utter rooting out and rejection of the external and political church-state of the Jews." Lastly, the passage shows "that none of the fleshly seed as such should be heirs and partakers with the true spiritual seed of Abraham under the Gospel, or have a being in Abraham's true spiritual house or Gospel church."[137] John Owen confirms this interpretation, Keach claims, when he asserts that the efficacious "dispensation of the grace of the covenant, is peculiar to them only, who are the children of promise, the remnant of Abraham, according to election, with all that in all the nations were to be blessed with him and his seed, i.e., Jesus Christ; Ishmael, tho circumcised, was cast out."[138] In the light of all of this, Keach asks, can anybody still argue for church affiliation for the children of believers? Whatever benefits or legal rights were accorded to the Jews by the old covenant cannot be extended to the new; otherwise, since the Jewish legal covenant granted the priesthood to the children of priests, why not claim the ministry to the children of Gospel's ministers?[139]

By way of clarification, a word should be said about the meaning of "seed" of Abraham (Gen.17.7). We have noted John Owen using it to describe Christ. Keach, prior to Owen, used the same word to describe Abraham's spiritual and carnal descendants. Burkitt uses the term indiscriminately as a depiction of separation: the seed of Abraham is a nation set apart "from all other people under heaven."[140] The Athenian Society affirms that the offspring of Christians "are the spiritual seed of Abraham, till they by actual sin, unrepented of, are otherwise."[141] Knowing that perseverance of the saints was axiomatic among his opponents, Keach accuses the Athenians of making the covenant of grace uncertain. That is, one may belong to it and yet be damned; for, does not experience show that many of the children of believers live and depart this life

---

[135] Keach, *Ax Laid to the Root*, I: 14. Cf. Idem, *Rector Rectified*, 43.

[136] Keach, *Rector Rectified*, 48-49.

[137] Keach, *Ax Laid to the Root*, I: 14. In a different place, Keach puts this point thus: Ishmael represents all fleshly descendants of Abraham and the Jewish church state constituted by them. This church has been dismantled together with its circumcised membership. *Rector Rectified*, 60-61. Cf. Idem, *Pedobaptism Disproved*, 19-20. Contra, Shute, *Replication to Benjamin Keach*, 65; idem, *Antidote to Anabaptism*, 99-104.

[138] Owen, *Works*, XI: 284; cited by Keach, *Light Broke Forth*, [303].

[139] Keach, *Ax Laid to the Root*, I: 14-15.

[140] Burkitt, *Argumentative Discourse*, 4.

[141] Bridgewater, *Athenian Oracle*, IV: 176. Cf. ibid., p. 190.

in great profanity? Therefore, *pace* the Athenians, the covenant is certain "for all the seed" (Rom.4.16).[142] Now, to return to the meaning of "seed," it may be understood in four ways, Keach claims. Firstly, by dint of pre-eminence, Christ is said to be the seed (Gal.3.16). This is the case because "he is the head and representative of the Gospel-covenant."[143] Secondly, Christians, as elected by God, are the seed (Rom.9.7). In addition to these two categories, the fleshly seed of Abraham comprises the remaining two groups: those, thirdly, who had a right to his inheritance who are after the lineage of Isaac and, fourthly, those without such a right, after Ishmael. These four possibilities are exhaustive; "add, if you can," Keach challenges Burkitt, "a fifth" one. The immediate question, then, is, "can the infant-seed of believers, as such, be said to be the seed of Abraham in any of these four respects?" If not, Keach maintains, the argument for pedobaptism based on the Abrahamic covenant is undone.[144]

The offspring of Christians do not fit the first category. Christ is the seed of Abraham (Gal.3.16) by virtue of the fact that God promised to the patriarch that he would be Abraham's God and bless him: this blessing would come to fruition ultimately in Christ, according to the eternal covenant made between the persons of the Trinity. The descendants of Christians do not suit the second category, but rather the elect or those "who have the faith of Abraham and walk in his steps..." (Gal.3.29).[145] It cannot be all the offspring of Christians, since many of them do not walk righteously. Finally, the mere fact that the children of Christians are Gentiles eliminates the third and fourth possibilities, since both Isaac and Ishmael were *natural* seed of Abraham. In that light, Keach concludes: "If the children of believing Gentiles, as such, are not the natural nor the spiritual seed of Abraham, then they can have no right to baptism or church-membership, by virtue of any covenant-transaction God made with Abraham. But the children of believing Gentiles, as such, are not the natural nor spiritual seed of Abraham." Therefore, "they can have no right to baptism nor church membership, by virtue of any covenant-transaction God made with Abraham."[146]

To further demonstrate the dual nature of the Abrahamic covenant, Keach says that the *promises* of this covenant are differentiable: some of the promises made to the patriarch are exclusive to his natural progeny and, distinctively, other promises pertain to his spiritual seed or the elect. The first set of promises is legal, earthly, home-oriented and civic. The second is spiritual, Gospel oaths or "better promises" (Heb.8.6).[147] In the first place, then, to the first covenant

---

[142] Keach, *Ax Laid to the Root*, I: 28; and *Rector Rectified*, 45.
[143] Keach, *Rector Rectified*, 44.
[144] Keach, *Rector Rectified*, 44.
[145] Keach, *Rector Rectified*, 44.
[146] Keach, *Rector Rectified*, 44-45. Cf. Idem, *Answer to two Athenian Mercuries*, syllogism # 10, p. 4; and, *Ax Laid to the Root*, II: 48.
[147] Keach, *Ax Laid to the Root*, I: 15. Cf. Idem, *Rector Rectified*, 47-48.

belongs the promises (1) that Sarah would conceive and have a child, (2) that Abraham would have countless children through Isaac, (3) that God would maintain this covenant with the descendants of Isaac, (4) that the Messiah would descend from Isaac, (5) that the offspring of Isaac would be liberated from Egypt and (6) that these offspring would be given possession of the promised land. It is inconceivable to imagine, Keach argues, that these promises were given to the spiritual children of Abraham. That is, no Gentile would think, for example, that the actual liberation from Egypt was a promise to him or her. It is to this covenant—to this alone—that the sign of circumcision belongs (Gen.17.10-11). On the other hand, to the second pact or the covenant of grace belongs the promises that (1) Abraham would father many nations (i.e., non-Jewish believing nations) and that (2) in his "seed all the nations of the earth [would] be blessed" (Gen.12.3).[148] At this junction, Keach calls upon Paul to support his hermeneutic. Does not the Apostle explicitly teach that there was an evangelical promise made to Abraham's spiritual seed? "And the Scripture foreseeing that God would justifie the heathen through faith, preached the Gospel to Abraham saying, 'in thee shall all the nations of the earth be blessed'" (Gal.3.8). That the promise was made to the elect or Abraham's spiritual seed is further elucidated by the rest of Genesis 3. "Now to Abraham and to his seed was the promise made; he said, not to seeds, as of many (meaning his fleshly seed, as such) but to the seed which is Christ...And if ye be Christ's, then you are Abraham's seed and heirs according to the promise" (Gal.3.16,29).[149] In other words, having made the connection between Abraham and Christ, Paul, then, asserts that Christians are the (spiritual) seed of Abraham (Gal.3.29).[150] In the light of these verses, Keach claims, it is clear that God made a mixed compact or—to put it differently—a double covenant with Abraham.[151] As usual, Keach uses syllogistic reasoning to make the point.

> If the covenant takes its denomination from the promises and the promises are mix'd, some evangelical, belonging to those to whom the Gospel belongeth; some domestick or civil promises, specially and absolutely respecting the house and natural seed of Abraham and policy of Israel; then 'tis a mix'd covenant. But the covenant takes its denomination from the promises and the promises are mix'd, some evangelical, belonging to those to whom the Gospel belongeth; some domestick or civil promises, especially and absolutely respecting the

---

[148] Keach, *Ax Laid to the Root*, I: 15-17. Cf. Idem, *Rector Rectified*, 43; and, *Counter-Antidote*, 25-26.

[149] Keach, *Ax Laid to the Root*, I: 17. Parenthetical interpolation by Keach. Cf. Idem, *Rector Rectified*, 42-43. For a different interpretation, see, for example, Flavell, *Vindiciarum Vindex*, 291-292.

[150] Keach, *Rector Rectified*, 42-43.

[151] Keach, *Ax Laid to the Root*, I: 17.

house and natural seed of Abraham and policy of Israel. Ergo, 'tis a mix'd covenant.[152]

However, the Jews may object, Keach supposes, alleging that they could not have seen or understood this double pact and, hence, complain that in rooting them out, God had not been faithful. This objection is easily rebutted, Keach purports, for Paul says, "[t]hey are not all Israel, which are of Israel...Neither because they are the seed of Abraham, are they all children" (Rom.9.6-7). It is incontestable, then, that the descendants of Abraham are divided into two groups, spiritual and carnal. Consequently, to be a Jew or to have Christian parents does not entail Gospel rights or privileges.[153] Keach calls on Luther to endorse his position,

> Paul therefore concludeth with this sentence that they that are of faith, are the children of Abraham; that corporal birth, or carnal seed, make not the children of Abraham before God; as if he would say there is none before God accounted as the child of Abraham (who is the servant of God, whom God hath chosen and made righteous by faith) through carnal generation; but such children must be given before God, as he was a father; but he was a father of faith, was justified and pleased God, not because he could beget children after the flesh, not because he had circumcision under the law, but because he believed in God. He therefore that will be a child to believing Abraham, must also himself believe, or else he is not a child of the elect; the believing and justified Abraham, not the begetting Abraham, which is nothing else but a man conceived and born and wrap'd in sin, without the forgiveness of sins, without faith, without the Holy Ghost, as another man is, and therefore condemned. Such also are the children carnally begotten of him, having nothing in them, like unto their father, but flesh and blood, sin and death; therefore these are also damned: this glorious boasting then, we are the seed of Abraham, is to no purpose.[154]

In conclusion, then, what answer should be given to our first question—was the Abrahamic pact the covenant of grace? The reply is yes and no! This covenant was not monolithic, but rather twofold: some of its promises were fleshly and others spiritual, the former to all the patriarch's natural children, and the latter to his spiritual offspring. This interpretation, Keach affirms, "is owned by all true Protestant writers."[155]

---

[152] Keach, *Rector Rectified*, 42. *Contra*, Flavell, *Vindiciarum Vindex*, 190.
[153] Keach, *Ax Laid to the Root*, I: 17. Cf. Idem, *Ax Laid to the Root*, II: 48.
[154] Luther, *Luthers Werke*, XXVI: 374; quoted by Keach, *Ax Laid to the Root*, I: 17-18.
[155] Keach, *Ax Laid to the Root*, I: 18. Elsewhere Keach says that before the coming of Christ the pact of grace "was only contained in promise, by which covenant all that lived under the Old Testament who had faith in it were saved..." *Counter-Antidote*, 47.

Is Circumcision Part of the Covenant of Grace?

Keach turns to address the objection that, whether or not there were two covenants with Abraham, circumcision belonged to the *foedus gratiae*. Flavell, for example, insists that Paul would not otherwise have taken the liberty to circumcise Timothy (Gal.2.3-4).[156] In effect, the rite of circumcision did not bind humanity to keep the Law, or else it would have "bound Timothy to keep the Law" in order to be justified. This is an "unanswerable objection from Paul's circumcising Timothy, Act.16.2-3."[157]

At the outset, Keach states simply that there is no question that circumcision indeed obligated the one circumcised to maintain the entire Law (Gal.5.3). Secondly, Paul had the freedom to circumcise Timothy because he was persuaded that the Law, as to justification, had been abrogated and thus circumcision, as such, was an *adiaphoron*. On the other hand, when the Apostle commands the Gentile Christians not to circumcise themselves, he does so because they were thinking that those old covenant rites and regulations had not been abolished and by them justification could be attained. Therefore, in the case of Gentiles who falsely thought to attain righteousness by the Law, Paul says "if they were circumcised, they were obliged to keep the whole Law, tho his great design was to take them off from seeking justification by works."[158] Thirdly, Timothy's circumcision was done for *political reasons*, i.e., to accommodate the consciences of weak Jewish believers, and not in obedience to the Mosaic code. Once it was believed that the Law was terminated, it could do no harm. Thus, Paul himself underwent certain "rites...of the ceremonial Law, as shaving the head and purifying himself, which," like circumcision, had been revoked (Act.21.24). The whole difficulty—to go back to the second point—was that the recipients of Paul's epistles saw the Law as still in force and, in this context, circumcision would "be destructive to them, upon the obligation it lay them under, if it was as they conceived. This being so, what is become of Mr Flavell's argument, which he makes such a boast of, as if unanswerable?"[159]

Nevertheless, Flavell maintains, since the objective of circumcision is to teach "man the corruption of his nature by sin, and the mortification of sin," it follows that this rite can only be part of the covenant of grace.[160] To begin with, no one can prove, Keach contends, that the fundamental aim of the rite of circumcision was to teach humanity the corruption of its nature with the need for mortification thereof. At most, circumcision was a type or representation of the aforementioned things. More importantly though, as long as circumcision is not proved to be part of the covenant of grace, objections such as this are

---

[156] Flavell, *Vindiciarum Vindex*, 226. Cf. Rothwell, *Paedobaptismus Vindicatus*, 13.

[157] Flavell, *Vindiciarum Vindex*, 230, 226, 229. Cf. Ibid., pp. 177-178, 303.

[158] Keach, *Ax Laid to the Root*, II: 18-19.

[159] Keach, *Ax Laid to the Root*, II: 19.

[160] Flavell, *Vindiciarum Vindex*, 231.

worthless. The rite of circumcision, the paschal meal, as well as the legal ceremonies were ultimately figures of the coming Messiah. With the advent of Christ, these signs and types were abolished. The Mosaic code or "the Law as written in the two Tables was given in mercy...to Israel, in subserviency to the Gospel, and to it was annexed the ceremonies, to shew that a plenary satisfaction must be made for the breach of God's holy Law, and that this must be by blood..." All of which point to Christ's atoning sacrifice.[161]

Keach has much more to say against the claim that circumcision is part of the covenant of grace. He proceeds to amass nine arguments. First, circumcision is not part of the Gospel because it was given to the Israelites in order to set them apart from the other nations. On this basis, an all-encompassing state church was established. In contradistinction, in the covenant of grace, the church is to be a gathered community where the wicked are excluded. Are the offspring of Christians, however ungodly, to be included in the New Testament church merely on account of their descent? This would be contrary to the teaching of "the Church of England (whatever her practice is)." For according to her doctrine, "[t]he church of God is a company of godly Christians, among whom the Word of God is truly preach'd and the Sacraments duely administered."[162] Keach asks rhetorically, "[d]id Christ...constitute any one nation consisting of believers and their carnal offspring (some godly and some ungodly) into a church?" Study the Scriptures "and see whether the direct contrary is not apparent; for they were only such who believe, were converted and professed faith in Christ and so were baptised, that were added to the church; and such only doth the Gospel church consist."[163]

Second, circumcision is not part of the covenant of grace since reprobates were circumcised and some of the elect were not. Esau and Ishmael fit the first group and are said to be excluded (Gen.17.20-21). Additionally, a great number of circumcised men in Jesus' time are said to be Satan's children (Joh.8.44). The second group includes the multitude of the elect daughters of Abraham and all chosen boys who passed away before the eighth day. Conjectures apart, people like Job and Melchisedek were not circumcised though they were godly; for "had circumcision been a law or precept of the covenant of grace, all these would God have required to have been circumcised as well as others..." Ergo, circumcision is no part of the Gospel.[164]

Third, John's baptism testifies that circumcision does not belong to the *foedus gratiae*, because the Baptizer completely ignored circumcision, as

---

[161] Keach, *Ax Laid to the Root*, II: 26-27.
[162] Keach, *Ax Laid to the Root*, I: 18-19. Article XIX of the XXXIX Articles. Cf. Keach, *Answer unto two Athenian Mercuries*, 2.
[163] Keach, *Ax Laid to the Root*, I: 18-19. Cf. Idem, *Rector Rectified*, 47-48; idem, *Answer unto two Athenian Mercuries*, syllogism # 7, p. 2; idem, *Counter-Antidote*, 28, 43.
[164] Keach, *Ax Laid to the Root*, I: 20, 26. Cf. Idem, *Counter-Antidote*, 28; idem, *Rector Rectified*, 49.

demonstrated when he refuses to baptise many of the circumcised Pharisees and, at the same time, many people who were circumcised were nonetheless baptised. It ought to be concluded, Keach asserts, "that circumcision was no Gospel law, nor did it appertain to the covenant of grace, but was part of the old legal covenant, which the ax was laid to the root of and is gone."[165]

Fourth, circumcision does not belong to the covenant of grace since the Bible explicitly teaches that the members of it know God (Jer.31.32-33). Babies, however, know nothing. When infants were introduced into the old covenant, for a long time afterwards, they did not know God. On the other hand, with the new covenant it is not that way, because "all whom he would make that covenant with should know him before they were received as members of that church, tho afterwards 'tis granted, they stand in need of further teaching."[166]

Fifth, the covenant of circumcision resembles the covenant of Sinai, i.e., both covenant prescribe, *inter alia*, life as reward to obedience, death to disobedience, and material things, such as health, land, etc. (Gen.17.8,9,14). The covenant of grace, on the other hand, prescribes faith. Keach says, "[t]hat covenant that was in the nature and quality of it, as much a covenant of works as the Sinai covenant, could not be the covenant of grace. But so was the Law and the covenant of circumcision. Therefore, circumcision was no Gospel law or covenant."[167]

Sixth, circumcision in not part of the Gospel since Paul says that this pact is "of the letter and not of the Spirit" (Rom.3.29). The meaning of "letter" is made clear, according to Keach, by an analogous passage: "Who hath made us able ministers of the New Testament, not of the letter but of the Spirit..." (2Cor.3.6). Thus, "letter" pertains to the Law, which kills and not to the Spirit or the Gospel, which gives life. Hence, circumcision has no place in the Gospel.[168] Gyles Shute objects, saying that circumcision must be a Gospel institution, seeing that "nothing could be more a type of baptisme than circumcision, because all the subjects of that ordinance were passive, as all the subjects of baptisme are...Gen.17.13."[169] Keach replies by saying that baptism cannot be such a type, since Scripture declares that the removing of the foreskin corresponds not to baptism but rather to the "circumcision of the heart." What is more, circumcision is not a type of baptism for the mere fact that they coexisted for a time; that is to say, circumcision and baptism overlapped as

---

[165] Keach, *Ax Laid to the Root*, I: 20. Cf. Idem, *Ax Laid to the Root*, II: 42; idem, *Counter-Antidote*, 28; idem, *Rector Rectified*, 49.

[166] Keach, *Ax Laid to the Root*, I: 21. Cf. Idem, *Counter-Antidote*, 29; idem, *Rector Rectified*, 50-51. Contra, Rothwell, *Paedobaptismus Vindicatus*, 15.

[167] Keach, *Ax Laid to the Root*, I: 21-22. Cf. Idem, *Rector Rectified*, 52.

[168] Keach, *Ax Laid to the Root*, I: 22. Cf. Idem, *Counter-Antidote*, 29.

[169] Shute, *Antidote to Anabaptism*, 136. Cf. Ibid., pp. 16, 52; idem, *Replication to Benjamin Keach*, 62; Bridgewater, *Athenian Oracle*, I: 306, IV: 198.

valid institutions from the days of John's ministry all the way to Jesus' death. It is a given, according to Keach, that the arrival or appearance of the *res* obliterates the figure. This did not happen with the appearance of baptism and, thus, circumcision is not a type of baptism.[170] As to Shute's argument that circumcision and baptism are passive and hence correspond to each other, it is rather the case, Keach claims, that baptism requires *active* faith.[171]

Seventh, circumcision does not grant righteousness, for faith is not part of it. What greater evidence could be provided, Keach asks, that circumcision is not part of the Gospel? "...faith was reckoned to Abraham for righteousness...How then was it reckoned, when he was in circumcision or in uncircumcision? Not in circumcision but in uncircumcision" (Rom.4.9-10). There would have been no need for the Apostle to oppose this Jewish rite, "if it were as our brethren say, a Gospel law, precept or covenant."[172]

Eighth, the pact of circumcision depends on the Law for benefits. If the Law is broken, no benefit is accrued from circumcision. As a result, circumcision is not part of the Gospel of grace. "For circumcision verily profiteth if thou keep the law," as Paul says, "but if thou break the law, thy circumcision is made uncircumcision, that is, of none effect" (Rom.2.25). The covenant of circumcision could benefit those who kept the Law perfectly, for thereby justification could be obtained. But this justification needs no Messiah to keep the Law in the stead of the sinner. The benefits of the Gospel, however, are dependent on Christ and thus circumcision has no part to play in the Gospel.[173] Flavell argues that since circumcision is "a part of the ceremonial law and the ceremonial law was dedicated by blood, and whatsoever is do dedicated" cannot be part of the *foedus operum*, therefore circumcision is rather part of the compact of grace.[174] This objection, Keach says, begs the question, is the ceremonial law part of the covenant of grace? No one has ever made an attempt to prove such a thing! The ceremonial law was rather an "appendix" to the covenant of works and, as such, it has been uprooted with the said covenant. In addition to that, did not the ceremonial law belong to "that law St Paul calls '[t]he hand-writing of ordinances that was against us, which was contrary to us, and [Christ] took it out of the way, nailing it to his cross?'" (Col.2.14)[175] Granting, Keach proceeds, that the rite of circumcision was an ingredient of that law Paul refers to, then it does not belong to the pact of grace. As to the

---

[170] Keach, *Ax Laid to the Root*, II: 2. Cf. Idem, *Counter-Antidote*, 31; idem, *Rector Rectified*, 11-12.
[171] Keach, *Counter-Antidote*, 42.
[172] Keach, *Ax Laid to the Root*, I: 22. Cf. Idem, *Rector Rectified*, 56; idem, *Counter-Antidote*, 29-30. Concerning the concept that circumcision is a Gospel precept or covenant, see, for example, Flavell, *Vindiciarum Vindex*, 234.
[173] Keach, *Ax Laid to the Root*, I: 23. Cf. Idem, *Counter-Antidote*, 30.
[174] Flavell, *Vindiciarum Vindex*, 214-215.
[175] Keach, *Ax Laid to the Root*, II: 3.

claim that circumcision is not part of the covenant of works since it was dedicated by blood, it should be noted that it was so dedicated with "typical blood, blood of bulls and goats, that could not take away sin, purge the conscience [and could] not make anything perfect." Can such a blood be part of the perfect covenant of grace?[176]

Ninth, the Apostles regarded circumcision as an unbearable yoke of slavery and, therefore, it could not be part of the free covenant of grace (Act.15.10 and Gal.5.1-2). There is no advantage for Gentiles in circumcision as some were claiming,[177] otherwise the Apostles would have said so. The Jews were given circumcision as an ingredient of the *foedus operum*. Other components of this pact, such as the Ten Commandments, were given later on. This whole legal structure was put into place by God to restrain the wickedness of the Jews, to teach them the awfulness of sin, and to show them that they were in covenant with a holy God. The entire apparatus did not provide salvation, it only cursed. Circumcision, as part of this scheme, "is not an evangelical or Gospel privilege but only a legal or old covenant rite and privilege."[178]

Has Baptism Replaced Circumcision?

"Now, our blessed Saviour substituted baptism in the room of circumcision," Rothwell affirms in no uncertain terms.[179] Burkitt put it more elaborately: if Jewish babies had the right to partake "of circumcision, then the infants of Christians may and ought to be partakers of baptism. But the Jewish infants were partakers of circumcision. Therefore, Christian infants may and ought to be partakers of baptism."[180]

Where is the Scriptural basis for the first premise, Keach asks Burkitt, or should it be believed merely because the Rector says so? Keach volunteers to present a finer syllogism than Burkitt, but equally worthless. "If the Jewish infants had a right to the possession of the land of Canaan, the infants of Christians have a right to the possession of the land of Canaan. But the former is true; ergo," so is the latter. He continues sarcastically: "And if this were so, let us make another holy war and take possession of it for our children."[181] The logic here is flawed, Keach claims, because the reason behind Jewish circumcision was not the mere fact that they were descendants of Abraham.

---

[176] Keach, *Ax Laid to the Root*, II: 3-4.
[177] For example, Shute, *Antidote to Anabaptism*, 52-53.
[178] Keach, *Ax Laid to the Root*, I: 24-25. Cf. Idem, *Rector Rectified*, 56-57; idem, *Counter-Antidote*, 30.
[179] Rothwell, *Paedobaptismus Vindicatus*, 6. See Ibid., pp. 17, 28, 62. Cf. Exell, *Serious Enquiry*, 56; Flavell, *Vindiciarum Vindex*, 295; Bridgewater, *Athenian Oracle*, IV: 158; Shute, *Antidote to Anabaptism*, 35.
[180] Burkitt, *Argumentative Discourse*, 2.
[181] Keach, *Rector Rectified*, 3. Cf. Idem, *Counter-Antidote*, 49-50.

Rather, Jewish infants received circumcision on account of the explicit "positive command of God to Abraham; for evident it is, no godly male child, before Abraham's days, had any right to be circumcised." If Abraham or anybody else had circumcised children without God's command, it would have been a human invention and, as such, "will-worship."[182] Similarly, the Scripture does not contain any command from God to baptise the infants of Christians, therefore, to do so would be a mere human invention and thus "will-worship."[183] Jeremy Taylor notes, Keach says, that "[i]f baptism came in the room of circumcision, you must baptise your children always on the eighth day: and you must not baptise your female infants at all, because none but male infants were then circumcised."[184]

Burkitt recognises that there is no positive command for pedobaptism. He writes, "I acknowledge that the New Testament, tho it be not wholly silent, yet speaks very little touching the case of infants," and this is so for a double reason: since "the Old Testament spake so much in their case, therefore the New Testament speaks so little;" and secondly, because the "Old Testament plainly informs us that children in their infancy were admitted members of the visible church." There is no necessity, therefore, to reiterate it in the New,

---

[182] Keach, *Rector Rectified*, 4. This "positive command" is just another name for the Reformed "regulative principle of worship," that is, nothing should be done in worship other than what God has commanded in the Bible. Keach's understanding of a "positive command" is important for his argument hereafter. Both circumcision and baptism fall within this category: the rite of circumcision was to be performed on the eighth day, neither before nor after this day; in the same way, the rite of baptism is to be given solely to those "who believe or make profession of their faith." A positive command does not allow room for manoeuvring: that which was instituted must be strictly performed, or—to use Keach's words and illustrations—one ought "not to venture to do no more, nor no less, nor do any thing in any other way, than God hath commanded, as appears in Nadab and Abihu, and Uzzah's case; the first [two] for offering strange fire, which thing God commanded them not," were slain, though God had never forbidden them to present such an offering. Likewise, Uzzah, for touching the Ark, met the same disapproval. *Rector Rectified*, 6-7. See also Keach's syllogisms #s 2, 13 and 18 in *Answer unto two Athenian Mercuries*, 1, 4, 5; *Pedobaptism Disproved*, 11, 23; *Counter-Antidote*, 28-29, 32; *Ax Laid to the Root*, I: 25-26. Contrast Keach's "positive command" with Rothwell's "institution of latitude," *Paedobaptismus Vindicatus*, 16-19. On the whole, Puritanism "demanded a Scriptural warrant for every part of worship, believing it to be a repudiation of original sin for man to assume he was capable of deciding what was appropriate in the service of God, and arrant impudence to legislate for himself when God had already decided for him in the Word of God in the Holy Scriptures. The inflexible Puritan motto was: *Quod non iubet, vetat*." Horton Davies, *Worship and Theology in England*, 5 vols. (Princeton, NJ.: Princeton University Press, 1961-75), II: 254.

[183] Keach, *Rector Rectified*, 4.

[184] Taylor, ΘΕΟΛΟΓΙΑ ΕΚΛΕΤΙΚΗ, 326-327; quoted by Keach, *Rector Rectified*, 4-5.

especially when it is known that Christian doctrine derive from both collections.[185]

That is not correct, Keach claims, "for the New Testament speaks nothing at all touching infant-baptism; if a man read it over a thousand times, he shall not find one word, or the least hint given to it: therefore the New Testament, contrary to what you boldly affirm, is wholly silent in the case of infant-baptism and church-membership." Keach continues: what "a shame for a man who calls himself a minister, to speak falsely, but much more, to publish falsehood to the world. In this, Mr Rector, you must be corrected."[186] Certainly, the fact that the New Testament says nothing about including children as church members, does not allow the inference that they should be included on account of their membership in the Old Testament church. This would be an argument from silence, which positive commands would invalidate. As to the contention that Christian doctrine is to be derived from both Testaments, Keach says that Burkitt is partially right; for there are many precepts given to the Jews that do not pertain to Christians. To ground the Christian church on Old Testament commands can transform her into a Jewish church and the consequences of it may be far wider than the error, according to Keach, of pedobaptism. Christians may even start to circumcise their infants, "as some of late here in England were deluded to do. Therefore, we say as to all precepts of the Gospel that are meer positive laws, the New Testament is our only rule without the help of the Old."[187] Undoubtedly, the Old Testament can legitimately be used to establish moral principles as seen in the Ten Commandments and, additionally, to provide instructions on "prayer, singing God's praising, fasting days, &c. But for you to intimate in the case of circumcision that the Old Testament is a rule of practice, or in respect of Jewish church membership, you strangely betray your ignorance..."[188]

The New Testament speaks little about pedobaptism, Burkitt maintains, because it was common among the Jews to baptise proselytes before and during the first century. Whereas the rite of circumcision was the sign of the covenant, the rite of baptism was the sign of purification; "for when any of the Gentiles were admitted into the Jewish church, both parents and children were first circumcised and then wash'd, in token of cleaning them from the filth of their heathenism; so that baptism among the Jews constantly went along with circumcision till our Saviour's time."[189]

---

[185] Burkitt, *Argumentative Discourse*, 5. Cf. Rothwell, *Paedobaptismus Vindicatus*, xviii; Flavell, *Vindiciarum Vindex*, 52-53.
[186] Keach, *Rector Rectified*, 17.
[187] Keach, *Rector Rectified*, 18, 20.
[188] Keach, *Rector Rectified*, 20.
[189] Burkitt, *Argumentative Discourse*, 5. Cf. Smythies, *The Non-Communicant*, 88-89; Rothwell, *Paedobaptismus Vindicatus*, 7; Bridgewater, *Athenian Oracle*, I: 306, IV: 157, 179.

Is there any command from God, Keach interrogates, to this practice of washing away heathenism? The Jews invented this ritual without any warrant from God, just as the precursors of the Church of England invented pedobaptism for the washing of original sin. Both practices are "meer humane tradition."[190] Nothing unwarranted by the New Testament should be taken as a Christian doctrine, be it a Jewish or a Popish tradition. The Church of Rome, lacking any warrant from the Scripture, "received infant-baptism as an unwritten Apostolical Tradition," as Bellarmine himself admits.

> That though the arguments of the Anabaptists, from the defects of command or example, have a great use against the Lutherans, for as much as they use that rite every where, and having no command or example, theirs is to be rejected; yet is of no force against the Catholics, who conclude that Apostolical Tradition is of no less authority with us than the Scripture, &. This of baptising infants is an Apostolical Tradition.[191]

As for Jewish traditions, it is a disgrace what learned men such as "Hammond, Taylor and Lightfoot have said" in support of pedobaptism, as they take refuge in the Talmud. Is not the totality of Christian doctrine contained in Holy Scripture? Why include the Jewish Talmud, Keach asks, to support dubious, nay, wrong teaching, as infant baptism?[192] If this Jewish washing cannot be proved to be *Jure Divino*, there is no reason to give it any credence.[193] Keach attempts to refute the Talmudic washing as basis for pedobaptism with a syllogism.

> That custom among the Jews that God never commanded, nor is any where given by Moses unto them, who was faithful in all his house, was no ordinance of God, but a meer human tradition. But the custom among

---

[190] Keach, *Rector Rectified*, 21.

[191] Bellarmine, *De Controversiis Christianae Fidei*, De Sacramento Baptismi, Caput IX: 'Soluuntur objectiones Anabaptistarum,' s.v. Keach mistakenly attributes this quote to Bellarmine's previous division, i.e., Caput VIII: 'De Baptismo infantium, contra Anabaptistas.' See Keach, *Light Broke Forth*, [325-326]. Cf. Idem, *Counter-Antidote*, postscript, 3; idem, *Rector Rectified*, 21.

[192] Keach, *Rector Rectified*, 22-23. For Henry Hammond, see *Letter of Resolution to Six Quaeres, of Present Use in the Church of England* (London: Printed by J. Flesher for R. Royston at the Angel in Ivy-lane, 1653), 176-211. For John Lightfoot, see 'In Evangelium S. Matthaei Horae Hebraicae et Talmudicae,' Cap. III, ver. 6, in *Joannis Lightfooti, Opera Ominia*, Tomus II (Roterodami: Typis Regeneri Leers, 1686). For Jeremy Taylor, cf. e.g., *Antiquitates Christianae: Or the History of the Life and Death of the Holy Jesus, as Also the Lives, Acts and Martyrdoms of His Apostles*, In Two Parts, 9th ed. (London: Printed by J. Leake, for John Meredith, in Trust for Royston and Elizabeth Meredith. And are to be sold by S. and J. Sprint, et. al., 1703), Part I, 'Discourse VI: Of Baptism,' 8.

[193] Keach, *Pedobaptism Disproved*, 19.

the Jews of baptising the heathen and their children who were admitted into the church, was never commanded of God, nor any where given unto them by Moses who was faithful in all his house. Ergo, that custom was no ordinance of God but a meer human tradition.[194]

There is no command from God, Burkitt says, barring the children of Christians from God's church; that is, God has "no where declared that infants...should be excluded now from baptism, they being as capable of the visible sign of Gods invisible favours now, as they were then."[195] In other words, it is beyond doubt that if Christ, who was faithful in all things, had wanted the "exclusion of infants out of the visible church, he would have acquainted her with this alteration..."[196]

"You mean," Keach clarifies, that God "has no where forbid in express words the baptising of infants; no more, say I, has he" forbidden the baptism of chimes or the consecration of water.[197] Worse still, God has no where forbidden pedocommunion. Allowing for something to be done in the house of God, just because it is not prohibited and resembles a Jewish ceremony, would justify every Romish innovation imaginable; "for the Pope, Popish vestures, candle and candlesticks, &c. they no doubt will tell you are of like signification with the high priest under the law, with the priest's vestures and other ceremonies among the Jews."[198] Moreover, if that which is not forbidden can be practised, "how could we deny or oppose the Papists seven Sacraments? or condemn salt, oil and spittle to be used in baptism, which they use in it, seeing these are not forbidden? But well said Tertullian, 'Is it lawful because it is not forbidden? 'tis therefore not lawful, because it is not commanded.'"[199] Concerning Burkitt's point that undoubtedly Christ would have acquainted his church if he had wanted her to exclude infants, Keach says, "I must retort it back upon you with much better reason: doubtless, say I, had our Saviour intended the admission of infants, he would at this time have acquainted his disciples (and so us), that it was still his will" that babies were to be part of his church. This would have to be made clear since he explicitly required his church to be constituted by disciples.[200]

Following on, Burkitt makes a similar argument, but with an emphasis on the *need* for the replacement of circumcision by baptism. "If baptism succeeds

---

[194] Keach, *Rector Rectified*, 23-24. Cf. Idem, *Answer to two Athenian Mercuries*, 5; and, *Pedobaptism Disproved*, 2.

[195] Burkitt, *Argumentative Discourse*, 4. Cf. Smythies, *The Non-Communicant*, 89, 90; Rothwell, *Paedobaptismus Vindicatus*, 28-29, 34, 37.

[196] Burkitt, *Argumentative Discourse*, 27.

[197] Keach, *Rector Rectified*, 7.

[198] Keach, *Rector Rectified*, 7-8. Cf. Idem, *Light Broke Forth*, 88-89.

[199] Keach, *Rector Rectified*, 66-67. Tertullian, *Liber De Corona*, c. ii, P.L.2. Cf. Keach, *Counter-Antidote*, 42; and, *Light Broke Forth*, 21.

[200] Keach, *Rector Rectified*, 124.

not in the room of circumcision, then either circumcision is not abolished or else some other ordinance succeeds in the room of circumcision." However, to assert "that circumcision is not abolished is virtually to deny that Christ is come in the flesh; and no other ordinance is pretended to succeed in the room of circumcision. Therefore, baptism undoubtedly succeeds or nothing succeeds in the room of circumcision."[201]

The major premise must be denied, Keach avers, since there is no necessity of a Jewish rite to be replaced by a Christian one. Otherwise, each Jewish ceremony, rite and precept would require a corresponding Christian match. In other words, Christianity would have to have "more than three hundred" commands, ceremonies and rites, in order to correspond with its Jewish counterpart.[202]

Still on the question of baptism superseding circumcision, Burkitt insists that the New Testament explicitly authorised baptism to replace it. He says, "to put the matter out of all dispute, namely, that baptism doth succeed in the room of circumcision, take St Paul's testimony. Col.2.11,12, 'In whom also ye are circumcised with the circumcision made without hands, by the circumcision of Christ, buryed with him in baptism'. Observe here," Burkitt proceeds, "that the design of the Apostle is to take the Colossians off from the old sacramental rite of circumcision." Paul explains to them that they lack nothing, since baptism is more appropriate to their new condition. In effect, "Christians may now be said by baptism to be spiritually circumcised, as the Jews of old might be said by circumcision to be spiritually baptised."[203]

Keach begins his answer by affirming that Paul's intention in this text, *pace* Burkitt, was to assert the completeness or wholeness of Christians without Jewish accretions. In order to show how whole believers are, Paul "mentions faith as well as baptism, or such a faith that should always attend baptism; and therefore infant-baptism from hence cannot be proved or inferred, nor the least ground for your bold conclusion from hence, viz., that baptism came in the room of circumcision."[204] This Jewish rite has ceased, but not because it has been replaced by baptism; it rather came to an end on account of the fact that it has fulfilled its purpose. That is, the ceremony of circumcision was a figure of the promised circumcision of the heart (Rom.2.28-29). Paul wants to demonstrate in Col. 2.11-12, Keach claims, "that these believing Colossians had through Christ by the Spirit obtained the anti-type thereof or the thing figured out in the circumcision of the flesh; which baptism clearly represent." This Christian circumcision of the heart is visually represented by baptism as a

---

[201] Burkitt, *Argumentative Discourse*, 2-3. Cf. Smythies, *The Non-Communicant*, 88; Shute, *Replication to Benjamin Keach*, 60; idem, *Antidote to Anabaptism*, 136-137.
[202] Keach, *Rector Rectified*, 4.
[203] Burkitt, *Argumentatiye Discourse*, 4. Cf. Rothwell, *Paedobaptismus Vindicatus*, 14, 19; Bridgewater, *Athenian Oracle*, I: 306, IV: 158.
[204] Keach, *Rector Rectified*, 8.

person is buried under the water and is raised to new life. This act parallels Christ's burial under the earth and his rising from the dead.[205]

Is Circumcision a Seal of the Foedus Gratiae?

The Athenians affirm that "infants have now the same right to the seal of the covenant under the Gospel, as they had before under the Law."[206] In typical syllogistic fashion, Burkitt says, "[i]f the infants of believing Christians under the Gospel are in covenant with God, as the Jewish infants under the Law were; then the seal of the covenant, which is baptism, may and ought to be applied to them. But the infants of believers under the Gospel are in covenant with God, as well as the Jewish infants under the Law were." Consequently, "baptism, the seal of the covenant, ought to be applied to these, as circumcision was to them."[207] As a matter of fact, "if the covenant which God made with Abraham be a covenant of works (as the Anabaptists affirm) how comes circumcision, the seal of that covenant, to be called a seal of righteousness of faith, Rom.4.11."[208]

Even if the offspring of Christians, Keach supposes, were in covenant with God, baptism would not automatically be the seal of this covenant; for God has not ordained this rite to be such a seal. The only seal given to the *foedus gratiae* is the Holy Spirit (Eph.1.13-14; 4.30).[209] More to the point, the error here, Keach alleges, has to do with the assumption that the seal of the pact of grace is circumcision. This rite is rather designated the "seal of the righteousness of the faith he had (that is, Abraham) and which he had, being yet uncircumcised" (Rom.4.11).[210] Observe that Paul does not say that circumcision is the seal of the *covenant*, he rather affirms that it is the seal of the *faith* of Abraham. Additionally, it is the faith of nobody else, but Abraham's alone; for there were many godly people who were not circumcised and yet were in covenant with God. Moreover, the children of these pious men—e.g., Job's—were not circumcised because their parents did not *know* they should do so, but because their parents had not been *ordained* so to do. It is "God's command only," Keach continues, "and not their being in covenant, made their duty to circumcise their children; and had God given us such a command or any

---

[205] Keach, *Rector Rectified*, 8-9. Cf. Idem, *Pedobaptism Disproved*, 4.

[206] Bridgewater, *Athenian Oracle*, IV: 187. Cf. Ibid., 190, I: 306; Exell, *Serious Enquiry*, [43], 66, 71; Rothwell, *Paedobaptismus Vindicatus*, 5, 13, 21, 38; Flavell, *Vindiciarum Vindex*, 289-290.

[207] Burkitt, *Argumentative Discourse*, 8. Cf. Rothwell, *Paedobaptismus Vindicatus*, 10; Shute, *Replication to Benjamin Keach*, 59; idem, *Antidote to Anabaptism*, 26; Flavell, *Vindiciarum Vindex*, 292.

[208] Burkitt, *Argumentative Discourse*, 13. Cf. Flavell, *Vindiciarum Vindex*, 220, 234.

[209] Keach, *Rector Rectified*, 39, 2. Cf. Idem, *Counter-Antidote*, 15.

[210] Keach, *Rector Rectified*, 39. Cf. Idem, *Counter-Antidote*, 50.

authority to baptise our children, we ought and would baptise them; [but] must not, dare not, without such positive command."²¹¹

Keach also wants to refute Burkitt's minor proposition, sc., that the descendants of Christians are in covenant with God. This assumption is backed by the widely used argument that infants were never explicitly cast away from God's covenant. The Athenians articulate that argument using a general principle. "An ordinance once enjoin'd and never repeal'd is always in force: but the ordinance of children incovenanting was once in the Old Testament enjoin'd and was never repeal'd; ergo, 'tis yet in force."²¹² Burkitt, on the other hand, particularises it:

> They who by circumcision were once solemnly taken into covenant with God and never since were solemnly cast out, do undoubtedly continue in a covenant state. But infants under the Law were solemnly by God's appointment taken into covenant with himself and were never since by any command of God cast out. Therefore, they do still continue in covenant.²¹³

To the general point put forth by the Athenians, Keach replies rhetorically: "If the ordinance of children incovenanting under the Law was circumcision, that ordinance is repealed. Is not circumcision repealed?"²¹⁴ To Burkitt, Keach insists that the fact that Jewish infants were part of the covenant of works does not make them, or anybody else, part of the covenant of grace. In effect, in accordance with "that maxim *omnis privatio intimat habitum*, you know that every dispossession implieth a possession. Infants therefore cannot be cast out of the Gospel church, before it can be proved they were ever admitted."²¹⁵ Moreover, covenant status does not guarantee participation in the rite of baptism; otherwise John would have indiscriminately baptised all circumcised adults. This is due to the fact that the rites of baptism and circumcision belong to different churches and, therefore, membership in one does not warrant membership in the other.²¹⁶

The task of the advocates of infant baptism, as Keach envisages it, is to demonstrate that pedobaptism indeed seals babies. When you can attest that your babies possess "such faith as Abraham had, and that their baptism doth seal that faith to them for righteousness—which circumcision sealed

---

²¹¹ Keach, *Rector Rectified*, 39-40. Cf. Idem, *Ax Laid to the Root*, II: 9-10. *Contra*, Bridgewater, *Athenian Oracle*, IV: 195.
²¹² Bridgewater, *Athenian Oracle*, IV: 158. See also, ibid., 160, 164, 199, 201, 202, 204. Cf. Rothwell, *Paedobaptismus Vindicatus*, 24.
²¹³ Burkitt, *Argumentative Discourse*, 8-9. Cf. Exell, *Serious Enquiry*, 26-27; Rothwell, *Paedobaptismus Vindicatus*, 13; Flavell, *Vindiciarum Vindex*, 290; Bridgewater, *Athenian Oracle*, IV: 188; Shute, *Antidote to Anabaptism*, 45.
²¹⁴ Keach, *Pedobaptism Disproved*, 19.
²¹⁵ Keach, *Rector Rectified*, 59.
²¹⁶ Keach, *Rector Rectified*, 27-28.

Abraham—you do your business. But sirs, pray what blessings of the covenant of grace doth baptism now seal to your infants?"[217] Obviously it seals nothing, since many baptised infants grow up to be profane. Keach lets his interlocutor speak. "O, says one, the covenant is theirs, it belong to them and shall we deny them the seal?" However, "you must first prove the covenant of grace doth indeed belong to believers children as such, before you talk at such a rate as you do." It is imperative to note that a seal is something that confirms or guarantees something else, but pedobaptism does not guarantee piety, as experience attests. Hence, "take heed you do not blind the minds of people and deceive them, by making them think they are in covenant, when indeed it may be no such a thing."[218]

We close this section with Burkitt's claim that there is parity or equivalence between circumcision and baptism because the Abrahamic pact and the covenant of grace are essentially the same concerts.[219] In order to deny Burkitt's allegation, Keach lists thirteen disparities. First, the rite of circumcision was a figure of the coming Messiah; "baptism is a sign he is already come, was dead and buried." Second, the Jewish rite was a token of the compact established "with Abraham and his natural seed; baptism is a sign of the peculiar spiritual privileges made to saints, as such, no others."[220] Third, the rite of circumcision was a household affair; the rite of baptism is a church affair. Fourth, removing the foreskin was to be performed by the genitors; but the rite of baptism is to be performed solely by a minister of the Gospel. Fifth, the rite of circumcision entailed drawing blood as the flesh was cut; "baptism is to done by dipping the whole body into the water without drawing of any blood."[221] Sixth, the rite of circumcision was exclusively given to boys, but baptism is to be given to both sexes. Seventh, the cutting of the foreskin was to be performed on a precise day; the baptismal rite is not bound to any day or age. Eighth, the Jewish rite left a visible mark, the Christian rite makes no bodily mark. Ninth, the rite of circumcision was exclusively given "to Abraham's house, to his male infants only or such who were bought with his money, and not the male infants of any other godly men in his days, unless they join themselves to his family;" the baptismal rite is inclusive of all Christians from all ethnicities.[222] The Jewish rite obligated all included therein to fulfil the Mosaic code; baptism, on the other hand, liberates Christians "from the yoke of bondage." Eleventh,

---

[217] Keach, *Ax Laid to the Root*, II: 11.
[218] Keach, *Ax Laid to the Root*, II: 11. For the argument that the children are in covenant and thus have a right to the seal thereof, see, for example, Rothwell, *Paedobaptismus Vindicatus*, 93-94.
[219] Burkitt, *Argumentative Discourse*, 14. Cf. Rothwell, *Paedobaptismus Vindicatus*, xxvii-xxviii, 28, 119.
[220] Keach, *Light Broke Forth*, 86-87.
[221] Keach, *Light Broke Forth*, 87.
[222] Keach, *Light Broke Forth*, 87.

circumcision cannot stand in parity with baptism, for if this were the case, there would be no need for baptism. If circumcision made people part of the *foedus gratiae*, the rite of baptism would be useless; but the fact that Jesus and many of his followers, though circumcised, were nevertheless baptised negates any parity between the two rites. Twelfth, the cutting of the foreskin is a symbol of cleansing from sin or removing the sin of the flesh; but the baptismal rite symbolises Jesus' dying, being buried and rising again. Thirteenth, and finally, the Jewish rite "was to be a partition wall betwixt Jew and Gentile; but baptism testifieth that Jew and Gentile, male and female, Barbarian and Scythian, bond and free are all one in Christ Jesus. Therefore, there are divers disparities and different significations between circumcision and baptism."[223]

The Great Commission

Herein the arguments for pedobaptism rest ultimately on the universal inclusiveness of the commission: when Christ ordered the baptism of all, infants are, presumably, not excluded. (i) Owen and (ii) Burkitt appeal to this inclusiveness, (iii) Rothwell to the bountifulness of it.

(i). To Keach's objection that there is no command for the baptising of infants, James Owen replies that "there is not one particular command, *totidem verbis*, naming infant-baptism and that is not necessary; but there is an universal command...[to] baptise all nations, of which children are a great part." Moreover, granting that "there is a command for the baptism of the parents, then there is a command for the baptism of infants; for the children are included in the parents, even as part of them, being partakers of the privileges of good parents and of the judgement of wicked parents."[224]

There is no need, Keach retorts, to present a command in *totidem verbis*, "let infants be baptised." However, the inference introduced by Owen is invalid for several reasons. At the outset, the text of the commission requires the preaching of the Gospel in the first place, then, and only then, baptism is to be administered. Next, the point that infants are an inescapable part of all nations and, consequently, ought to receive baptism, is completely false, since no one would justify the baptism of the heathen or unbelievers on the same basis.

---

[223] Keach, *Light Broke Forth*, 87-88. All thirteen points *ipsis litteris* in *Rector Rectified*, 5-6.

[224] "Nid oes un *gorchymyn neullduol* mewn cnifer o eiriau yn enwi bedydd plant, ac nid yw hynny angheorheidiol; eithr y mae *gorchymyn Cyffredinol*,...[i] fedyddio yr holl genhedloedd, o ba rai mae plant yn rhan fawr." Os "oes gorchymyn am fedyddio'r rhieni, mae gorchymyn am fedyddio'r plant, Canys cynhwysir y plant yn y rhieni, megis rhannau o honynt, sy gyfrannogion o ragorfreintiau rhieni da, ac o farnedigachau rhieni drwg." Owen, *Bedydd Plant or Nefoedd*, 166-167. Cf. Rothwell, *Paedobaptismus Vindicatus*, xvii-xviii, 6, 23-26; Shute, *Replication to Benjamin Keach*, 52; idem, *Antidote to Anabaptism*, 28, 50; Flavell, *Vindiciarum Vindex*, 293; Bridgewater, *Athenian Oracle*, IV: 188, 189, I: 307, 308.

Finally, as to the reasoning that children are included in the parents as part of them and as such do not need a specific command to be baptised, that is "very ridiculous ...for any man to assert it;" for absurd consequences would follow from this logic, as, for example, the baptism received by parents would serve their children and thus children would not need to be baptised.[225]

(ii). William Burkitt presents a similar argument to Owen's. The commission commands to baptise all people and given the fact that infants are part of all—as the particular is part of the universal—they must be baptised though they are not mentioned. Burkitt presents an analogy to prove his point. "Suppose the king should grant his Royal Charter to make this your market-town a corporation and all the inhabitants of it free-men; would any be so idle as to suppose that this Royal Grant doth not include your children because it doth not particularly name them?" He continues rhetorically, "[i]s not the son of a free-man, a free-man as well as his father? Thus here in the sacred charter and Royal pattent of the covenant of grace, which is sealed by baptism." The promises and benefits given to believers are also extended to their offspring (Act.2.38).[226]

Keach accuses Burkitt of presenting a sophistical argument. For it is undeniable that "all nations" must include "pagans, Turks and infidels, with the profane and ungodly men and women and their children," all of which are not specifically named in the commission. Should they also be baptised?[227] Additionally, Burkitt's analogy is flawed, Keach purports, for his civil Royal Charter does not parallel the spiritual Christian charter, i.e., the regulations for the establishment of the Christian church. That is, fleshly lineage does not make a person part of the *foedus gratiae*, since participation in it is not by natural but by spiritual birth. Keach puts this point thus: it is "not the first birth that brings us into the covenant of grace, but the second; not generation, but regeneration; not being born of believers, but by being born of God."[228]

Burkitt, however, argues that the Great Commission has to be understood in the context in which it was given. Christianity was being introduced to pagans and, in that case, the announcement of the Word would have to antecede the practice of baptism; hence, Jesus commanded his disciples to preach first then baptise. Likewise, if the Christian faith were to be taken to a foreign land, where the Gospel was unknown, then teaching would have to precede baptism. However, once the adults are instructed and manifest faith in Christ,

---

[225] Keach, *Light Broke Forth*, [241]. Cf. Idem, *Counter-Antidote*, 15.

[226] Burkitt, *Argumentative Discourse*, 6-7. Cf. Ibid., 123. Note the twist Exell put on this same argument, when he asserts that on the basis of Luk.3.7 it must be granted "that children are contained in and intended by the 'multitude' in Scripture as well as the adult." *Serious Inquiry*, 18.

[227] Keach, *Rector Rectified*, 29-30. This point is made syllogistically in idem, *Answer unto two Athenian Mercuries*, 1. Cf. Idem, *Pedobaptism Disproved*, 6; and, *Counter-Antidote*, postscript [1].

[228] Keach, *Rector Rectified*, 31. Cf. Idem, *Ax Laid to the Root*, II: 48.

then their offspring may receive baptism followed by instruction, like the sons of "the Jewish Proselytes were first circumcised and then taught; for tho Abraham was first taught and then circumcised, yet Isaac was first circumcised and then taught: so that the sense of our Saviour is this, teach such as are capable of teaching and baptise such as are capable of baptism."[229]

Keach accuses Burkitt of inconsistency, for he sometimes advocates pedobaptism on the basis of a "habitual faith [or] faith *in semine*,"[230] however now Burkitt is prepared to have infants baptised not on the basis of faith but capability. Secondly, in the case of Abraham, whom Burkitt cites, he was explicitly commanded to circumcise his son. But there is no command in the New Testament saying that once adults are evangelised, then infants may be baptised without teaching. Granted that there is no command, "how dare you," Keach asks Burkitt, make "such additions to Christ's commission without his authority and so make the world believe, if you could, our blessed Saviour gave forth an imperfect commission to his disciples, which all men must confess is the only warrant and rule of all ministers to act by in the case of baptising to the end of the world."[231]

(iii). John Rothwell, on the basis of Mat.28, makes the following argument: the great commission is more comprehensive and more bountiful than the *foedus operum*. Suppose Moses had given a commission "to twelve elders of Israel, as the blessed Jesus gave to his disciples, go teach all nations, circumcising them; this" would have "been no prohibition to the circumcising of Jewish children," though no mention of infants were made. Under the covenant of works, circumcision was the sign of its membership; under the covenant of grace, which is "a more merciful dispensation," baptism plays the same role.[232]

Keach sarcastically asks Rothwell, "[i]s this that the mountains have brought forth? We were big in expectation by your title page, wondering what new notion or argument you had found out from the Commission...but truly sir, the log is still too heavy, you cannot lift it up." For you are right in conceding that circumcision belongs to the *foedus operum*, however, as you grant this, your cause is lost.[233]

Both Burkitt and Rothwell failed to see, Keach claims, that the Great Commission has a sequence, viz., teaching precedes baptism. When the Commission was given, Christ did not say, "go, baptise all nations; mark, but 'go ye therefore, teach all nations, $\mu\alpha\theta\eta\tau\varepsilon\acute{\upsilon}\sigma\alpha\tau\varepsilon$' (Mat.28.19); that is, disciple, make disciples in all nations baptising them, that is, such who are so

---

[229] Burkitt, *Argumentative Discourse*, 20. Cf. Rothwell, *Paedobaptismus Vindicatus*, xl-xlv, 10, 28, 84; Flavell, *Vindiciarum Vindex*, 293.
[230] See infra under the heading, 'Incipient faith as basis for baptism,' pp. 173ff.
[231] Keach, *Rector Rectified*, 96-97.
[232] Rothwell, *Paedobaptismus Vindicatus*, 4-7. See also, ibid., 2-3, 26-29.
[233] Keach, *Ax Laid to the Root*, II: 29.

taught or made disciples."²³⁴ As to Rothwell's proposition, let us suppose that the Israelites had received a commission along the lines of, "go and teach all nations, circumcising them..." Can anyone suppose that this commission would have granted the Jews the right to pedocircumcision? Obviously not, for children are not able to be taught and, again, the sequencing in the said commission is teaching first, then circumcising.²³⁵

Burkitt objects to the necessity of strict observance to a sequence in the Great Commission. Considering that there is an inversion of words by the Evangelists, word sequence proves nothing: for "St Matthew sets teaching before baptising, but St Mark sets baptising before teaching, Mar.1.4, so that no conclusive argument can be drawn from hence either way."²³⁶

Keach examines the said inversion done by the Evangelists. "Pray, good reader, observe the text: John 'did baptise in the wilderness and teach the baptism of repentance for the remission of sins.'" Obviously, Keach claims, the text is not saying that John baptised people in order to make them repent. The fact that his baptism is "baptism of repentance," means only that repentance was the chief message he preached and that which he required from everyone who came to him for baptism. Moreover, both Jesus and John made *disciples* (Joh.4.1-2) and then baptised them. Furthermore, there is no Scriptural evidence that ever a person, adult or otherwise, was baptised without a profession of faith. All of this being the case, the argument based on the sequence of words in the Commission to baptise is definitive.²³⁷ To support his point, Keach quotes Perkins on the sequence of words to baptising. "First, teach them; that is, make them my disciples by teaching them to believe and repent. Here we are to consider the order which God observes in making with men a covenant in baptism." Initially, God calls everyone "by his Word and Spirit to believe and repent; then, in the second place, he makes a promise of mercy and forgiveness; and then, thirdly, he seals his promise by baptism." Those who ignore this sequence, Keach continues to quote Perkins, "deal preposterously, over-flipping the command of repenting and believing and [this] is the cause of so much prophanes in the world."²³⁸

To Rothwell, Keach says, if the Commission is to be made, as you say, more "full...(or rather more) beneficial and extensive than the covenant of works,"²³⁹

---

²³⁴ Keach, *Rector Rectified*, 30. For a syllogistical argument for the priority of teaching before baptism, see idem, *Answer unto two Athenian Mercuries*, syllogism # 1, p.1. Cf. Idem, *Pedobaptism Disproved*, 6-7.

²³⁵ Keach, *Ax Laid to the Root*, II: 30.

²³⁶ Burkitt, *Argumentative Discourse*, 19-20. Cf. Rothwell, *Paedobaptismus Vindicatus*, 39-40.

²³⁷ Keach, *Rector Rectified*, 93-94. On Exell's view of repentance as an ingredient for baptism, see *Serious Inquiry*, 80.

²³⁸ Perkins, *A Commentarie upon Galatians*, 257; cited by Keach, *Rector Rectified*, 94-95.

²³⁹ Rothwell, *Paedobaptismus Vindicatus*, 4.

what would stop any Christian minister going to the pagans and baptising "them and their children," making them automatically believers? "You may teach them...faith and repentance, afterwards, as you do your children; but the truth is, there is no need to teach them afterwards the way of faith and regeneration (if your doctrine be true) because the chief thing they receive in baptism, you say, is divine grace," that is, "regeneration, adoption and a title to the inheritance of eternal life..." And it is granted by all that these "divine habits can never be lost."[240] Concerning Rothwell's hypothetical commission given to twelve Israelite elders, it cannot be equated with Christ's Commission. The simile is flawed because the Mosaic Law is ethnically bound, whereas Christ's Commission is for all ethnicities, or, to put it differently, the Law was exclusively granted to the Jews but the Gospel is not exclusive of any nation. Confirming the former, the Scripture asserts that God "shewth his word unto Jacob, his statutes and judgements to Israel: He hath not dealt so with any nation..."(Psa.147.19-20). Proving the latter, Jesus commissioned his disciples to preach the Gospel to every country—promising that whoever believe would be saved (Mar.16.16).[241]

The inclusion of infants in the command to baptise all nations may be proved by what Burkitt calls "necessary consequence." Sometimes Christ himself argues that way. For example, when discussing the resurrection with the Sadducees, Jesus says that his Father is the living God of the Patriarchs and, therefore, they are alive. The Arians refused to accept consequential reasoning, and the Anabaptists, doing likewise, find themselves hard pressed to maintain their own practices, such as praying before meals, altering the Sabbath or allowing women to participate at the Lord's Table. These lawful practices cannot be directly proved from Scripture, but rather inferred from necessary consequences.[242]

In typical polemical mood, Keach answers Burkitt: "You basely misrepresent those you call Anabaptists; for we do not deny, nor never did, necessary consequences deduced from the Scripture;" however, a difference must be made between a legitimate and an illegitimate biblical inference. There are issues of faith, e.g., Christ's divinity, which can be genuinely inferred from the Scriptures, but the establishment of a law or institution is not to be done by inference. Considering that no Old Testament institution was inferred, but, on the contrary, they were all ordained (Hab.2.2), we should expect no less of New Testament institutions.[243] As to prayer, the Bible unambiguously commands believers to pray always (1The.5.17-18). Concerning the Sabbath, the Christian practice is amply illustrated in the New Testament: the gathering at Pentecost

---

[240] Keach, *Ax Laid to the Root*, II: 30.
[241] Keach, *Ax Laid to the Root*, II: 31.
[242] Burkitt, *Argumentative Discourse*, 7-8. Cf. Rothwell, *Paedobaptismus Vindicatus*, xviii-xix, 7, 11-12, 64-66; Bridgewater, *Athenian Oracle*, I: 309, IV: 160, 172.
[243] Keach, *Rector Rectified*, 33-34.

(Act.2.1-2), the church meeting for the Eucharist (Act.20.7), the Corinthian collection for the needy (1Cor.16.1-2), etc. are all examples of church meetings on the first day of the week. As to women's participation at the Table, Scripture clearly includes them: when Paul commands self-examination (1Cor.11.28), although he uses the word "man," he means both sexes, "for so the word Ἄνθρωπος in the Greek, and in the Hebrew signify. There 'is one mediator between God and man' [1Tim.2.5]. Is not the woman comprehended as clearly as the man?"[244] Moreover, Keach asks Burkitt, have "you never read of the figure *Sylepsis* or *Conceptio*, that comprehends the less worthy under the more worthy, *indignioris sub dignioris*?" The husband plays this role in a marriage, as seen, Keach claims, in 1Cor. 6.16: οἱ δύο εἰς σάρκα μίαν, they two shall be one flesh. Lastly, since men and women were disciples (Act.2), there can be no doubt that both sexes received communion.[245]

Federal Holiness

"If the infants of Christian parents," Burkitt argues, "are federally holy, then are they subjects qualified for baptism. But the Scripture pronounces such children federally holy. Therefore, they are qualified for baptism and may be admitted to it."[246] Both the Fathers and Scriptures witness federal holiness. James Owen says, "Tertulian gave evidence for the baptism of children around the year 192. *Ex sanctificato altero sexu sanctos procreari ait, ex seminis praerogativa.* From holy parents are born holy children according to the privilege of the seed of the faithful."[247] As to the Scriptures, two texts allegedly substantiate this claim: (i) Romans 11.16. and (ii) 1Corinthians 7.14.

(i). In the first passage, ("For if the first fruit is holy, the lump is also holy; and if the root be holy, so are the branches"), Burkitt argues that the "branches" referred to by Paul are to be understood as the Jewish people. They were cast aside on account of unbelief and the Gentiles were engrafted in their place. On this account, the Gentiles came to be inheritors of the holiness that the Jews possessed by being part of the holy root. Thus, Christians are now sanctified, "not with an internal and inherent holiness passing by natural generation from

---

[244] Keach, *Rector Rectified*, 35. Cf. Idem, *Pedobaptism Disproved*, 20.
[245] Keach, *Rector Rectified*, 35-36. Cf. Idem, *Gold Refin'd*, 161-162; idem, *Pedobaptism Disproved*, 20-21.
[246] Burkitt, *Argumentative Discourse*, 23-24. Cf. Owen, *Bedydd Plant or Nefoedd*, 68; Rothwell, *Paedobaptismus Vindicatus*, 72; Bridgewater, *Athenian Oracle*, I: 307, IV: 160.
[247] Tertulian a dystiolaethodd tros fedydd plant ynghylch y flwyddyn 192. Ex sanctificato altero sexu sanctos procreari ait, ex seminis praerogativa. O rieni sanctaidd y genir plant sanctaidd, yn ol rhagorfraint hád y ffyddloniaid. Owen, *Bedydd Plant or Nefoedd*, 150. Cf. e.g., Tertullian, *De Anima*, c. xl (719), P.L.2.

parent to child, but with an external, relative, covenant-holiness, grounded on the promise made to the faithful and their seed."[248]

This so-called external federal holiness, Keach affirms, does not grant admission to baptism. There are several reasons for denying this privilege to infants. First, admission to baptism, as said before, is a positive command, i.e., explicitly made in sure terms (repentance and faith). Second, many Jews—the "holy" branches—came to John the Baptist and were denied baptism. That is, "that external relative covenant-holiness which qualified under the Old Testament persons for circumcision and Jewish church-membership, will not qualify old or young under the New Testament for baptism and Gospel church-membership."[249] Third, the text cited, Rom.11.16, does not explicitly say that infants of Christians are holy. Though a pedobaptist, when Goodwin deals with the issue of federal holiness, he says that "in the New Testament there is no other holiness spoken of, but personal or real by regeneration; about which he challenged all the world to shew to the contrary."[250] Finally, this concept of federal holiness and the argument that baptism produces holiness are mutually exclusive; that is, if holiness is produced by baptism, then infants are not holy on account of being the offspring of Christians. On the other hand, if the descendants of Christians are holy by merely having Christian parents (i.e., if federal holiness is true), then baptism is irrelevant.[251]

The context of the passage in question (Rom.9-11), Keach thinks, rather deals with the gracious aspect of the Abrahamic covenant. The fact that believing Gentiles are the people of God now, does not mean that God has rejected the Jews, for the acceptance of both are based on election. The evidence of this is what God told Elijah, "…seven thousand have I reserved…" (Rom.11.4). The Apostle shows that the majority of the descendants of Abraham were rejected on account of unbelief, but that eventually the Jewish chosen ones will "in God's due time be brought in and so partake of the blessings of the Gospel-covenant or the covenant of grace made with Abraham."[252] Observe, Keach adds, what Paul states in Rom.11.16: "For if the first fruit is holy, the lump is also holy; and if the root be holy, so are the branches." Keach understands the metaphor "root" as Abraham, whom God has appointed father of a spiritual seed. By "first fruit," it is denoted "Isaac, Jacob and the holy patriarchs, for they were given as the first fruits to Abraham, of that covenant and free promise of God."[253] The other metaphor, "lump," means, Keach continues, the entire chosen portion of the Israelites, from Abraham's

---

[248] Burkitt, *Argumentative Discourse*, 24.

[249] Keach, *Rector Rectified*, 106-107. Cf. Idem, *Ax Laid to the Root*, II: 20, 48.

[250] Keach, *Rector Rectified*, 107. Thomas Goodwin, *The Works of Thomas Goodwin*, 12 vols. (Edinburgh: James Nichol, 1864), IX: 455ff.

[251] Keach, *Light Broke Forth*, 112.

[252] Keach, *Rector Rectified*, 109-110.

[253] Keach, *Rector Rectified*, 110. Cf. Idem, *Ax Laid to the Root*, II: 23.

days until the coming of Christ. Two types of "branches" are mentioned: holy and broken ones. Both of them were contemporaries of Paul. The former was constituted of spiritual Jews and the latter of carnal ones; i.e., people that were descendants of Abraham but did not have his faith.[254] Keach draws a parallel between these broken branches and the ones Christ affirms that "bear no fruit" (Joh.15.2-4). These broken and fruitless branches are not part of the covenant of grace. However, what does Paul mean, then, when he said that some of the Jewish branches were "broken off" if they were never part of the covenant to begin with? They were separated from the external privileges of belonging to the Jewish state church, for this church was obliterated and a new church established on the basis of faith only. Having said all of this, Keach asks, "what doth this text do to prove the natural seed of believers are in Gospel-covenant; for if the natural seed of Abraham can lay no claim, nor have any right to Gospel-privileges, but are gone or broken off, what grounds is there for us to think that our natural offspring (as such) should be taken in?" The holiness of the branches referred to by Paul is not "an external federal holiness," but rather the holiness illustrated by Abraham, viz., faith in God.[255]

Additionally, Keach says that Burkitt's argument for pedobaptism on the basis of the federal holiness of the parents, makes parents now the "common head or root of their natural" progeny, just like Abraham was then.[256] Has God anywhere declared that every or any Christian father is to have special carnal progeny as Abraham had? If this were the case, faith would be obfuscated by ascribing undue value to the flesh. As it is, the only gate to the church, both past and present, is faith and not federal holiness. Although in the Jewish state church, all Jews had an external right to membership, yet only those who had faith were the spiritual descendants of Abraham and, as such, part of the invisible church. Likewise, in the New Testament, faith and faith alone grants entrance in the church.[257]

(ii). Burkitt's next argument for federal holiness is taken from the Corinthian correspondence. "The unbelieving wife is sanctified by the believing husband, & else were your children unclean, but now are they holy" (1Cor.7.14). Here, Burkitt thinks that Paul is addressing the same issue that Ezra addressed, namely, if it were licit to remain in a marriage when the wife was an unbeliever. The Apostle's answer was affirmative, for "the unbelieving wife is sanctified to the believing husband." How can this be, Burkitt asks. The wife is sanctified "not in her nature, but in her use," in order that as a couple they may have legitimate sexual relations. Second and most importantly, the children also

---

[254] Keach, *Rector Rectified*, 111. Cf. Idem, *Ax Laid to the Root*, II: 20-23.
[255] Keach, *Rector Rectified*, 111-112. Cf. Idem, *Counter-Antidote*, 37-40. Contrast Keach's hermeneutical approach to Rom. 11 with, for example, Shutte, *Antidote to Anabaptism*, 79-99.
[256] Keach, *Rector Rectified*, 113. Also *contra*, Shute, *Antidote to Anabaptism*, 186.
[257] Keach, *Rector Rectified*, 109.

benefit from this sanctifying presence; that is, the infants "are holy, not with an inherent, internal personal holiness; for the holiest man child is born in sin and by nature a child of wrath. But with an external, relative, federal holiness they are not common and unclean, like the children of infidels, but fit to be partakers of the privileges of the church," a privilege that heathen progeny do not have.[258]

It is obvious that the holiness in question, Keach inveighs against Burkitt, "is no such external relative federal holiness you dream of." The text merely speaks about holiness in the context of matrimony, that is, mixed marriage is considered legitimate in God's sight. This fact entails two things. First, a Christian spouse may commune with the unbeliever (herein Keach agrees with Burkitt). Second, the descendants of the couple are not "unclean or illegitimate, i.e., bastards."[259] This second part is the bone of contention. Burkitt thinks that the sanctification spoken about by Paul makes the children federally holy and thus with a right to baptism.[260] Keach, on the other hand, sees this holiness as nothing other than legitimacy. Besides this disagreement, Keach adds that whatever holiness the offspring derive from a believing parent, the partner also derives. Ergo, if the child would have a right to baptism on account of this holiness, then the unbelieving partner would have the same. How absurd is it?[261]

The Anabaptists object to our interpretation saying that Paul simply means that infants referred to are "not bastards. To which I answer," Burkitt proceeds, "this is not an interpreting, but a racking of the Scriptures to maintain a private opinion; it is to make the Scripture speak what you think and not what the Apostle intends, for according to this interpretation of the word 'holy,' the Apostle spake neither pertinently nor truly."[262]

This contention, Keach replies, deserves careful exegesis of 1Cor.7.14. For "Musculus...confesseth that he formerly abused this place against the Anabaptists."[263] Here Paul uses a type of verbal tense ($\dot{\eta}\gamma\iota\alpha\sigma\tau\alpha\iota$, has been made sanctified) to express the holiness of the partners within marriage. This verbal form equally refers to "present or past" actions and thus the partners are

---

[258] Burkitt, *Argumentative Discourse*, 24. Cf. Bridgewater, *Athenian Oracle*, I: 308, IV: 158, 191-192; Flavell, *Vindiciarum Vindex*, 292-294; Rothwell, *Paedobaptismus Vindicatus*, xix-xx, xxxvi-xxxvii, xliii, 57-58, 71, extensive discussion in pp. 124-136; Shute, *Antidote to Anabaptism*, 44; idem, *Replication to Benjamin Keach*, 34-35.

[259] Keach, *Rector Rectified*, 114. Cf. Idem, *Pedobaptism Disproved*, 8; and, *Counter-Antidote*, 40.

[260] Burkitt, *Argumentative Discourse*, 24.

[261] Keach, *Rector Rectified*, 114-115.

[262] Burkitt, *Argumentative Discourse*, 25.

[263] Keach, *Rector Rectified*, 119. "Abusus sum aliquando praesenti loco contra errorem anabaptistarum, infantes Christianorum baptismo arcentium, putans illud: nunc autem sancti sunt, idem esse atque, de populo Dei sunt propter fidelem parentem." Wolfgang Musculus, *In ambas Apostoli Pauli ad Corinthios epistolas commentarii. Cum indice rerum & verborum locupletissimo* (Basileae: Hervagius, 1559), s.v. 1 Ad Corinthios, VII: 14.

holy or sanctified even before one of them became a Christian. They are holy because they are legitimately married and chaste. This meaning may be confirmed by the fact "that Ἁγισμῷ, sanctification, is the same with chastity, 1The.4.7."[264] The partners can legitimately enjoy each another without the fear of fornication. Within the confines of a lawful or sanctified marriage, lawful or sanctified children may be produced; otherwise these children would be "unclean, but now are they holy: the particle νῦν δὲ, 'but now,' is not an adverb of time here, as Beza rightly speaks," it only stands in apposition to ἐπεὶ ἄρα, else were, they unclean.[265] "So νῦν δὲ, but now, is a particle of reasoning used in the assumption of arguments, which shews it is the assumption of the Apostle's argument and therefore it" ought to "be understood of holiness opposite to uncleanness mentioned; but that being no other than bastardy, the holiness can be meant no other than legitimation."[266] This interpretation is agreeable to other parts of Scripture, for "bastards were reckoned among unclean persons, Det.23.2. and the Apostle's expression is allusive to the Jewish speaking and estimation;" thus, it may be asked, "why it should be thought strange that 'holy' should signify legitimation...when Mal. 2.51. זרע אלהים, *a seed of God*, is rendered by some pedobaptists, *a holy seed*," as reference to the progeny of married couples? Moreover, although dismissive of credobaptism, many authors find this text unrelated to the issue. That is, the literal sense of the word "holy" herein advocated, Keach claims, in upheld by Ambrose, Jerome, Anselm, Aquinas and Melanchthon.[267] See, for example, what Erasmus asserts: children "born of such parents, as one being a Christian, the other not, are legitimately holy; for the conversion of either

---

[264] Keach, *Rector Rectified*, 115.
[265] Keach, *Rector Rectified*, 116-117. Theodore Beza, *Iesu Christi Novum Testamentum Interpretationes duae, una vetus, altera nova, T. Bezae* (Geneva: Estienne, 1565), s.v., Ad Corinth. I, VII: 14. Idem, *Testamentum Novum, sive Novum Foedus Iesu Christi, D.N. Cuius Graeco contextui respondent interpretationes duae: una vetus: altera, Theodori Bezae, nunc quartò diligenter ab eo recognita* (Geneva: s.n., 1589), s.v., Ad Corinth. I, VII: 14.
[266] Keach, *Rector Rectified*, 117-118.
[267] Keach, Rector Rectified, 118-119. Ambrose, *Commentaria In Epistola Ad Corinthios Primam*, 134, P.G.17; Jerome, *Commentarius in Primam Epistolam ad Corinthios*, c.vii, P.L.30; Anselm, *D. Anselmi Cantuariensis archiepiscopi, Theologorum omnium sui temporis facile Principis, neminique eorum qui post eum fuerunt, vel sanctitate, vel eruditione, vel eloquentia secundi, luculentissimae, in omnes sanctissimi Pauli Apostoli epistolas, & aliquot Euangelia, enarrationes* (Parisiis: Apud Ioannem Roigny, via Iacobea sus insigni quatuor Elementorum, 1549), s.v., 'I Ad Corinthios,' VII:14, col. c.; Thomas Aquinas, *Corpus Thomisticum* (Subsidia studii ab Enrique Alarcón colecta et edita Pampilonae ad Universitatis Studiorum Navarrensis aedes, 2005), s.v., Super I Epistolam ad Corinthios, Caput 7, Lectio 2; Philip Melanchthon, Argumentum et Brevis Explicatio Prioris Epistolae Ad Corinthios, VII, 14, in Philippi Melanchthonis Opera, *CR*, 15.

husband or wife, doth not dissolve the marriage which was made when both were in unbelief."²⁶⁸

The interpretation of the Baptists, Keach addresses Burkitt, "is not 'a racking of the Scripture to maintain a private opinion;' therefore what you speak is not true," for the term "holy" can indeed mean legitimate. Even though "the Greek word doth signify in so many places you mention, spiritual sanctification and separation to God, shew us where it signifies external federal holiness" in the Scriptures.²⁶⁹ What must be stressed, Keach urges, is that the Greek word is not limited to "spiritual sanctification and separation," as Burkitt asserts,

> for ἁγισεύω is used for *castimonian servo*, as Stephanus in his *Thesaurus* observes out of Demosthenes, κατὰ Νεάιρας, where a priest of Bacchus speaks thus, ἁγισεύω καί καθαρά εἰμί τοῦ ἀνδρὸς συνουσίας, I am holy and pure from the company of men: and the words ἁγνός, ἁγνεύω, ἁγνίζω, ἁγνεία, chaste, to be chaste, to make chaste, chastity, coming from the same root with ἅγιος, holy; whether ἅζω, to reverence, or ἅγαμαι, to admire, as grammarians conceive, are used for holiness very frequently, both in Scripture and in all sorts of Greek writers. So that what you say as to the signification of the word ἁγία, holy, that it cannot be taken for 'legitimate' is fully cleared and we are justified from your unjust accusation, viz., that we wrested the word to favour our private opinion; neither we are out in our Logik, as you infer; but now the inference may be that you are weak in your Greek.²⁷⁰

Benefits Accrued by Pedobaptism

"I shall prove," Burkitt contends, "that it is much more useful and beneficial to baptise a child in infancy, than to omit it till riper years." To start with, pedobaptism is useful because it functions as "a prae-engagement upon the

---

²⁶⁸ Keach, *Rector Rectified*, 119. Cf. e.g., Erasmus, 'Apologia pro Declamatione Matrimonii,' p. 109, cols, B-E, in *Desiderii Erasmi Roterodami Opera Omnia*, Tomus Nonus (Lugduni Batavorum, Curam & impresis Petro Vander, 1706).

²⁶⁹ Keach, *Rector Rectified*, 119-120.

²⁷⁰ Keach, *Rector Rectified*, 120. Ἁγισεύω. F. σω. P. κα, pro ἁγιάζω, inquit Suidas. Idem exponit, perago quae ad sacrificium pertinent. Hesychius, veneror. Item, pietatem colo; intellige autem pietatem in deos; & ita fortasse exponi in hoc Platonis loco possit,...Item, castimoniam servo, in qua significatione videtur sumi apud Demosthenem, κατὰ Νεάιρας; ubi tale est iusiurandum sacerdotis Bacchi, ἁγισεύω, καί καθαρά καί ἁγνή τῶ ἄλλων τῶ οὐ καθαρουόντων καί ἀπ' ἀνδρὸς συνουσίας. Scribitur & Ἁγισεύω, ῶ, unde ἁγισεῖν infinituus apud Hesychium. Henricus Stephanus, *Thesaurus Graecae Lingua* (Geneva: Excudebat Henr. Stephanus, 1572), s.v., Ἁγισεύω.

Christian to repel and resist temptations of Satan."[271]

Keach retorts that Burkitt might as well put infants "under an hundred engagements and covenants," and additionally, as soon as they grow up and acquire some understanding, ask them to make a vow "that they shall not yield to temptations and pretend 'tis Gods law they should do so; and if you can deceive their judgements, they will dread as much (nay, may be more) the breaking of those oaths and covenants, than this [baptism] you bring them into, without any authority from Jesus Christ."[272]

Pedobaptism is advantageous, Keach's opponents argue, for several other reasons: through it, baptism per se is not overlooked; infants participate in the church's prayers and care; children receive the effectual bond of holiness, have their nature regenerated, their sins forgiven, and thus they have the hope of heaven if called out of this world. These and other alleged benefits of pedobaptism will be now considered.

Burkitt maintains that pedobaptism "appears to be most beneficial and advantageous, because it prevents such shameful and scandalous neglect of baptism, …to the great blemish of Christianity."[273] Shame is rather the keeping of a human tradition, Keach replies, as the commands of Jesus "are neglected and his precious ordinance of baptism exposed to contempt and shame, as it is by you and thousands more," while "the statutes of Omri are zealously kept and observed, as the prophet complained; I mean, human rites and traditions…which the wisdom of your church and many corrupt churches have been zealous for to this day."[274]

Pedobaptism, Burkitt insists, is of benefit in that (1) a baptised infant has an "interest in all the prayers put up in and by the church;" (2) he or she benefits from "that special providential care which Christ exercises over his church;" (3) the child acquires a position nearer to God than those outside the church as the Scripture asserts: your "children shall be taught of God…" (Isa.54.13).[275]

Keach says in turn that, first, since God has never made infants members of his church, there is no reason to believe he will listen to prayers on behalf of children by virtue of the fact they are conscripted into her; second, obviously Jesus cares for children, but not on account of unauthorised church membership, and; third, it is impossible to make a child come closer to God by a human act. As for Isa.54.13, it is not a reference "to infants, not to our children as such, but to those godly Christians who being born in Sion, are indeed truly her children."[276]

---

[271] Burkitt, *Argumentative Discourse*, 38.

[272] Keach, *Rector Rectified*, 145-146.

[273] Burkitt, *Argumentative Discourse*, 41. Cf. Owen, *Bedydd Plant or Nefoedd*, 164-165.

[274] Keach, *Rector Rectified*, 153. The Scriptural allusion is Micah 6.16.

[275] Burkitt, *Argumentative Discourse*, 35-36. Cf. Bridgewater, *Athenian Oracle*, I: 309-310.

[276] Keach, *Rector Rectified*, 142.

As a benefit of enduring validity, James Owen says, baptism is a "witness of our faith in Christ, Mark 16.16...And therefore it is to remain as long as faith is to remain on the earth."[277] Assuming that baptism is a witness of our faith, then, Keach concludes, infants cannot be the subjects of it, since they are incapable of both knowing the object of faith, Christ, and of exercising faith in him.[278]

James Owen maintains that sin's remission is signified by baptism (Mk.1.4), and that those who reject baptism are ungrateful to such a gracious Father, "who offers them the seal of pardon and they will not receive it."[279] Indeed, Keach agrees, the rite of baptism is a sign of the forgiveness of sins; however, it is such a sign to those who repent and believe. In addition, "[y]ou exhort," Keach continues, "the subjects of baptism to be thankful, lest they despise the seal of pardon. Now take from your reasoning the following argument," namely, "such persons that baptism belong unto, may neglect and despise the ordinance and seal of pardon; but infants cannot neglect or despise the ordinance and seal of pardon. *Ergo*, baptism doth not belong to infants."[280]

Baptism is beneficial, Owen insists, on account of its effectiveness. The baptismal rite "is a bond of holiness, 1Pet.3.21. The Apostle [Paul] exhorts Christians to be dead unto sin and alive to righteousness because they have been baptised...There is a virtue in the ordinances of God answerable to the end for which they are appointed. The ordinances are not unfruitful, except to the unbelieving and negligent."[281] This being the case, Keach replies, infants cannot receive baptism since they can neither die to sin nor be made alive to righteousness. "Ordinances have not more virtue in them to an infant, than if you should water a dead tree." The infant's nature has to be changed by the grace of God and then the ordinances would become appropriate. However, since babies cannot evince such a change, the ordinance of baptism is not to be imparted to them.[282]

Nonetheless, God is able to regenerate a child, Burkitt claims, and considering that the unclean shall not come into heaven, pedobaptism then is greatly advantageous. For either God effectuates the salvation of infants without any cooperation from them, or children are to perish without the hope

---

[277] Y mae'n "dystiolaeth o'n ffydd ni yn Ghrist, Mar.16.16...Ac am hynny i barhau tra parhao ffydd ar y ddaiar." Owen, *Bedydd Plant or Nefoedd*, 17.

[278] Keach, *Light Broke Forth*, 6.

[279] Mae bedydd yn arwyddocau maddeuant pechod, Mar.1.4...Onid anniolchgar yw rheini i ras Duw yr "hwn fydd yn cynnig sél o bardwn iddynt, ac nis derbyniant." Owen, *Bedydd Plant or Nefoedd*, 18.

[280] Keach, *Light Broke Forth*, 8.

[281] Y mae "yn rhwymyn sancteiddrwydd, 1 Pet.3.21. Y mae'r Apostl yn cynghori'r Christnogion I farw I bechod, ac I fyw I gyfiawnder, o herwydd eu bod wedi eu bedyddio...Y mae rhinwedd yn Ordinhadau Duw I atteb y dibennion I ba rai yr appwyntiwyd hwynt. Nid ydynt yn anffrwythlon ond ir anghrediniol ar esgeulus." Owen, *Bedydd Plant or Nefoedd*, 17.

[282] Keach, *Light Broke Forth*, 6.

of heaven. But children can be regenerated by God and thus "they are capable of baptism, for the outward and visible sign ought not to be denied to such as are capable of the inward spiritual grace."[283]

Keach responds that as "a free agent" God can do anything, including the regeneration of babies. However, it is impossible to know if or how God does it. Furthermore, even if it could be known which infants God regenerates, nevertheless there is no support in Scripture to either pedobaptism or pedocommunion.[284] As to little children, "God (as Dr Jeremy Taylor observes) may have many ways to magnify his grace, through Jesus Christ, to them, which we know not of, who die in their infancy, yet have we no authority to baptise them, any more than to give them the Lord's Supper."[285] Keach then proceeds to attack Burkitt for denying the doctrines of his church, as she maintains that "'[r]epentance, whereby a person forsakes sin, and faith, whereby he steadfastly believes the promise of God made to him in that sacrament,' is required of those who are to be baptised; nay and of little ones too,"[286] thus the Godparents say in their stead "that they do 'believe and repent or forsake the Devil and all his works, &c.' the child answers by proxy. Your church baptises no child but as a believer and as a true penitent person." Therefore, the Church of England agrees with the Baptists, Keach affirms, that the subjects of baptism, whether infants or adults, must exercise faith. However, Burkitt "saw the snake in the grass, viz., that Godfathers and Godmothers is a tradition and none of God's appointment...And made use of another argument and would have them baptised without faith or upon their parents faith, of which your church speaks nothing."[287] This baptismal covenant, i.e., the promises made during baptism, as done by sureties is "an humane invention and not appointed by God, as Mr Perkins himself confesseth."[288] Keach purports that, ultimately, Burkitt is inconsistent; for, on the one hand he argues that children have the right to baptism because they are in covenant just like their Christian parents, but on the other hand, children must have their nature regenerated by water baptism or else remain outside the covenant. "Your

---

[283] Burkitt, *Argumentative Discourse*, 15-16.
[284] Keach, *Rector Rectified*, 79.
[285] Keach, *Rector Rectified*, 89. Cf. e.g., Taylor, ΘΕΟΛΟΓΙΑ ΕΚΛΕΤΙΚΗ, 328.
[286] See *The Anglican Catechism*, 1549, in Schaff, *Creeds of the Evangelical Protestant Churches*, 521.
[287] Keach, *Rector Rectified*, 89. Cf. Idem, *Answer unto two Athenian Mercuries*, syllogisms 4 and 6, pp. 1, 2; idem, *Ax Laid to the Root*, II: 50; idem, *Counter-Antidote*, 20. Contrast with Rothwell, *Paedobaptismus Vindicatus*, xxxix, 75, 80; Bridgewater, *Athenian Oracle*, IV: 172-173, I: 306.
[288] Keach, *Rector Rectified*, 144. Cf. e.g., William Perkins, *The Whole Treatise of the Cases of Conscience, Distinguished into Three Bookes* (London: Iohn Legatt, Printer to the University of Cambridge, 1606), 318.

play the part of a fencer and resolve to try your skill with every weapon, one while you are a Presbyterian, another time a Church-of-England-man."[289]

Through baptism, Rothwell alleges, God bestows grace, forgives sins, adopts and gives life eternal. Children and adults need these benefits and are qualified to receive them. Infants "are fitted for all the purposes of baptism, as it is appointed by heaven for a sign to us to convey unto us the advantages of the New Covenant."[290] How can anybody prove, Keach queries, the things hereby claimed? Where can one find in Scripture that, through baptism God bestows grace or gives eternal life? "You minister of the Church of England, if this be so, can do as strange things as the Popish priests in transubstantiation; you can, by sprinkling a little water on the face of a babe," it seems, "change the evil and vitious habits, form Christ in the soul, raise the dead to life and of a child of wrath make a child of God." Keach adds, how sad it is to see that "a minister of the Gospel should teach such a corrupt doctrine and deceive the ignorant."[291] There is disagreement, Keach contends, even among the pedobaptists concerning baptism's power to confer grace. Charnock, for example, thought that the water of baptism could neither regenerate nor confer grace to a person. As an external thing, water could not wash the inward parts of an individual; for otherwise all infants would automatically be converted (turn out Christians) which is contrary to experience.[292]

A similar case to Rothwell's is presented by Burkitt with an analogy. Since children are capable of benefiting from baptism in that thereby they have their sins forgiven, it is therefore incumbent upon parents to baptise them. Consider this simile between the progeny of a traitor and that of a Christian: as the child of a traitor could receive pardon from the king, likewise the child of a believer can be forgiven by God. That is, suppose a traitor whose offspring would by law lose all rights and benefits of citizenship, but instead receives forgiveness from the offended king; who would say that the forgiveness was without significance for lack of understanding on the part of the child?[293]

The simile is defective, Keach claims, for if baptism remits sins, why not baptise the children of the heathen? What is more, one does not receive a benefit merely because one is capable of receiving it; rather a benefit is to be received only by the command from whom the benefit comes. The fact that an infant is capable of being the recipient of a blessing does not make it *eligible*

---

[289] Keach, *Rector Rectified*, 80.

[290] Rothwell, *Paedobaptismus Vindicatus*, 20. See also ibid., 11. Cf. Exell, *Serious Enquiry*, 7; Bridgewater, *Athenian Oracle*, IV: 159.

[291] Keach, *Ax Laid to the Root*, II: 30.

[292] Stephen Charnock, 'A Discorse of the Nature of Regeneration,' in vol. II: 45, of *The Works of late Learned Divine Stephen Charnock, B.D. Being Several Discourses upon Various Divine Subjects* (London: Printed for Ben. Griffin, in the Old-Baily; et al., 1699); cited by Keach, *Ax Laid to the Root*, II: 30-31.

[293] Burkitt, *Argumentative Discourse*, 15. Cf. Rothwell, *Paedobaptismus Vindicatus*, 21-23.

for the blessing. Capability plays a role in baptism, but as it relates to repentance: baptism is to be given to those who are able to repent "and profess faith in Christ; these we say and none else ought to be baptised, if the royal charter or grant of the Lord Jesus be observed in the case of a regal right to baptism."[294] Great care must be exercised, as said before, when analogies are used to establish Christian practices based on Jewish ordinances. Otherwise, Protestants will have to accept "the arguments of the papists for a universal bishop, because the Jews had such; and justify a linen garment at Mass," on account of a Jewish parallel. What could deter a minister from giving communion to infants, "since Samuel [and] Jesus Christ under age were partakers of the Passover?" Error such as these, Keach purports, would be multiplied if strict care were not taken with analogies.[295]

Pedobaptism, according to Burkitt, is of greater benefit than credobaptism, for "it is an early remedy against the malady of original sin, that hereditary contagion of the soul."[296] This is a contentious doctrinal point and Keach challenges Burkitt. "Speak; doth baptism take away original sin, or free them of that malady, or not? You know, some of the ancient Fathers were carried away with such a dream;" but it is obvious that baptism has no power to wash such pollution (1Pet.3.20). Otherwise, how can anybody explain the fact that this "contagion appears so soon and to be so strong in your children as in ours who never were baptised at all?"[297] Keach requests the support of John Owen against the alleged power of baptism to confer grace: the Congregationalist affirms "that the Father of lies himself could not well have invented a more pernicious opinion, or which might pour in a more deadly poyson into the minds of sinners."[298] The truth is, Keach claims, that infants are simply not fit to undergo

---

[294] Keach, *Rector Rectified*, 77-78. Cf. Idem, *Ax Laid to the Root*, II: 53.

[295] Keach, *Rector Rectified*, 15-16.

[296] Burkitt, *Argumentative Discourse*, 39. Cf. Shute, *Replication to Benjamin Keach*, 33; Rothwell, *Paedobaptismus Vindicatus*, 11. As an aside, although the Particular Baptists had published a Reformed confession and were known to be orthodox, when James Owen makes the same argument Burkitt is making, he attempts to characterised the baptised churches as Pelagic: pedobaptism, Owen asserts, "was common in the church of God, that the Pelagians could not deny it, though they denied original sin, against the which it is a medicine." Yr oedd bedydd pland "mor gyffredinol yn eglwys Dduw, na allei y Pelagiaid wadu o honaw, er eu bod yn gwadu pechod gwreiddlol, yn erbyn pa un y mae yn feddyginiaeth." *Bedydd Plant or Nefoedd*, 153.

[297] Keach, *Rector Rectified*, 146. See also, idem, *Light Broke Forth*, 111-112.

[298] John Owen, ΘΕΟΛΟΓΟΥΜΕΝΑ ΠΑΝΤΟΔΑΠΑ. *Sive de Natura, Ortu, Progressu, et Studio Verae Theologiae Libri Sex* (Oxoniae, Excudebat Hen. Hall, Academiae Typograghus, Impensis Tho. Robinson, n.d.), s.v., lib.vi.c.iii.; quoted by Keach, *Gold Refin'd*, 129.

any Gospel ordinance. "We *challenge all the world*, by God's Word, to prove they are capable of baptism, any more than of the Lord's Supper."[299]

The much-disputed question of infants who die without baptism is presented by Burkitt: pedobaptism, "as a channel of grace," is advantageous in that it grants to a "parent a good ground of hope that his children dying in infancy are certainly saved..."[300]

Keach maintains that the same problem is to be found here as elsewhere, namely, there is no warrant from Scripture to affirm such a thing. Who made baptism "a channel of grace?" Is salvation to be found in baptism or in Christ? If this doctrine were true, all babies who die in the womb and all infants who died without baptism would forthwith be damned. It is far better to leave aside issues that are unknown, such as the lot of "dying infants and idiots;" which are "secret things that are not revealed."[301] Although children do not belong to the visible church, "I know no cause," Keach supposes, "why unbelieving parents should doubt the salvation of their dying infants. They may (so far as I see) have as much ground of hope God's election may reach their dying infants, as any believer can have it may reach theirs." Very hesitantly, Keach risks an opinion. "What if I should exercise so much charity as to hope that God hath comprehended in his electing love all the dying infants both of believers and unbelievers and that, through the blood and merit of Christ, they are sanctified and shall be saved?"[302] Finally, "[m]y opinion, were it so, could not justly be condemned by any; but I say secret things belong to God and I shall forbear to pass judgement in the case, but leave it to God; but I am sure no child shall be damned for the parent's fault."[303] What is most important, Keach avers, in the

---

[299] Keach, *Rector Rectified*, 146. His emphasis. The aforesaid type of assertion is typical of Keach. To give another example, denying that infants are to be brought into covenant via baptism, Keach says to Burkitt: "I challenge you and all pedobaptists in the world to prove God hath anywhere, directly or indirectly, required any such thing at your hands." Ibid., 148

[300] Burkitt, *Argumentative Discourse*, 40. The controversy over pedobaptism generated a huge dispute on the lot of dying infants. See, Shute, *Replication to Benjamin Keach*, 26-35; idem, *Antidote to Anabaptism*, 43, 46, 57, 65, 66-69, 70, especially 121-134 and 161-181; Keach, *Counter-Antidote*, 12, 19-20, 31; idem, *Ax Laid to the Root*, I: 25; idem, *Ax Laid to the Root*, II: 31; idem, *Rector Rectified*, 46, 57, 89, 146; etc.

[301] Keach, *Rector Rectified*, 153. "...what have we to do with dying infants?...How doth God sanctify dying infants...no mortal man I am sure can tell; if it is by infusing grace, let it be so, tho it can't be proved whilst the world stands..." Idem, *Counter-Antidote*, 13, 14. See also Vaughn, 'Public Worship and Practical Theology,' 54-60.

[302] Keach, *Light Broke Forth*, 122. Elsewhere, Keach says, surely "elect infants that die have union with Christ in a way we are ignorant of, but what is this to the infants of believers as such?" Ibid., 7

[303] Keach, *Light Broke Forth*, 122-123. A subtle but important soteriological difference is to be noted, between Keach (Reformed) and—for example—the Athenians (Arminians): both agree that only the applied merits of Christ can save infants, but

discussion of dying infants is that salvation for both young and old is one and the same: the applied merits of Christ to the elect. As to how this relates to the covenant of grace, there are two aspects to be considered: first, the true beneficiaries of this covenant are only known to God (the elect); second, the *external* benefits of the same pact belong to those who profess faith in Christ and, in so doing, receive the right to the said benefits (baptism, etc).[304]

It seems then, Burkitt asserts, that the children of believers have lost out with the advent of Christ, for if the infants of Christians are no longer in covenant with God as they were before, it follows that "the privileges of the Gospel are straiter and narrower than those of the Law, which in the judgement of judicious Calvin is a degree of blasphemy to affirm..."[305] What is more, in the light of Jesus' gracious acts toward children and, moreover, his words to them that heaven is theirs, can anybody believe that he would have left infants out of his church? "Therefore, as Calvin very well observes upon this place, 'tis no less than audacious sacrilege in the ministers of Christ to drive them from the sheep-fold, which he so lovingly owns to be part of his flock."[306] The Anabaptists, Burkitt proceeds, have an "unkind and uncharitable opinion, which robs parents of their comfort, infants of their right, the church of its members and God of his glory."[307]

To begin with, Keach retorts, it does not "matter what Calvin spoke, 'tis no sin to keep out of Christ's (visible) fold, whom he has given no authority to take in. Nor have any people a more charitable opinion of the state of dying infants than those sti'd [styled] Anabaptists."[308] As far as privileges are concerned, Keach admits that there were greater earthly benefits in the legal covenant with the Jewish national church than with Christians in the covenant of grace: for example, the Jews were given a right to put to death all who disobeyed the covenant, they had a right to Canaan, "they were promised outward peace, riches, ...they had a glorious external temple and what not; also all their natural off-spring were born members of their church." None of these benefits can be claimed under the covenant of grace. Gospel believers are rather to expect tribulations and all sort of wants. Nevertheless, "our privileges are better and greater under the Gospel, than theirs were under the Law, the Gospel covenant being established upon better promises: our children grow up, sit under the clear and glorious light and preaching of the Gospel;" a Gospel which

---

Keach is ultimately *unsure* of their destiny, whereas the Athenians unhesitantly affirm that "the kingdom of heaven" belongs to all who die in infancy. *Athenian Oracle*, I: 309. See Keach, *Counter-Antidote*, 12, 20.

[304] Keach, *Ax Laid to the Root*, I: 25.
[305] Burkitt, *Argumentative Discourse*, 9. Calvin, *Institutes*, IV.xvi.6. Cf. Exell, *Serious Enquiry*, 79; Bridgewater, *Athenian Oracle*, IV: 167; Flavell, *Vindiciarum Vindex*, 289.
[306] Cf. e.g., Calvin, *Institutes*, IV.xvi.6-7.
[307] Burkitt, *Argumentative Discourse*, 22.
[308] Keach, *Light Broke Forth*, 131. Cf. Idem, *Rector Rectified*, 104.

the Jews had "but in dark shadows; moreover 'the partition wall being now broken down,' the Gospel church is not confin'd to one people or nation only, but now all...who" trust and accept the Son "by saving faith...are joint-heirs together... Alas! What privileges had the poor Gentiles under the Law, and their children? Is not the matter well amended with us?"[309]

Incipient Faith as Basis for Pedobaptism

Pedobaptism and infant church membership, Exell says, are proper practices because children have "supernatural grace" or the "habit" of faith, "and if the habits cannot constitute us members" nothing else can do it.[310] That infants are able to have this habit and so be given baptism and membership may be "exemplified and proved by the filling of John with the Holy Ghost from his mother's womb" (Luk.1.15).[311]

Certainly it is impossible to judge, Keach claims, if babies have, or do not have, this habit. Moreover, even if it were possible to demonstrate that such habit existed, a further difficulty would ensue; namely, one would have to prove that this habit could be lost, for many baptised infants grow up to be wicked. Furthermore, why is it that often times this so-called habit lay dormant for so many years without the least hint of its presence? That is, why do so many people from the time of baptism to the time of conversion, live a licentious life, despite the purported presence of this habit? These questions make these arguments implausible, for a holy "habit is a principle of divine life; yea, a most active and lively principle. Can the weakness of nature hinder the operations of the Holy Ghost in infants, when the power of the Devil can't in the adult?...Can there be fire and no heat?" Definitely, if Exell were right, the offspring of Christians would be visibly impacted by this habit.[312] It is noteworthy to mention the cases of Judas Iscariotes and Simon Magus in the New Testament, to further refute the thesis that baptism conveys grace. Unquestionably both had been baptised but proved in themselves to have received no grace. If the habit of grace is not given to adults upon baptism, it

---

[309] Keach, *Ax Laid to the Root*, II: 25-26. Cf. Idem, *Pedobaptism Disproved*, 19; and, *Counter-Antidote*, 17.

[310] Exell, *Serious Enquiry*, 31-32.

[311] Exell, *Serious Enquiry*, 75. Cf. Rothwell, *Paedobaptismus Vindicatus*, 100. See Shute, *Antidote to Anabaptism*, 18-24, for extensive discussion on habitual faith; see also his further comments on, and helpful illustrations of, habitual faith on pp. 58-63. The word used by all these authors, *habitus*, is a term that indicates a capacity or disposition of the soul to receive spiritual life. They argue that infants *innately* possess this habit merely on account of being the progeny of believers.

[312] Keach, *Ax Laid to the Root*, II: 38-39. Cf. Idem, *Counter-Antidote*, 12-13, and especially, proscript, 2. Keach is not dealing with the general *habitus*, rather he is talking about *habitus infusus*, which is a God-given virtue implanted in the soul. His following illustrations (Judas, Simon and John the Baptist) confirm our suspicion.

can be inferred that it is not similarly given to babies.³¹³ Assuredly, God may choose to infuse grace into an infant (as he did in John's case) if it is part of the elect, but the exception cannot be made into the norm. The Scriptures tell us of an "animal that spoke, must all animals speak therefore?" Exell's argument can only stand, Keach affirms, if he is able to show that somehow infants have the evidence of grace in their lives. As a general principle, grace must *already* be present in the lives of those "Christ commands to be baptised, ...they must act, must believe, must repent or must be actually discipled, that baptism belong unto..."³¹⁴

Pedobaptism, Burkitt argues, can be granted on the basis of incipient faith, and the following analogy exemplifies the point. He says, although infants do not possess "actual faith, yet they have habitual faith, faith *in semine*, and so are potentially believers..." That is, even though little children do not display reason, "yet because they have a principle, we call them reasonable creatures, the first day they are born. Thus infants, whilst such, have not the use and exercise of faith, but have it in the root and may be called believers initially."³¹⁵

Keach starts his answer quoting Taylor: habitual faith is a "strange invention... absolutely without art, without Scripture, reason or authority."³¹⁶ Secondly, if Burkitt is right concerning this habitual faith, then who can prove that pagans do not have the same faith and thus, on that basis, be baptised? That is, instead of baptising people upon repentance and faith, why not baptise them on the assumption of a habit of faith? Thirdly, if the argument for habitual faith were true, there would be no need for further infusion of grace, for this incipient habit would develop into piety and godliness, and manifest itself in the lives of children as they grow up. Experience, however, teaches the opposite: as infants grow up they rather manifest "the evil habits of sin, but no sacred habits of grace of divine faith or seed of regeneration sown into them at all."³¹⁷ Anything unprovable by Scripture, Keach argues, or not "directly or indirectly spoken about it, is absurd and vain for any person to assert. But it cannot be proved from the Word of God that one infant of believers or any other, have habitual faith;" for there is "nothing directly or indirectly spoken about it. Ergo, 'tis absurd and vain for any person to assert that any infant of believer hath habitual faith."³¹⁸

---

³¹³ Keach, *Ax Laid to the Root*, II: 40.
³¹⁴ Keach, *Ax Laid to the Root*, II: 49.
³¹⁵ Burkitt, *Argumentative Discourse*, 19. Cf. Bridgewater, *Athenian Oracle*, I: 310; Smythies, *The Non-Communicant*, 91; Rothwell, *Paedobaptismus Vindicatus*, 45-46, 100; Shute, *Replication to Benjamin Keach*, 55.
³¹⁶ Taylor, ΘΕΟΛΟΓΙΑ ΕΚΛΕΤΙΚΗ, 343-344; in Keach, *Counter-Antidote*, 14. Cf. Idem, *Rector Rectified*, 90.
³¹⁷ Keach, *Rector Rectified*, 90-91. Cf. Idem, *Counter-Antidote*, 12-13.
³¹⁸ Keach, *Counter-Antidote*, 21.

Burkitt insists that children "born within the bosom of the church, of believing parents; the faith of the parents is to them (at present) instead of an outward profession in their own persons...for tho no child is saveable by its parents faith, yet the child is baptizable by virtue of its parents faith," for God's oath (Act.2.39) includes the parents and their descendants.[319]

Two things must be said in response to this: first, there is a great danger, Keach says, in relying on the faith of the parents in order to baptise their offspring; for if the parents later on deny the faith, the children will surely question their right to church membership and inclusion in the covenant of grace. Thus, the faith of the parents is no grounds for the baptism of their descendants.[320] Perkins claims, Keach says, that "[t]here is no reason that the wickedness of the parents should prejudice the child, in things pertaining to eternal life."[321] Second, the opposite danger is also true: children may rely on the fact that their parents are sincere Christians and conclude that they are automatically included in the covenant of grace and, as a result, "destroy their souls by looking for no other regeneration but that which they had in baptism in their infancy."[322] Additionally and more importantly, there is again an inconsistency, Keach alleges, on the part of Burkitt as to the basis of pedobaptism: sometimes he grounds it in God's covenant of circumcision, but now Burkitt bases it in "the immediate faith of the parents." The heat of the debate is illustrated by Keach's reaction to this perceived inconsistency: "...you build your childish practice upon your dream. Why not, as your church teaches, upon the faith and profession of sureties?"[323] Why the faith of the immediate parents?"[324] If the faith of the parents serves the child, why not their baptism? If their baptism does serve, why baptise children of baptised parents? When will pedobaptists agree as to what sort of faith is present in babies? "Is it the faith of the Church, as Thomas Aquinas asserts, which is intailed upon all who are within the pale thereof, or in her bosom, to use your words?" If not, "is it an imputative faith from the parents, as Musculus, you and other maintain?"[325]

---

[319] Burkitt, *Argumentative Discourse*, 19. Cf. Smythies, *The Non-Communicant*, 88; Rothwell, *Paedobaptismus Vindicatus*, xix-xx, 6, 50-53.

[320] Keach, *Ax Laid to the Root*, II: 35.

[321] Perkins, *A Commentarie upon Galatians*, 264; cited by Keach, *Light Broke Forth*, [313].

[322] Keach, *Ax Laid to the Root*, II: 35.

[323] See *The Anglican Catechism*, 1549, in Schaff, *Creeds of the Evangelical Protestant Churches*, 521.

[324] Keach, *Rector Rectified*, 91. For baptism grounded on the faith of the parents, see, e.g., Perkins, *Commentarie upon Galatians*, 263.

[325] Thomas Aquinas, *Summa Theologiae*, 3a. 68, 9; 3a. 69, 8; 3a. 71, 1. Cf. e.g., Wolfgang Musculus, *Loci Communes Theologiae Sacrae* (Basileae: Henricpetri, 15-?), s.v., 'De Baptismo: III. Quomodo debeat administrari Baptismus.' Idem, *In Evangelistam Mattaeum Commentarii* (Basileae: Hervagius, 1578), Cap.IX, 18. Perkins, *A Commentarie upon Galatians*, 263.

Do infants possess "justifying faith, as Mr Baxter intimates? Or a dogmatical faith only, as in Mr Blake's sense? Some say 'tis physical faith, some metaphysical, and some hyper-physical faith. Some say they are born believers, others say they are made believers by baptism."[326] Keach concludes thus: note "what confusion you pedobaptists are in. An actual faith you dare not say they have," since infants, obviously, cannot manifest to know or understand anything. "Young children, saith Luther, hear not, nor understand the word of God, out of which faith cometh; and therefore if the commandment be followed, children ought not to be baptised."[327]

Suffer Little Children

Arguably, the second most important argument for pedobaptism is that the kingdom of God belongs to little children (Mat.19.14) and, as a result, they have a supposed right to baptism. "The kingdom of heaven belongs to infants, which is the greater; therefore...baptism belongs to them also, which is the lesser."[328]

Nobody questions, Keach asserts, that little children are associated with heaven's kingdom. However, it cannot be inferred from this that they have a right to baptism. For a similar defective inference could be made *a majori ad minus*, namely, children "belong to the kingdom of heaven, which is the greater; therefore to them belongeth the Lord's Supper, which is the lesser." Certainly the proper candidates of baptism are undeniably fit to partake of the Supper as well. The fallacy of this type of argumentation is that it does not take into account that these ordinances can only be administered by the explicit command of God.[329] Secondly, it is impossible to know if the children referred to in the passage had believing parents. Thirdly, however, even if the parents were believers, the argument would not serve pedobaptists since there is still uncertainty over what defines "little children" in Mat.19.14. For "the Greek word doth not always signify a little child or infant, as appears by 2Tim.3.15,"

---

[326] Keach, *Rector Rectified*, 92. Cf. Idem, *Counter-Antidote*, 11-12; idem, *Answer unto two Athenian Mercuries*, 3-4; idem, *Pedobaptism Disproved*, 12. See, Thomas Blake, *Vindiciae Foederis: Or, a Treatise of the Covenant of Grace entered with Man-kind* (London: Printed for Abel Roper, at the Sun against St Dunstins Church in Fleet Street, 1658), 289.

[327] Unable to locate this quote from Luther; Keach, *Gold Refin'd*, 150-151.

[328] Keach presents this argument (*Gold Refin'd*, 125) without attributing it to anybody. It seems that this is a close paraphrase of Burkitt's, "...if Christ denies them not the kingdom of heaven which is the greater, what reason have I to deny them baptism which is the less?" *Argumentative Discourse*, 22. Slightly less plausible is Rothwell's, "...if the child when born hath a right to the covenant, he hath a right to the sign; for [it is] according to the logical maxim, *the greater includes the less*; and he that should deny this, would be as absurd as he that should say, he that receiveth ten Pounds receives not five." *Paedobaptismus Vindicatus*, xx. His emphasis. See also, ibid., 5-6.

[329] Keach, *Gold Refin'd*, 125-126.

wherein the identical term is employed to describe a teachable child. To conclude, let us hear, Keach asserts, what Taylor eloquently says: the fact that Jesus blessed children proves nothing as to pedobaptism. For a better argument could easily be made along the following lines: "Christ blessed children and so dismissed them, but baptised them not, therefore infants are not to be baptised."[330]

Arguing that infants should not be hindered to come to faith via baptism, James Owen says, "those who prevented children coming to him, excited his anger against them."[331] Keach replies that this is rather a good argument to prove that pedobaptism was not in place, otherwise the disciples would not have obstructed the children. What is far more likely is that the disciples hindered them on account of a possible disturbance they would have caused.[332]

How can a minister, Burkitt inquires, refuse to accept those whom Christ accepted! Little children were invited to come to him and were promptly welcomed by him; consequently, his ministers must not dare to reject those Christ accepted.[333] Additionally, children should be dedicated to God as the Israelites' first born were dedicated in the Old Testament. "Your children are Gods already by virtue of his choice, let them be his by virtue of your consecration."[334]

A host of people, Keach responds, came to Jesus and was accepted by him, yet were not part of his church. Often Christ received common people and religious authorities and healed a great number from all walks of life; nevertheless, the immense majority were not part of his flock. There is something else against the above argument, namely, the passage "[s]uffer little children to come unto me..." cannot be used to argue for pedobaptism; for if it implies that the children are already part of the church, what need is there for baptism? "If Christ owns them subjects or members of his visible church, you by baptism have no need, I say, to add them to it; for if they are the seed of believers, they are already (*fidem foederis*) not only in covenant with God, but also belong to his kingdom or church upon the earth," and therefore submitting infants to baptism or refusing to do so would not alter their position.[335]

---

[330] Taylor, ΘΕΟΛΟΓΙΑ ΕΚΛΕΤΙΚΗ, 327-328; in Keach, *Gold Refin'd*, 126-127.

[331] "[Y] rhai a rwystrand blant i ddyfod atto yn cyffroi ei ddigofaint yn eu herbyn." Owen, *Bedydd Plant or Nefoedd*, 84. Cf. Shute, *Antidote to Anabaptism*, 30; idem, *Replication to Benjamin Keach*, 62; Rothwell, *Paedobaptismus Vindicatus*, 124.

[332] Keach, *Light Broke Forth*, 127.

[333] Burkitt, *Argumentative Discourse*, 21. Cf. Exell, *Serious Enquiry*, [43], 73; Rothwell, *Paedobaptismus Vindicatus*, 14; Shute, *Replication to Benjamin Keach*, 62-63; idem, *Antidote Anabaptism*, 27-28, 75; Flavell, *Vindiciarum Vindex*, 294; Bridgewater, *Athenian Oracle*, IV: 159-160, I: 307.

[334] Burkitt, *Argumentative Discourse*, 36-37.

[335] Keach, *Rector Rectified*, 102. Elsewhere Keach maintains that, if baptism can produce holiness, then infants are not holy on account of being the offspring of Christians. On the other hand, if the descendants of Christians are holy merely for

Concerning the consecration of infants to Christ, there is no warrant from Scripture for this practice and, besides, the fact that Jesus laid his hands on children, does not imply that they were baptised.[336]

John's Confession and Baptism

The confession of sins required by the baptism of John must be such, as to include all ages young and old, for his baptism embraces all. Joshua Exell begins his argument along the following lines: pedobaptism can be inferred from the fact that all people came to John to be baptised, as the evangelists show, Mar.1.5 and Mat.3.5,6. In these passages, "all Jerusalem or all they of Jerusalem" means every person without exception. Among these people, there were adults as well as infants.[337]

Should the word "all" here be taken for every person? Somewhat condescendingly, Keach says that this author has "no better skill in Scripture rhetoric;" for "frequently *per synecdochen vel totius, vel partis*, a part is put for the whole," as in the case where Jesus "is said to die for all, yet we know he dyed (in a proper and true spiritual sense) but for a few, i.e., for none but the elect."[338] To put it differently, "God would have all men to be saved, i.e., some of all sorts and degrees, as kings, noble-men, old, young, rich or poor, &c." Another example of the hyperbole "all" would be the assertion, "when he were lifted up he would draw all men to him, πάντας ἑλκύσω πρὸς ἐμαυτόν, Joh. 12.32. Doth he mean every individual person, or some of all sorts, of Jews and Gentiles?"[339] Illustrations of these types could be multiplied, you "shall be hated of all men for my sake" (Mat.10.22). These "and many other Scriptures are to be taken synecdocally."[340] When the Evangelist affirms, Keach proceeds, that "all the land of Judea and they of Jerusalem were baptised of him in the river Jordan," it means that "many" people from these regions came and received the baptism of John.[341] Furthermore, the Scripture cited cannot be taken literally for yet another reason, the New Testament's broader context would validate rebaptism. Note the two following texts: "Behold him that thou bearest witness of…the same baptizeth and all men came to him, καὶ πάντες ἔρχονται πρὸς αὐτόν, i.e., to Jesus Christ" (Joh.3.26). The Gospel likewise says that "Jesus

---

having Christian parents, then baptism is irrelevant. *Light Broke Forth*, 112. Another example of this type of argumentation is Shute's assertion that "all the children of believing parents are church-members;" to which Keach replies, "…if all believers seed are born church members, ours are as good as yours, tho not baptised." *Antidote to Anabaptism*, 37; idem, *Counter-Antidote*, 17.

[336] Keach, *Rector Rectified*, 37.

[337] Exell, *Serious Enquiry*, 1-14, 74. Cf. Shute, *Replication to Benjamin Keach*, 54.

[338] Keach, *Ax Laid to the Root*, II: 36 and *Light Broke Forth*, 24.

[339] Keach, *Light Broke Forth*, 24.

[340] Among other passages, Keach gives, Exo.32.3,26; Isa.2.2; Phi.2.21.

[341] Keach, *Ax Laid to the Root*, II: 36-37.

made and baptised more disciples than John [Joh.4.1]. If John baptised them all and Jesus baptised them all, then they were all twice baptised, or all rebaptised and if so, were indeed properly all Anabaptists."[342] Moreover, although the evangelist says that "all" Jerusalem and Judea came to be baptised by John, it also says that Jesus and his disciples baptised and did so in greater numbers than John (Joh.4.1). If John had baptised all people, none would be left to be subsequently baptised.[343] Lastly, the immediate context of this passage reports that John urged repentance or confession of sins in order to baptise people. Infants cannot repent or confess their sins and thus cannot be baptised.[344]

Not every one could confess sins *viva voce*, Exell says. It is conceivable that some individuals had speech impediments on the one hand and, on the other, mere infants are incapable of confessing sins with their mouths. Both cases justify exemption from verbal confession. In addition to that, when little children came to be baptised by John, they had a moral confession to present, namely, they were not guilty of the grosser sins (e.g., "generation of vipers") John was levelling against the adults. In conclusion, then, the moral confession would suffice for infants.[345]

Keach affirms that, generally, the confession had to be verbal since confession of sins necessarily involves articulating them. The wider context of the idea of confession explicitly confirms its verbal nature. "With the heart man believeth and with the mouth confession is made to salvation" (Rom.10.10). Therefore, it may be said that the people whom "John baptised confessed their sins, but infants could not confess their sins; ergo, John did not baptise infants."[346] As to the particular want of, or difficulties with, speech—the confession, nevertheless, has to be communicated to the one receiving it, either written down or somehow imparted; otherwise it is impossible to know what is in a person's heart.[347]

The confession, Exell maintains, ought to be consistent "with the capacity of them that were represented to John to be the objects of his ministry, which were parents and children, Mal.4.6. Luk.1.17." Otherwise, it would have been impossible for John to turn their hearts to God.[348] Furthermore, the confession required by John ought not to be transformed into a command, else the covenant would no longer be gracious but legal. If the confession, that is, were made into a command, then the Gospel would be mutated into a covenant of works, for access to it would be gained by performing such a command. As a

---

[342] Keach, *Light Broke Forth*, 25.
[343] Keach, *Ax Laid to the Root*, II: 41-42.
[344] Keach, *Ax Laid to the Root*, II: 37-38.
[345] Exell, *Serious Enquiry*, 37, 41, [46], [47], 49.
[346] Keach, *Ax Laid to the Root*, II: 40, 43.
[347] Keach, *Ax Laid to the Root*, II: 43, 40.
[348] Exell, *Serious Enquiry*, 37. See also ibid., pp. 34, 60-64, 73.

result, the people baptised would be children of duty, instead of children of promise.[349]

Whatever level of understanding and intelligence the listeners had, Keach retorts, the confession John expected from them was compatible with their capacity to respond and, as to babies, they had no capacity whatsoever and so were excluded from confessing and consequently from baptism. Concerning the texts cited, was there any need for John to turn the hearts of babies to their parents? In addition, as to obeying commands, God gives the grace for such an accomplishment. In other words, the Holy Spirit enables a person to do whatever God wills. It should be noted, however, that the obedience to the said commands takes place without violation of the will. Keach rhetorically asks, does "free grace destroy the noble faculty of the will, because it over-powers its vitious habits and strongly inclines it to that which is good? Do not saints freely and voluntarily by the help of the Spirit and grace of Christ, will do that which is good and well-pleasing to him?"[350]

Exell raises the question that if the confession of sins is commanded, it follows that "the performance of it externally could not make a change upon their state and relation towards God, anymore than the performance of any duty." That is, one's state—saved or otherwise—is not changeable upon performance of a duty, for God alone can make such a change.[351]

The fact, Keach affirms, that a command or duty does not make a change in one's state or relationship towards God, does not make such a command void. "Must we not make an external confession of that which God's Spirit hath wrought internally upon our souls?" Must a confession or a duty, in order to be valuable, change our state before God? What happens with confessions or duties is that they actually reveal "what blessed change the grace of God hath wrought or made on the soul. Besides, it is not universally true, i.e., because a thing is commanded it can't make a change; for sometimes a command is attended with power to change the soul" (Joh.6.28, for example).[352] In addition, qualification for baptism is not obtained by confession, but by "inward grace of faith in the Lord Jesus Christ; this is the only qualification which ought to be in all the subjects of baptism, and this faith must be made manifest by the confession of the mouth and the holy fruits of the life." Thus, John the Baptist requested not only a mere confession of sin as a token of their turning to God, but also lives bringing "forth fruits meet for repentance" (Mat.3.8). In other words, in order to baptise, John wanted the evidence of genuine reformed lives.[353] To conclude, Keach affirms, well said Jerome, Christ ordered "his Apostles first to instruct and teach the nations and afterward should baptise

---

[349] Exell, *Serious Enquiry*, [43].
[350] Keach, *Ax Laid to the Root*, II: 44, 47.
[351] Exell, *Serious Enquiry*, [43].
[352] Keach, *Ax Laid to the Root*, II: 47.
[353] Keach, *Ax Laid to the Root*, II: 47-48.

such who were instructed into those great mysteries of the faith; for it cannot be that the body should receive the sacrament of baptism, till the soul has receive the true faith."[354]

Households

James Owen affirms that it has been "God's way from the beginning of the world, to receive whole households into covenant, the children were received in with their parents; so Noah and his family were in the same covenant. For his sake his family was received with him into the ark and were baptised with him in the depth of the flood."[355]

To begin with, in the Noetic pact, Keach claims, God covenants not only with Noah, but with the rest of the animal kingdom as well (Gen.9.9-10). This temporal salvation of all in the ark, does not entail a spiritual salvation; that is, the fact that the entire family of the patriarch was spared from drowning does not mean that each one had faith or was in any way part of the covenant of grace. Rather the opposite, Noah's faith did not save his cursed son Cham.[356] Secondly, concerning "the ark being a type of baptism, or that his family were baptised in the ark," these two things do not prove anything, other than that man and beasts, good and bad people, could have been baptised. Thirdly, what is to be noted in this passage, Keach purports, is that the ark may be deemed a type of the church and so, as the ark was undoubtedly enveloped by water, likewise Christians are to be covered or immersed in water. There is a great difference, therefore, between God saving a family by an ark on the one hand and, on the other, trying to argue from this that entire families are included in the pact of grace.[357]

Burkitt maintains that pedobaptism is evident in the New Testament because the Apostles baptised whole households. This is illustrated by Lydia (Act.16.15) and the Philippian jailer (Act.16.33).[358] The argument would be of value, Keach replies, if there were infants in every household. As there are many families without babies, no definitive conclusions may be derived from

---

[354] Jerome, *Commentariorum in Evangelium Matthaei*, L.IV.c.xxviii, (243-244), P.L.26; in Keach, *Ax Laid to the Root*, II: 50.

[355] "Ffordd Duw o ddechreuad y byd oedd derbyn teuluoedd cyfain iw gyfammod, yr oedd y plant yn cael eu derbyn i mewn gydâ eu rhieni, felly yr ydoedd Noah ai deulu yn yr un cyfammod. Er ei fwyn ef derbyniwyd eu deulu gydâg ef ir Arch, a bedyddiwyd hwynt gydâg ef yn nyfroedd y diluw." Owen, *Bedydd Plant or Nefoedd*, 132. Cf. Shute, *Replication to Benjamin Keach*, 40, 44-45, 55-56; Rothwell, *Paedobaptismus Vindicatus*, 86.

[356] Keach, *Light Broke Forth*, 190. See also ibid., pp. 154-155.

[357] Keach, *Light Broke Forth*, 190-192.

[358] Burkitt, *Argumentative Discourse*, 27. Cf. Rothwell, *Paedobaptismus Vindicatus*, xvi, 89-90; Flavell, *Vindiciarum Vindex*, 293; Bridgewater, *Athenian Oracle*, I: 307.

these passages.³⁵⁹ Secondly, sometimes the Scripture speaks synecdocally as in the case where it says that "the man Elkana and all his household went to offer unto the Lord;" but "in the next verse 'tis as expressly said that Hannah and her child Samuel went not up; and yet 'tis said, all his house went up" (1Sam.1.21, 22).³⁶⁰ Thirdly, concerning the jailer, the text explicitly states that Paul announced the Gospel to him and to all the others in his house. Should one suppose that Paul announced the good news to the jailer's babies if there were any in the house? Fourthly, it is even more difficult to derive conclusions from Lydia's case. It is not known if she was a widow, a single woman, or if she had a husband. Even if it were assumed she had children, it is implausible that they were with her, since she was from Thyatira which was a great distance from Philippi, where she was baptised. Furthermore, it is unlikely that babies would be called "brothers" as Lydia's companions were, Act.16.40. Should pedobaptism be inferred from such questionable evidence? Therefore, "it appears to all impartial persons," Keach concludes, that the practice of the New Testament church does not include pedobaptism since there is "no mention made of one infant baptised, nor the least colour of reason to conclude there were [infants] in those families."³⁶¹

Gyles Shute—just like Exell, Burkitt, Rothwell and others—demands that the "Anabaptists" prove a negative, namely, "that ever Christ or any of his Apostles by his authority, did ever forbid baptising the infant seed of believers," or that no infant received the baptismal rite.³⁶² Keach retorts, "we might as well have desire him to give proof that there never was any infant ordained an elder or pastor of a church... Where is the extream unction forbid, or auricular confession, or the use of beads in prayer and a hundred more such Roman fopperies?"³⁶³

Owen asserts that God did not leave Jewish children free to decide their religion and, likewise, "let none take upon them to be wiser than God by leaving children at this time to follow their fancies, to choose their own religion, without having God's covenant upon them. For man's nature is as corrupt at this time as formerly..."³⁶⁴

First, Keach repeats that there was an explicit command from God to initiate babies into the national Jewish church through circumcision, but this is not the

---

³⁵⁹ Keach, *Rector Rectified*, 124. Cf. Idem, *Pedobaptism Disproved*, 7.
³⁶⁰ Keach, *Rector Rectified*, 125.
³⁶¹ Keach, *Rector Rectified*, 125.
³⁶² Shute, *Antidote to Anabaptism*, 49; Exell, *Serious Enquiry*, 29-30; Burkitt, *Argumentative Discourse*, 28; Rothwell, *Paedobaptismus Vindicatus*, xxxviii, 26; Flavell, *Vindiciarum Vindex*, 294; Bridgewater, *Athenian Oracle*, IV: 161, 178.
³⁶³ Keach, *Light Broke Forth*, 210. Cf. Idem, *Rector Rectified*, 138.
³⁶⁴ "...na chymmered neb arnynd fod yn ddoethach nâ Duw, trwy adel plant yn awr i wysc eu pennau eu hunain, i ddewis eu chefydd heb rwyn Cyfammod Duw arnynt. Mae'r natur ddynol mor llygredic yr awrhon ac oedd gynt..." Owen, *Bedydd Plant or Nefoedd*, 163.

case with the congregational Christian ecclesia. "[I]f therefore there was the like authority from God for the one as there was for the other, we would contend with you no longer." Second, as to how God should build his church, it is "you that would seem wiser than God," Keach says, "whose wisdom hath not led him to erect his Gospel church of such materials or of such matter, and in such form now, as it was his wisdom to built the Jewish legal church."³⁶⁵ Third, has "not God freely left us and our children to choose to be his servants or to choose our religion? Are not the saints to be all volunteers? Will Christ accept of prest-soldiers into his service? Or have you any power to force or compel your children to be of what perswasion in religion you please?" It is correct to say that God did not leave his people to pursue their own ways, neither in the past nor present; rather, he has ordained for them now to place their faith in Christ and receive baptism, and never "follow the fancies of their parents any more than to follow their own fancies, nor [follow] ministers who teach them contrary doctrine to that which the Word of God doth."³⁶⁶ Fourth, concerning the corrupt state of human nature, it has indeed not changed. However, there is no profit in baptising or rantizing children; for this rite cannot cleanse them from their nature's corruption. Lastly, "I affirm," Keach says to Owen, that "God hath not commanded us to bring our children into the bond of the covenant by baptism until they believe, and you can never disprove us while you live from God's Word."³⁶⁷

James Owen insists that God has blessed pedobaptism as a means to preserve Christianity "from the days of the Apostles even to this day. The Lord only bestows his particular blessing on his own ordinances. He does not stamp the seal of heaven on earthly inventions. No one can deny but that there are thousands baptised in their infancy that feel in themselves the virtue of their baptism..."³⁶⁸ It is not possible, Keach claims, to prove that God owns or approves pedobaptism. The fact that God maintained a remnant through the ages cannot be ascribed to infant baptism, but rather it is to be attributed to his bountiful and sovereign grace and the powerful influence of the Holy Spirit. Additionally, the fact that some infants who were baptised turn out to be godly when the age of reason comes, does not validate this practice. This is rather to be reckoned to God's mercy. For myriads of people "remain ungodly, and so

---

³⁶⁵ Keach, *Light Broke Forth*, 233.
³⁶⁶ Keach, *Light Broke Forth*, 233. In the light of assertions such as these, it is difficult to accuse Keach of "hyper Calvinism."
³⁶⁷ Keach, *Light Broke Forth*, 233.
³⁶⁸ Y mae'r Arglwydd wedi bendithio bedydd plant bychain i fod yn fodd i barhau'r wir grefydd, ar eglwys Gristnogol ar y ddaiar "o ddyddiayu'r Apostolion hyd y dydd hwn. Nid yw'r Arglwydd yn rhoddi ei fendith neullduol ond ar ei Ordinhadau ei hun. Nid ydyw yn argraphy sêl y Nefoedd ar ddychymyggion daiarol. Ni all neb ammeu nad oes miloedd a fedyddiwyd yn blant yn teimlo ynthynt eu hunain rinwedd eu bedydd..." Owen, *Bedydd Plant or Nefoedd*, 164. Cf. Rothwell, *Paedobaptismus Vindicatus*, 82; Shute, *Antidote to Anabaptism*, 53.

live and die, notwithstanding their parents faith and their reception of their infant-baptism."³⁶⁹

Keach closes this section saying that his adversary James Owen had, as it were, presented his case before a jury, and once this jury read his book and Keach's reply, they would pass "their verdict on our side and against your infant-baptism..." All things are to be judged ultimately by the Scriptures and the readers are to convince themselves about what is right. "For matters of faith and things that concern our souls, every Christian is to judg for himself."³⁷⁰

Antiquity

From ancient times, Burkitt affirms, it has been God's expressed desire that the new-born be made members of his church.

> That which has been the constant and immemorial practice of the church of God in all ages of the world, is unquestionably an ordinance of God and agreeable to his will. But infants initiation or admission of infants into the Jewish church by circumcision and into the Christian church by baptism, has been the immemorial practice of the universal church from the days of Abraham to this day. Therefore, it is undeniably an ordinance of God and agreeable to his will.³⁷¹

Secondly, it should be noted that from the time of John the Baptist all the way to the death of John the Apostle, there is no mention of an infant not being baptised; i.e., the New Testament does not disapprove of pedobaptism.³⁷²

Keach initially criticises Burkitt's syllogism: the minor premise lacks "all ages of the world." Although a defective syllogism, Keach snobs, "I shall pass that by and give you" an appropriate reply. This argument confuses two distinct things, initiation and baptism: for if baptism were to replace circumcision as rite of initiation, it is worth noting that not all babies received such initiation. Most notably, female infants were surely initiated into the Jewish church without circumcision or baptism. What is more, the Christian church—as already stated—is different from the Jewish one in that its membership is constituted not from natural, but spiritual offspring.³⁷³ Keach relies on John Owen for support: our Saviour himself has established an eternal regulation, "that unless a man be born again, he cannot enter the kingdom of God, Joh.3.3; requiring regeneration as an indispensable condition in a member of his church, a subject to his kingdom; for his temple now is built of living stones,

---

³⁶⁹ Keach, *Light Broke Forth*, 234-235.
³⁷⁰ Keach, *Light Broke Forth*, 237-238.
³⁷¹ Burkitt, *Argumentative Discourse*, 26. Cf. Exell, *Serious Enquiry*, [i]; Bridgewater, *Athenian Oracle*, I: 308; Owen, *Bedydd Plant or Nefoedd*, ii, 149.
³⁷² Burkitt, *Argumentative Discourse*, 28.
³⁷³ Keach, *Rector Rectified*, 121-122.

1Pet.2.5."[374] Secondly, as to the non-prohibition of pedobaptism from the Baptizer to John the Apostle, this is rather, Keach claims, "a great argument against infant-baptism and not for it." Is it reasonable to imagine that infants were being baptised then without any mention of it? Indubitably, "it could not stand consistent with the care, wisdom and faithfulness of Jesus Christ, to have hid and concealed such a practice, had there been one infant by his authority or allowance baptised."[375]

James Owen comes up with what appears to be new arguments for the cause of pedobaptism. He says that the model to be followed by the Gospel church has to mirror the model which preceded it. To put it differently, since baptism had anteceded the Law and, then, coexisted with it; baptism, therefore, is to proceed in like manner under the aegis of the Gospel. Owen puts his argument tortuously thus. "Considering the form of baptism before the Law, and under the Law, from which comes the duty of baptising children under the Gospel."[376]

It may also be equally inferred, Keach responds, "that clothes, pots, tables and vessels ought to be baptised under the Gospel, as an ordinance of Christ, because they were dipped, washed or baptised before and under the Law." Additionally and more importantly, Keach continues, the allegedly coexistence of sign and *res* destroys the argument Owen is trying to make.[377]

Owen affirms that "Jacob received little children into God's covenant by baptism [as seen in] Gen.35.2. Then Jacob said unto his household...put away the strange gods that are among you, and clean yourselves, and change your garments."[378]

Keach asks, how can one know that this charge was made against infants? How can one access that infants had polluted themselves by worshipping strange gods? Indeed, though "the Hebrew word signifies cleansing or washing with water, was it therefore formally the ordinance of baptism? Did ever any man argue after this manner before? 'Tis a sign you want proofs for your childish baptism in the New Testament that you go to Genesis for it, and to such a remote text that includes nothing of the controversy."[379]

Again, Owen asserts that "circumcision had become abominable in the sight of the Gentiles, because the children of Jacob made it to be an ordinance of death unto the Sichemites, Gen.34, therefore Jacob received their wives and children (having killed their husbands) into God's covenant through the

---

[374] Owen, *Works*, XV: 617; cited by Keach, *Rector Rectified*, 122. Keach also quotes Taylor to support his argument, ΘΕΟΛΟΓΙΑ ἘΚΛΕΤΙΚΗ, 346.
[375] Keach, *Rector Rectified*, 126-127.
[376] "Am ffurf bedydd Cyn y Gyfraith a than y gyfraith, oddiwrth ba un y dengys y dylid bedyddio plant tan yr Efengyl." Owen, *Bedydd Plant or Nefoedd*, 111.
[377] Keach, *Light Broke Forth*, 154, 156.
[378] "Derbyniodd Jacob blant bychain i Gyfammod Duw trwy fedydd, Gen.35.2. Yna Jacob a ddywedodd wrth ei deulu...bwriwch ymaith y Duwiau deithr sydd yn eich plith chwi, ac ymlanhewch, a newidiwch eich dillad." Owen, *Bedydd Plant or Nefoedd*, 113.
[379] Keach, *Light Broke Forth*, 155-156.

washing with water or baptism." In keeping with "the example of Jacob, the Jews used to baptise all the Gentiles that received circumcision; for their wise men spake thus, *none are proselytes until circumcised and baptised.*"³⁸⁰

Keach responds: at the outset, it is true that circumcision and baptism were used by the Israelites to introduce Gentiles to Judaism. However, the suggestion that Jacob replaced circumcision by the ordinance of baptism is utterly unfounded. "What an abominable innovation had he been guilty of should he have done this thing, which you seem positively to affirm?"³⁸¹ Secondly, it also appears, Keach maintains, that Owen has inferred that the Israelites approved of the innovation brought about by Jacob of baptising proselytes, though they did not obliterate circumcision. In reaction to Owen's suggestion, Keach inveighs, "I challenge you or any man under heaven to prove that God commanded Jacob or any patriarch, or Jewish rabbies, to baptise any proselyte, either young or old, when received into the church."³⁸² Thirdly, the above argument grounds baptism neither on a command from Jesus nor on circumcision; rather this rite, according to Owen, owes its origin to "Jacob's commanding his whole household and all that were with him to be clean," i.e., "to be baptised all of them. So that infant-baptism hath its rise not from the command of Christ, but from the command of Jacob; and that not from circumcision, for Jacob laid that aside...[and] contrived baptism in its stead."³⁸³

James Owen calls upon the authority of the Reformers to validate his position. Pedobaptism has been inherited from the Jewish ecclesia and, further, "the custom continue in the Christian church, in her purest age, and was kept through every age until the time of Luther and Calvin and many other godly scholars, whom the Lord raised up to reform the church of God and to call her out of Babylon." All these men agreed on pedobaptism, and all of them upheld the privileges of infants.³⁸⁴

---

³⁸⁰ Yr oedd yr "Enwaediad wedi mynd yn ffiaidd yngolwy y Cenhedloedd, o herwydd ei feibion Jacob ei gwneuthur yn Ordinhad o farwolaedth ir Sichmiaid, Gen.34, am hynny y mae Jacob yn derbyn ei gwragedd ai plant (canys lladdafid y gwyr) i gyfammod Duw trwy olchiad dwfr, neu fedydd. Yn ol siampl Jacob arferei'r Iddewon fedyddopawb or Cenhedloedd a dderbynient enwaediad. Canys fel hyn y dywed eu gwyr doethion hwynt, *nid yw neb yn broselyt, nes ei enwaedu ai fedyddio.* Owen, *Bedydd Plant or Nefoedd,* 114. Owen's italics is reference to the axiomatic Jewish statement, *Non est quis Proselytus, usque dum circumcidatur & baptizatur.* See John Lightfoot's list of authorities in his, 'In Euangelium S. Matthaei Horae Hebraicae et Talmudicae,' Cap. III: Ver. 6, *Opera Omnia.*
³⁸¹ Keach, *Light Broke Forth,* 156-157.
³⁸² Keach, *Light Broke Forth,* 157.
³⁸³ Keach, *Light Broke Forth,* 158.
³⁸⁴ "...a pharhaodd yr Arferiad o honaw yn yr Eglwys Gristnogawl, yn yr oesoedd puraf o honi, ac i wared drwy bob oes hyd yr amser yr ymddangosodd Luther a Calvin, a llawer eraill o wyr duwiol a dyscedig y rhai a cyfododd yr Arglwydd i ddiwygio eglwys Dduw, ac iw galw allan o Babylon. Yr oeddent hwy oll yn cydsynnio ynghylch bedydd

The antiquity of a practice or custom, Keach claims, is not a proof or warrant of its practices. "What, tho Calvin and Luther, two famous Protestant Reformers, and many other modern divines were, and many godly and learned men are now for this tradition; must it be therefore a truth? Must our faith stand in the wisdom of men in this matter or in the power of God and in the authority of his sacred Word?" As Keach proceeds, he again hints at the primary role of the original Reformers and the secondary role played by the Baptists in pushing forward the Reformation. "Our first Protestants Reformers were raised up to restore those grand fundamentals of faith, more than to reform matters of discipline and about the rite of infant-baptism and some other ceremonies. The path of the just is a shining light, that shines more and more to the perfect day, Pro.4.18."[385]

Still connected with the antiquity of pedobaptism, Burkitt asserts that in sub-Apostolic times, children received laying on of hands. Through this rite, grown up children confirmed the covenant into which their God-parents had entered as their representatives. Accordingly, after the laying on of hands, children "were received in *Ecclesiam Adultorum* and so were admitted to the Lords Supper, and thus by a regular transition they passed out of a state of infant membership into a state of adult membership, by a personal owning of their baptismal covenant." Secondly, Burkitt adds that in the early church infants were given the Eucharist and, thus, it could be assumed that they were also baptised.[386]

The evidence of the laying on of hands, Keach indicates, is inconsequential, "for the Fathers changed the ordinance of baptism from believing men and women to ignorant babies, so they changed imposition of hands...to such young people who in their minority had learned the Articles of the Christian faith." Relevant to the discussion of pedobaptism is that, in the early church, only "baptised believers were admitted to that ordinance of laying on of hands, as Acts 8.14 & 19.6 witnesses."[387] Secondly, knowing that the Church of England did not give Communion to infants, Keach takes advantage of this argument to ask Burkitt, "[w]hy do you not from hence give infants the Lords Supper?" The basis upon which you deny the Supper to infants, Keach says, "I have before proved insignificant."[388] There is as much reason to give one sacrament as to give the other, "as Dr Taylor says," and the logical conclusion is that as the Fathers erred "in the one, so they did in the other."[389]

---

plant, ac nid oedd yr un o hnynt yn ammeu rhagorfreintiau plant." Owen, *Bedydd Plant or Nefoedd*, 156. Martin Luther, *Luther's Works*, Theodore G. Tappert, ed. and trans. (Philadelphia: Fortress Press, 1967), LIV: 55-58.

[385] Keach, *Light Broke Forth*, 226-227.

[386] Burkitt, *Argumentative Discourse*, [31].

[387] Keach, *Rector Rectified*, 137.

[388] Keach, *Rector Rectified*, 138. See this last point, viz., Keach's denial of the Supper to infants, immediately hereafter.

[389] Keach, *Rector Rectified*, 138. Cf. e.g., Taylor, ΘΕΟΛΟΓΙΑ ΕΚΛΕΤΙΚΗ, 331-332.

James Owen had actually replied to Keach's objection that, since babies were to receive the baptismal rite, why is the Eucharist not given them? Owen answered that the Apostle Paul rules that, "those who receive the Lords Supper must examine themselves and to recognise the body of the Lord, which little children cannot do."[390]

Keach argues that just as infants are commanded to examine themselves (which they cannot do and consequently are rightly denied the Eucharist), so also all who come to baptism are commanded to repent and believe, an act little children likewise cannot do. As a result, infants cannot be the subjects of baptism.[391]

However, Owen insists, the baptismal rite "is the sacrament of our regeneration and of our admission into the visible church of God; the Lords Supper is the sacrament of our growth and spiritual food."[392] This parallels the Old Testament, Owen affirms, for though "circumcision belonged to infants, yet the Paschal Lamb belonged only to those of age."[393]

This argument is actually against pedobaptism, Keach alleges, "unless you Presbyterians do believe as the Church of England doth...viz., that baptism doth regenerate the child..."[394] How does baptism work? Does it regenerate the subject or does it proclaim this regeneration? In other words, is baptism a sacrament or is it an ordinance? If infants are regenerated by baptism, they cannot be denied the Lord's Supper. The rite of baptism, Keach proceeds to define his position, "holds forth, 'tis clear, a person born again, or a baby of grace." The Lord's Supper, on the other hand, "is food, fit and proper for that new born or regenerated person, that he may grow thereby; therefore they belong both to one and the same subject, and neither of them, it appears from hence, do belong to infants..."[395] Concerning the parallel between the Jewish and Christian ordinances, it is not true that little children were not allowed to eat the Passover meal; for the Scripture says "that the whole house of Israel were to eat thereof, even a lamb for an house" (Exo.12.3-4). What is more,

---

[390] O herwydd bod yr Apostl yn gorchymyn ir "rhai a dderbyniant Swpper yr Arglwydd eu holi eu hunain, a dirnad Corph yr Arglwydd yr hyn ni all plant bychain ei wneuthur." Owen, *Bedydd Plant or Nefoedd*, 171-172.

[391] Keach, *Light Broke Forth*, [251].

[392] Bedydd "yn Sacrament ein hadenedigaeth ni, a'n derbyniad i eglwys weledig Dduw. Swpper yr Arglwydd yw Sacrament ein tyfiant an hymborth ysprydol ni." Owen, *Bedydd Plant or Nefoedd*, 172.

[393] Felly yr oedd gynt, "er bod enwaediad yn perthyn i blant bychain, nid oedd oen y Pasc yn perthyn ond i rai o oedran." Owen, *Bedydd Plant or Nefoedd*, 172. Cf. Shute, *Antidote to Anabaptism*, 181-182.

[394] Article XXVII of the XXXIX Articles. See also question 2 of *The Anglican Catechism*, 1549: "Who gave you this name? My Godfathers and Godmothers in my baptism; wherein I was made a member of Christ, the child of God and an inheritor of the kingdom of heaven." Schaff, *Creeds of the Evangelical Protestant Churches*, 517.

[395] Keach, *Light Broke Forth*, [251-252].

even though the children were to partake of the Passover, this is unimportant to the discussion, for it is a rite that belongs to the Jewish, not the Gospel church.[396]

Church Fathers

William Burkitt (and others) calls upon the testimony of the Fathers as a witness to the validity of infant baptism. Pedobaptism has been a sub-Apostolical observance and done "so early that none could ever yet define when the practice began."[397]

Before embarking on the subject of Fathers vs. pedobaptism, Keach makes the following observation: the church slowly allowed error to creep into herself after the second and third centuries.[398] "Curcaeleus saith, *Paedobaptismus duobus primus a Christo nato saeculis fuit in cognitus*, &c. Pedobaptism was unknown in the two first centuries after Christ, but in the third and fourth, it was approved by a few, in the fifth and following ages, it began to be generally received." Thus, pedobaptism "is indeed observed by us as an ancient custom, but not as an Apostolic Tradition." Moreover, Keach continues, this Protestant affirms, "*morem infantes baptizandi non coepisse ante tertium a Christo nato saeculum*, &c. That the custom of baptising infants did not begin till the third age after Christ, but in the two former no footsteps of it appear." He adds, Keach concludes, "that *sine ipsius [Christi] mandato introducta est*; it was introduced without the command of Christ."[399] The point of all of this, Keach says, is that pedobaptism may or may not be proved from post-Apostolic testimonies. However, it must be kept in mind, Keach addresses Burkitt, that "now you are without Book, you are forced to quit the Holy Bible, that sacred history and great Charter of the church; and therefore all your proof out of humane history...signifies just nothing." Nevertheless, "you had best take heed lest we carry the cause against you here too..."[400] By the expression, "carry the cause here too," Keach is attempting to say that the Baptists have the support of the earliest part of the Tradition. There was no unanimity among the Reformed Orthodox about the precise era up to which a respective figure would be considered *Ecclesia Patrum*, but the rough general agreement would be 600

---

[396] Keach, *Light Broke Forth*, [253].
[397] Burkitt, *Argumentative Discourse*, 28. For other author's appeal to the Fathers, see, for example, Owen, *Bedydd Plant or Nefoedd*, 149ff.; Bridgewater, *Athenian Oracle*, IV: 163-164, 189.
[398] Keach, *Rector Rectified*, 127.
[399] Stephanus Curcaelleus, *Opera Theologica: Quorum pars praecipua Institutio Religionis Christianae. Cum indicibus necessariis* (Amstelodami: Apud Danielem Elsevirium, 1675), s.v., 'Segunda Dissertatio Theologica: De Peccato Originis,' LVI; cited by Keach in, *Light Broke Forth*, 222; and, *Rector Rectified*, 135.
[400] Keach, *Rector Rectified*, 127-128.

A.D. Nonetheless, it was not unusual to appeal only to the first three centuries.[401] That is the case with Keach.

Burkitt's first witness for pedobaptism is Irenaeus (c.130-c.200): *"Omnes venit Christus per semetipsum salvare, omnes que per eum renascuntur ad Deum infantes & parvulos juniores & seniores.* That is, Jesus Christ came to save all by himself, all who by him are born again unto God, infants and little ones, young and old."[402]

Keach points out that Ireneus does not mention pedobaptism; Burkitt is simply making an inference. The expression, "born again," Keach claims, does not refer to pedobaptism as Burkitt is trying to presume. The interpretation of this passage requires a careful analysis of context, Keach maintains. Ireneus is combating the Gnostic doctrine that Jesus did not live beyond thirty-one years of age. Against this teaching, Ireneus asserts that the Son of God "lived in every age, of infancy, youth and old age; that by his age and example, he might sanctify every age." Consequently,

> Ireneus speaks not of being born again by baptism, for he saith, *Omnen inquam qui per eum renascuntur in Deum*; i.e., I say all which are born again by him to God, i.e., by Christ, not as if he had baptised infants, but because he (i.e., Christ) was an infant, that by the example or virtue of his age, he might sanctify infants, as the whole discourse in Latin plainly shows, viz., *Magister ergo existens, magistri quoque habebat aetatem, non reprobans nec supergrendiens hominem, neque solvens suam legem in se humani generis, sed omnem aetatem sanctificat per illam,* &c.[403]

James Owen quotes Origen (c.185-c.254) saying, *"de infantibus baptizandis Ecclesia traditionem accepit ab Apostolis,* the church received infant baptism by Tradition from the Apostles. We have already proved this was a Scripture Tradition, for the Apostles baptised little children."[404]

---

[401] See this issue in E. P. Meijering, 'The Fathers and Calvinist Orthodoxy: Systematic Theology,' in *The Reception of the Church Fathers in the West*, 867-869. Turretine says, "...paucissima habemus Veterum scripta, praesertim eorum, qui vel secundo aut tertio seculo vixerunt, quorum tamen potior quam inferiorum habenda est ratio, utpote ad aetatem apostolorum proxime accedentium." François Turrettini, *Institutio theologiae elencticae* (Utrecht: s.n., 1696), II: 21, 16. Cited by Meijering, ibid.

[402] Burkitt, *Argumentative Discourse*, 29. James Owen also uses this quotation in a more expanded form to make the same point. *Bedydd Plant or Nefoedd*, 149-150. The citation of Ireneus is to be found in *Contra Haereses*, L.II.c.xxii (147-148), P.G.7.

[403] Keach, *Rector Rectified*, 128-129. Cf. Idem, *Light Broke Forth*, 215.

[404] Sid yn dywedyd, de infantibus baptizandis Ecclesia traditionem accepit ab Apostolis. "Derbyniodd yr Eglwys fedydd plant trwy draddodiad oddiwrth yr Apostolion. Ni a brofasom or blaen mae traddodiad scrythurol oedd hwn, Canys bedyddiodd yr Apostolion blant bychain." Owen, *Bedydd Plant or Nefoedd*, 150. Origin, *In Leviticum Homilia*, VIII (230), P.G.12.

Historical records have been so corrupted, Keach responds, that Origen may be quoted against himself. Examples of contradiction would be him saying that those "that are rightly baptised are washed unto salvation, but so was not Simon Magnus; he that is baptised unto salvation receives the water and the Holy Ghost, which Simon did not but water only..."[405] On the other hand, Origen says that "such baptism that was accompanied with crucifying the flesh and rising again to newness of life, was the approved baptism."[406] When one is dealing with the Fathers, Keach insists, it ought to be done carefully: the works of Origen were not available in Greek, and, to make matters worse, were adulterated by Ruffinus, as Erasmus says. Moreover, Perkins affirms that works attributed to this or that Father are often spurious and of dubious authorship.[407] The important relationship, Keach proceeds, between pedobaptism and Apostolic tradition depends on the testimony of two Fathers only, as Taylor says, Origen and Augustine. Since the latter took it from the former, the claim that pedobaptism is an Apostolic tradition relies—ultimately—on Origen. However, Tertullian, who preceded Origen, seemed to have opposed it: surely, had this tradition been accurate, Tertullian would have concurred with Origen.[408]

Bernard of Clairvaux, Owen says, "who lived between the year 1091 and the year 1153, declares it was the practice of the church in those ages and expressed strong opinions concerning those who were in opposition to it."[409] It is undeniable, Keach concedes, "that the baptism of infants was in the church long before that time. And remarkable 'tis that about 1091 or 1100, Popish darkness was at its greatest height." Nobody should marvel that "those Fathers gave baptism to infants when it was the practice of those times before Bernard, to give the Lords Supper also, as well as baptism."[410]

---

[405] Origen, *Homiliae in Ezechielem*, VI.5, in *GCSEDJ*.
[406] Cf. e.g., Origen, *Ad Romanos*, Liber VI, 579, P.G.14.
[407] Keach, *Light Broke Forth*, 217. Cf. e.g., Erasmus, 'Novum Testamentum Juxta Graecorum Lectionem: Ad Ephesios,' p. 834, col. C, in *Desiderii Erasmi Opera Omnia*, Tomus Sextus. Perkins, *Forged Catholicisme*, 491ff.
[408] Keach, *Light Broke Forth*, 219. Jeremy Taylor, *The Second Part of the Dissuasive from Popery: In Vindication of the First Part and further Reproof and Conviction of the Roman Errors* (London: Printed for R. Royston, Bookseller for the Kings most excellent Majesty, at the Angel in S. Bartholomew's Hospital, 1657), 118. Origen has at least three *loci* where pedobaptism is presented as Apostolic Tradition: *In Leviticum Homilia*, VIII, (230), P.G.12; *Ad Romanus*, Liber V, 565, P.G.14; *In Lucam Homilia*, XIV, *GCS*. For Augustine's *locus*, see *De Genesi ad Litteram*, L.X.c.xxiii, P.L.34.
[409] Bernard "yr hwn a fu fyw rhwng y flwyddyn 1091 ar flwyddyn 1153, sydd yn dangos arferiad yr Eglwys yn yr Oefoedd hynny, ac yn rhoddi barn galed ar y rhai a wrthwynebant fedydd plant." Owen, *Bedydd Plant or Nefoedd*, 154. Cf. Rothwell, *Paedobaptismus Vindicatus*, 74-75.
[410] Keach, *Light Broke Forth*, 225.

However, if it is true, Burkitt interjects, that the Fathers erred in allowing pedobaptism, it would follow that "they in suffering such an error to pass uncensured and uncondemned were guilty of the greatest impiety and hypocrisie."[411] And what of it? Keach queries, "I ask you, whether you do not believe for several centuries those Fathers who admitted infants to the Lords Supper without censuring or condemning it, were not guilty also of great impurity? Besides, did not the same Fathers hold to other errors?" Keach proceeds to quote Perkins saying that "some Fathers, viz., Ireneus, Justin, Clement, Tertullian, held that the Law of Nature had power to save the Gentiles without Christ."[412]

What about the testimony of Cyprian (d.258), Burkitt inquires. Discussing the validity or otherwise of a baptism executed before the eighth day, Cyprian asserts that an infant may be baptised even at the moment of birth. Moreover, he adds the following "words: *Null hominum Nato, misericordiam & gratiam Dei denegandam esse*, that is, the mercy and grace of God (dispensed by baptism), is to be denied to no child of man, namely upon the account of its age."[413]

Keach affirms that Cyprian lived in the third century and by that time, pollutions were penetrating the church. As much as anyone can tell, it was during Cyprian's time that pedobaptism "was first introduced, without any ground or warrant from Christ and it was strongly opposed, which appears by the debates and doubts about it.[414] Concerning these "pollutions," Keach presents Perkins saying that some Fathers practised "rites and ceremonies which are now omitted, as kissing of the child, which was baptised...use of milk and hony...milk and wine..." Furthermore, during baptism, it was common "for the Baptizer to blow in the face of the baptised, and the party baptised used to exufflate, whom he renounced. What credit is to be given to such Fathers? They gave the Eucharist to children likewise."[415]

---

[411] Burkitt, *Argumentative Discourse*, 33.

[412] Keach, *Rector Rectified*, 139. Perkins, *Forged Catholicisme*, 488.

[413] Burkitt, *Argumentative Discourse*, 29. On baptising at the moment of birth, see Cypriot, *Cyprianus et Ceteri Collegae qui in Concilio Adfuerunt numero LXVI Fratri S.*, Epistula LXIII, c.5; the Latin quotation is to be found in ibid., c.2. in C.S.E.L.3. Cf. Owen, *Bedydd Plant or Nefoedd*, 151-152.

[414] Keach, *Rector Rectified*, 129. Cf. Idem, *Light Broke Forth*, 215-216. See the debates and doubts referred to by Keach, in Perkins, *Forged Catholicisme*, 549.

[415] Keach, *Rector Rectified*, 138-139. Perkins, *Forged Catholicisme*, 549. For kissing infants, see Cyprian, *Cyprianus et Ceteri Collegae qui in Concilio Adfuerunt numero LXVI Fratri S.*, Epistula LXIII. c.4, C.S.E.L.3. For milk and honey, Tertullian, *Liber De Corona*, c.iii (79), P.L.2. For milk and wine, Jerome, *Commentariorum in Isaiam Prophetam*, L.XV. c.lv (644), P.L.24. For blowing and exufflating, Rabanus Maurus, *De Clericorum Institutione*, L.I. c.xxvii, P.L.107. Keach deals with these issues also in *Pedobaptism Disproved*, 20.

Next, Burkitt presents the Milevetan Council, which pontificated as follows: *Quicumque parvulos recentes ab uteris matrum baptizandos esse negat, anathema sit.* That is, anyone who would deny baptism to new born infants, let him be accursed.[416] "If you come," Keach berates, "but a little lower, you have proof enough in the Popish Councils, Decrees and Canons. But 'tis to be observed that those Fathers pleaded for infant-baptism, *as that which took away original sin, and gave children the Eucharist too*;" and did this based on a bad interpretation of Joh.3.5. (for pedobaptism) and Joh.6.53 (for pedocommunion).[417] However, Keach says, if testimonies of the Councils are to be sought, we can present them as well. For example, "[a]s to those who are big with child, they ought to be baptised when they will; for in this sacrament there is nothing in common to her that brings forth and that which shall be brought forth from her womb, because in that confession, the liberty of every one's choice is declared."[418] From the Council's statement, Keach makes two inferences. First, the fact that the Council had to deal with unwillingness for pregnant women's baptism indicates that there was hostility towards pedobaptism, since it may appear that in baptising the mother, the child would be baptised as well. Second, the importance of a confession of faith as preparation for baptism seems to be the cause of excluding the infant in the womb as the mother is baptised; that is, it was deemed "necessary to have the consent and choice of those who were to be baptised."[419]

Concerning the approval of the Fathers, Keach challenges Burkitt as follows: there are more "ancient Fathers against infant-baptism, than you have brought for it, and some of them nearer the Apostles days." Only 150 years after Jesus, Justin Martyr (d.c.165) says,

> I will declare unto you how we offer up our selves to God, after that we are renewed through Christ; those amongst us that are instructed in the faith and believe that which we teach them is true, being willing to live according to the same, we do admonish to fast and pray for forgiveness of sins, as we also pray with them: and when they are brought by us into

---

[416] Burkitt, *Argumentative Discourse*, 29. A.D.416, 'Milevitanum Concilium,' Can. II, (87) in *Isidori Mercatoris Collectio Decretalium*, P.L.130.

[417] Keach, *Rector Rectified*, 129. His emphasis.

[418] Keach, *Rector Rectified*, 133-134. *Canones Synodi Neocaesariannae* (c.311 A.D.), VI: Περὶ κυοφορούσης, ὅτι δεῖ φωτίζεσθαι ὁπότε βούλεται οὐδὲν γάρ...κοινωνεῖ ἡ τίκτουσα τῷ τικτομένῳ, διὰ τὸ ἑκάςτουἰδίαν τὴν προαίρεσιν τὴν ἐν τῇ ὁμολογίᾳ δείκνυσθαι. That is, "A woman with a child may be baptised when she pleases, for her baptism concerns not the child...Because every one in that confession is to give a demonstration of this own choice and election." Translation by Taylor, *ΘΕΟΛΟΓΙΑ ΕΚΛΕΤΙΚΗ*, 339. A Latin version of the Greek text in *Collectio Canonum S. Isidoro – Concilium Neocaesariense*, 'De praegnantibus baptizantis,' c.vi (25-26), P.L.84. See also, Keach, *Light Broke Forth*, 221.

[419] Keach, *Rector Rectified*, 134.

the water and there, as we were new born, are they also; and then in calling upon God the Father, the Lord Jesus Christ and the Holy Spirit, they are washed in water, &.[420]

Regarding the Lord's Supper, the same Justin asserts, "[t]his food we call the Eucharist, to which no man is admitted but only he that believeth the truth of the doctrine, being washed in the laver of regeneration of remission of sins and so liveth as Christ hath taught;" which leads one to infer, Keach claims, that pedobaptism was not in place at that time and, therefore, it follows that the Baptists are not innovators, but rather restorers.[421]

Keach proceeds to cite other early Fathers. Discussing Jesus' invitation to children, Mat.19.14, Tertullian insists that the response must be voluntary. That is, children ought to be mature enough to appreciate Christian commitment and to know Christ, before they have their transgressions forgiven. "Men will deal more warily in worldly affairs: so that they who are not trusted with an earthly inheritance, are trusted with an heavenly one: let them ask for salvation, that thou mayst appear to have given it to them."[422] Next, Keach calls upon Ignatius (c.107), who says that baptism must "be accompanied with faith, love and patience, after preaching."[423] Basil the Great (c.330-379) asserts, Keach says, that "baptism is the seal of faith, faith is the necessary confession of the Godhead; it is necessary we should first believe and then be sealed in baptism."[424] In a different place, Basil affirms that,

> [f]aith and baptism are the two means of salvation inseparably cleaving together; for faith is perfected by baptism, but baptism is founded by faith; and by the same names both things are fulfilled: for as we believe in the Father, Son and Holy Spirit, so also we are baptised in the name of the Father, Son and Holy Spirit; and indeed there goeth before, a confession leading us unto salvation; but baptism followeth, sealing our confession and covenant.[425]

In support of pedobaptism, James Owen presents the testimony of Gregory of Nazianzus, who "said, *omni aetati baptisma convenit*, baptism is answerable

---

[420] Keach, *Rector Rectified*, 129-130. Justin Martyr, *Apologia Prima Pro Christianis*, 61, P.G.6.

[421] Keach, *Rector Rectified*, 130. Justin Martyr, *Apologia Prima Pro Christianis*, 66, P.G.6.

[422] Tertullian, *Liber De Baptismo*, XVIII, P.L.1; cited by Keach in, *Gold Refin'd*, 151; *Light Broke Forth*, 130; and *Rector Rectified*, 131.

[423] Cf. e.g., Ignatius, *Ad Philadelphenses*, IV, P.G.5; quoted by Keach in, *Rector Rectified*, 131; and *Light Broke Forth*, 219.

[424] Basil, *Adversus Eunomium*, L.III. c.v. (276), P.G.29; referred to by Keach in, *Light Broke Forth*, 220; *Rector Rectified*, 132.

[425] Basil, *Liber De Spiritu Sancto*, c.xii (23-24), P.G.32; cited by Keach in, *Light Broke Forth*, 219-220; *Rector Rectified*, 132.

unto every age: and again, *da infantis custodiam trinitatem, magnam & praestantissimam custodiam*, give infants the baptism of the Trinity and that will be a great and excellent guard unto them."[426]

The same Gregory, Keach replies, also asserts that "the baptised used in the place to confess their sins and to renounce the Devil and all his works before many witnesses, and that none were baptised of old but they did confess, and how dangerous it was headlong and without preparation to partake thereof." Thus Gregory recommends "that baptism of infants be deferred till they did not only make a confession of their faith, but were to desire the same," as Jeremy Taylor affirms.[427] The truth is, Keach insists, it is difficult to ascertain the position of some Fathers due to the adulteration of their works. The Lord has kept the Scriptures "from corruption, but not the humane history of the Fathers."[428] Although Gregory's position on pedobaptism is not clear, Keach says, observe what he affirms in the following statement: discussing the case of "those who die without baptism," Gregory "gives us an instance in those to whom baptism was not administered, *by reason of infancy*."[429] What is more, in spite of being the son of a bishop, Gregory himself did not receive baptism until he was an adult. The same thing happened to Basil the Great and John Chrysostom; these men had had Christian parents and, additionally, Chrysostom had been educated by the bishop of Melitus—nevertheless, all of them were baptised only as adults.[430] The same happened to Jerome, Ambrose and Augustine, "who were born of Christian parents and consecrated to Christian discipline, even from their childhood, were not baptised before thirty years of age, as Dr. Taylor, Bishop of Down" affirms.[431]

All those examples, stances and opinions, Keach purports, show that the practice of pedobaptism was not in place in sub-Apostolic times. People coming to baptism had to confess their faith and baptism would follow.[432] Consider, further, the opinion of St. Athanasius. Christ "did not slightly

---

[426] Gregory Nazianzus, *Oratio XL: In Sacrum Baptisma*, XVII (703-704), P.G.36. "[M]edd ef, Omni aetati baptisma covenit, y mae bedydd yn gyfattebol i bob oedran: a thrachefn, da infanti trinitatem, magnam & praestantissimam custodiam. Dyro fedydd y drindod i blant bychain, a bydd hynny yn ddiogelwch mawr a rhagorol iddynt." Owen, *Bedydd Plant or Nefoedd*, 152.

[427] Gregory cited by Taylor, ΘΕΟΛΟΓΙΑ ΕΚΛΕΤΙΚΗ, 341; in Keach, *Light Broke Forth*, 217.

[428] Keach, *Light Broke Forth*, 217-218.

[429] Gregory Nazianzus, *Oratio XL: In Sacrum Baptisma*, XXXIII, (708-709), P.G.36; quoted by Keach in, *Light Broke Forth*, 118, 220. Keach's emphasis.

[430] Keach, *Rector Rectified*, 132-133. Keach's source is Du Veil, *Exposition of Acts*, 280.

[431] Taylor, ΘΕΟΛΟΓΙΑ ΕΚΛΕΤΙΚΗ, 341; cited by Keach in, *Light Broke Forth*, 220; and *Rector Rectified*, 133.

[432] Keach, *Rector Rectified*, 133.

command to baptise, but first of all said, teach and then baptise, that the true faith might come by teaching, and baptism be perfected by faith."[433]

However, according to James Owen, Jerome asserts that "we maintain that there is only one baptism and this sacrament should be given to little children in the same way as it is ministered to adults."[434] As we have already seen, Keach says, Jerome maintains that Christ ordered his disciples "that they should first instruct and teach the nations, and afterwards should baptise those that were instructed into the mysteries of the faith; for it cannot be that the body should receive the sacrament of baptism, till the soul have received the true faith."[435] On the whole, the early tradition agrees with the position held by the Baptists, Keach claims. In addition to all the testimonies so far provided, consider the following Fathers. The Venerable Bede maintains that "all those who came to the Apostles to be baptised were instructed and taught concerning the sacrament of baptism, then they received the holy administration thereof."[436] Rabanus emphasises that teaching and Christian doctrine must precede baptism, in order that "he that is to be baptised (i.e., Catechumens) may first learn the mysteries of the faith."[437] Arnobius says to the baptismal candidate: "thou art not...baptised and then beginnest to effect and embrace the faith; but when thou art to be baptised, thou signifie unto the priest what thy desire is and makest thy confession with thy mouth."[438]

Having given the evidence of the sub-Apostolic church, Keach asks his pedobaptist opponents, "what think you now of the testimony of the ancient Fathers and the practice of the churches after the Apostles days? Sure the reader must needs conclude we have the advantage here too, and you must yield whether you will or no and give up the controversie."[439] The conclusion can be no other than that pedobaptism—Keach reiterates—was adopted by the church "in the third or forth century, with many other fopperies,...the church was adulterated from the true Apostolical faith and practice in many respects in those and after times downwards."[440]

---

[433] Athanasius, *Contra Arianus Oratio Secunda*, 42 (403-404), P.G.26; quoted by Keach in, *Light Broke Forth*, 223; and *Rector Rectified*, 135-136.

[434] "...yr ydym ni yn dal bod un bedydd, ac y dylid rhoddi y Sacrament hwn i blant bychain, yn yr un geiriau, ac gweinir ef i rai o oedran." Owen, *Bedydd Plant or Nefoedd*, 152-153.

[435] Jerome, *Commentariorum in Evangelium Matthaei*, L.IV. c.xxviii (243-244), P.L.25; cited by Keach in, *Rector Rectified*, 136-137.

[436] Keach, *Light Broke Forth*, 223. Cf. e.g., Bede, 'Homilia feriae sextae Pasched,' 219-220, in *Quarta Centuria Ecclesiasticae Historiae* (Basileae, Per Annem Oporinum, 1560). This work is commonly known as *Magdeburg Centuries*.

[437] Rabanus Maurus, *Liber De Sacris Ordinibus, Sacramentis Divinis et Vestimentis Sacerdotalibus*, c.v., P.L.112; in Keach, *Light Broke Forth*, 223.

[438] Keach, *Light Broke Forth*, 223. We were unable to locate this reference.

[439] Keach, *Light Broke Forth*, 223-224. Cf. Idem, *Rector Rectified*, 137.

[440] Keach, *Light Broke Forth*, 224.

Having dealt with the *subjects* of baptism, Keach turns to the *administration* of this rite. "I shall prove," he avers, that to sprinkle or to pour water on the candidate, "either on the face or any part of the body, is not *baptising* but *rantizing*."[441]

Mode of Execution

The rite of baptism, Burkitt affirms, is not to be taken as an immutable ordinance. Both immersion and sprinkling are to be accepted. Besides the error of rebaptizing, the Anabaptists want to ascribe such importance to immersion as to dismiss the ancient custom of the churches of the Reformation as "null and void," but in order to do this they must demonstrate that baptism cannot be changed.[442]

This argument is "against your self," Keach retorts. "How dare you change a divine institution of Jesus Christ?" Changing one ordinance "opens a door to make all Christ's institutions *null and void*." For immersion alone was practised for 1300 years in the majority of countries, as we shall see.[443] As to church custom, Keach calls upon the testimony of Gregory, who said that in the case that "there be an offence taken at the truth, it is much better that offence be taken, than that the truth should be deserted." Moreover, Gregory continues, "[t]he custom of the churches ought to submit to the words of Christ, not the words of Christ to be wrested to the custom of the church; in regard the words of Christ are the foundation upon which all customs are to be built."[444] Additionally, "Tertullian says, [w]hatsoever favours contrary to truth is heresy, though it be an ancient custom.'"[445] Concerning Burkitt's accusation of rebaptizing, Keach replies that both credoand pedobaptists deem it wrong, "sinful and unlawful." Thus, "Perkins said, if the external form of administration be observed, a person baptised by a heretick, must not be baptised again."[446] However, Keach addresses Burkitt, "since yours is no baptism, but meer rantism," there is no need of much contention, save a demonstration of the meaning of the word "baptism."[447] We turn now to Keach's examination of the said word.

---

[441] Keach, *Rector Rectified*, 158.

[442] Burkitt, *Argumentative Discourse*, 47, 50. Cf. Shute, *Antidote to Anabaptism*, 12; Owen, *Bedydd Plant or Nefoedd*, 30.

[443] Keach, *Rector Rectified*, 174. His emphasis. Cf. Idem, *Pedobaptism Disproved*, 11.

[444] In Keach, *Rector Rectified*, 158-159. Unable to trace Gregory.

[445] Tertullian, *De Virginibus Velandis Liber*, c.i., P.L.2; quoted by Keach, *Rector Rectified*, 159.

[446] Keach, *Rector Rectified*, 159. Cf. e.g., Perkins, *A Commentarie upon Galatians*, 262.

[447] Keach, *Rector Rectified*, 159. Cf. Idem, *Counter-Antidote*, 32.

Immersion vs. βαπτίζω: Linguistic Consideration

That the meaning of the term baptism is immersion, can be ascertained from the fact that it is a transliteration of "the Greek word βαπτίζω, *baptizo*; [which] comes from βάπτω, to dip, [and] signifies *mergo, immergo, submergo, obruo, item tingo quod sit immergendo*; that is, to immerse, plunge, overwhelm, as also to dip, which is done by plunging." In addition, Keach continues, there is a secondary meaning to βαπτίζω. "We grant in a less proper or more remote sense, because things that are said to be washed, are commonly dipped or plunged all over in water, it is put for washing..."[448] What must be stressed, Keach claims, is that βαπτίζω never means to "sprinkle," for the Greek language has a different term "to express sprinkling, viz., ῥαντίζω, *rantizo*, as Heb.9.19...τὸ βιβλίον καὶ πάντα τὸν λαὸν ἐράντισεν; that is, '[h]e sprinkled the book and all the people.'"[449] Another example, Keach proceeds, would be, καὶ ῥαντισμὸν αἵματος Ἰησοῦ Χριστοῦ, that is, "and sprinkling of the blood of Jesus Christ" (1Pet.1.2). Again, Keach insists, "there is not one place in Scripture wherein the word ῥαντίζω, *rantizo*, is rendered to baptise; nor is there one Scripture wherein the word βαπτίζω, *baptizo*, is rendered sprinkling."[450] Hammond asserts "that βαπτίσμος signifies an immersion or washing of the whole body, and which answereth to the Hebrew word לבטו׳ used for dipping in the Old Testament;" thus, he adds, Jesus' cousin used the Jordan as the environment for baptism, on account of the abundance of waters, or, as Hammond puts it, "because 'tis said there was much water, which the Greeks called the Lakes where they used to wash."[451]

The German language calls baptism "Tauff," a word whose etymology comes from "Tieff," deepness, and from which one gets the sense that baptismal candidates should be deeply immersed. Luther asserts, Keach continues, that the name "baptism is a Greek word, it may be termed a dipping when we dip something in water that it may be wholly covered with water." Whilst the tradition of immersion "is now altogether abolished among most

---

[448] Keach, *Rector Rectified*, 159-160. For the aforesaid definition, Keach relies on Stephanus and Scapula, *Lexicon Graecolatinum Recentiis* (Apud Guillelmum Laemarium, 1593), s.v., βαπτίζω. For a syllogistical argument on *baptizo*, see Keach, *Answer unto two Athenian Mercuries*, 8.

[449] Keach, *Rector Rectified*, 160. There is a Greek misprint, viz., ἐρράντισε. Cf. Idem, *Pedo-baptim Disproved*, 22.

[450] Keach, *Rector Rectified*, 160.

[451] Keach, *Rector Rectified*, 166. Henry Hammond, *A Paraphrase and Annotations upon all the Books of the New Testament, Briefly Explaining all the Difficult Places thereof*, 4th ed. (London: Printed by E. F., T. R. and J. M for R. Roston, Bookseller to his most Sacred Majesty, at the Angel in Amen-Corner, 1675), s.v., Jo.13.10; Mk.1.5; Mat.3.1; Jo.3.23.

part, for neither do they dip the whole children, but only sprinkle them with little water, they ought nevertheless to be dipt and presently drawn out again."[452]

A German Synod was called in Hamburgh by several ministers on account of sprinkling. After some deliberation, the ministers assembled agreed "that the judgement of Luther and of the divines of Wittemburgh should be demanded about this point. Which thing being done, Luther wrote to Hamburgh, that this sprinkling was an abuse, which they ought to remove."[453] Keach then moves on to give a practical example to drive home the point that the rantizing of an infant is an act of disobedience to God. He says, suppose I ordered "my maid to dip my handkerchief into the water and she only takes a little water in her hand and sprinkles a few drops upon it, doth she do what I command her? Was that the thing or is it another act? Even so 'tis here, you do not do the thing, you rantize, and baptise none, unless you dip them into the water."[454]

The Dutch language, Keach affirms, translates $\beta\alpha\pi\tau i\zeta\omega$ as dipping. This may be illustrated by looking at Mat.3.16 and 3.6 respectively: *Ende Jesus gedoopt zijnde, is terstont opgeklomen vit hit wter*; "And when Jesus was dipp'd, he came out of the water." *Erde wierden van hemge doopt in de Jordan*; "And [the people] were dipped of him in Jordan." This translation of $\beta\alpha\pi\tau i\zeta\omega$ is not restricted to the Gospel. Likewise, Act.8.12, reads: *Maer do sy Philippo getrofden die Euangeliam van het koninckrycke Godts ende [van] don name Jesus Christi verkondigh de wier den sy de doop begde manan endevrouwen*; that is, "when they heard Philip preaching the things concerning the kingdom of God, and the name of Jesus Christ, they were dipped both men and women."[455] In addition to that, John the Baptist is called John the Dipper: *Ende in die dayen quam Jonnes de Dooper predikenn in de woeffijue van Judea*..."In those days came John the Dipper, preaching in the wilderness of Judea." Keach adds that if the Dutch way of translating $\beta\alpha\pi\tau i\zeta\omega$ had been done by English translators, the English Bibles would have read "John the Dipper, and for 'baptising them in the name of the Father &c.' it would have been read, 'dipping them in the name of the Father...' and the people would not have been deceived."[456] The Greek word was not translated into English, Keach says, but rather transliterated. "What difference is there between *Baptisma* (Greek) and *Baptism*?"[457]

Burkitt affirms, however, that there must be a distinction made between "that which is of the essence of baptism and that which is accidental in baptism; the Word and element of water are of the essence of baptism." Thus says Augustine, *accedat verbum ad elementum & sit sacramentum*, i.e., add the

---

[452] Keach, *Rector Rectified*, 164. Luther, *Luther's Works*, XXXVI: 64.
[453] Keach, *Rector Rectified*, 165. Keach is quoting Du Veil, *Exposition of Acts*, 286-287.
[454] Keach, *Rector Rectified*, 166.
[455] Keach, *Light Broke Forth* 23. Cf. Idem, *Rector Rectified*, 199.
[456] Keach, *Rector Rectified*, 167.
[457] Keach, *Counter-Antidote*, 7. Cf. Idem, *Light Broke Forth*, 23.

Word to the element and it turns into a sacrament. Even though the element of water is fundamental, "yet the *modus applicanti*, that is, the manner of applying the water to the person baptised, is only circumstantial."[458] To pour water or to sprinkle is called baptism in the Scripture, consequently both practices are "lawful and sufficient, and dipping [is] not necessary."[459]

Burkitt is right, Keach concedes, concerning the fact that secondary things are not essential for a rite to be legitimate. However, immersion is not incidental to baptism, it is rather part of the *res*, it is an essential component of baptism. There can be no Word and element without the proper mode being used, for "rantizing is rantizing and baptising is baptising, they are two different things and the one will never be the other while the world stands. And tho you dare affirm," Keach continues, "that the child that is only rantized, i.e., sprinkled, is baptised, yet you cannot prove it; and altho you do assert it and attempt to make it out, yet a multitude of learned writers and critics in the Greek tongue do fully contradict you."[460] For example, "Grotius says it signifies to dip over head and ears."[461] Similarly, Pasor has it as "immersion, dipping or submersion."[462] Likewise, "Vossius says it implieth a washing the whole body."[463] "Minceaus in his dictionary saith that βαπτισμός à βαπτίζω, is in the Latin *Baptismus*, in Dutch droopsit or droopen...to dive or duck in water, and the same with the Hebrew לבט *tabal*, which is the Septuagint or seventy interpreters, render βαπτίζω, to dip."[464] The renowned Du Veil—Keach continues on with his entourage of lexicographers—affirm that "the word βαπτίζειν is to dip, as if it were to dye colour; and any dyer will tell you, if there is any small bit of cloth not dipped, it is not dyed."[465] Keach also cites Leigh, who says that βαπτίζω means "'to dip into the water or plunge under the water,'...for which he quotes Casaubon, Bullinger, Zanchy, Spanhemius." Leigh adds, Keach says, that "some would have it signify washing, which sense

---

[458] Augustine, *In Iohannis Evangelium Tractatus*, LXXX, 3, C.C.S.L.36; in Burkitt, *Argumentative Discourse*, 49. Cf. Bridgewater, *Athenian Oracle*, IV: 162, I: 309.

[459] Burkitt, *Argumentative Discourse*, 51.

[460] Keach, *Rector Rectified*, 161. Cf. Idem, *Counter-Antidote*, 7.

[461] Cf. e.g., Hugo Grotius, *Operum Theologicorum*, Tomi II (Amstelaedami: Apud Heredes Joannis Blaev, 1679), s.v., Mat.3.6.

[462] Georgius Pasor, *Lexicon Graeco-Latinum, Novum Domini Nosti Jesu Christi Testamentum*, Editio quarta (Herbornae Nassoviorum: Typis Georgii Corvini & Johan-Georgii Muderspachii, 1632), s.v., βαπτίζω.

[463] Gehardus Joannes Vossius, *Etymologycon Linguae Latinae. Praefigitur Ejusdem de Literarum Permutatione Tratactus*, Editio Nova (Amstelodami: Ex typographia P. & I. Blaev, Prostant apud Ianssonio-Waesbergios, Boom, à Someren & Goethals, 1695), s.v., *Baptismus*.

[464] All preceding authorities quoted by Keach in, *Gold Refin'd*, 27; and *Rector Rectified*, 161. Unable to track down Minceaus.

[465] Cf. e.g., Du Veil, *Exposition of Acts*, II: 76; cited by Keach in, *Rector Rectified*, 162; and *Gold Refin'd*, 28.

Erasmus opposed, affirming that it was not otherwise so than by consequence; for the proper signification was such a dipping or plunging as dyers use for dying of clothes."[466] Furthermore, when Ambrose alludes to immersion, he says that "water is that wherein the body is plunged to wash all sin away, there all vice is buried." One may guess, Keach adds, that Ambrose intends to convey the idea that baptism is a picture of sin's burial.[467] Moreover, Tomasso de Vio maintains that "Christ ascended out of the water, therefore Christ was baptised by John, not by sprinkling or pouring water upon him, but by immersion, that is, by dipping into the water."[468] In the last place, "[y]our church," Keach addresses Burkitt, asserts that "dipping into the water is the proper (as I conceive) signification of the word."[469]

A syllogistic conclusion to this linguistic consideration is befitting. "If the proper, literal and genuine signification of the Greek word *Baptizo* is dipping or to dip;" Keach argues, "then sprinkling is not baptising. But the proper, literal and genuine signification of the Greek word *Baptizo* is dipping or to dip. Ergo, sprinkling is not baptising."[470]

Immersion vs. the Practice of the Early Church

During Jesus' earthly days, Keach remarks, the Jordan river was the environment where baptism took place. Here, John the Baptist received candidates for baptism and, as Diodati affirms, "he plunged them in water."[471] The same thing, Keach proceeds, is said by Piscator and the Westminster

---

[466] Edward Leigh, *Critica Sacra: Or, Philologicall and Theologicall Obervations upon all the Greek Words of the New Testament, in Order Alphabeticall*, 2nd ed. corrected and much enlarged by the author (London: Printed by James Young, for Thomas Underhill, and are to be sold at the Signe of the Bible in Wood-Street, 1646), s.v., βαπτίζω; quoted by Keach in, *Rector Rectified*, 162; and *Gold Refin'd*, 28.

[467] Cf. e.g., Ambrose, *De Spiritu Sancto: Ad Gratianum Augustum*, L.I. c.vi, 76, P.L.16; cited by Keach in, *Counter-Antidote*, 10; *Light Broke Forth*, 31; *Gold Refin'd*, 53; and *Rector Rectified*, 164.

[468] Thomas de Vio Cajetan, *RR. DD. Thomae de Vio Caietani in Quattor Evangelia et Acta Apostolorum* (Lugduni: Sumptibus Iacobe & Petri Prost, 1639), s.v., Matt.3.16; in Keach, *Rector Rectified*, 172. Keach continues to pile up other witnesses in support of his point that *baptizo* means immersion. Among others, he calls on Wolfgang Musculus, William Ames, Daniel Rogers, Jeremy Taylor, Isaac Casaubon, Henry Pool, John Ball, Joseph Mede, Daniel Chamier. See references in *Rector Rectified*, 161-172.

[469] Keach, *Rector Rectified*, 167.

[470] Keach, *Rector Rectified*, 168.

[471] Giovanni Diodati, *Pious Annotations upon the Holy Bible: Expounding the difficult places thereof Learnedly and Plainly. With other things of great importance* (London: Printed by T. B. for Nicholas Fussel; and are to be sold at the Green Dragon in St. Paul's Church-yard, 1643), s.v., Mat.3.6; cited by Keach, *Gold Refin'd*, 33.

Assembly.[472] There would be no need to go to a river if sprinkling were practised, but as the Scriptures says, "John baptised in Aenon near Salim, because there was much water" (Joh.3.23).[473]

Burkitt protests by saying that "many waters" is the correct translation. "[L]et the original be considered," he says, for the Greek does not say, "there was πόλυ ὕδωρ, much water; but πολλὰ ὕδατα, many waters; that is, many streams or rivolets..."[474] Secondly, Burkitt adds the testimony of *Sandys Travels*, which reports that Judean rivers were so shallow that the waters could not "reach above the ankles; so that the small quantity of water would hardly admit of baptism by dipping."[475]

This is an useless objection, Keach claims, for what matters is that the Scripture emphasises that the rite "could not be administered with a little water, but that it required many waters or much water, a great deal more than a bason could hold, or you hold in your hand."[476] In effect, "the Greek words ὕδατα πολλα signifies many waters, but not rivulets, but rather the tumultuousness and raging of the seas, which fully signifies the abundance and confluence of waters, contrary to what you affirm. See Rev.14.2..."[477] As to the testimony of *Sandys Travels* Keach replies that as time elapses, things change. Thus, it is better to believe in the Scripture's testimony which says "many or much," than in a voyager's who says the opposite. Moreover, Keach addresses Burkitt, "for your seeking after this manner to contradict the Sacred Text, to defend your childish practice of rantism, you deserve greatly to be blamed."[478]

To allude again to the baptismal practice of the early church, Keach says that Fisher did well to note that it would not make any sense "for St. Mark to say that Jesus was baptised in Jordan, if it had been sprinkled, because the Greek reads it εἰς τὸν Ἰορδάνην, into Jordan. Could Jesus be said to be sprinkled into the river Jordan?" It is rather much more logical to affirm that he was immersed

---

[472] Johannes Piscator, *Analysis Logica Evangelii Secundum Johannem* (Londini: Impresis Geor. Bishop, 1595), s.v., Joh.3.23; Westminster Assembly, *Annotations upon all the books of the Old and New Testament* (London: Printed by Evan Tyler, 1657), s.v., Matt.3.6; both works quoted by Keach in, *Gold Refin'd*, 33, and *Rector Rectified*, 168.

[473] Keach, *Rector Rectified*, 168. Cf. Idem, *Counter-Antidote*, 6; and *Light Broke Forth*, 24.

[474] Burkitt, *Argumentative Discourse*, 59.

[475] Burkitt, *Argumentative Discourse*, 59. Cf. e.g., George Sandys, *Sandys Travels, Containing an History of the Original and Present State of the Turkish Empire: Their Laws, Government, Policy, Military Force, Courts of Justice and Commerce*, 7th ed. (London: Printed for John Williams Junior, at the Crown in Little-Britain, 1673), 110.

[476] Keach, *Rector Rectified*, 169.

[477] Keach, *Rector Rectified*, 203.

[478] Keach, *Rector Rectified*, 169-170.

into the river.[479] Additionally, there would have been no need for Philip (Act.8) to take the Ethiopian Eunuch out of his chariot and into the river, if a few drops of water would suffice. Keach says of Philip's action that, "he might have fetch'd a little water in his hand, or otherwise, and have sprinkled him in his chariot, as some ministers do now in their publick places of worship. And thus," Keach addresses Burkitt, "you and they make void the command of Christ by your traditions, to the abuse of Christian baptism and reproach of us that keep to his sacred institution."[480]

Keach also refers to the Synod of Caelichyth. In it, the Archbishop of Canterbury states: "let the Presbyters beware that when they administer the sacrament of baptism, they do not pour water upon the heads of the infants, but let them be always plunged in the font, according to the example of the Son of God himself, who was plunged into the waters of Jordan, thus must the ceremony be performed according to order."[481] Du Veil asserts, Keach says, that dipping was universally practised by the church, until "the time of Clem.5. who was crowned Pope An. 1305, under whom first of all the second Synod of Ravenna approved the abuse introduced into some churches about an hundred years before, that baptism without any necessity should be administered by aspersion."[482] Thus, Keach proceeds, this distortion of the natural illustration of baptism came into being and, as a result, "all the West for the most part has in this age the use of rantism...to the great scandal of the Greeks and Russians, who to this day plunge into the water those they baptise and deny, mark it, any one to be rightly baptised, who is not plunged into the water," as Jesus ordains.[483]

---

[479] Keach, *Rector Rectified*, 170. Samuel Fisher, *Christianismus Redivivus* (London: Printed by Henry Hills, and are to be sold by Francis Smith at his shop in Flying Horse court in Fleetstreet, 1655), 310.

[480] Keach, *Rector Rectified*, 170-171. Cf. Idem, *Gold Refin'd*, 34-35.

[481] "Sciant etiam presbyteri quando sacrum baptismum ministrant, ut non effundant aquam sanctam super capita infantium, sed semper mergantur in lavacro, sicut exemplum praebuit per semetipsum Dei Filius omni credenti, quando esset ter mersus in undis Jordanis. Ita necesse est secundum ordinem servari & haberi." Synodus Apud Celichyth (A.D. 816): 'Canon XI.' Taken from Johannes Dominicus Mansi, ed. *Sacrorum Conciliorum Nova et Amplissima Collectio*, 54 vols. (Paris: Apud Antonium Zatta, 1903), s.v. vol. 15; cited by Keach in, *Counter-Antidote*, 6; *Rector Rectified*, 170-171; and *Gold Refin'd*, 34-35.

[482] Consilium Ravennate II (A.D1311): 'De Sacramento baptismi & forma conferenda:' "Cum sacramentum baptismi ominium sacramentorum sit principium & fundamentum, & ideo propter summan necessitatem forma ejusdem, a Christo institutore tradita, a nullo fidelium maxime debeat ignorari: ipsam formam, quae infra scriptis verbis complectitur, recensemus: Petre vel Maria, ego baptizo te in nomine Patris, & Filii, & Spiritus sancti, sub trina aspersione, vel immersione, nihil interposito, vel detracto." Mansi, *Sacrorum Conciliorum Nova*, s.v. vol.25.

[483] Keach, *Gold Refin'd*, 29. Du Veil, *Exposition of Acts*, II: 76.

At this point, it is noteworthy to point out that, though highly antagonistic towards sprinkling, which he considers a betrayal, Keach avidly pursues unity and Reformation among Protestants. "O what abundance of the betrayers of the truth and of churches too, have we in these, as well as in former days! How little is the institution of Christ or practice of the primitive churches minded by many good men? Where is the spirit of the Reformation?"[484] Why is it, Keach inquires, that the church finds herself in this situation? This is the case because those presiding over her usurped authority and made undue alterations. However, no one was given license to change her baptismal ordinance; rather, the church should have been "kept exactly to the institution" as prescribed by Christ.[485] To illustrate the "error" of changing God's ordinances, Keach refers to the command to build God's altar out of the earth or out of undressed stones (Det.20.24-25). Years later, the Lord rebukes the people for altering his ordinances. Israel is a nation "that provoked me to anger continually to my face, that sacrificed in gardens and burn incense upon altars of brick" (Isa.65.3). Keach then addresses the sprinklers. "O tremble ye who adventure to transgress God's precept in as bad or worse a manner! Who commanded you to baptise or dip believers in 'in the name of Father, &c.' and you rantize or sprinkle infants. Alas you know not how you hereby provoke God..."[486] To complicate matters further, it is very difficult to admit the wrongfulness of a practice when this practice has been in place for a long period of time, and "especially when carnal ease and profit attends the keeping of it up and also when the true way of baptism is reproached and look'd upon to be so contemptible a practice, and those who own it and dare not do otherwise, vilified and reproached ...with the scurrilous name of Anabaptists, &c."[487]

In conclusion to this section, granting that the one baptising and the one receiving baptism "in the days of Christ and his Apostles went both down into the water, and the person baptised was dipp'd; then is baptism not sprinkling but dipping. But the baptizer and the baptised in the days of Christ and the Apostles went both down into the water, and the person baptised was dipp'd. Ergo, baptism is not sprinkling but dipping."[488]

Immersion: Typical and Metaphorical

Keach's last arguments for dipping lie in the concepts of (i) typical and (ii) metaphorical baptisms found in Scripture. Both types are usually portrayed as a kind of immersion.

---

[484] Keach, *Rector Rectified*, 171.
[485] Keach, *Rector Rectified*, 171. Cf. Ibid., 180-181; idem, *Light Broke Forth*, 31-32.
[486] Keach, *Light Broke Forth*, 32.
[487] Keach, *Rector Rectified*, 171-172.
[488] Keach, *Light Broke Forth*, 20.

(i). He provides two illustrations of typical baptism. The first example is the one at "the red sea, wherein the Fathers were buried, as it were, unto Moses in the sea and under the cloud." Pool comments, Keach says, that this passage relates to "the great analogy betwixt baptism (as it was used), the persons going down into the waters, and being dipped in them," on the one hand; and, on the other, "the Isrealites going down into the sea, the great receptacle of water, though the water at that time was gathered on heaps on either side of them; yet they seemed buried in the water, as persons seemed buried in the water" when baptism takes place.[489] The second illustration comes from the ark of Noah. Keach quotes Knatchbull, who said that both baptism and Noah's ark symbolise "the resurrection, not a sign of the washing away of sin, though so taken metonymically, but a particular signal of the resurrection of Christ; of this again is baptism a lively and emphatically figure, as also was the ark of Noah," whence "he returned as from a sepulchre."[490]

(ii). There are two kinds of metaphorical baptism: the baptism of the Holy Spirit and the baptism of affliction. First, the baptism of the Holy Ghost is not the common sanctification of, nor the gifts given to, every believer by the Spirit. The reference, Keach alleges, is rather to "the miraculous effusion of the Holy Spirit, like that at the Pentecost, Act.1.4-5." Keach quotes Casaubon saying that the "word $\beta\alpha\pi\tau i\zeta\epsilon\iota\nu$...is to dip or plunge, &c. in which sense...the Apostles might be truly said to have been baptised, for the house in which this was done was filled with the Holy Ghost. So that the Apostles might seem to have been plunged into it, as in a large fish-pond."[491] Keach continues, it is "not a sprinkling of the Spirit that is the baptism of the Spirit, for so doubtless the Apostles had the Spirit before they were said to be baptised with it."[492] This is what Oecumenius asserts, as he comments on Acts 2: "A wind filled the whole house, that it seemed like a fish-pond, because it was promised to the Apostles, that they should be baptised with the Holy Ghost."[493] Second, the Scriptures testify to the baptism of affliction in this way: "I have a baptism to be baptised with and am I strained till it be accomplished!" (Mat.20.22) From the true meaning, Keach proceeds, "of the word *baptizo, immergo*, plunge under, overwhelm; great afflictions come to be called baptism, and signifies, as

---

[489] Matthew Pool, *Annotations upon the Holy Bible*, 3 vols. (Edinburgh: s.n., 1700-01), s.v., vol. 3, 1Cor.10.2; cited in Keach, *Rector Rectified*, 204-205; and *Gold Refin'd*, 61-62.

[490] Norton Knatchbull, *Annotations upon Some Difficult Texts in all the Books of the New Testament* (Cambridge: Printed by J. Hayes, Printer to the University; for W. Graves, Bookseller there, 1693), s.v., 1Pet.3.20; referred to by Keach in, *Light Broke Forth*, 43; and *Rector Rectified*, 205.

[491] Isaac Casaubon, 'Notae in Novum Testamentum: In Acta Apostolorum,' s.v., 1.5, 2.2, in *ΤΗΣ ΚΑΙΝΣ ΔΙΑΘΗΚΗΣ ΑΠΑΝΤΑ* (Londini: Apud Richardum Whittakerum, 1633); cited by Keach in, *Counter-Antidote*, 5; and *Rector Rectified*, 205-206.

[492] Keach, *Rector Rectified*, 206.

[493] Oecumenius Triccae, *Commentaria in Acta Apostolorum*, Cap. III (14), P.G.118.

Vossius shews, not every light affliction, but like that of David, Psa.32.6, 'he drew me out of deep water.'"[494] On that account, "great afflictions are called waves...(Psa.42.7). 'Tis spoken of Christ's sufferings," which is metaphorically called baptism of affliction.[495] Pool concurs, Keach notes, for he says, "to be baptised is to be dipped in water, metaphorically to be plunged in affliction."[496]

Immersion: Objections to It

James Owen presents our first objection.

> Baptism, according to the meaning of the word, is *washing*, because of that, the Apostle said, we are saved through the washing of regeneration. This is how the word βαπτίσμοις is rendered in Heb.9.10. 'through various washings,' [yet] according to the Greek [it should read] 'through various baptisms;' not all of which were through dipping under the water, but through sprinkling water on those who were washed or baptised, as the Apostle showed, Heb.9.19: 'he took the blood of the calves and of goats with water—and sprinkled the book and all people.' That which the Apostle called baptism in the 10th verse, is called the 'sprinkling of water' in verse 19.[497]

First, it is true, Keach agrees, that although the term βαπτίζω may secondarily mean washing, "yet I challenge you and all that know (or pretend to know) the Greek tongue, whether in every place in the New Testament where the word is mentioned, or any derivative from it (as it refers to Christ's ordinance of baptism), it doth not directly and properly signify immersion, and accordingly rendered by Beza in his translation."[498] Second, Keach accuses Owen of great error as he confuses "sprinkling" (v.19) with "divers baptisms" (v.10). Keach then asks him, "do you find the Greek word βαπτίσμοις (which is in v.10) in v.19, where sprinkling is mentioned? Or is it not in vv.13, 19 as also 1Pet.1.2. καὶ πάντα τὸν λαὸν ἐράντισεν?" It can be said "that no Greek author,

---

[494] Vossius, *Etymologicon Linguae Latinae*, s.v., *Baptismus*, in Keach, *Gold Refin'd*, 5.
[495] Keach, *Rector Rectified*, 206. Cf. Idem, *Counter-Antidote*, 5.
[496] Pool, *Annotations*, vol. 3, s.v., Mat.20.22; in Keach, *Rector Rectified*, 206.
[497] "Bedydd yn ol arwyddocáid y gair yw *golchiad*, am hynny ebe'r Apostl, achubir ni trwy olchiad yr adenedigath. Felly y troir y gair βαπτίσμοις, Heb.9.10. 'trwy amryw olchiadau,' yn ol y groeg, 'trwy amryw fedyddiadau,' yrhai oeddent nid yn unig trwy ymdrochi tan ddwr, ond trwy daenellu dwr ar y rhai a olchwyd neu a bedyddiwd, fel y dangos yr Apostl, Heb.9.19: 'efe a gymmerodd waed lloi a geifr, gydá dwr—ac ai taenellodd ar y llyfr ar bobl oll.' Yr hyn a alwodd yr Apostl bedyddiadau yn y 10 wers a elwir 'taenelliad dwfr' yn y wers hon." Owen, *Bedydd Plant or Nefoedd*, 3.
[498] Keach, *Light Broke Forth*, 2. Beza affirms that *baptizo* means "to immerse" as "to dye." *Testamentum Novvum, sive Novvum Foedus Iesu Christi, D.N.* (Geneva: s.n., 1589), s.v., Mat.3.11.

whether Heathenish or Christian, has ever put baptising for sprinkling or use those words promiscuously," and if only biblical texts are considered, there is not a single occasion when "the word ῥαντίζω, is rendered baptism, nor is there one Scripture where βαπτίζω is rendered sprinkling."[499] Moreover, concerning the occasional instances when βαπτίζω signifies washing, it does so in the sense that washing involves the total plunging of an artefact, like a piece of cloth that is to be dyed.[500]

Like James Owen, Burkitt also objects to immersion saying that there are instances when the Greek βαπτίζω means to wash or sprinkle. "Sometimes blood was sprinkled, sometimes water was poured forth. No person were dipped or plunged in blood, yet those sprinklings are called baptising."[501]

Keach replies that whenever the Scripture talks about "sprinkling of blood," the Greek word employed is not βαπτίζω.[502] Furthermore, Keach denies that Jewish washings (which the Scripture calls baptism), were done by any means other than dipping. He quotes Ainsworth, who says that all kinds of pollutions, in things or persons, were made clean "by dipping or baptising in water and wheresover the Law speaketh of washing a man's flesh, or washing of cloaths for uncleanness, it is not but by dipping the whole body therein." Additionally, regardless of reference to utensils or persons, "there may not be anything between them and the water to keep them asunder, as clay, pitch or the like, that cleaveth to the body or vessel; if there be, then they are...unclean and their washing profiteth them not."[503]

Burkitt argues that when it comes to the "sacrament it is not the quantity of elements, but the significancy of them that ought to be attended; in circumcision it was not the quantity of flesh cut off so much as the signification of it that the Jews were to concern themselves about." In the same way, when dealing with the Eucharist, "it is not the quantity of bread and wine, but the right apprehension of the thing signified thereby that we should labour after." Finally, it is no different, Burkitt continues, with the sacrament of baptism: a drip of water sprinkled "upon me, may signify, seal, conveigh and confirm to me a right and interest in all the benefits of my Saviours death and resurrection as fully as if, with Jonah, I were plunged into the main ocean."[504]

If the Eucharist is in view, Keach affirms, surely it is "not the quantity of bread and wine" that makes it valid; rather, the Eucharist is valid if done in the way Jesus commanded it, i.e., "to represent his body broken and his blood

---

[499] Keach, *Light Broke Forth*, 2-3. Cf. Idem, *Gold Refin'd*, 25.
[500] Keach, *Light Broke Forth*, 3.
[501] Burkitt, *Argumentative Discourse*, 52.
[502] Keach, *Rector Rectified*, 177.
[503] Henry Ainsworth, *Annotations upon the Third Book of Moses, called Leviticus* (Amsterdam: Imprinted by Giles Thorp, 1618), s.v., Lev.9.31-33; cited by Keach, *Rector Rectified*, 176.
[504] Burkitt, *Argumentative Discourse*, 51.

poured forth." Similarly, there is no need to have rivers of water to have proper baptism, only enough of it to immerse one's body completely, in order to illustrate "the burial and resurrection of Christ, which was the very thing it was appointed to hold forth or represent when administered."[505] As to Burkitt's illustration, Keach asks, should the Israelites "in circumcision only have cut a little bit of the fore-skin of the flesh, and not round, or quite off, or only have paired off the nails of the childrens fingers with a little skin with it, would that have answered the mind of God in that rite?"[506] Likewise, the intention of God is frustrated when baptism is not done by immersion. The institution of both ordinances was made in such a way as to make visible to the senses the word preached. "And that baptism doth hold forth this, together with our death unto sin and rising again to walk in newness of life, I shall now prove," Keach avers, in two ways: by the testimony of the Scripture and "by the consent, agreement and arguments of a cloud of witnesses, both ancient Fathers and modern divines, and worthy Protestant writers."[507]

To start with Scripture, Paul says that "...we are buried with him in baptism, &c." (Rom.6.3-6). That is, the Christians in Rome were to count themselves lifeless concerning sin and its power and, further, were to live new lives. As a result, baptism signifies, first, the burial and resurrection of Jesus and, second, "our death unto sin and our rising again to walk in newness of life."[508] Curiously, Keach turns Paul into a syllogistic thinker: the Apostle herein speaks in such way, "[a]s if he should say, as many of us as are baptised, must know this, that we were baptised into Christ's death and, therefore, must die to sin and live a new life. But we have been baptised or buried with him in baptism; therefore must all die to sin and live a new life."[509] Keach adds that, on this text, Pool comments that Paul "seemed to allude to the manner of baptising in those warm countries, which was...to dip or plunge the party baptised and, as it were, to bury him for a while under the water."[510] On this same passage, Cajetan maintains that "[w]e are buried with Christ by baptism into death; by the ceremony of baptism, because he (i.e., the party baptised) is put under the water, and this carries a similitude of him that was buried, who was put under the earth. Now because" no one "is buried but dead men, from this very thing, that we are buried in baptism, we are assimilated to Christ buried, or when he was buried."[511]

---

[505] Keach, *Rector Rectified*, 175.

[506] Keach, *Rector Rectified*, 175.

[507] Keach, *Rector Rectified*, 177. Cf. Idem, *Answer unto two Athenian Mercuries*, syllogism 26, pp. 7-8.

[508] Keach, *Rector Rectified*, 177-178. Cf. Idem, *Counter-Antidote*, 7.

[509] Keach, *Rector Rectified*, 178. Cf. Idem, *Light Broke Forth*, 29.

[510] Pool, *Annotations*, vol. 3, s.v., Rom.6.4; cited by Keach, *Rector Rectified*, 178.

[511] Cajetan, *Epistolae Pauli et aliorum Apostolorum ad Graecam veritatem castigatam & per Reverendissimum Dominum Thoman de Vio, Caietanum Cardinalem sancti Sisti, iuxta sensum literalem enarratae* (Apud Iod. Badium Ascensium & Ioan. Paruum &

As to the Fathers, Keach asserts, "St. Bernard saith, immersion is a representation of death and burial."[512] St. Ignatius maintains that we are to believe in the death of Christ, in order that "we may be made partakers of his resurrection by baptism.[513] Baptism was given in memory of the death of our Lord; we perform the symbols of his death."[514] Not the pouring forth of his blood, Keach comments, or pouring the "Holy Spirit, or sprinkling the Spirit on us, or the blood of Christ: No, this that authors says, is not signified in baptism, but the burial and resurrection of Jesus Christ; which sprinkling no manner of ways can represent."[515] Moreover, "Justin Martyr saith, we know but one saving baptism, in regard there is but one resurrection from the dead, of which baptism is an image."[516] Basil the Great, Keach claims, has Paul saying that the Israelites went "through the sea, and were all baptised in the cloud, and in the sea." Basil of Seleucia reiterates that the same Apostle "calls baptism the passage of the sea, for it was a flight of death caused by water."[517] John Chrysostom affirms that "[t]o be baptised, and so plunged, and to return up, and rise out of water, is a symbol of the descent into the grave, and returning from thence."[518] Lactantius maintains that "baptism is a pledg and representation of the resurrection."[519] In conclusion to the Fathers, Keach says, "[i]nnumerable are the testimonies which might be added."[520]

Ioannem Roigny, 1532), s.v., Ad Romanos, C.VI. col.c-e; cited by Keach in, *Counter-Antidote*, 9; *Rector Rectified*, 178; *Light Broke Forth*, 29-30; and *Gold Refin'd*, 45.

[512] Cf. e.g., Bernard, *In Cantici Canticorum Priora Duo Capita Brevis Commentatio*, 277; in Keach, *Light Broke Forth*, 33.

[513] Ignatius, *Epistula Ad Trallianos*, II: 1, *PAO*; in Keach, *Light Broke Forth*, 37.

[514] Keach attributes the whole quote to Ignatius, *Ad Philadelphenos*, (no chapter given). He has misquoted Knatchbull, *Annotations*, 301-302. The first sentence (viz., 'baptism was given in memory of the death of our Lord'), Knatchbull says that it comes from "*Epistola Ad Philadelphenses* in the name of Ignatius," 302. However, we did not find this sentence in the said letter, but rather (an allusion to it?) in Ignatius, *Ad Philippenses: De Baptismo*, I: ...*unum quoque et baptisma, quod datur in morte Christi*, there is one baptism, which is given for the death of Christ; i.e., that we may have fellowship with the death of Christ. Ignatii Epistula Supposticiae et Interpolatae in, Fas. II, *PAO*. The second sentence (viz., 'we perform the symbols of his death'), which Natchbull, ibid., 302, attributes to Justin Martyr, we were unable to locate.

[515] Keach, *Rector Rectified*, 187.

[516] Keach, *Rector Rectified*, 187. Keach has wrongly attributed this quote to Justin Martyr, whereas Natchbull—from whom Keach lifted the quote—rightly attributes it to Basil the Great [*Liber De Spiritu Sancto*, XV, P.G.32], *Annotations*, 302.

[517] Keach, *Gold Refin'd*, 48. Basil the Great is not responsible for the first quote; both quotations are to be found in Basil of Seleucia, *Orationes XIII* (75), P.G.85.

[518] John Chrysostom, *Argumentum Epistolae Primae Corinthios*, Homilia XL, P.G.61; cited by Keach in, *Rector Rectified*, 188; and *Gold Refin'd*, 48-49.

[519] Keach, *Gold Refin'd*, 49. Unable to track down Lactantius.

[520] Keach, *Gold Refin'd*, 49.

Concerning modern divines, Keach carries on, Perkins affirms that the immersion of the person symbolises "mortification or fellowship with Christ in his death; the staying under the water signifies the burial of sin; and coming out of the water, the resurrection from sin to newness of life."[521]

Finally, Keach asserts, let us hear what the erudite Zanchy has to say on this issue.

> There are two parts in regeneration, *mortification* and *vivification*; that is called *a burial with Christ*, this *a resurrection with Christ*. The sacrament of both of these is baptism, in which we are overwhelmed or buried, and after that do come forth and rise again. It may not be said truly, but sacramentally of all that are baptised that they are buried with Christ and raised with him, but only of such as have true faith.[522]

---

[521] Perkins, *A Commentarie upon Galatians*, 257; cited by Keach in, *Light Broke Forth*, 38; and *Rector Rectified*, 188. Keach proceeds to bury his opponents under a heap of quotations in support of the point that baptism means burying. Among others he cites, Daniel Tilenus, *Syntagmatis Tripertii Disputationum Theologicarum in Academia Sedanensi habitarum*, Pars Prima (Geneva: Apud Petrum & Jacobum Chouet, 1622), 886, 889; the Archbishop of York, John Sharp, *A Sermon Preach'd before the Queen at White-Hall* (London: Printed for Walter Kettilby at Bishop's Head in St. Paul's Church-Yard, 1692), 9; Edward Fowler, Lord-Bishop of Glocester, *The Design of Christianity* (London: Printed for R. Royston, Bookseller to his most Sacred Majesty, at the Angel in Amen-Corner, 1878), 90-91; William Sherlock, Dean of St. Paul's, *The Charity of Lending without Usury* (London: Printed for William Rogers at the Sun, over-against St. Dunstan's Church in Fleetstreet, 1692), 1; John Tilloston, Archbishop of Canterbury, *Sermons Preach'd upon Several Occasions*, 5th ed. corrected (London: Printed for Ed. Gellibrand, at the Golden Ball in St. Paul's Church-Yard, 1681), I: 188-189; Du Veil, *Expostion of Acts*, VIII, 292-293; Jean Daillé, *A Treatise Concerning the Right Use of the Fathers* (London: Printed for John Martin, and are to be sold by Robert Boulter at the Turks Head in Cornhill, 1675), L.II.148; Wilīliam Cave, *Primitive Christianity: or, the Religion of the Ancient Christians* (London: Printed by J.H. for R. Chriswel, at the Rose and Crown in St. Paul's Church-Yard, 1682), Part I, 312. All these and other authors in Keach, *Light Broke Forth*, 30-41; *Gold Refin'd*, 41-52; and *Rector Rectified*, 179-193.

[522] The text cited is a loose paraphrase of the original: "Docet, quo ad spiritualem circumcisionem, seu, quo ad eius sanctificationem, eam constare duabus partibus, mortificatione, imo & sepelitione veteris hominis, quam antea vocavit exuitionem seu exspoliationem carnis: Et vivificatione in novam vitam: primam vocat sepelitionem cum Christo: altera resurrectionem cum eodem Christo, utriusque signum ac sacramentum facit Baptismum. In eo enim & immergimur, ac sepelimur, & deinde extrahimur ac ceu resurgimus. Docet, quanquam omnes sacramentaliter in Baptismo moriuntur & sepeliuntur cum Christo, & cum eo etiam resurgere dicuntur, non omnes tamen reipsa, nempe, illos qui non habent fidem." Jerome Zanchi, 'In Epistolam Ad Colossenses Commentarius,' II.12, in *Operum Theologicorum D. Hieronymi Zanchii, Tomus Sextus Tripertius, Commentarios in Epistolas Apostolicas* (Geneva: Sumptibus Samvelis

"Now we may appeal to all the world, whether Zanchi and all the rest do not clearly and evidently testify the same thing that we assert," namely, that the rite of baptism must be done by immersion, for "sprinkling, all must confess, doth not represent in a lively figure the burial and resurrection of Christ, nor our dying or being dead to sin, and vivification to newness of life, said he [i.e., Zanchi] sacramentally, i.e., analogically, in respect of the near resemblance between baptism and a death and resurrection."[523]

Therefore, Keach purports, the change of mode of baptism obliterates what it signifies. For a few drops of water in one's face cannot represent the burial and resurrection of Christ. "O how is Christ's holy baptism abused by this devised rantism, and the signification thereof destroyed!"[524]

Again, Burkitt objects by saying that to pour water onto the face, which stands for the entire individual, fulfils the objective of baptism, as much as immersion. For the aim of baptism is "to represent to our minds the effusion of Christ's blood, for the taking away the guilt of sin; and the pouring forth of the Holy Spirit, for the purging away of the filth of" the said sin. What is more, "the sprinkling of the blood of Christ and the pouring forth of the Holy Spirit upon the infant, are more fully and plainly represented by baptism, as administered by sprinkling, than by dipping."[525] Considering that "the inward and spiritual grace signified by baptism...[is] more lively represented by sprinkling than by dipping, then surely sprinkling is not only as lawful, but more expedient than dipping. But the inward and spiritual grace signified by baptism," namely, "the cleansing of the soul by the grace and Spirit of Christ is more lively represented by sprinkling than by dipping. Therefore more expedient."[526]

Keach claims that he has already shown that immersion alone represents the significance of baptism. Burkitt's position—that sprinkling would represent the aim of baptism—is denied by the witness of the Bible "and almost all learned men, both ancient Fathers and modern divines..."[527] Secondly, the effusion of Christ's blood is not represented by baptism but by the Eucharist. "Will you confound the use and end of one sacrament with the other, to maintain you own innovation and abuse of Christ's holy baptism?"[528] Thirdly, "[y]ou are not,"

Crispini, 1617). Quoted by Keach in, *Gold Refin'd*, 52-53; *Rector Rectified*, 193; and *Light Broke Forth*, 41.

[523] Jerome Zanchi, *Operum Theologicarum D. Hieronymi Zanchii Tomus Quartus. In quo de primi hominis lapsu, de Peccato & de Lege Dei prolixè agitur. Opus solidum, primam tractatus de redemptione partem continens, multiplici doctrina refertum* (Genevae: Sumtibus Samvelis Crispini, 1617), s.v., Liber Primus, 'De Baptismo;' cited by Keach in, *Light Broke Forth*, 41-42; *Rector Rectified*, 193-194; and *Gold Refin'd*, 53.

[524] Keach, *Rector Rectified*, 180. Cf. Idem, *Counter-Antidote*, 10.

[525] Burkitt, *Argumentative Discourse*, 52-53, 183.

[526] Burkitt, *Argumentative Discourse*, 53.

[527] Keach, *Rector Rectified*, 183-184.

[528] Keach, *Rector Rectified*, 184. Cf. Idem, *Light Broke Forth*, 34.

Keach addresses Burkitt, "to devise new signs or symbols of spiritual mysteries, of which God speaks nothing in his Word, nor ever instituted to such ends. I affirm, he has appointed no rite or ordinance in the Gospel to represent the sprinkling or pouring forth of the Holy Spirit."[529] Significantly, Keach proceeds to attack the Roman Church and praise Thomas Aquinas in the same breath: the Romanists own

> seven sacraments and they tell us of the use and end of them, and how wonderful significant they are; and yet all their use and expediency of them were the contrivances of their own wicked hearts. And I must tell you that they prove what they do and say of those sacraments, as well as you do what you speak of pouring or sprinkling. Take what Tho. Aquinas most excellently hath said on this account. 'It belongs to the signifier (says he) to determine what the sign is to be used for the signification; but God it is, who by things sensible, signifies spiritual things in the sacrament.'[530]

Keach continues, "Christ hath ordained baptism to be a sign, symbol or lively representation of his own death, burial and resurrection, as I have proved and confirmed by a cloud of witness." How dare anybody say that sprinkling or aspersion is "not only lawful, but more expedient than dipping?" By this, Keach concludes, "you seem to teach God wisdom, or to magnify your above his."[531]

If immersion were indispensable, Burkitt insists, "then in all the baptisms recorded in Scripture, we should meet with full proof or at least with fair possibility that the parties baptised were dipped."[532] On many occasions, however, the Bible gives no such evidence, rather the opposite; it reveals immersion as improbable in some cases. Let us consider the following three passages: (i) Act.9.18-19, (ii) Act.16.33, and (iii) Act.2.41. In the first text, the Apostle is ill and feeble and so is baptised inside the house. Hence, it is unlikely that he would have been taken out to be plunged into a pond.[533]

There is not Scriptural evidence, Keach replies, for these assertions. In the first place, the verses do not affirm that Paul "was baptised in his lodgings; therefore you strive to make the Scripture speak what it doth not."[534] Secondly, again nothing is said as to Paul being ill or feeble. However, "if he had been weak, yet when God commanded him to be baptised or dipp'd in water...he had no cause to fear or doubt of any harm." Thirdly, Keach testifies, "I have

---

[529] Keach, *Rector Rectified*, 184-185.
[530] Keach, *Rector Rectified*, 185. Thomas Aquinas, *Summa Theologiae*, 3a.60.5.
[531] Keach, *Rector Rectified*, 185. Cf. Idem, *Light Broke Forth*, 35.
[532] Burkitt, *Argumentative Discourse*, 53.
[533] Burkitt, *Argumentative Discourse*, 53-54. Cf. Owen, *Bedydd Plant or Nefoedd*, 29.
[534] Keach, *Rector Rectified*, 194-195.

known sickly and weak people baptised in this cold climate, and yet received not the least hurt thereby."[535]

In the second passage (Act.16.33), Burkitt maintains, the Scripture shows that the Apostle, though sorely wounded by lashes, baptised the Philippian jailer without delay. The possibility that Paul would take the jailer and his household in the middle of the night, to immerse the whole company into a brook, "is to be believed by such as have their credulity at their own dispose and can believe what they list."[536]

"This is such a silly reasoning," Keach contends, "that 'tis not worth naming. He was not so sore, but he might go into the water to baptise the jayler and those in his house." Even though Paul baptised the jailer right way, this is not a reason to presume that immersion did not take place; for there might have been a stream close to the household.[537]

Third, Burkitt presents Act.2.41, a text which states that in a single day three thousand individuals received baptism. This baptism, in all likelihood, happened in the same area where the message was preached, perhaps in the temple or around it. Where in this area of Jerusalem could be found such an immense amount of water to dip all these people? Furthermore, they were all baptised right way; but not by immersion, for it would take many days to plunge such a number.[538]

Surely, Keach replies, a great city like Jerusalem had enough water to baptise the said number. Besides, he asks, "could not the twelve Apostles and the seventy disciples dip more than 3000 persons in one day? Sir, 'tis enough, the Holy Ghost says they were baptised, that is, dipped not rantized: therefore you do but go about to contradict the Holy Spirit and fight with your own shadow."[539]

Yet again Burkitt claims that immersion is not necessary, since it is too troublesome and awkward. There are regions of the world where there is not much water to satisfy thirst, let alone to immerse people. What is more, when immersion takes place, there is great risk of violating the sixth and the seventh commandment: thou shalt not kill, thou shalt not commit adultery. As to the former, why should lives be endangered by cold water? Christ, "who prefers mercy before sacrifice, allows the administration of the ordinance in such way as is consistent with his peoples lives; which must in some countries, especially at some sessons of the year, be in extreme danger by dipping." On account of this danger, a law enacted in "Zurich, Switzerland, [says] that if any Anabaptist dipp'd any of their people, he should be punish'd with drowning."[540] As to the

---

[535] Keach, *Rector Rectified*, 195. Cf. the whole paragraph with *Light Broke Forth*, 22.
[536] Burkitt, *Argumentative Discourse*, 54. Cf. Shute, *Antidote to Anabaptism*, 6-7.
[537] Keach, *Rector Rectified*, 195. Cf. Idem, *Counter-Antidote*, 6.
[538] Burkitt, *Argumentative Discourse*, 54. Cf. Owen, *Bedydd Plant or Nefoedd*, 28.
[539] Keach, *Rector Rectified*, 195. Cf. Idem, *Light Broke Forth*, 21.
[540] Burkitt, *Argumentative Discourse*, 54-55. Cf. Shute, *Antidote to Anabaptism*, 6.

commandment against adultery, why should Christian chastity be imperilled by temptation? Surely immoral thoughts are unavoidable when immersion takes place if the candidates are naked. If they are clothed, where does the command to baptise their clothes come from?[541] Shute adds that all candidates ought to come naked, stripped of all things before God, and thus the naked face—not the body—is the most appropriate and modest place to represent the person in baptism.[542]

First, "[y]ou should have told us," Keach retorts, "what countries they are who have not water enough to baptise people in." Usually these areas are not habitable.[543] Second, as to the difficulties faced by the inaccessibility of rivers, Jesus covered a great distance to be baptised by John. If it is one's duty to be immersed, he or she should not be hindered by obstacles. Third, regarding the health risk, a warm season may be chosen for baptism; otherwise, if immersion were to be performed in the bitterest temperatures, we have countless testimonies of people who underwent the rite in such conditions without any harm. Considering that babies cannot endure such temperatures, this is rather "a good argument they were not the subjects Christ intended" for baptism.[544] Fourth, the same reasoning that God prefers mercy rather than sacrifice could have been used by the Jews, since circumcision would be a very risky act, as Zipporah testifies, "[a] bloody husband thou art to me because of circumcision" (Exo.4.25-26). Yet, God would have none of it. Fifth, as to the Swiss law, there have been similar laws "also in England" as seen in the 'Acts' which prohibits the assemblies for prayer and preaching of more than five people, giving them fines, imprisonment and confiscating their property. Little wonder that these laws come into existence, since "wicked men always hated Christ's truth and people."[545] Concerning modesty, Keach invites Shute to come to a baptismal service and see for himself the sober and modest manner in which the candidates undergo this rite.[546]

If the objective of baptism, Burkitt contends, is to represent the burial of Christ, then aspersion can represent it, "for the pouring of water" on a person may portray "the pouring forth [of] the earth upon a dead body."[547] In effect, this metaphor of burial cannot be applied in every detail; else the person being baptised would have to be carried to the water in an utterly passive manner. That is, as a dead body is taken into the arms of those burying it, likewise the

---

[541] Burkitt, *Argumentative Discourse*, 55-56.
[542] Shute, *Antidote to Anabaptism*, 13.
[543] Keach, *Rector Rectified*, 196.
[544] Keach, *Rector Rectified*, 196-197.
[545] Keach, *Rector Rectified*, 197. Keach must be referring to the First (1664) and Second (1670) 'Conventicle Acts.' For details, see Watts, *The Dissenters*, 225-227; and Howson, *Erroneous and Schismatical Opinions*, 44.
[546] Keach, *Counter-Antidote*, 53.
[547] Burkitt, *Argumentative Discourse*, 58.

baptised would have "to put neither foot nor leg nor thigh into the water himself, but the dipper ought to take him up in his arms and lay his entire body into the water, as a man is laid into his grave;" but the "Anabaptists" let the candidates walk into the water, and therefore, they are baptising from the waist upwards.[548]

Keach partially concedes that if, as the water is poured, the infant is completely covered, then something akin to a burial is represented. However, a burial does not take place when a mere portion of earth is thrown upon a corpse, as is the case in aspersion. For "the body must be covered under the earth before it can be said to be buried, and so must the person baptised be covered, or 'tis not baptised..."[549] As to the appropriate procedure for immersion, what does the Scripture say? "They went both into the water, both Philip and the Eunuch, and he (that is, Philip) baptised or dipped him." The baptizer then is not to carry the candidate into his arms, rather both are to enter into the water but only the one to be baptised goes completely under it. The metaphor of burial is not "to be strained further than the design and purport of the Holy Spirit; but you by sprinkling destroy and utterly make void that sacred allusion of the Holy Ghost..."[550]

Evaluation and Conclusion

Our evaluation and concluding thoughts on Keach's doctrine of baptism will involve considerations on, first, his rejection of pedobaptism as well as the connection between his covenantal conception and believer's baptism; second, his position on immersion as the only mode of baptism; and, third, his ecumenical bent together with his uncompromising stance on the need for reformation.

Keach's View of Pedobaptism and his Covenantal Conception

There are two distinct sets of arguments in support of pedobaptism. The first set relates to circumcision, baptism of families, and regenerative baptism. We shall deal with this group immediately below. On a different level altogether, the second group of arguments relates to the Great Commission, federal holiness, benefits accrued by baptism, incipient faith, "suffer little children," John the Baptist's confession, and tradition: This second set of reasons are unconvincing, well refuted by Keach, and generally no longer used even by those who argue for pedobaptism.[551]

---

[548] Burkitt, *Argumentative Discourse*, 58.
[549] Keach, *Rector Rectified*, 201.
[550] Keach, *Rector Rectified*, 202.
[551] See, for example, *Catechism of the Catholic Church: revised in accordance with the official Latin text promulgated by Pope John Paul II*, 2nd. Ed. (Vatican City: Libreria

We pointed out that the Abrahamic covenant or circumcision was by far the most significant argument used by Reformed pedobaptists to argue their case. Over three hundred years have elapsed since Keach fought with his opponents, and circumcision remains the most important evidence for the baptism of infants.[552] The second and third most significant arguments are respectively, the baptism of families and regenerative baptism. Keach correctly considers familial baptism problematic and inconclusive: First there are families without infants; and second, in many instances the Bible uses synecdoche—the part for the whole—to narrate facts. We would add that the baptism of families is at best an argument from silence and, as such, is questionable evidence. As to regeneration or washing of original sin, the Reformed tradition loosened—though did not entirely break—the close instrumental connection between sacrament and grace or between baptism and regeneration that existed in Roman Catholic, and, to a lesser extent, in Lutheran theology. Sacraments came to be perceived as having *some* instrumental function in Reformed theology in relation to the elect, but no effect on the non-elect. In that light, the urgency that drove the Medieval church to rescue babies from original sin, less they go to hell or limbo, disappeared and a new prominence was given to election. Thus, a space emerged in which it became possible to ask: is childhood the right time to baptise? The Baptists answered negatively. After all, it makes no difference in an ultimate sense whether an elect child is baptised or not.[553] As a matter of fact, when we presented the arguments dealing with the lot of dying infants, we saw Keach affirming that it is impossible to be certain of the lot of "dying infants and idiots," that these are secret things belonging to the Lord. He allowed for the possibility of God including all infants "in his electing love."[554] It is clear then that election, as we are suggesting, is the fundamental element to be considered regarding regeneration. It seems, then, that with the weakening of sacramental instrumentality and the emphasis on election, the Baptists pushed Reformed theology to at least one of its possible logical conclusions.

Editrice Vaticana, 1997), 318-320. The argument from tradition is still very important in the case of the Roman Catholic and Eastern Orthodox churches, but not so within Reformed and Lutheran circles.

[552] See, for example, Donald Bridge and David Phypers, *A Survey of the Doctrine of Baptism: The Water that Divides*, in the Mentor Series (Christian Focus Publication: Genies House, Fean, Ross-shire, 1998), 26-41.

[553] See Calvin, *Institutes*, IV.xvi.26.

[554] Supra, p. 171. It is to be stressed that the Reformed did not become casual about the administration of the sacraments. For the Reformed who assumed the necessity of a state church, it was almost taken for granted that just as the Word had to be preached to all alike, elect or otherwise, the sacraments had to be administered to all alike. However, with the fear of damning infants removed, it was at least possible to ask the question whether it really was necessary or appropriate to administer baptism in such an apparently heedless manner.

Finally, of all the arguments mentioned, we are left with circumcision, to which we now turn.

To begin with, it is worth reiterating that Reformed pedobaptists deem the Abrahamic covenant and the pact of grace as identical, and thus circumcision and baptism are equivalent—standing in a continuum—with the latter replacing the former. On the other hand, the rationale between Keach's covenant theology and his credobaptism relies heavily on the twofold character of Abraam's covenant. Circumcision has to be understood as a sign meant to be applied to all Israelites, independent of their faith or inclusion in the covenant of grace. In other words, the concert made with Abraham cannot exactly parallel the covenant of grace, otherwise Keach's position collapses. This is the reason he spills so much ink on this subject, as we saw. Keach's understanding is not farfetched: "Abraam took Ishmael his son, all who were born in his house and all who were bought with his money, every male among the men of Abraham's house, and circumcised the flesh of their foreskins..." (Gen.18:24). Nothing whatsoever is said of whether all these people had Abraham's faith. Furthermore, Ishmael, Esau, great numbers of Pharisees, and a multitude of others are explicitly excluded from the pact of grace though circumcised (Gal.4:21-31; Rom.9:6-24; Luc.3:7-9; Joh.8:42-47). Thus, circumcision was an ethnic rite unconnected with faith. In effect, circumcision was part and parcel of the covenant of works—a covenant Christ came to fulfil. With the fulfilment of the said covenant and the full implementation of the pact of grace, the covenant of circumcision had run its course. Karl Barth put it well saying that circumcision is a reference to "natural birth; it is the sign of the election of the holy lineage of Israel, which with the birth of the Messiah achieved its goal, so that therewith this sign [had] lost its meaning."[555] Therefore, as baptism is not a racial rite and—unlike circumcision—has faith as a prerequisite, it is not equivalent to circumcision, and consequently did not replace it.[556]

Underlying Keach's contention for believer's baptism is his covenantal concept that—to repeat ourselves again—Christ came to discharge the *foedus operum* and to implement fully the *foedus gratiae*: in this new phase, church membership is to be made up only of those who worship "in spirit and truth," i.e., converted people. That is the driving force behind his insistence on

---

[555] Karl Barth, *The Teaching of the Church regarding Baptism*, Ernest A. Payne, trans. (London: SCM Press, 1948), 56.

[556] In addition to all the arguments already presented by Keach, an appendix could be made in the following way: it is highly likely that early Jewish Christians continued to both circumcise and baptise their children, as it may be inferred from the first Jerusalem Council (Act.15). Here the subject of circumcision is brought out, but baptism—as a replacement rite—is not even suggested. It seems likely, if baptism had replaced circumcision, that the Jewish Christians would not have insisted on circumcising Gentiles. Furthermore, the opposition to the Judaizers would have argued that there would be no need to circumcise now since Christian baptism replaced Jewish circumcision.

believer's baptism. A direct consequence of this is that baptism *qua* baptism is not the main issue in Keach's mind, but rather baptism as an element of the properly constituted, visible church—as we proposed at the very beginning of this chapter. His ecclesiological dispute is that pedobatism undermines the congregational nature of the church, thus reformation is imperative.

Immersion as the Only Mode of Baptism

Concerning the mode of baptism, Keach is at times vague and even weak in his disputes with his adversaries. One example would be Burkitt's point that the text of Acts 9: 18-19 does not seem to suggest immersion at all. Here Saul is without food and drink during a three-day blindness. At this junction, Ananias came to him, prayed and so he "got up and was baptised, and after taking some food, he regained his strength." Keach replies that the Bible does not say that Paul was baptised in his lodgings. Also, Keach continues, Paul's strength makes no difference as to God's command to be baptised, i.e., immersed. This seems an inadequate answer. Another example would be Burkitt's citation of Acts 2:41, where three thousand were baptised, in all likelihood in the same area where they were (Jerusalem) and on the same day. The practice of immersion in this context appears to be doubtful. Keach retorts, as we saw, that it is "enough, the Holy Ghost says they were baptised, that is, dipped not rantized." That reply seems even weaker than the previous one. In these and other places, it seems to us that Keach forces his point though he does not have an adequate counter argument.[557] In our judgment, either Keach's polemical context of fierce antagonism did not allow room to make the mode *adiaphoron*; or, more likely, he *failed* to see this possibility. Within the options of affusion, aspersion and immersion, it seems best to us to let churches decide which tradition to embrace in accordance with their context and experience.

An objection may be raised at this point. One of the burdens of this dissertation is to demonstrate that Keach is part of the Reformed tradition. He clearly stands outside of it as to pedobaptism and, to a certain extent,

---

[557] Incidentally, should we believe that John the Baptist dipped one by one the hordes of individuals that came to him, or is it not better to accept the early depictions showing him pouring water on the heads? See Berkhof, *Systematic Theology*, 630. We have evidence for both total immersion and affusion/aspersion in the early church. Concerning immersion, we have, for example, the well-preserved ruins of a 4th century baptismal tank in Sbeitla (Tunisia). See the picture and comments in Christopher Howse, ed. *The Daily Telegraph*, Supplement - May 29th 1999, 'AD: 2000 years of Christianity', Part One: 1-400. From the time of Jesus to the Vandal invasions,' p. 22. Regarding affusion/aspersion, the third century depictions in the catacombs of Calixtus, of Saint Peter and Saint Marcellinus, as well as the depiction of the baptism of Christ in a sarcophagus in Rome—all of them show figures receiving aspersion/affusion. See the pictures and comments in Hendrick F. Stander and Johannes P. Louw, *Baptism in the Early Church* (Leeds, England: Carey Publications, 1994), 172-173.

immersion (bearing in mind that the Reformed only objected to immersion as the sole valid mode). Regarding pedobaptism, we have already demonstrated that he deemed himself a reformer simply restoring the biblical practice and ecumenically inviting Christians to join him. What about the mode of baptism? It is a known fact that the Particular Baptists were the ones who "recovered" the practice of immersion circa 1640.[558] Is the concept extraneous to the Reformed tradition? We do not think so. Note, for example, how Calvin uses the language of mortification and renewal in Christ as he discusses baptism: "we have been baptised into his death...buried with him into death...that we may walk in newness of life." The citation is commented by Calvin thus: The Apostle

> not only exhorts us to follow Christ as if he had said that we are admonished through baptism to die to our desires by an example of Christ's death, and to be aroused to righteousness by the example of his resurrection. But he also takes hold of something far higher, namely, that through baptism Christ makes us shares in his death, that we may be engrafted in it. And, just as the twig draws substance and nourishment from the root to which it is grafted, so those who receive baptism with right faith truly feel the effective working of Christ's death in the mortification of their flesh, together with the working of his resurrection in the vivification of the Spirit.[559]

Although one could arrive at different conclusions, this association of baptism, on the one hand, with the death, burial and resurrection of Christ, on the other, may lend itself to the conclusion that immersion is the perfect picture for the baptismal rite. "This would not have been a stretch for them [the Baptists] given their Reformed tradition on baptism using the above Scriptures, and their belief in believer's baptism."[560]

Comments on Both Keach's Ecumenical Leaning and his Uncompromising Stance on the Need of Reformation

Regarding believer's baptism, there seem to be two main impulses in Keach's actions: first, his conscience and, second, the Reformation. Note his answers to James Owen's reflections. First, Owen had appealed to the conscience of credobaptists in the following way. "Let their consciences dictate and reprove them of this sinful carelessness, that they never made a right use of their first baptism, if they had received profit from the first, they would not have

---

[558] McBeth, *The Baptist Heritage*, 44.
[559] Calvin, *Institutes*, IV.xv.5.
[560] Howson, *Erroneous and Schismatical Opinions*, 326.

renounced it at all."[561] Keach replies to Owen in the following way: "I will take this appeal to be made to me...even to my conscience; and I do solemnly declare...that the reason why we cast out infant baptism or rather rantism, was because we were fully convinced it was no ordinance of Christ and, therefore, knew it could be of no profit to us."[562]

Second, Owen also accuses the "Anabaptists" of breaking away not only from a particular congregation, but also "from the Universal Catholic Church in every age and country upon the face of the earth, which is cleansed with the washing of water through the Word, and continues in the union of baptism. Can you think this to be a small sin for you to separate yourself from the body of Christ?"[563] Should separation from the Church of England, Keach rhetorically queries, and from the Roman Church, be considered a sin? Although "we believe there are many holy and gracious Christians of the communion of the Church of England and they are members of the invisible universal church, yet we do not believe the Church of England, nor any national church is an orderly true constituted visible church of Jesus Christ," thus separation from these communities is unavoidable.[564] What is more, he adds, separation from *any* church which does not practice adult baptism by immersion is urgent, otherwise the Reformation will not move forward.

We see then that Keach understands catholicity not as maintaining ties to particular institutions, but rather conscientious adherence to what he perceives to be catholic truth: this is what makes a church catholic. Otherwise, the earliest Reformers would never have broken with Rome. However, is Keach's ecclesiology consistent with such a view? We believe it is, for we saw that he reckoned the rite of cardinal importance to a properly constituted visible church, but not essential to salvation.[565] He gave evidence of this view when he affirmed that pedobaptist congregations "are true churches, as well as we [i.e., Baptists], they being godly Christians, tho I believe they are less compleat churches, than those who are baptised upon the profession of faith, or not so orderly in their constitution..."[566] Ultimately, the whole issue of baptism—to

---

[561] "Gadawent iw cydwybodau ddywedyd a hwy ai argyhoeddant or esgeulusdra pechadurus hwn, na ddarfu iddynt erioed iawn ddefnyddio eu bedydd Cyntaf, pe derbyneasent leshad oddiwrth y cyntaf ni ymwrthodasent âg ef byth." Owen, *Bedydd Plant or Nefoedd*, 175. Cf. Rothwell, *Paedobaptismus Vindicatus*, 140-141; Burkitt, *Argumentative Discourse*, 47.

[562] Keach, *Light Broke Forth*, [256].

[563] "...ond oddiwrth yr Eglwys Gatholic gyffredinol o bob oes a gwlad ar wyneb y ddair, yr hon sydd wedi ei glauhau â'r olchfa ddwfr, trwy'r gair, ac yn parhau mewn undeb bedydd. A gelli di feddwl mae pechod bychan yw hwn, iti dy rwygo dy hun oddiwrth gorph Christ?" Owen, *Bedydd Plant or Nefoedd*, 182-183.

[564] Keach, *Light Broke Forth*, [266]. Cf. Ibid., 'Epistle to all godly Christians who are pedobaptists in South and North Wales,' iii.

[565] Supra pp. 123-124.

[566] Keach, *Counter-Antidote*, 54. Cf. supra p. 118, footnote 38.

reiterate—hangs on ecclesiology. Time and again, Keach calls his adversative brothers to ponder his position and join his cause: he desires to rid the visible church of infant baptism by sprinkling, in order to give her what he believes to be an adequate visible organization.

Conclusion

Our short concluding thoughts will observe a sort of symmetry with our introduction. We began this dissertation drawing attention to the paucity of studies on Benjamin Keach. The importance of this man—it was shown—was undisputed: he was one of the signatories of the most important Baptist Confession of all times (1689 London Confession); Keach was the most prolific Baptist writer of the seventeenth century; his Baptist peers looked up to him when controversy broke out—as we saw in the case between Burkitt and Tredwell; he was nominated by the Baptist Assembly of 1689 to found congregations and strengthen existing churches; some of his books were of outstanding quality (e.g., *The Jewish Sabbath abrogated*)—in short, he was a talented man, revered by his Baptist colleagues and respected by his foes. In light of his importance the want of research was surprising.

We examined recent research on Reformation and post-Reformation periods. These studies have increased our knowledge of the periods, so that both historical segmentation and appeals to John Calvin as touchstone of "Calvinism," have become difficult to maintain. We assessed the current discussion within Reformation studies and demonstrated that there were deep streams of thought flowing from Patristic and medieval tributaries, and extending in different ways into the Reformation and beyond. Regarding post-Reformation studies, we also examined arguments against the traditional way of viewing the entire Reformed tradition as subservient to the Genevan Reformer: Other thinkers and confessions of faith were responsible together with him for defining the contours of Reformed Orthodoxy.

The claim that the Baptist tradition as a whole, and Keach in particular, is sectarian was scrutinised and deemed problematic. Using Keach as representative of the said tradition, we demonstrated that the employment of consensual, exegetical and dogmatic tradition made catholicity an integral part of his thought. Next, we attacked the assumptions that Keach was either a "moderate Calvinist," or a near "hyper-Calvinist." It is better, we argued, to regard Keach as a Reformed thinker, working within the parameters of Reformed Orthodoxy.

Two of Keach's *loci* were explored. In the first case, namely federalism, Keach attempted to stand roughly at the centre of conventional Reformed theology—even fiercely defending this theology against any perceived deviation. In examining Keach's federalism, we saw that he leaned towards Antinomianism, though he was far from becoming Antinomian. Two pieces of evidence were presented to this inclination: first, he equates the eternal and the temporal covenants; and second, Keach only occasionally makes strictures against the Antinomians. Rather, Baxterianism, the other extreme, is the aim of his vitriolic attacks. Nevertheless, we concluded that Keach stood near the center of Reformed Orthodoxy.

In the case of the second, baptism, Keach departs from the traditional Reformed position, viz., pedobaptism. This departure, we believe, was done on the basis of a conscience captive to *sola Scriptura* and a sincere intention to reform the church. It is abundantly clear—as we heard Keach's many pleas for union among Orthodox Protestants—that he desired that the whole company of post-Reformation Reformed Protestantism would join him in adopting credobaptism by immersion. Moreover, it could be argued that Keach understands that believer's baptism is a consequence of the Reformed "regulative principle of worship".[1] In addition to all of that, as the Reformed allowed for a slackening of the connection between sacrament and grace, baptism lost its instrumental power to convey regeneration: if the elect, and *the elect alone*, is the one who will be renewed, it makes no difference if he or she is baptised. Thus the door was opened to the possibility of inquiring if infants should indiscriminately be granted the baptismal rite. The Reformed Baptists denied it. It could be said that what Keach is doing is not creating something new, but rather pushing Reformed thought at least to one of its potential conclusions.

To sum up, on the basis of conscience, Scripture alone, Reformation, the regulative principle, election, and ecumenicity, Keach's defence of believer's baptism does not make him a deviator from the Reformed tradition.

On account of the necessarily limited scope of this study, we have left a number of avenues of investigation unexplored. Thus, for example, Keach's *A Golden Mine Opened* (1694), in which he deals at length with 'perseverance of the saints,' may turn out to be well-worth investigating. The study of Keach's exegetical method in his two-volume set *Exposition of the Parables* (1701), may also be fruitful. The largest Protestant tradition—the Baptist family with 47 million members—could benefit from a better knowledge of its history, in order to illumine its future.[2] It is hoped that the historical reconstruction presented in this dissertation will provide grounds for further Baptist and "Keachean" studies.

Finally, to come full circle, based on our re-evaluation of Keach's theology, we expect to have demonstrated that he is neither a sectarian nor a Calvinist, but rather a *catholic Reformed theologian*.

---

[1] See supra p. 147, footnote 182.
[2] Isabella Rocha and Lélis Dutra Moura, *Informativo da Primeira Igreja Batista do Rio de Janeiro*, VI, number 19; May, 2005, p. 14.

Bibliography

Primary Sources
Benjamin Keach

An answer to Mr. Marlow's Appendix Wherein his arguments to prove that singing of psalms, hymns, and spiritual songs, was performed in the primitive church by a special or an extraordinary gift, and therefore not to be practised in these days, are examined, and clearly detected. Also some reflections on what he speaks on the word hymnos: and on his undue quotations of divers learned men. London: printed for the author, and sold by John Hancock in Castle-Alley on the west side of the Royal-Exchange, and by the author at his house near Horselydown in Southwark, 1691.

An appendix to the answer unto two Athenian Mercuries concerning pedo-baptism containing twenty seven syllogistical arguments proving infant-baptism a mere humane tradition: the gentlemen called the Athenian Society desiring in the last of the said Mercuries to have syllogism. London: Printed for the author and sold by John Harris, 1692.

Antichrist Stormed: or, Mystery Babylon the Great Whore, and the great City, proved to be the present Church of Rome. London: Printed for Nath. Crouch at the Bell in the Poultrey near Cheapside, 1689.

The articles of the faith of the Church of Christ, or, Congregation meeting at Horsley-down, Benjamin Keach, pastor, as asserted this 10th of the 6th month, 1697. London: [s.n.], 1697.

The Ax Laid to the Root, or, One blow more at the foundation of infant baptism, and church-membership. Containing an exposition of that metaphorical text of Holy Scripture, Mat. 3. 10. being the substance of two sermons lately preached, with some additions, wherein is shewed that God made a two-fold covenant with Abraham, and that circumcision appertained not to the covenant of grace, but to the legal and external covenant God made with Abraham's natural seed, as such : together with an answer to Mr. John Flavel's last grand arguments in his Vindiciarum Vindex, in his last reply to Mr. Philip Cary, also to Mr. Rothwell's Paedo-baptismus Vindicatur, as to what seems most material. London: Printed for the author, and are to be sold by John Harris, 1693.

The Banquetting-House, Or A Feast of Fat Things: A Divine Poem. Opening many Sacred Scripture Mysteries. Profitable for all who would attain to the Saving Knowledge of God and of Jesus Christ. London: Printed by J. A. for H. Barnard at the Bible in the Poultrey, 1692.

The Baptist Catechism, Or, a Brief Instruction in the Principles of the Christian Religion. London: s.n., 1793.

Beams of Divine Light: Or, Some Brief Hints of the Being and Attributes of God, and of the Three Persons in the God-head. Also proving the Deity of Christ and of the Holy Ghost. London: Printed by K. Astwood, and Sold by William Marshall at the Bible in New-gate-street, 1700.

Believers Baptism: Or, Love to the Antient Britains Displayed. London: Printed for John Marshall, 1705. [This is a reprint of *Light Broke Forth in Wales*, 1696, below.]

The breach repaired in God's worship: or, Singing of psalms, hymns, and spiritual songs, proved to be an holy ordinance of Jesus Christ Wherein the chief arguments of ma- ny learned divines, who have wrote on that subject, are recited, as Mr. Cotton of New England, Mr. Sidenham, Dr. Roberts, Dr. Owen, Mr. Caryl, Dr. Du-Veil, Mr. Wells, &c. With an answer to all objections. As also, an examination of Mr. Isaac Marlow's two papers, one called, A discourse concerning singing, &c. the other, An appendix: wherein his arguments and cavils are detected and refuted. With an appendix, by Thomas Winnell. London: Printed by John Marshall, at the Bible in Grace-Church-Street: where is sold most of the author's works, 1700.

A call to weeping: or A warning touching approaching miseries. In a sermon preached on the 20th of March, 1699. At the funeral of Mrs. Elizabeth Westen, late wife of Mr. John Westen, who departed this life on the 17th of the said month, in the 38th year of her age. London: Printed for, and sold by John Marshal at the Bible in Grace-Church-street, 1699.

The Child's Instructor: or, a new and easie Primmer. London: s.n., 1664.

Christ alone the way to Heaven, or, Jacob's Ladder improved containing four sermons lately preach'd on Genesis XXVIII, XII: wherein the doctrine of free-grace is display'd through Jesus Christ: also discovering the nature, office, and ministration of the holy angels: to which is added one sermon on Rom. 8, 1: with some short reflections on Mr. Samuel Clark's new book intituled Scripture justification. London: Printed and sold by Benja. Harris, 1698.

A Counter-Antidote, to purge out the malignant effects of a late counterfeit, prepared by Mr. Gyles Shute ... being an answer to his vindication of his pretended Antidote to prevent the prevalency of Anabaptism, shewing that Mr. Hercules Collins's reply to the said author remains unanswered: wherein the baptism of believers is evinced to be God's ordinance, and the baptized congregations proved true churches of Jesus Christ: with a further detection of the error of pedo-baptism: to which is added, An answer to Mr. Shute's reply to Mr. Collins's half-sheet. London: Printed for H. Bernard, 1694.

The counterfeit Christian, or, The danger of hypocrisy opened in two sermons: containing an exposition of that parabolical speech of our Blessed

Saviour, Matth. XII, 43, 44, 45. London: Printed and are sold by John Pike, 1691.

Darkness vanquished: or, Truth in it's primitive purity, being an answer to a late book of Mr. Henry Danvers, intituled A treatise of laying on of hands. Wherein his mistakes and cloudy apprehensions about it, are in a faithful and friendly manner rectified, his grand obiections answered, and imposition of hands upon baptised believers, as such with prayer for the spirit of promise is proved, to be a holy and divine institution of Jesus Christ, and accordingly practiced by the apostles and primitive saints. Together with the testimony of many famous writers, both antient, and of later times concerning it. London: Printed, and are to be sold by Benjamin Harris in Swithins Rents, at the Stationers Arms in Corn-hill, near the Royal Exchange, 1675.

The Display of Glorious Grace, or, The covenant of peace opened in fourteen sermons lately preached in which the errors of the present day about reconciliation and justification are detected. London: Printed by S. Bridge and sold by Mary Fabian and Joseph Collier and Willam Marshall, 1698.

Distressed Sion Relieved, or, The garment of praise for the spirit of heaviness wherein are discovered the grand causes of the churches trouble and misery under the late dismal dispensation: with a compleat history of, and lamentation for those renowned worthies that fell in England by popish rage and cruelty, from the year 1680 to 1688. London: Printed for Nath. Crouch, 1689.

An elegy on the death of that most laborious and painful minister of the gospel, Mr. John Norcot who fell asleep in the Lord the 24th day of this instant March, 1675/6. London: Printed for Ben. Harris, 1676.

Exposition of the Parables. 2 vols. Grand Rapids: Kregel Publications, 1991.

The everlasting covenant, a sweet cordial for a drooping soul, or, The excellent nature of the covenant of grace opened in a sermon preached January the 29th, at the funeral of Mr. Henry Forty, late pastor of a Church of Christ, at Abingdon, in the county of Berks, who departed this life Jan. 25th 1692/3 and was interr'd at Southwark ... : to which is added, An elegy on the death of the said minister. London: Printed for H. Barnard, 1693.

A feast of fat things full of marrow containing several Scripture songs taken out of the Old and New Testaments, with others composed by t[he author]: together [with o]ne hundred of divine hymns, being the first century. London: Printed by B.H., 1696.

The French Impostour Detected, or Zach. Housel Tried by the Word of God. London: Printed for Ebenezer Tracy, 1702.

The glorious lover A divine poem, upon the adorable mystery of sinners redemption. By B. K. author of War with the Devil. London: Printed by F.L. for Christopher Hussey, at the Flower-de-Luce in Little-Britain,

1685.

The glory of a true church, and its discipline display'd wherein a true gospel-church is described: together with the power of the keys, and who are to be let in, and who to be shut out. London: [s.n.], 1697.

God acknowledged, or, The true interest of the nation and all that fear God opened in a sermon preached December the 11th, 1695: being the day appointed by the king for publick prayer and humiliation. London: Printed for William Marshal, 1696.

A golden mine opened, or, The glory of God's rich grace displayed in the mediator to believers, and his direful wrath against impenitent sinners. London: For the author, 1694.

Gold Refin'd; Or, Baptism in its Primitive Purity. Proving Baptism in Water an Holy Institution of Jesus Christ, and to continue in the Church to the End of the World. London: Printed for the Author, and are to be sold by Nathaniel Couch, at the sign of the Bell in the Poultry, 1689.

The Gospel Minister's Maintenance Vindicated. London: John Harris, 1689.

The Grand Impostor Discovered or the Quakers Doctrine weighed in the Balance and found wanting. London: s.n., 1674.

Instructions for Children: Or, The Child's and Youth's Delight. London: John Marshall, 1710.

The Jewish Sabbath abrogated, or, The Saturday Sabbatarians confuted in two parts: first, proving the abrogation of the old seventh-day Sabbath: secondly, that the Lord's-Day is of divine appointment: containing several sermons newly preach'd upon a special occasion, wherein are many new arguments not found in former authors. London: Printed and sold by John Marshall, 1700.

Laying on of hands upon baptized believers, as such, proved an ordinance of Christ in answer to Mr. Danvers's former book intituled, A treatise of laying on of hands: with a brief answer to a late book called, A treatise concerning laying on of hands, written by a nameless author. London: Printed, are to be sold by Benj. Harris, 1698.

Light Broke Forth in Wales, expelling darkness, or, The Englishman's love to the antient Britains being an answer to a book, iutituled Children's baptism from Heaven, published in the Welsh tongue by Mr. James Owen. London: Printed and sold by William Marshall at the Bible in Newgate-street, 1696.

The Marrow of Justification. Or Justification without Works. Containing the Substance of Two Sermons Lately preached on Rom.4.5. And by the Importunity of some gracious Christians, now published with some Additions. London: Printed for Dorman Newman, at the King's Arms in the Poultrey, 1692.

A Medium Betwixt TwoEextremes. London: Printed for Andrew Bell, 1698.

Pedo-baptism disproved being an answer to two printed papers (put forth by some gentlemen called the Athenian Society, who pretend to answer all questions sent to them of what nature soever) called the Athenian Mercury, one put forth November 14, the other November 28, 1691: in which papers they pretend to answer eight queries about the lawfulness of infant-baptism: likewise divers queries sent to them about the true subjects of baptism, &c. London: Printed for the author, and sold by John Harris, 1691.

A Pillar set up, to Keep in Remembrance his first dear and beloved wife. London: s.n., 1670.

Preaching from the Types and Metaphors of the Bible. Grand Rapids: Kregel, 1972.

The Progress of Sin, or, The travels of ungodliness wherein, the pedigree, rise (or original) antiquity, subtilty, evil nature, and prevailing power of sin, is fully discovered, in an apt and pleasant allegory: together with the great victories he hath obtained, and abominable evils he hath done to mankind, by the help of the Devil: as also, the manner of his apprehension, arraignment, tryal, condemnation, and execution. B.K., author of War with the Devil, and Travels of true godliness. London: Printed for John Dunton, 1684.

The Rector Rectified and Corrected, or, Infant-baptism unlawful being a sober answer to a late pamphlet entituled An argumentative and practical discourse of infant-baptism, published by Mr. William Burkit, rector of Mildin in Suffolk: wherein all his arguments for pedo-baptism are refuted and the necessity of immersion, i.e. dipping, is evidenced, and the people falsly called Anabaptists are cleared from those unjust reproaches and calumnies cast upon them: together with a reply to the Athenian gazette added to their 5th volume about infant-baptism: with some remarks upon Mr. John Flavel's last book in answer to Mr. Philip Cary. London: Printed and sold by John Harris, 1692.

A short confession of faith containing the substance of all the fundamental articles in the larger confession put forth by the elders of the Baptist churches, owning personal election and final perserverance. London: [s.n.], 1697.

Sion in distress, or, The groans of the Protestant church. London: Printed by George Larkin, for Enoch Prosser, 1682.

Spiritual songs being the marrow of Scripture in songs of praise to Almighty God from the Old and New Testament: with a hundred divine hymns on several occasions as now practised in several congregations in and about London: with a table of contents. London: Printed for John Marshal, 1700.

A summons to the grave, or, The necessity of a timely preparation for death demonstrated in a sermon preached at the funeral of that most eminent and faithful servant of Jesus Christ Mr. John Norcot who departed this life March 24, 1675/6. London: Printed for Ben Harris, 1676.

The travels of true godliness, from the beginning of the world to this present day in an apt and pleasant allegory. London: Printed for John Dunton, 1684.

A trumpet blown in Zion, or, An allarm in God's holy mountain containing an exposition of that metaphorical Scripture, Matth. III, 12: lately delivered in two sermons. London: [s.n.], 1694.

War with the devil or, The young man's conflict with the powers of darkness In a dialogue. Discovering the corruption and vanity of youth, the horrible nature of sin, and deplorable condition of fallen man. Also, a description, power, and rule of conscience, and the nature of true conversion. To which is added, an appendix, containing a dialogue between an old apostate, and a young professor worthy the perusal of all, but chiefly intended for the instruction of the younger sort. The tenth impression. London: Printed and sold by Benj. Harris, at the Golden Boar's-head in Grace-church-street, 1700.

Other Primary Works

A Declaration against the Antinomians, and their doctrine of liberty their chief tenents briefly and fully answered and the danger of those erronoeus points manifested: with a caution to such as are or have been so misled, to persvvade with them to turn from that evill into which they are or have been seduced ..., London: Printed for Iohn Iones, 1644.

The History of the Athenian Society: For the Resolving of all Nice and Curious Questions. By a Gentleman who got Secret Intelligence of their Whole Proceedings. London: Printed for James Dowley and are to be sold by the Booksellers on London and Westminster, n.d.

Quarta Centuria Ecclesiasticae Historiae. Basileae, Per Annem Oporinum, 1560.

The Racovian Catechisme: Wherein You have the substance of the Confession of those Churches, which in the Kingdom of Poland, and Great Dukedome of Lithuania, and other Provinces appertaining to that Kingdom, do affirm, That no other save the Father of our Lord Jesus Christ, is that one God of Israel, and that the man Jesus of Nazareth, who was born of the Virgin, and no other besides him, is the onely begotten Sonne of God. Amsterdam: Brooer Janz, 1652.

Ainsworth, Henry. *Annotations upon the Third Book of Moses, called Leviticus.* Amsterdam: Imprinted by Giles Thorp, 1618.

Ames, William. *Medulla Theologica.* Amsterdam: Apud Ioannem Ianssonium, 1648.

Anselm, *Sancti Anselmi ex Beccensi Abbate Canturiensis Archiepiscopi Opera.* Parisiis: Sumptib. Ludovici Billaine et Joannis Du Puis, 1675.

_____. *D. Anselmi Cantuariensis archiepiscopi, Theologorum omnium sui temporis facile Principis, neminique eorum qui post eum fuerunt, vel sanctitate, vel eruditione, vel eloquentia secundi, luculentissimae, in omnes sanctissimi Pauli Apostoli epistolas, & aliquot Euangelia, enarrationes*. Parisiis: Apud Ioannem Roigny, via Iacobea sus insigni quatuor Elementorum, 1549.

Barclay, Robert. *Theses Theologicae, or, Some Solid Positions of Sound Divinity Asserted*. Aberdeen: s.n., 1675.

Baxter, Richard. *Aphorismes of justification, with their explication annexed wherein also is opened the nature of the covenants, satisfaction, righteousnesse, faith, works, &c.: published especially for the use of the church of Kederminster in Worcestershire / by their unworthy teacher Ri. Baxter*. Hague: Printed by Abraham Brown, 1655.

_____. *Confirmation and Restauration, the necessary means of Reformation and Reconciliation*. London: Printed by A. M. for Nevil Simmons Bookseller in Kederminster, and are to be sold by Joseph Cranford, at the Kings-Head in Pauls Church-yard, 1658.

_____. *Plain Scripture proof of infants church-membership and baptism being the arguments prepared for and partly managed in the publicke dispute with Mr. Tombes at Bewdley on the first day of Jan., 1649: with a ful reply to what he then answered and what is contained in his sermon since preached in his printed books, his MS. on 1 Cor., 7, 14 which I saw, against M. Marshall, against these arguments: with a reply to his valedictory oration at Bewdley, and A corrective for his antidote / by Richard Baxter; with An appendix of animadversions on Mr. Bedfords tractate, and part of Dr. Wards, which seem to give too much to baptism; wherein is added An examination of Mr. Ts. Praecursor and A friendly accommodation with Mr. Bedford*. London: Printed for Robert VVhite, 1653.

_____. *Rich: Baxter's confesssion of his faith, especially concerning the interest of repentance and sincere obedience to Christ, in our justification & salvation. Writ- ten for the satisfaction of the misinformed, the conviction of calumniators, and the explication and vindication of some weighty truths.*, London: Printed by R.W. for Tho. Underhil, and Fra. Tyton, and are to be sold at the Anchor and Bible in Pauls Church-yard, and at the three Daggers in Fleetstreet., 1655.

_____. *A Treatise of Justifying Righteousness*. London: Nevil Simons and Johath Robinson, 1676.

Bellarmine, Robert. *Disputationum Roberti Bellarmini, De Controversiis Christianae Fidei, Adversus huius Temporis Haereticos, Quatuor Tomis Comprehensarum*. Coloniae Agrippinae: Sumptibus Ioannis Gymnici, sub Monocerote, 1628.

Beza, Theodore. *Iesu Christi Novum Testamentum Interpretationes duae, una vetus, altera nova, T. Bezae*. Geneva: Estienne, 1565.

_____. *Testamentum Novum, sive Novum Foedus Iesu Christi, D.N. Cuius Graeco contextui respondent interpretationes duae: una vetus: altera, Theodori Bezae, nunc quartò delegenter ab eo recognita*. Geneva: s.n.,

1589.

Blake, Thomas. *Vindiciae Foederis: Or, a Treatise of the Covenant of Grace entered with Man-kind*. London: Printed for Abel Roper, at the Sun against St Dunstins Church in Fleet Street, 1658.

Bridgewater, John. *The Athenian Oracle: being an entire collection of all the valuable questions and answers in the old athenian mercuries. Intermix'd with many cases in divinity, history, philosophy, mathematicks, love, poetry, never before publish'd. To which is prefix'd, the History of the Athenian Society and an essay upon learning*, 3rd ed., 4 vols. London: Printed for J. and J. Knapton, et. al., 1728.

Britten, William. *Silent meeting, a wonder to the world yet practised by the apostles, and owned by the people of God scornfully called Quakers*. S.l.: s.n., 1675.

Bullinger, Heinrich. *In Acta Apostolorum Heinrychi Bullingeri Commentariorum Libri VI: ab authore recogniti ac denuo iam recusi*. Tiguri: Excudebat Christophorus Froschoverus, 1583.

_____. *De Testamento seu Foedere Dei unico & aeterno Heinrychi Bullingeri breuis expositio*. Tigurini: In Aedibus Christ. Frosch. Mense Septemb. An., 1534.

Bunyan, John. *Differences in Judgment About Water-Baptism, No Bar to Communion: Or, To Communicate with Saints, as Saints, proved lawful. In Answer to a Book written by the Baptists and published by Mr. T. P. and Mr. W. K., entituled, 'Some serious Reflections on that parts of Mr. Bunyan's "Confession of Faith," touching Church-Communion with Unbaptized Believers.' Wherein Their Objections and Arguments are Answered, and the Doctrine of Communion still Asserted and Vindicated. Here is also Mr. Henry Jesse's Judgment in the Case fully declaring the Doctrine I have Asserted*. London: Printed for John Wilkins, and are to be sold at his shop in Exchange-Alley, next door to the Exchange-Coffee-House, over against the Royal Exchange, 1673.

Burkitt, William. *An argumentative and practical discourse of infant-baptism in which I. The lawfulness of infant-baptism is demonstrated, II. The objections against infant-baptism are answered, III. The usefulness of the ordinance is asserted, IV. The sinfulness of re-baptizing manifested, V. The non-necessity of dipping evidenced, VI. The practical use of infant-baptism urged and inforced*. London: Printed by T.M. for Tho. Parkhurst, 1695.

Cajetan, Thomas de Vio, Cardinal. *Epistolae Pauli et aliorum Apostolorum ad Graecam veritatem castigatem & per Reverendissimum Dominum Thoman de Vio, Caietanum Cardinalem sancti Sisti, iuxta sensum literalem enarratae*. Apud Iod. Badium Ascensium & Ioan. Paruum & Ioannem Roigny, 1532.

_____. *RR. DD. Thomae de Vio Caietani in Quattor Evangelia et Acta Apostolorum*. Lugduni: Sumptibus Iacobe & Petri Prost, 1639.

Calvin, John. *Institutes of the Christian Religion*. Ed. John T. McNeill, trans. F. L. Battles. 2 vols. Philadelphia: Westminster, 1950.

───────. *The Gospel According to St John 11-21 and The First Epistle of John*. T. H. L. Parker, trans., D. W. Torrance and T. F. Torrance, eds. Grand Rapids: Eerdmands Publishing Co., 1959.

Casaubon, Isaac. *ΤΗΣ ΚΑΙΝΣ ΔΙΑΘΗΚΗΣ ΑΠΑΝΤΑ*. Londini: Apud Richardum Whittakerum, 1633.

Charnock, Stephen. *The Works of late Learned Divine Stephen Charnock, B.D. Being Several Discourses upon Various Divine Subjects*. London: Printed for Ben. Griffin, in the Old-Baily; et al., 1699.

Clark, Samuel. *Scripture Justification: Or, A Discourse of Justification, According to the Evidence of Scripture-Light. Wherein the Nature of Justification is fully open'd; the Great Point of Justification by Works, both of the Law and Gospel, is clearly Stated. All those Scriptures which concern Justification, with divers others, are Explained; and the whole Managed with Scripture-materials, in a Plain and Peculiar Method. Together with a Thesis concerning the Interest of Christ's Active Obedience in our Justification*. London: Printed by S. Bridge, for Tho. Parkhust at the Bible and Tree Crowns in Cheapside, near Mercers Chapel, 1698.

Crisp, Tobias. *Christ alone exalted being the compleat works of Tobias Crisp, D.D., containing XLII sermons*. London: Printed for William Marshal, at the Bible in Newgate-street, 1690.

Crosby, Thomas. *The History of the English Baptists: From the Reformation to the Beginning of the Reign of King George I*. 4 vols. London: Printed and sold by the author, 1738-1740.

Davis, Horton. *Worship and Theology in England*, 5 vols. (Princeton, NJ.: Princeton University Press, 1961-75.

Curcaelleus, Stephanus. *Opera Theologica: Quorum pars praecipua Institutio Religionis Christianae. Cum indicibus necessariis*. Amstelodami: Apud Danielem Elsevirium, 1675.

Denne, Henry. *The man of sin discovered whom the Lord shall destroy with the brightnesse of his coming: the root and foundation of antichrist laid open in doctrine*. London: Printed for John Sweeting, 1646.

───────. *Seven Arguments to prove, that in order of working God doth justifie his elect, before they doe actually believe. With some answers to the objections that some make against the same. For the confirmation of those that doe truly beleeve, lest they should attribute any part of the office of Christ to the act of their beleeving*. London: s.n., 1643.

Diodati, Giovanni. *Pious Annotations upon the Holy Bible: Expounding the difficult places thereof Learnedly and Plainly. With other things of great importance* London: Printed by T. B. for Nicholas Fussel; and are to be sold at the Green Dragon in St. Paul's Church-yard, 1643.

Erasmus, Desiderius. *Desiderii Erasmi Roterodami Opera Omnia*, Tomus

Nonus. Lugduni Batavorum, Curam & impresis Petro Vander, 1706.
Exell, Joshua. *Plain and Exquisite Scripture Proof that St. John the Baptist and the blessed Apostles and all the Primitive Baptizers, did baptize by sprinkling or pouring water upon the person or persons they baptized and not by dipping the person into the water*. London: Printed for the author, to be sold by Thomas Parkhurst and William Langford, 1693.

_____. *A Serious Enquiry into, and containing plain and express Scripture-proofs, that John the Baptist did as certainly Baptize Infants, as the Adult*. London: Printed for R. Man, and are to be sold by many booksellers in London, 1693.

Du Moulin, Peter. *The Accomplishment of the Prophecies, Or the Third Booke in defense of the Catholicke faith*. Printed at Oxford by Ioseph Barnes and are to be sold by Iohn Barnes dwelling neere Holborne Conduit, 1613.

Featley, Daniel. *The Dippers dipt: or the Anabaptist Duck'd and Plung'd over Head and Ears, at a Disputation in Southwark*. London: Printed for N. B. and Richard Royston at the Angel in Ivy-Lane, 1647.

Fisher, Samuel. *Christianismus Redivivus*. London: Printed by Henry Hills, and are to be sold by Francis Smith at his shop in Flying Horse court in Fleetstreet, 1655.

Flavell, John. *ΠΛΑΝΗΛΟΓΙΑ, A Succinct and Seasonable Discourse of the Occasions, Causes, Nature, Rise, Growth and Remedies of Mental Errors. Written some months since, and now publick, both for the healing and prevention of Sins and Calamities which have broken in this way upon the Churches of Christ, to the great scandal of Religion, hardening of the wicked and obstruction of Reformation. Whereunto are subjoined by way of appendix: I. Vindiciarum Vindex, being a succinct but full answer to Mr. Philip Cary's weak and impertinent exceptions to my Vindiciae legis & foederis. II. A Synopsis of Ancient and Modern Antinomian Errors, with Scriptural Arguments and Reasons against them. III. A Sermon composed for the preventing and healing of Rents and Divisions in the Churches of Christ*. London: Printed by R. Roberts for Tho. Cockrill, 1691.

Gillespie, Patrick. *The Ark of the Covenant Opened: Or, A Treatise of the Covenant of Redemption Between God and Christ, as the Foundation of the Covenant of Grace*. London: Printed for Tho. Parkhurst at the Bible and three Crowns, in Cheapside, near Mercers Chappel, 1677.

Goodwin, Thomas. *The Works of Thomas Goodwin*, 12 vols. Edinburgh: James Nichol, 1864.

Grotius, Hugo. *Operum Theologicorum*. Amstelaedami: Apud Heredes Joannis Blaev, 1679.

Hammond, Henry. *Letter of Resolution to Six Quaeres, of Present Use in the Church of England*. London: Printed by J. Flesher for R. Royston at the Angel in Ivy-lane, 1653.

_____. *A Paraphrase and Annotations upon all the Books of the New Testament, Briefly Explaining all the Difficult Places thereof*, 4th ed. London: Printed by E. F., T. R. and J. M for R. Roston, Bookseller to his most Sacred Majesty, at the Angel in Amen-Corner, 1675.

Leigh, Edward. *Critica Sacra: Or, Philologicall and Theologicall Obervations upon all the Greek Words of the New Testament, in Order Alphabeticall*, 2nd ed. corrected and much enlarged by the author. London: Printed by James Young, for Thomas Underhill, and are to be sold at the Signe of the Bible in Wood-Street, 1646.

Lightfoot, John. *Joannis Lightfooti Opera Ominia*. Roterodami: Typis Regeneri Leers, 1686.

Luther, Martin. *D. Martin Luthers Werke: kritische Gesamtausgabe*. Weimar: Bohlau, 1883—

_____. *Luther's Works*, Theodore G. Tappert, ed. and trans. Philadelphia: Fortress Press, 1967.

Mansi, Johannes Dominicus. ed. *Sacrorum Conciliorum Nova et Amplissima Collectio*. 54 vols. Paris: Apud Antonium Zatta, 1901-27.

Mason, John. *Mentis Humane Metamorphis sive Conversio. The History of the Young Converted Galland or Directions to the Readers of that Divine Poem written by Benjamin Keach, Intittled Warre with the Devil*. London: B. Harris, 1676.

Melachthon, Philip. *CR*, XV.

Musculus, Wolfgang. *In ambas Apostoli Pauli ad Corinthios epistolas commentarii. Cum indice rerum & verborum locupletissimo*. Basileae: Hervagius, 1559.

_____. *In Evangelistam Mattaeum Commentarii*. Basileae: Hervagius, 1578.

An Orthodox Creed, or, A Protestant Confession of Faith. London: s.n., 1679.

Owen, John. ΘΕΟΛΟΓΟΥΜΕΝΑ ΠΑΝΤΟΔΑΠΑ. *Sive de Natura, Ortu, Progressu, et Studio Verae Theologiae Libri Sex*. Oxoniae, Excudebat Hen. Hall, Academiae Typograghus, Impensis Tho. Robinson, n.d.

_____. *The Works of John Owen*. 16 vols. Rio, WI.: Ages, 2000.

Park, James. *False Fictions and Romances Rebuked: In Answer to Pretended Matter Charged against the Quaker in a book Intitled, The Progress of Sin, &c. Written by B. K. His Lies and Slanders therein returned back upon him and the Speakers of Yea and Nay in Truth Vindicated*. London: s.n., 1684.

Pasor, Georgius. *Lexicon Graeco-Latinum, Novum Domini Nosti Jesu Christi Testamentum*, Editio quarta. Herbornae Nassoviorum: Typis Georgii Corvini & Johan-Georgii Muderspachii, 1632.

Perkins, William. *A Commentarie or Exposition upon the Five First Chapters of the Epistle to the Galatians: penned by the godly, learned and iudicial Diuine, M. W. Perkins. Now Published for the Benefite of the Church, and Continued with a Supplement vpon the Sixth Chapter*. London: Iohn

Legatt, Printer to the University of Cambridge, 1613.

_____. *Whole Treatise of the Cases of Conscience, Distinguished into Three Bookes*. London: Iohn Legatt, Printer to the University of Cambridge, 1606.

_____. *William Perkins: His Probleme of the Forged Catholicisme, or Uniuersalitie of the Romish Religion*. London: Iohn Legatt, Printer to the University of Cambridge, 1613.

Piscator, Johannes. *Analysis Logica Evangelii Secudum Johannem*. Londini: Impresis Geor. Bishop, 1595.

Pool, Matthew. *Annotations upon the Holy Bible*, 3 vols. Edinburgh: s.n., 1700-01.

Rothwell, John. *A Catalogue of Approved Divinity Books which have been printed or reprinted about twenty years past, and continue down to this present year, 1657, mensis Junii 18*. London: Printed for John Rothwell, 1657.

_____. *Paedobaptismus Vindicatus, or, Infant-baptism stated in an essay to evidence its lawfulness from the testimony of the Holy Scripture, especially St. Matthew, XXVIII, 19: the grand, if not sole place, so much insisted on by the antipaedobaptists, to prove their mistaken principle: handled in a different method form other tracts on the subject, as appears in the contents: with an account of a conference publickly held with an antipaedobaptist of no small fame*. London: Printed for John Dunton at the Raven in the Poultrey, 1693.

Rutherford, Samuel. *The Covenant of Life Opened: Or, A Treatise of the Covenant of Grace*. Edinburgh: Printed by Andro. Anderson, for Robert Broun, and are to be sold at his shop, at the Sign of the Sun, 1654.

_____. Rutherford, *A Survey of the Spiritual Antichrist. Opening the secrets of Familisme and Antinomianisme in the Antichristian Doctrine of John Saltmarsh, and Will. Del, the present Preachers of the Army now in England, and of Robert Town, Tob. Crisp, H. Denne, Eaton, and others*. London: Printed by J. D. & R. I. for Andrew Crooke, 1647.

Saltmarsh, John. *Free-grace or, the flowings of Christ's blood freely to sinners. Being an experiment of Jesus Christ upon one who hath been in the bondage of a troubled conscience at times for the space of about twelve yeers, til now upon a clearer discovery of Jesus Christ, and the Gospel: wherein divers secrets of the soul, of sin and temptations, are experimentally opened, and by way of observation, concerning a natural condition, and a mixed condition of law and Gospel: with a further revealing of the Gospel in its glory, liberty, freenesse, and simplicity for salvation*. London: Printed for Giles Calvert, dwelling at the black Spred-Eagle at the West-end of Pauls, 1645.

_____. *Sparkles of glory, or Some beams of the morning-star. Wherein are many discoveries as to truth, and peace. To the establishment, and pure enlargement of a Christian in spirit and truth*, 2nd. Ed. London: Printed for Giles Calvert, and are to be sold at the Black-spred-Eagle, at the West end of Pauls, 1647.

Sandys, George. *Sandys Travels, Containing an History of the Original and Present State of the Turkish Empire: Their Laws, Government, Policy, Military Force, Courts of Justice and Commerce*, 7th ed. London: Printed for John Williams Junior, at the Crown in Little-Britain, 1673.

Shute, Gyles. *An antidote to prevent the prevalency of anabaptism clearly vindicated from that foul aspersion of being a counterfeit, and the aspersors totally confuted, or, Another broad-side against anabaptism.* London: Printed by J.R., and are to be sold by Nathaniel Hiller, William Chandler, Samuel Norcut, Will. Wingod, James Wright, 1694.

_____. *A Replication to a Late Book written by Mr Benjamin Keach Against Infant-Baptism, Intituled A Counter-Antidote.* London: Printed for the author, 1694.

Smythies, William. *The Spirit of Meekness, Recommended for the Reducing of the Erroneous and Such as have Dissented from the Church of England.* London: s.n., 1684.

_____. *The Unworthy Non-Communicant. A Treatise Shewing the Danger of Neglecting the Blessed Sacrament of the Lords Supper, and Rectifying the Mistakes of many in This Age Concerning it.* 2nd impression corrected. London: Printed by T. Milbourn for Samuel Lee at the Feathers in Lumbard Street, 1683.

Stephanus, Henricus. *Thesaurus Graecae Lingua.* Geneva: Excudebat Henr. Stephanus, 1572.

Taylor, Jeremy. *Antiquitates Christianae: Or the History of the Life and Death of the Holy Jesus, as Also the Lives, Acts and Martyrdoms of His Apostles*, In Two Parts, 9th ed. London: Printed by J. Leake, for John Meredith, in Trust for Royston and Elizabeth Meredith. And are to be sold by S. and J. Sprint, et. al., 1703.

_____. *The Second Part of the Dissuasive from Popery: In Vindication of the First Part and further Reproof and Conviction of the Roman Errors.* London: Printed for R. Royston, Bookseller for the Kings most excellent Majesty, at the Angel in S. Bartholomew's Hospital, 1657.

_____. ΘΕΟΛΟΓΙΑ ΕΚΛΕΤΙΚΗ: *A Discourse of the Liberty of Prophesying, with its Just Limits and Temper. Showing the Unreasonableness of Prescribing to Other Men's Faith, and the Iniquity of Persecuting Differing Opinions*, new ed. London: Printed for Gale and Fenner, Paternoster Row, 1817.

Thomas Aquinas, *Corpus Thomisticum.* Subsidia studii ab Enrique Alarcón colecta et edita Pampilonae ad Universitatis Studiorum Navarrensis aedes, 2005.

Tombes, John. *Anti-Paedobaptism: or the Third Part. Being a full review of the dispute concerning infant-baptism. In which the Arguments for infant-baptism from the Covenant and initial seal, infants visible church-*

membership, antiquity of infant-baptism are referred. London: Printed by E. Aisop, 1657.

Ursinus, Zacharias. *Opera Theologica.* Heildelberge: Typis Johannis Lancelloti, 1613.

Vossius, Gehardus Joannes. *Etymologycon Linguae Latinae. Praefigitur Ejusdem de Literarum Permutatione Tratactus*, Editio Nova. Amstelodami: Ex typographia P. & I. Blaev, Prostant apud Ianssonio-Waesbergios, Boom, à Someren & Goethals, 1695.

Westminster Assembly, *Annotations upon all the books of the Old and New Testament.* London: Printed by Evan Tyler, 1657.

_____. *The Confession of Faith, And the Larger and Shorter Catechisme.* London: Company of the Stationers, 1651.

Williams, Daniel. *Gospel Truth stated and vindicated wherein some of Dr. Crisp's opinions are considered, and the opposite truths are plainly stated and confirmed.* London: Printed for John Dunton, 1692.

Woffius, Iohannis. *Lectionum Memorabilium et Reconditarum Centenarii XVI.* Palatinus: Impressit Leong. Reinmichel, 1660.

Zanchy, Jerome. *Hieronymi Zanchii Theologiclarissimi in D. Pauli Apostoli Epistolas Ad Philippenses, Colossenses, Thessalonicenses, Et Duo priora capita primae Epistolae D. Iohannis. Commentarii, in quibus et textus Apostoli accurate explicatur: & multi loci communes Theologiae solide pertractantur.* Editio Altera Recognita et Aucta. Neustadii Palatinorum: Apud haeredes Wilhelmi Harnisij, 1601.

_____. *Operum Theologicorum D. Hieronymi Zanchii Tomus Quartus. In quo de primi hominis lapsu, de Peccato & de Lege Dei prolixè agitur. Opus solidum, primam tractatus de redemptione partem continens, multiplici doctrina refertum.* Genevae: Sumtibus Samvelis Crispini, 1617.

_____. *Operum Theologicorum D. Hieronymi Zanchii, Tomus Sextus Tripertius, Commentarios in Epistolas Apostolicas.* Geneva: Sumptibus Samvelis Crispini, 1617.

Zwingli, Huldreich. *Sämliche Werke.* Berlim: Verlag von C. A. Schwetschke and Sohn, 1905.

Secondary Sources

Armstrong, Brian G. *Calvinism and the Amyraut Heresy: Protestant Scholasticism and Humanism in the Seventeenth-Century France.* Madison and London: The University of Wisconsin Press, 1969.

Asselt, Willem J. van. '*Amicitia Dei* as Ultimate Reality: An Outline of the Covenant Theology of Johannes Cocceius (1603-1669).' *URM* 21/1 (1998): 35-47.

_____. *The Federal Theology of Johannes Cocceius (1603-1669).* Raymond A. Blacketer, trans. Leiden: Brill, 2001.

Asselt, Willem J. van and Eef Dekker, eds. *Reformation and Scholasticism: An Ecumenical Enterprise*. Grand Rapids: Baker Academic, 2001.
_____. 'Scholasticism, Medieval.' s.v. *DHT*.
Baker, J. Wayne. *Heinrich Bullinger and the Covenant: The Other Reformed Tradition*. Athens, Ohio: Ohio University Press, 1980.
_____. '*Sola Fide, Sola Gratia*: The Battle for Luther in Seventeenth Century England.' *SCJ* 16 (1/1985): 115-133.
Bierma, Lyle D. Book review of, *The Age of Reform, 1250-1550: An Intellectual and Religious History of Late Medieval and Reformation Europe*. *CTJ* 16 (1981): 100-103.
_____. 'Federal Theology in the Sixteenth Century: Two Traditions?' *WTJ* 45 (1983): 304-321.
Bouyer, Louis. *The Spirit and Forms of Protestantism*, A. V. Littledale, trans. London: The Harvill Press, 1956.
Bozeman, T. D. '"The Glory of the Third Time:" John Eaton as Contra-Puritan,' *JEH* 47/4 (October 1996): 638-654.
Braaten, Carl E. and Robert W. Jenson. *The Catholicity of the Reformation*. Grand Rapids: Eerdmans, 1996.
Brackney, William Henry. *The Baptists*. New York: Greewood Press, 1988.
Bray, John S. *Theodore Beza's Doctrine of Predestination*. Nieuwkoop : De Graaf, 1975.
Breward, Ian. 'The Significance of William Perkins.' *JRH* 4 (1966-67): 113-128.
Brooks, Benjamin. *The Lives of the Puritans*. 3 vols. Morgan: Soli Deo Gloria Publications, 1997.
Brown, Louise Fargo. *The Political Activities of the Baptists and Fifth Monarchy Men in England During the Interregnum*. New York: Burt Franklin, 1911.
Brunner, Emil. *O Equívoco sobre a Igreja*. Paulo Arantes, trans. São Paulo: Novo Século, 2000.
Carpenter, Humphrey and Mari Prichard, eds. 'Keach, Benjamin (1640-1704).' s.v. *The Oxford Companion to Children's Literature*. Oxford: Oxford University Press, 1984.
Carnes, James. 'The Famous Mr. Keach: Benjamin Keach and his Influence on Congregational Singing in the Seventeenth Century England.' M.A. thesis, Denton, TX.: North Texas State University, 1984.
Cathcart, William. ed. *The Baptist Encyclopedia*. Single ed. Philadelphia: Louis H. Everts, 1883.
Christian, J. T. *A History of the Baptists Together with Some Account of Their Principles and Practices*. Nashville: Sunday School Board of the Southern Baptist Convention, 1922.
Close, Robert G. 'Covenant Theology.' s.v. *The International Dictionary of the Christian Church*, J. D. Douglas, ed. Exeter, Devon: Paternoster Press, 1974.

Cobbett, William and Thomas Bayly Howell, *Cobbett's Complete Collection of state trials and proceedings for high treason and other crimes and misdemeanours, from the earliest period to the present time.* 33 vols. S.l.: Printed by T. C. Hansard, 1809-26.

Cooper, Tim. *Fear and Polemic in Seventeenth-Century England: Richard Baxter and Antinomianism.* Aldershot: Ashgate, 2001.

Coughenour, Robert A. 'The Shape and Vehicle of Puritan Hermeneutics.' *RR* 30 (1976): 23-34.

Cragg, G. R. *From Puritanism to the Age of Reason: A Study of changes in Religious thought within the Church of England, 1660 to 1700.* Cambridge: Cambridge University Press, 1950.

Cramp, J. M. *Baptist History: From the Foundation of the Christian Church to the Close of the Eighteenth Century.* 2nd ed. complete and unabridged. Philadelphia: American Baptist Publication Society, 1869.

Dix, Kenneth. *Benjamin Keach and a monument to liberty.* Dunstable, Beds.: The Fouconberg Press, 1985.

Donnelly, John Patrick. *Calvinism and Scholasticism in Vermigli's Doctrine of Man and Grace.* Leiden: Brill, 1976.

Durston, Christopher and Jacqueline Eales, eds. *The Culture of English Puritanism, 1560-1700.* London: Macmillan Press, 1996.

Evans, B. *The Early English Baptists.* London: J. Heaton & Son, 1864.

Ferguson, Sinclair B. *John Owen on the Christian Life.* Edinburgh: Banner of Truth, 1987.

Fleming, Sandford. *Children & Puritanism: The Place of Children in the Life and Thought of the New England Churches, 1620-1847.* New Haven: Yale University Press, 1933.

George, Timothy. *Theology of the Reformers.* Nashville: Broadman Press, 1988.

Graves, J. R. *The Triemme; or Death by Three Horns.* Nashville: South-Western Publishing Co., 1869.

Greaves, Richard. *John Bunyan* (Appleford, Berkshire: The Sutton Courtenay Press, 1969.

_____. 'John Bunyan and Covenant Thought in the Seventeenth Century.' *CH* 36 (1967): 151-169.

_____. 'Keach (or Keeche), Benjamin (1640-1704).' s.v. *BDBR*

_____. 'The Origin and Early Development of English Covenant Thought.' *THis* 21 (1968): 21-35.

Griffiths, Olive M. *Religion and Learning: A Study in English Presbyterian Thought from the Bàrtholomew Ejections (1662) to the Foundation of the Unitarian Movement.* Cambridge: Cambridge University Press, 1935.

Griffiths, Steve. *Redeem the Time: Sin in the Writings of John Owen.* Fern: Mentor, 2001.

Hall, Basil. 'Calvin Against the Calvinists.' *John Calvin*, Gervase Dunffield, ed. Grand Rapids: Eerdmans, 1966. pp. 19-37.

Haller, William. *The Rise of Puritanism: Or, the way to New Jerusalem as set forth in Pulpit and Press from Thomas Cartwright to John Lilburne and John Milton, 1570-1643*. New York: Columbia University Press, 1938.

Hatch, Nathan O. and Mark A. Noll, eds. *The Bible in America: Essays in Cultural History*. Oxford: Oxford University Press, 1982.

Haykin, Michael A. G. ed. *British Particular Baptists*. 2 vols. Springfield, MO.: Particular Baptist Press, 1998.

_____. *Kiffin, Knollys and Keach—Rediscovering our English Baptist Heritage*. Leeds: Reformation Today Trust, 1996.

_____. ed. *The Life and Thought of John Gill (1697-1771): A Tercentennial Appreciation*. Leiden: E. J. Brill, 1997.

Helm, Paul. *Calvin and the Calvinists*. 2nd ed. Edinburgh: Banner of Truth, 1998.

Heppe, Heinrich. *Reformed Dogmatics*. G. T. Thompson, trans. London: George Allen & Unwin Ltd., 1950.

Hill, Christopher. *Society and Puritanism in Pre-Revolutionary England*. London: Secker & Warburg, 1964.

Holifield, E. Brooks. *The Covenant Sealed: The Development of Puritan Sacramental Theology in Old and New England, 1570-1720*. New Haven and London: Yale University Press, 1974.

Holmes, Stephen R. *Listening to the Past: The Place of Tradition in Theology*. Carlisle, Cumbria / Grand Rapids, MI.: Paternoster / Baker Academic, 2002.

Huehns, Gertrude. *Antinomianism in English History: With special reference to the period 1640-1660*. London: The Cresset Press, 1951.

Huizinga, Johan. *The Waning of the Middle Ages: A Study of the Forms of Life, Thought and Art in France and the Netherlands in the XIVth and XVth Centuries*. F. Hopman, trans. London: Edward Arnold & Co., 1924.

Hulse, Erol. *An Introduction to the Baptists*. Haywards Heath, Sussex: Carey Publications, 1973.

Ivimey, Joseph. *A History of the English Baptists*. Vol. 1. London: Printed for the author, 1811.

James III, Frank A. *Peter Martyr Vermigli and Predestination: The Augustinian Inheritance of an Italian Reformer*. Oxford: Claredon Press, 1998.

Karlberg, Mark. 'Reformed Interpretation of the Mosaic Covenant.' *WTJ* 43 (Fall, 1980): 1-57.

Kendall, R. T. *Calvin and English Calvinism to 1649*. Oxford: Oxford University Press, 1979.

Kevan, Ernest Frederick. *The Grace of the Law: A Study in Puritan Theology*. London: Carey Kingsgate Press, 1964.

Knatchbull, Norton. *Annotations upon Some Difficult Texts in all the Books of the New Testament*. Cambridge: Printed by J. Hayes, Printer to the University; for W. Graves, Bookseller there, 1693.

Knappen, Marshall M. *Tudor Puritanism: A Chapter in the History of Idealism*. Gloucester, Mass.: Peter Smith, 1963.

Lamond, William. *Puritanism and historical controversy*. London: UCL Press, 1996.

Lane, Anthony N. S. '*Sola Scriptura*? Making Sense of a Post-Reformation Slogan,' in *A Pathway into the Holy Scriptures*, Philip E. Satterthwaite and David F. Wright, eds. Grand Rapids: Eerdmans, 1994. pp. 297-324.

Lea, Thomas D. 'The Hermeneutics of the Puritans.' *JETS* 39/2 (June 1996): 271-284.

Lee, Jason Kenneth. 'The Theology of John Smith.' Ph.D. diss., University of Aberdeen, 1999.

Leff, Gordon. *The Dissolution of the Medieval Outlook: An Essay on Intellectual and Spiritual Change in the Fourteenth Century*. New York: s.n., 1976.

Lethan, Robert. 'Faith and Assurance in Early Calvinism: A Model of Continuity and Diversity.' *Later Calvinism*: International Perspectives. Sixteenth Century Essays & Studies. Vol. 22. Kirksville, MO.: Sixteenth Century Journal Publishers, 1994.

Lillback, Peter A. *The Binding of God: Calvin's Role in the Development of Covenant Theology*. Grand Rapids, Michigan and Carlisle, Cumbria: Baker Academic and Paternoster Press, 2001.

Lim, Paul. 'Baxter, Richard,' s.v., *DHT*.

Lopes, Hernandes Dias Lopes. *A Importância da Pregação Expositiva para o Crescimento da Igreja*. São Paulo: Editora Candeia, 2004.

Lortz, Joseph. *The Reformation in Germany*, Ronald Walls, trans., 2 vols. London: Darton, Longman & Todd, 1968.

_____. 'The Basic Elements of Luther's Intellectual Style.' *Catholic Scholars Dialogue with Luther*, Jared Wicks, com. Chicago: Loyola University Press, 1970. pp. 3-33.

MacCulloch, Diarmaid. *Reformation: Europe's House Divided 1490-1700*. London: Penguin Group, 2003.

MacDonald, Murdina. 'London Calvinistic Baptists, 1689-1727: Tensions within a Dissenting Community under Toleration.' Ph.D. diss., Regent's Park College, Oxford, 1983.

Macleod, Donald. 'Covenant Theology.' *Dictionary of Scottish Church History and Theology*, Nigel Cameron, David Wright, David Lachman, and Donald Meek, eds. Edinburgh: T&T Clark, 1993, s.v.

Martin, Hugh. *Benjamin Keach, 1640-1704: Pioneer of Congregational Hymn Singing*. London: Independent Press, 1961.

Maurer, Armand. *Medieval Philosophy*. New York: s.n., 1962.

McBeth, H. Leon. *The Baptist Heritage: Four Centuries of Baptist Witness*. Nashville: Broadman Press, 1987.

_____. *A Sourcebook for Baptist Heritage*. Nashville: Broadman Press, 1990.

McElrath, Hugh T. 'Turning Points in the Story of Baptist Church Music.' *BHH* 19 (January 1984): 4-16.
McGiffert, Michael. 'The Perkinsian Moment of Federal Theology.' *CTJ* 29 (1994): 117-148.
McGowan, Andrew T. B. 'Federal Theology as a Theology of Grace.' *SBET* 2 (1984): 41-50.
_____. *The Federal Theology of Thomas Boston*. Carlisle, U.K.: Paternoster Press, 1997.
McGrath, Alister E. *A Life of John Calvin: A Study in the Shaping of Western Culture*. Oxford: Blackwell, 1990.
_____. *Iustitia Dei: A History of the Christian Doctrine of Justification*. 2 vols. Cambridge: Cambridge University Press, 1986.
Mckim, Donald K. 'John Owen's Doctrine of Scripture in Historical Perspective.' *EvQ* 45 (1973): 195-207.
Meijering, E. P. 'The Fathers and Calvinist Orthodoxy: Systematic Theology.' *The Reception of the Church Fathers in the West: From the Carolingians to the Maurists*. I. Backus, ed. Leiden: E. J. Brill, 1997, II: 867-888.
Miller, Perry. *The New England Mind: The Seventeenth Century*. Cambridge, MA.: Harvard University Press, 1967.
Mitchell, Fraser W. *English Pulpit Oratory From Andrewes to Tillotson: A Study of Its Literary Aspects*. London: Society for Promoting Christian Knowledge, 1932.
Moltman, Jürgen. 'Theologia Reformata et Semper Reformanda.' *Toward the Future of Reformed Theology: Tasks, Topics, Traditions*. David Willis and Michael Welker, eds. Grand Rapids, MI./Cambridge, U.K.: Eerdmans Publishing Co., 1999.
Muller, Richard A. *After Calvin: Studies in the Development of a Theological Tradition*. Oxford: Oxford University Press, 2003.
_____. 'Arminius and Arminianism,' s.v., *DHT*.
_____. *Christ and the Decree: Christology and Predestination in Reformed Theology from Calvin to Perkins*. Grand Rapids: Baker Book House, 1986.
_____. 'Calvin and the "Calvinists:" Assessing Continuities an Discontinuities Between the Reformation and Orthodoxy – Part I.' *CTJ* 30 (1995): 345-375.
_____. *Dictionary of Latin and Greek Theological Terms: Drawn Principally from the Protestant Scholastic Theology*. Grand Rapids, Baker Books / Carlisle, Paternoster Press, 1985.
_____. 'The Federal Motif in Seventeenth Century Arminian Theology.' *NAK* 62 (1982): 102-122.
_____. *God, Creation, and Providence in the Thought of Jacob Arminius: Sources and Directions of Scholastic Protestantism in the Era of Orthodoxy*. Grand Rapids, MI.: Baker Book House, 1991.

_____. 'John Gill and the Reformed Tradition: A Study in the Reception of Protestant Orthodoxy in the Eighteenth Century,' in *The Life and Thought of John Gill (1697-1771): A Tercentennial Appreciation*, Michael A. G. Hayking, ed. Leiden: E. J. Brill, 1997.

_____. *Post-Reformation Reformed Dogmatics: Volume 1 Prolegomena to Theology*. Grand Rapids, MI.: Baker Book House, 1987.

_____. 'The Problem of Protestant Scholasticism—A Review and Definition.' *Reformation and Scholasticism*. W. van Asselt and E. Dekker, eds. pp. 45-64.

_____. *Scholasticism and Orthodoxy in the Reformed Tradition: An Attempt at Definition*. Grand Rapids, MI.: Calvin Theological Seminary, 1995.

_____. 'Scholasticism, Reformation, Orthodoxy, and the Persistence of Christian Aristotelianism.' *TJ* 19/1 (1998): 81-96.

_____. 'The Spirit and the Covenant: John Gill's Critique of the *Pactum Salutis*.' *FBJHT* 24/1 (January-March, 1981): 4-14.

_____. *The Unaccommodated Calvin: Studies in the Formation of a Theological Tradition*. New York: Oxford University Press, 2000.

Music, David. 'The Hymns of Benjamin Keach: An Introductory Study.' *Hymn* 34 (July 1983): 147-154.

Nettles, Thomas. *Baptist Catechisms: 'To Make Thee Wise unto Salvation.'* Forth Worth: For the author, 1982.

Nuttal, Geoffrey. *The Holy Spirit in Puritan Faith and Experience*. Oxford: Basil Blackwell, 1946.

Oberman, Heiko Augustinus. *Archbishop Thomas Bradwardine: A Fourteenth-century Augustinian. A Study of his Theology in its Historical Context*. Utrecht: Kemink en Zoon, 1957.

_____. *The Dawn of the Reformation*. Edinburgh: T. & T. Clark, 1986.

_____. *Forerunners of the Reformation*. New York: Holt, Rinehart, and Wilson, 1966.

_____. *The Harvest of Medieval Theology: Gabriel Biel and Late Nominalism*. Cambridge, MA.: Harvard University Press, 1963.

_____. *The Impact of the Reformation*. Grand Rapids: Eerdmans, 1994.

_____. *Masters of the Reformation: The Emergence of a New Intellectual Climate in Europe*. Dennis Martin, trans. Cambridge: Cambridge University Press, 1981.

_____. *The Reformation: Roots and Ramifications*. Andrew Gow, trans. Edinburgh: T. & T. Clark, 1994.

Nicollier, Béatrice. 'Beza, Theodore (1519-1605).' s.v. *DHT*.

Novak, Michael James. 'Thy Will be done: the Theology of the English Particular Baptists, 1638-1660.' Ph.D. diss., Harvard University, 1979.

Oliveira, Zaqueu Moreira de. *Liberdade e Exclusivismo: Ensaios Sobre os Batistas Ingleses*. Rio de Janeiro: Horizontal Editora, 1997.

Orchard, G. H. *A Concise History of the Baptists from the Time of Christ, Their Founder, to the Eighteenth Century*. Lexington: Ashland Avenue Baptist

Church, 1838.
Osterhaven, M. Eugene. 'Covenant.' s.v. *Encyclopedia of the Reformed Faith.* Donald K. Mckin, ed. Louisville, Kentucky and Edinburgh: Westminster/John Knox Press and Saint Andrew Press, 1992.
Ozment, Steven. *The Age of Reaform, 1250-1550: An Intellectual and Religious History of Late Medieval and Reformation Europe.* New Haven: Yale University Press, 1980.
Park, Hong-Gyu. 'Grace and Nature in the Theology of John Gill (1697-1771).' Ph.D. diss., University of Aberdeen, 2001.
Parker, G. Keith. *Baptists In Europe: History & Confessions of Faith.* Nashville: Broadman Press, 1982.
Patterson, W. Morgan. *Baptist Successionism: A Critical View.* Valley Forge, PA.: The Judson Press, 1969.
Pelikan, Jaroslav. *Obedient Rebels: Catholic Substance and Protestant Principle in Luther's Reformation.* London: SCM Press, 1964.
Persson, Erik Per. *Sacra Doctrina: Reason and Revelation in Aquinas*, Ross MacKenzie, trans. Oxford: Basil Blackwell, 1970.
Peter, J. F. 'The Place of Tradition in Reformed Theology.' *SJT* 18 (1965): 294-307.
Plum, Harry Grant. *Restoration Puritanism: A Study of the Growth of English Liberty.* Port Washington, N.Y.: Kennikat Press, 1972.
Preuss, Robert. *The Theology of Post-Reformation Lutheranism*, 2 vols. St. Louis: Con- cordia, 1970-72.
Ray, D. B. *Baptist Successionism: a Hand-Book of Baptist History.* S.l.: Geo. E. Stevens & Co., 1871.
Reniham, James. 'The Practical Ecclesiology of the English Particular Baptists, 1675-1705: the Doctrine of the Church in the Second London Confession.' Ph.D. diss., Trinity Evangelical Divinity School, 1997.
Robinson, H. Wheeler. *The Life and Faith of the Baptists.* London: Methuen & Co., 1927.
Rolston III, Holmes. *John Calvin versus the Westminster Confession.* Richmond, Virginia: John Knox Press, 1972.
_____. 'Responsible Man in Reformed Theology: Calvin versus the Westminster Confession.' *SJT* 23/2 (May, 1970): 129-156.
Routley, Erik. *Creeds and Confessions: The Reformation and Its Modern Ecumenical Implications.* London: Gerald Duckworth & Co. Ltd., 1962.
Ruland, Vernon Joseph. 'Covenant Theology.' s.v. *New Catholic Encyclopedia.* William McDonald, gen. ed. New York: McGraw-Hill Book Co., 1967.
Satterthwaite, Philip E. and David F. Wright, eds. *A Pathway into the Holy Scriptures.* Grand Rapids: Eerdmans, 1994.
Schaff, Philip. *Creeds of Christendom.* 3 vols. New York: s.n. 1877.
_____. *The Creeds of the Evangelical Protestant Churches.* London: Hodder & Stoughton, 1877.
Shaw, Robert. *An Exposition of the Confession of Faith of the Westminster*

Assembly of Divines. Inverness, Scotland: Christian Focus Publication, first pub., 1845, new ed., 1973.

Sohm, Rudolf. *Outlines of Church History*, Sinclair May, trans. London: Macmillan & Co., 1895.

Solt, Leo F. 'John Saltmarsh: New Model Army Chaplain.' *JEH* 2 (1951): 69-80.

Spears, William. 'The Baptist Movement in the Late Seventeenth Century as Reflected in the Work and Thought of Benjamin Keach, 1640-1704.' Ph.D. diss., University of Edinburgh, 1953.

Sprunger, Keith L. 'Technometria: A Prologue to Puritan Theology.' *JHI* 29 (1968): 115-122.

Steinmetz, David C. *Luther and Staupitz: An Essay in the Intellectual Origins of the Protestant Reformation*. Durham, N.C.: Duke University Press, 1980.

_____. *Luther in Context*. Bloomington: Indiana University Press, 1986.

_____. *Misericordia Dei: The Theology of Johannes von Staupitz in its Late Medieval Setting*. Leiden: Brill, 1968.

_____. 'The Scholastic Calvin,' in *Protestant Scholasticism: Essays in Reassessment*. Carl R. Trueman and R. Scott Clark, eds. 16-30. Carlisle, Cumbria: Paternoster Press, 1999.

Stevenson, W. R. 'Keach, Benjamin.' s.v. *A Dictionary of Hymnology*. John Julian, ed. 2nd ed. London: John Murray, Albemarle Street, 1907.

Stoever, William K. B. *'A Faire and Easie Way to Heaven': Covenant Theology and Antinominanism in Early Massachusetts*. Middletown: Wesleyan University Press, 1978.

_____. 'Nature, Grace and John Cotton: The Theological Dimension of the New England Antinomian Controversy.' *CH* 44 (1975): 22-33.

Strehle, Stephen. *Calvinism, Federalism, and Scholasticism: A Study of the Reformed Doctrine of Covenant*. Bern: Lang, 1988.

_____. 'Fides aut Foedus: Wittemberg and Zurich in conflict over the Gospel.' *SCJ* 23/1 (1992): 3-20.

_____. *The Catholic Roots of the Protestant Gospel: Encounter Between the Middle Ages and the Reformation*. Leiden: E. J. Brill, 1995.

Taylor, Adam. *The History of the English General Baptists*. 2 vols. London: T. Bore, 1818.

Toon, Peter, ed. *Puritans, the Millenium and the Future of Israel: Puritan Eschatology 1600-1660*. Cambridge & London: James Clarke & Co. Ltd., 1970.

Torbert, Robert G. *A History of the Baptists*. Philadelphia: The Judson Press, 1950.

Torrance, James B. 'Covenant or Contract? A Study of the Theological Background of Worship in the Seventeenth-Century Scotland.' *SJT* 23/1 (February, 1970): 51-76.

Torrance, T. F. 'The Distinctive Character of the Reformed Tradition.' *RR* 54/1

(2000): 5-16.
Trinkaus, Charles E. and Heiko Oberman, eds. *The Pursuit of Holiness in Late Medieval and Renaissance Religion*. Leiden: Brill, 1974.
Trueman, Carl R. 'Calvin and Calvinism.' s.v. *CCJC*.
_____. *The Claims of Truth: John Owen's Trinitarian Theology*. Carlisle, U.K.: Paternoster Press, 1998.
_____. *John Owen: The Man and His Theology*. Robert Oliver, ed. Darlington: Evangelical Press, 2002.
_____. 'Richard Baxter on Christian Unity: A Chapter in the Enlightening of English Reformed Orthodoxy.' *WTJ* 61 (1999): 53-71.
Tulloch, John. *English Puritanism and its Leaders: Cromwell, Milton, Baxter, Bunyan*. Edinburgh: William Blackwood and Sons, 1861.
Underwood, A. C. *A History of English Baptists*. London: Kings Gate Press, 1947.
Vaughn, James Barry. 'Benjamin Keach.' *Baptist Theologians*. Timothy George and David Dockery, eds. Nashville: Broadman & Holman Publishers, 1990. pp. 49-76.
_____. 'Public Worship and Practical Theology in the Work of Benjamin Keach (1640-1704).' Ph.D. diss., University of St. Andrews, 1990.
Wallace, Dewey D. *Puritans and Predestination: Grace in English Protestant Theology, 1525-1695*. Chapel Hill: The University of North Carolina Press, 1982.
Watts, Michael. *The Dissenters: From the Reformation to the French Revolution*. Oxford: Claredon Press, 1978.
Webber, Otto. *Foundations of Dogmatics*, Darrel L. Gudder, trans. Vol. 1. Grand Rapids: Eerdmans, 1981.
Weir, David A. *The Origins of the Federal Theology in Sixteenth Century Reformation Thought*. Oxford: Clarendon Press, 1990.
White, B. R. *The English Baptists of the Seventeenth Century*. Oxford: The Baptist Historical Society, 1996.
Whiting, C. E. *Studies in English Puritanism from the Restoration to the Revolution, 1660-1688*. London: Frank Cass & Co. Ltd., 1968.
Whitley, W. T. *The Baptists of London 1612-1928*. London: The Kingsgate Press, 1928.
William, D. H. *Retrieving the Tradition and Renewing Evangelicalism: A Primer for Suspicious Protestants*. Grand Rapids, MI. / Cambridge, U.K.: Eerdmans Publishing Co., 1999.
_____. 'The Search for *Sola Scriptura* in the Early Church.' *Interpretation: A Journal of Bible and Theology*, 52/4 (1998): 354-366
Willis, David and Michael Welker, eds. *Toward the Future of Reformed Theology: Tasks, Topics, Traditions*. Grand Rapids, MI./Cambridge, U.K.: Eerdmans Publishing Co., 1999.
Wilson, Walter. The History and Antiquities of Dissenting Churches and Meeting Houses in London, Westminster and Southwark. 4 vols.

London: s.n., 1808-14.

Index

Aberdeen 78
Adams, Richard 42
adiaphora 112, 142, 218
adoption 102
Ailsbury 36, 37
Ainsworth, Henry 117, 207
Albigenses 5, 58
Ambrose 164, 195
Ames, William 19, 20, 25, 79, 52, 53, 107, 126, 127
Amphilocus 54
Amrose 201
Amsterdam 115n
Amyraldian controversy 37n
Amyraut, Moise 21
Anabaptists 5, 20, 113, 115, 116, 117, 118, 119, 120, 121, 122, 130n, 149, 152, 159, 163, 172, 179, 182, 197, 204, 213, 215, 220
Anglicanism 44, 65
Anglicans 22n, 42, 78, 112, 169
Anselm 12n, 19, 58, 101, 164
Antinomianism 64, 65, 66, 68, 69, 70, 72, 75, 76n, 79, 80, 94n, 104, 108, 110, 222
  libertinism 65n, 66, 72
Antinomians 66, 67, 70, 71, 72, 75, 76, 80, 109
apostasy 58
Aquinas, Thomas 12n, 19, 58, 164, 175, 212
Arians 39, 159
Aristotelianism 14
Aristotle 14
Arminianism 25, 65, 67, 73, 77n, 78
Arminians 20, 33, 39, 47, 120
Arminius, Jacobus 20
Arnobius 196
assurance 24, 93
Athanasius 50, 195
Athenian Society, the 44, 120, 138, 139

Athenians, the 117, 120, 139, 152, 153, 171n
atonement 24, 89, 90
  limited atonement 25n, 28, 98
Augustine 12, 13, 23, 51, 53, 54, 57, 125, 131, 191, 195, 199
Augustinianism/Augustinian tradition 12, 63n

babies 112, 146, 174, 180, 182, 188, *see also children and infants*
baptism 2, 3, 6, 7, 35, 39, 44, 47, 52, 54, 111-221
  accidents of baptism 199
  administration of baptism 133, 213
  adult baptism 220
  baptism and regeneration 52
    laver of regeneration 194
  baptism not essential to salvation 220
  baptism of affliction 206
  baptism of Christ 133
  baptism of families 215, 216
  baptism of the Holy Spirit 205
  baptism of water 129, 132
  baptismal command 56n
  baptismal covenant 130, 168
  believer's baptism 1, 118, 119, 123n, 215, 217, 218, 219, 223
  benefits accrued by baptism 215
  candidates of baptism 176
  credobaptism 7, 44, 111, 164, 217
  essence of baptism 199, 200
  font 203
  household baptism 133, 181-84
  infant baptism 6, 112, 117, 122, 123, 124, 133, 147, 148, 149, 150, 151, 153, 155, 182, 183, 184, 185, 186, 187, 189, 190, 191, 193, 216, 221
  christening 124
  pedobaptism 33n, 111, 112, 113, 115, 116, 118, 119, 121, 123, 124, 133, 134n, 139, 139, 148,

149, 153, 154, 165-76, 178, 181, 182, 185, 186, 187, 188, 189, 191, 192, 193, 194, 195, 215-18, 219, 223
initiation 184, 125n
John's baptism 132, 133, 143, 153, 161, 178-81, 201, 202, 214, 218n
metaphorical baptisms 204-206
mode of baptism 112, 197-215, 218-19
  affusion 218
  aspersion 203, 214, 215, 218
  bason of water 202
  dipping 198, 199, 200, 201, 202, 204, 205, 206, 207, 211, 212, 213, 215, 218
  immersion 111, 125, 126, 130, 131, 197, 198-215, 218-19, 220
  immersion of adults 132
  naked baptism 115n, 118
  pouring water 197
  sprinkling 112, 130, 169, 197, 198, 199, 200, 203, 204, 206, 207, 209, 211, 221
outward baptism 129
rebaptism 117, 197
  anabaptism 117
regenerative baptism 215, 216
subjects of baptism 116, 130, 133, 167
  credobaptists 117, 118, 219
unbaptised, the 53
washing of regeneration 206
water of baptism 169
Baptist historiography 4
Baptist tradition 2, 3, 40, 41
Baptists 4, 5, 6n, 35n, 40, 42, 67, 78, 83, 111, 113, 114, 115, 117, 123n, 126, 165, 168, 187, 216, 219, 222, 223
Antipaedobaptists 121
Calvinistic Baptists 6n, 47
General Baptists 33, 34. 41n, 130n
Particular Baptists 6n, 33, 34, 41n, 42, 44, 62, 76, 124n, 130n, 170n, 219
Reformed Baptists 1, 4

Sabbatarian Baptists 36, 45
Barclay, Robert 32
Barth, Karl 19, 217
Basil of Seleucia 209
Basil the Great, 50, 51, 194, 195
Baxter, Richard 25, 68, 69, 73, 74, 76, 109, 117, 176
Baxterianism 48, 60, 65, 72-75, 78, 80n, 104n, 108, 110, 222
Baxterians 39, 70n, 75, 76, 79, 99, 101, 103
Bede 196
Bellarmine, Robert 20, 98, 99, 100n, 149
Bernard of Clairvaux 12n, 58, 191, 209
Beza, Theodore 14n, 18n, 19, 20, 21, 22n, 26, 27, 164, 206
biblical exclusivism 4
biblicism 1, 4, 7, 57
Biel, Gabriel 10, 11
Blake, Thomas 176
Bogomils 5
Bradwardine, Thomas 10, 11, 12n, 13n
Brinkworth 67
Bucanus 21
Bucer, Martin 17n, 18n, 21, 22n
Buckinghamshire 35
Bullinger, Heinrich 13, 17, 19, 20, 22, 23, 24n, 25, 31n, 200
Bunyan, John 1, 46
Burkitt, William 112, 113-16, 122, 123, 135, 136, 138, 139, 146, 147, 148, 150, 151, 152, 153, 154, 156, 157, 158, 159, 160, 162, 163, 165, 166, 168, 169, 170, 171, 172, 174, 175, 177, 181, 182, 184, 187, 189, 190, 192, 193, 197, 199, 200, 201, 202, 203, 207, 208, 211, 212, 213, 218, 222
Burmann, Franz 22
Burroughs, Jeremy 79

Caffin, Matthew 39
Cajetan, Tomasso de Vio 19, 201, 208
Calvin, John 2, 13, 17, 18n, 19, 20, 22, 23, 24, 25, 26, 27, 28, 29n, 30, 31n, 47, 48, 49, 51n, 52, 79, 106n, 112, 113, 172, 186, 187, 219, 222

Calvinism 2, 5, 21n, 49, 62, 76n, 78, 222
  five point Calvinism 6
    TULIP 62
Calvinists 23, 29, 30, 47, 48, 50, 223
  hyper-Calvinists 222
  moderate Calvinists 2, 222
Cambridge 67, 74, 113
Carnes, James 6n
Caryl, Joseph 79
Casuabon, Isaac 200, 205
catacombs 218n
catechumens 125, 196
catholic Reformed theologian 2, 223
catholicity 1, 2, 6, 42n, 58, 59
causality 98n
  instrument(s) 131
charismatics 67
Charles II 65
Charnock, Stephen 169
Chauncy, Isaac 64, 76, 77, 78, 106n, 107
children 124, 133, 134, 140, 141, 147, 150, 153, 154, 155, 156, 159, 160, 162, 164, 166, 167, 168, 169, 172, 173, 174, 175, 176, 177, 181, 183, 185, 188, 189, 190, 196, 199, 208, 215, 217n
  children of duty 180
  children of promise 105n, 180
  little children 176-78
Christendom 58, 122-28
Christology 55
  Monophysitism 55
church constitution 118n, 119
church membership 1, 111n, 137, 139, 148, 153, 161, 175
  infant church membership 173
Church of England 35, 39, 65, 67 77, 78, 115, 117, 121, 123, 125, 129, 143, 149, 168, 188, 220
Church of Scotland 78
church tradition 9
circumcision 113, 119, 125n, 128n, 133, 134, 136, 140, 142-52, 157, 175, 184, 185, 186, 188, 208, 214, 215, 216, 217
  circumcision of the heart 144, 151

Clark, Samuel 73, 74, 79, 99
cleansing 155
  washing 149, 198, 200, 206, 207, 216
Clement of Alexandria 192
Cocceian federalists 21
Cocceius, Johannes 22
Collins, Hercules 42
confession of sins 178-81, 194
confessionism, canons and catechisms
  First Helvetic Confession 31
  French Confession of Faith 49
  Confession of Dort 2
  Belgic Confession 20n, 21n, 49
  Canons of Dort 21n, 25, 31n
  Genevan Catechism 49
  Heidelberg Catechism 20n, 24n, 49
  Helvetic Confession 2, 21n
  London Confession (1689) 222
  Scots Confession 23n, 31, 49
  Second Helvetic Confession 20, 31, 49, 59
  Westminster Catechism 104
  Westminster Confession 2, 21n, 23n, 31, 48n
  Westminster Shorter Catechism 116
Congregationalists 35n, 76, 78, 120, 170, *see also Independents*
Constantine 5
conversion 110, 164, 173
Counter-Reformation, the 1, 11, 12, 16
covenant(s) 2, 21, 22, 23, 29, 30, 48, 63, 64, 65, 71, 72, 80, 83, 84, 85, 86, 87, 88, 93, 94, 96, 97, 100, 102, 103, 104, 105, 106, 110, 131n, 133, 134, 136, 137, 138, 139, 140, 142, 144, 145, 148, 152, 153, 166, 172, 175, 177, 181, 182, 183, 185, 187, 194, 216, 217
  covenant blessings 92n
  covenant holiness 161
  covenant of grace 63, 69, 72, 74, 79, 82n, 83n 96n, 97, 103, 105n, 108, 119, 134-46, 154, 156, 161, 172, 181
  covenant of peace 81, 83, 84, 85, 93, 96, 100, 101-106

covenant of peace and reconciliation 79
covenant of promise 96n
covenant of redemption 63, 69, 72, 79, 93, 103, 104
covenant of works 63, 71, 74, 82n, 103, 146, 153, 158, 217
covenant theology 108
covenant transaction 139
covenantal conception of believer's baptism 215-18
covenantal scheme 109, 100
compact 63n, 134, 135, 140, 145, 154
compact of grace 82
compact of redemption 82
compact of works 81
eternal covenant 81, 82, 83, 96, 103, 139
everlasting covenant 84, 97
Gospel covenant 134, 135, 139, 161, 162
new covenant 89, 144, 169
pact 63n, 69, 83, 84 85, 93, 102n, 103, 106, 119, 181
  pact of grace 141n, 217
  pact of redemption 108
creeds 2n
  Apostles' Creed 16n, 31
  Athanasian Creed 32, 56
  Chalcedonian definition 15
  ecumenical creeds 15
  Nicene Creed 31, 56
Crisp, Tobias 66, 67, 69, 70, 72, 75, 79, 107, 109
Crispianism 76
Cromwell, Oliver 77
Crosby, Thomas 33, 34, 40n
Cyprian of Carthage 125, 192

d'Ally, Pierre 11
Daneu 21
de Bruys, Pierre 10
de Vio, Tomasso 201
death, burial and resurrection 130, 131, 208, 209, 211, 212, 215, 219
Dedham, Essex 113
Denne, Henry 66, 67, 71, 75, 109

Diodati, Giovanni 201
Dionysius, bishop of Corinth 54
dispensation 107n
  old dispensation 96
dissent 36
Dissenters 35, 42, 73, 76n
Donatists 5
Donnelly, John Patrick 14n
Du Veil 200, 203

Earl of Nottingham 41
Eastern Orthodox Church/Orthodoxy 5, 216n
ecclesiology 16, 118n, 122, 220, 221
  invisible universal church 220
  gathered community 143
  mystical body of Christ 126
  visible church 111, 126, 129
ecumenism 219
Edinburgh 78
efficiency 25n
effusion of Christ's blood 211
elect, the 63, 68n, 71, 82, 86, 90, 95, 98, 105n, 107, 109, 110, 172
  elect child 216
  elect infants 171n
election 24, 74, 216
Elizabeth I 43
Epiphanius 54
Episcopalians 118
Erasmus, Desiderius 15n, 164, 191, 201
Essex 40n
Eutychus 55
evangelical piety 66
evangelical righteousness 75
excommunication 124
Exell, Joshua 121-22, 156n, 173, 174, 179, 180, 182

faith 24, 69, 71, 75, 80, 90, 98, 99, 100n, 101, 102, 104, 107, 109, 112, 131, 133, 141, 143, 152, 157, 159, 161, 162, 167, 168, 170, 172, 173-76, 195, 196, 215
  witness of faith 167
Fall, the 63n, 81
Featley, Daniel 118n
federal holiness 113, 133, 160-65, 215

Index

federal theology 6, 23n, 62, 63-110
federalism 3, 15n, 30, 48, 64n, 65, 76, 77, 222
Federalists 22, 29
Fifth Monarchianism 35
Flavell, John 119-20, 142
Franciscanism 15n
Franciscans 12n

Gansfort, Wessel 11
Gehard, Johann 12n
Gerson, Jean Charlier 11
Gill, John 2, 6n, 47, 48
Gillespie, Patrick 64, 76, 78-79
Glasgow 78
Gnostics 77n
godparents 168, 188n
Gomarus 21
Goodman's Field 45
Goodwin, Dr 79
grace 22, 67, 80, 82, 85, 89, 98, 100, 100n, 102n, 103, 105, 136, 145, 169, 171, 172, 173, 211, 216, 217
  channel(s) of grace 171
  inward grace 129, 168
Grantham, Thomas 47
Gravesend 39
Great Commission, the 128, 129, 133, 155-60, 215
Gregory Nazianzus 51, 194, 195, 197
Gregory of Rimini 13n
Grotius, Hugo 200

Hall, Basil 25, 27, 28, 48n
Hammond, Henry 149, 198
Harderwyck 78
Harvard 78
historiography 7, 9
holiness 80, 87, 94n, 104, 131, 136, 161, 162, 163, 165, 166, 177n
Holland 117
Hooper, John 24n
Horsley-down, London 40
Hugh of St Victor 12n
Huguenots 58
humanism 15n
  Renaissance humanism 26
Huss, John 10

hymn singing 42, 43n, 44n, 45n, 47
hymnody 44
Hyperius, Andreas 17

Ignatius 209
Independents 35n, 76n, 118, 125, *see also Congregationalists*
infants 127, 133, 139, 144, 146, 150, 152, 154, 155, 156, 157, 166, 168, 169, 172, 173, 174, 176, 177, 178, 179, 182, 183, 184, 185, 187, 188, 189, 191, 192, 193, 195, 216, *see also babies and children*
  dying infants 171
  infancy 171
Ireland 73
Irenaeus 190, 192

James, John 36
Jerome 51n, 53, 164, 180, 195, 196
John Chrysostom 51, 54, 55, 195, 209
Junius 20n
Jurieu, Pierre 58
justification 47n, 49, 60, 64, 65n, 68, 69, 71-72, 75, 79, 80, 94n, 96, 98, 100, 100n, 101, 102, 103, 107, 108, 142, 145
  justification by works 142
  justification from eternity 109-110
  partial justification 99
Justin Martyr 52, 192, 193, 194, 209

Keach, Elias 45
Keach, Fedora 33
Keach, Jane (née Grove) 34, 40
Keach, John 33
Keach/Partridge, Susanna (née Skidmore) 40
Kendall, R.T. 24, 25, 48n
Kiffin, William 45
Knatchbull, Norton 205
Knollys, Hanserd 40, 41, 45, 76

Lactantius 209
latitudinarianism 65
Law, the 63n, 69-70, 72, 74, 108-109, 142, 143, 145, 152, 153, 159, 172, 173, 185

Law of Nature 192
laying on of hands 34, 187
Leigh, Edward 200
Lightfoot, John 149
Limehouse, London 40n
Lincoln, Abraham 3
Lollards 5
Lombard, Peter 12n, 27
London 33, 39-44, 67
Lord's Prayer, the 16n
Lord's Supper 54, 112, 125, 130, 131, 168, 171, 176, 187, 188, 191, 192, 194
  communion 126
    infant communion 51, 151, 187, 188
  Eucharist, the 15n, 51, 112, 121, 128, 131, 160, 188, 192, 193, 194, 207, 211
  Lord's table 159
  transubstantiation 169
Luther, Martin 13, 14n, 15n, 52, 57n, 58, 59, 75, 79, 99, 112, 122, 132, 141, 176, 186, 187, 198, 199
Lutheran Church 216n
  Lutheran churches 17
Lutheranism 18, 216
  Lutheran Orthodoxy 20n
Lutherans 14n, 27, 43, 149

Martinius 21
Mason, John 46
mediatorial role of Christ 87-89, 90n, 91, 105, 106
Melanchthon, Philip 13, 14, 15n, 16n, 79, 164
mercy 82, 90
merit 95
metaphor(s) 47n, 161, 214, 215
  metonymy 99, 205
  synecdoche 178, 182, 216
Milden, Suffolk 113
Milevetan Council 193
Mincaeus 200
Moltmann, Jürgen 57n
Monophysitism 55
Montanists 5
moralism 79

moralistic theology 65
mortification 131, 142, 210, 219
Muller, Richard A. 17, 18n, 22
Mullet, Michael 32
Münster 117, 118
Musculus, Wolfgang 17n, 19, 163, 175
mysteries of the faith 196
  spiritual mysteries 212

neonomianism 72, 76, 78
Newgate Prison, London 36
nominalism 15n
non-conformists 78
Norton, Thomas 79
Novatians 5

obedience 71, 74, 75, 80, 83n, 89, 97, 101, 103, 104, 105n, 107, 144
  sincere obedience 60
Oberman, Heiko A. 9, 10, 12n
Oecolampadius, John 22n
opus operatum 131
ordinance(s) 105n, 126, 132, 137, 151, 153, 167, 183, 184, 185, 186, 187, 188, 197, 208, 212, 213
  Gospel ordinance 171
Origen 51n, 190, 191
original sin 147n, 149, 170, 216
Orthodox Protestants 79, 223
Orthodox tradition 108
Orthodoxy 2n, 16, 17, 19, 22, 62, 64, 76, 77, 93, 94, 99, 100, 110
  Trinitarian orthodoxy 62
Owen, James 116-19, 132, 155, 156, 160, 167, 177, 181, 182, 183, 184, 185, 186, 188, 191, 194, 196, 206, 207, 219, 220
Owen, John 19, 20, 23, 35n, 47, 52, 56n, 64, 76, 77-78, 79, 83, 84 85, 86, 87, 88, 92, 95, 107, 138, 170, 184
Oxford 67, 73, 77, 78, 119

Papists 20, 38, 98, 99, 119, 150
parents 162, 171, 175, 176, 184
Park, Hong-Guy 2
Pasor, Georgius 200
Patrick, St 5

Index

peace 83, 90, 93, 97, 105, 106
pedobaptists 39, 117, 122, 126, 127, 136, 164, 169, 196, 197, 220
  Reformed pedobaptists 216, 217
Pelagianism 73, 170n
Pelagians 77n
Pelikan, Jaroslav 16n, 57
Pemble, William 79
Pentecostalism 67
perfection 69-70
Perkins, William 19, 20, 22n, 23, 25, 27, 79, 107, 129, 158, 168, 175, 191, 192, 210
persecution 40
perseverance of the saints 138
Philadelphia Baptist Association 46
Photinians 77n
Pinner's Hall, London 73, 76n
Piscator, Johannes 201
Polanus, Amandus 19, 21
Pool, Matthew 205
Pope, the 54, 150, 203, 215n
popery 73
popish 4, 58, 75, 149, 150, 169, 191, 193
predestination 17n, 20n, 23, 25, 31n, 64
  double predestination 21, 48, 49
  infralapsarianism 20n, 21
  lapsarianism 15n
  supralapsarianism 20n, 21
Presbyterianism 79
Presbyterians 35n, 73, 76, 78, 116, 118, 125, 169, 188
Preston, John 79
profession of faith 118n
promise(s) 85, 105, 106, 107
prophetic office of Christ 91-92
proselytes 148, 157
Protestant churches 11
Protestant divines 79n
Protestant ecumenicity 44
Protestant Orthodoxy 18
Protestant scholasticism 6, 18n
Protestantism 15, 47, 62
  magisterial Protestantism 17
Protestants 7, 31, 55n, 60, 114n, 118, 123, 125, 127, 132, 170, 204

free church Protestants 4
purification 148
Puritan theology 65
Puritanism 7n, 18n, 20, 31, 42, 59, 63n, 68, 70, 147n
Puritans 7, 13, 18, 22, 24n, 25, 32, 43, 57n, 73, 122n, 128n, 134n
Pyntius, bishop of Knossos 54n

Quakers 32, 35n, 38, 39, 99
Quakerism 45

Rabanus Maurus 196
Ramism 24n
rantism 198, 200, 202, 203, 204, 213, 218
reconciliation 48, 70, 90, 91, 96, 97, 98, 103
redemption 48, 64n, 74, 80n, 84, 94n, 103, 105
  particular redemption 15n
Reformation, the 1, 10, 11, 12, 13, 15, 16n
Reformed catholic faith 57n
Reformed churches 17, 77, 78, 123, 216n
Reformed confession 179n
Reformed divines 96, 127
Reformed federalists 7, 77
Reformed Orthodox 18, 19n, 21, 24, 25, 31, 32n, 64, 74n, 82n, 98, 107n, 110, 127, 189
Reformed Orthodoxy 1, 2, 6, 13n, 20, 39, 50, 62, 75, 77, 96, 102, 222, 223
Reformed Protestantism 223
  post-Reformation Reformed Protestantism 1, 2n, 3
Reformed scholasticism 14n
Reformed scholastics 26
Reformed theology/thought 20, 23, 40, 41, 65, 72, 222
Reformed tradition 20n, 21, 22, 107, 216, 218, 219, 223
regeneration 104, 107, 161, 166, 168, 174, 188, 210, 216
  mystery of regeneration 131
Remonstrants 33

renewal 219
Renihan, James M. 124n
repentance 102, 104, 112, 158, 159, 161, 168, 170, 179, 180
representation 212
reprobation 74
resurrection 209, 210
righteousness 73, 86, 94n, 97, 98, 104, 105, 145, 152, 153, 219
  imputation 26, 76, 97, 98
  imputation of righteousness 65, 74, 79n, 94, 105
  righteousness of Christ 99
  righteousness of faith 119
  righteousness of the law 106n
Roberts, John 41
Rolston, Holmes 28, 29
Roman Catholic Church 7, 12, 15n, 99, 114n, 117, 123, 124, 212, 216n, 220
  Roman Catholic churches 11
Roman Catholicism 216
  Romanism 66
  Romish 123, 124, 150
Roman Catholics 39, 149
Romanists 118, 212
Rome 37, 38, 53, 54, 55, 58, 59, 114, 137, 220
Rotherhithe 40n
Rothwell, John 121, 146, 155, 157, 158, 159, 169, 182
Ruffinus 191
Rutherford, Samuel 64, 67, 76, 77, 78

Sabbath 21n, 159, 222
sacerdotal office of Christ 90-91
sacrament(s) 16n, 22, 52, 54, 111n, 112, 123, 131, 143, 181, 196, 200, 207, 211, 216
  sacrament of initiation 52, 126
  sacrament of regeneration 188
  sacramental theology 16
  seven sacraments 150
  Word and sacrament 16
sacrifice 83n, 87
Saltmarsh, John 66, 67, 72, 107, 109
salvation/soteriology 13, 15n, 16, 23, 24, 49n, 61, 64, 65, 70, 72, 73, 76, 81, 89, 94, 96, 97, 103, 105, 109, 118n, 122n, 130, 146, 171, 172, 181, 191, 194, 220
ordo salutis 64
sanctification 64, 67, 69, 99, 164, 165
Sandys, George 202
satisfaction 24, 25, 75, 81, 86, 87, 88, 89, 95, 143
scholasticism 9, 14, 15n, 19, 20, 26, 50-61
scholastics 19
Scotists 15n
Scotus, Duns 12n
Scriptura nuda 50
seal 134, 152, 167, 194, 207
sectarian 223
sectarianism 1, 2, 6
Shalder, Robert 36n
Sheer's Alley, London 40n
Shute, Gyles 120, 144, 145, 182
Sibbs, Richard 79
sign(s) 131, 167, 185, 207, 209, 212, 217
  outward sign 129, 168
sin(s) 63n, 68, 69, 70, 90n, 91, 102, 112, 131, 142, 168, 211
  forgiveness of sins 94n, 167
  remission of sins 96, 158, 167, 194
Smith, Elias 4
Smyth, John 117
Smythies, William 121
Snyder, Hendricks 115n
Socinianism 93, 108
Socinians 20, 39, 94
sola Scriptura 2, 4, 11, 12n, 18, 50, 111, 118, 223
solafideism 65
solafideists/solifidians 75, 80
Southwark 40n
Spanhemius 200
Spears, William 2, 5n, 42, 46, 47
Spurgeon, C.H. 40n
St Andrews 78
St. Michael Cornhill, London 121
Stadhampton 78
Staupitz, Johannes 13n
Steinmetz, David C. 9
Stennett, Joseph 42, 45

Stoke Hammond, Buckinghamshire 33
successionism 1, 2, 5, 7, 9, 38, 50-61, 123n
sufficiency 25n
surety/suretyship of Christ 92-95, 103, 106, 109
symbol(s) 131, 155, 209, 212
symbolism 210
Synod of Caelichyth 203
Synod of Ravenna 203
Synod of Utrecht 31n

Talon, Harry 46
Taylor, Jeremy 112, 131, 147, 149, 168, 174, 187, 191, 195
teaching 196
Tertullian 54, 150, 160, 191, 192, 194, 197
Theodosius 5
Thomists 12n
Toleration Act, the 41
Tombes, John 47, 59
Tooly-street, London 40
Torrance, James 28, 29
tradition 3, 10, 11, 12, 50-61
treaty of peace 83
Tredwell, John 113, 114, 222
Trent, Council of 16
Trinity, the 6, 15, 55, 57, 62, 82n, 84, 195
Tyndale, William 24n

union with Christ 72, 80, 85, 102
universal catholic church 220
universalism 21. 67
Ursinus, Zacharias 19, 24n, 125
Ussher, James 79

Utrecht 78

Vaughn, James Barry 2, 6n, 42, 47, 48, 49, 111n
Vermigli, Peter Martyr 14n, 17, 19
vivification 131, 210, 219
Voetians 21
Vossius, Gerhardus Joannes 200, 206

Waldensians/Waldenses 5, 58
Waldo, Peter 58, 59
Wapping, Middlesex 45
water 181, 186, 191, 194, 198, 199, 200, 201, 202, 203, 205, 207, 208, 214, 215, 220
Western Catholicism 5
Western schism 17
Westminster Assembly 31n, 75, 76, 78, 79, 126, 201, 202
Westminster divines 29n, 67, 100
White Street, London 40n
William of Occam 11
Williams, Daniel 73, 76, 78
Winslow 34
Witsius, Herman 22
Woffius 54n
women 160
works 97, 102n
  good works 80, 99
Wycliffe, John 10, 11

Zanchy, Girolamo 14n, 18n, 19, 20, 21, 79, 100, 112, 200, 210, 211
Zurich 213
Zwingli, Huldrych 13, 15n, 17, 19, 21 22n

www.ingramcontent.com/pod-product-compliance
Lightning Source LLC
Chambersburg PA
CBHW071245230426
43668CB00011B/1592